American Law

Second Edition

By the Same Author

A History of American Law
Law & Society: An Introduction
Crime and Punishment in American History
The Republic of Choice
Total Justice

American Law

An Introduction

Second Edition

Lawrence M. Friedman
STANFORD UNIVERSITY

W. W. Norton & Company
New York   London

Printed in the United States of America

The text of this book is composed in 11/13 New Caledonia, with the display set in Bulmer.
Composition and manufacturing by The Maple-Vail Book Manufacturing Group.

Library of Congress Cataloging-in-Publication Data

Friedman, Lawrence Meir, 1930–
    American law : an introduction / Lawrence M. Friedman. — 2nd ed.
     p. cm.
    Includes bibliographical references and index.
    ISBN 0-393-97273-9 (pbk.)
    1. Law—United States—Popular works. I. Title.
KF387.F74   1998
349.73—dc21   98-9481

W. W. Norton & Company, Inc., 500 Fifth Avenue, New York. N.Y. 10110

W. W. Norton & Company Ltd., 10 Coptic Street, London WC1A 1PU

3 4 5 6 7 8 9 0

Contents

Acknowledgments

The staff of the Stanford Law Library, headed by Lance Dickson, was enormously helpful as I prepared this new edition. I want to mention, in particular, Andy Eisenberg, Paul Lomio, and David Bridgman. Stan Mallison, my research assistant, was a tremendous help as well. Peter Bouckaert helped with some stubborn footnotes. And, as always, I want to thank my wife, Leah, for embodying the very concept of social support.

Preface

This book is a general introduction to the law and the legal system of the United States. In a way, writing another book about American law would seem to be like bringing another coal to Newcastle. There is certainly no shortage of books about our legal system. The Harvard Law School library, which is just about the biggest in the country except for the Library of Congress, has almost two million volumes. Hundreds of thousands of these are books about American law. Every year, Harvard adds thousands more to its collection. Of the making of law books, there seems to be no end. Do we really need more?

Perhaps we do. Almost all of those thousands and thousands of books are meant for the specialized eyes of the lawyers. Very few are written for the layman. True, in recent years, flocks of "how to do it" books have appeared: how to get your own divorce, how to avoid probate, how to deal with your landlord, how to resolve the legal problems of cohabitors, and the like. There are also some popular handbooks about people's rights, how to "win big" in small-claims courts, and so on. Books of this kind are no novelty. In the nineteenth century, too, there were "how to do it" books, with names like *Every Man His Own Lawyer.* Some were extremely popular. One such book, published in 1867, claimed it would be valuable for just about everybody: the "city wholesale merchant," the retailer, the country merchant, attorneys, justices of the peace, farmers, mechanics, even the "discharged soldier or sailor" of the Civil War, who would find "all the instructions and forms necessary" to get back pay or pension, in language "so plain as to make the whole matter perfectly clear and simple."[1]

Yet in this vast storehouse of literature, this ocean of print, now supplemented by all sorts of databases, computerized gadgets, and electronic aids, only a handful of books are designed to explain the system to general readers (and students) who presumably do not have some immediate, practical goal. True, there are some books on specialized subjects—constitutional law and business law, for example. Others of these books confine themselves more or less to what we might call the official story: the law on the books. They do not ask some of the difficult but important questions about the way the legal system meshes with its society. This book, written specifically for the general reader, tries to give an overall picture of the American legal system as it was and as it is, focusing on the law in operation—the living law.

This book is about the American legal system as a working system. But exactly what is a legal system? Where does a legal system come from? What is it made out of? Where does it begin, and where does it end? There are no simple answers to such questions even for any particular legal system, and certainly none that would apply to all legal systems, wherever they are in the world, and all the systems that have ever been, including extinct ones. I doubt that we could come up with a definition of a "legal system" that would fit the law of small tribes of nomads as well as the law of giant industrial societies; that would fit both modern legal systems and the systems of the ancient Hittites and Chinese. Building a conceptual structure that would bridge all of these would be a tall order indeed. Of course, some scholars have tried. There is no general agreement on whether their results have been worth the effort.

The goal of this book is more modest. It is an introduction to *American* law, and it has a right, then, to focus on the United States and neglect radically different societies. After all, "law," "legal system," and "legal process" are all mental constructs. They are not things that exist in the real world. You cannot touch, taste, smell, or measure law. Any definition, in short, has to be more or less conventional—which is to say artificial. This does not mean that such a definition is wrong; it simply means that a definition is good if it is useful, and if we make clear to ourselves and to others exactly what we are trying to accomplish with our definition.

Our first job, then, is to lay out a kind of map of the American legal system—to catalog the subject of this book. Roughly, the criterion for including and excluding will be based on popular understanding: what scholars and laymen would agree is inside the circle of law. The starting point must include the body of rules (statutes, regulations, ordinances) that come out of the halls of government; these are obviously part of what people mean when they talk about "'the law." Clearly, too, whatever is concerned with making and carrying out these rules is inside the legal system. This means the courts, of course, and the legislatures, city councils, and county boards; also administrative agencies such as the Internal Revenue Service and the Securities and Exchange Commission; state agencies that license doctors, teachers, and plumbers; and even the rather lowly zoning boards and sewer districts. They all make rules and regulations.

A legal system cannot enforce or implement these rules and regulations without the work of a lot of men and women who carry out orders from above—policemen, for example, or elevator inspectors, or auditors who work for the tax bureau. We also include as part of the system our huge corps of lawyers. Their work—even their private dealings in the snug confines of a Wall Street office—is directly relevant to the legal system. Law is, after all, the lawyer's stock in trade. Lawyers advise their clients and tell them how to use law or how to pick a path among legal minefields. They work in the shadow of the law, and what they do is necessarily a part of the working legal system—indeed, a vital part.

But the activities of official agents of the law are not the whole story. Ordinary citizens participate in the legal system not just by their actions, which may be law-abiding or not, but also by their attitudes and beliefs. The American legal system in operation is thus a very complex organism. It has many parts, many actors, and many aspects. The actors range from judges of the Supreme Court to the desolate army of the homeless. The institutions include courts, prisons, zoning boards, police departments, and countless others. As in all legal systems, what gives the organism life is the way rules, people, and institutions interact. How they do so—how they combine, chemically as it were—is the general theme of this book.

· · ·

This book was first published in 1985. The world does not stand still, nor do legal systems. A lot has happened since then. Since 1985, the Soviet Union has collapsed, and both the fifty-five-mile-an-hour speed limit and the Interstate Commerce Commission have vanished into the black hole of history, to mention only two examples. The basic structure of the legal system remains the same, and so I have kept the basic structure of this book. But I have thoroughly revised and reworked the text. I have tried to reflect what has happened in the years since the first edition was born, but also, perhaps more significantly, to reflect what light events and evolutions have shed on our basic understanding of the things that make the legal system tick.

American Law

Revised and Updated Edition

1

What Is a Legal System?

*I*N MODERN AMERICAN SOCIETY, the legal system is everywhere with us and around us. To be sure, most of us do not have much contact with courts and lawyers except in emergencies. But not a day goes by, and hardly a waking hour, without contact with law in its broader sense or with people whose behavior is modified or influenced by law. Law is a vast, though sometimes invisible, presence.

For example, when we go to the grocery and buy bread, milk, soups, and potato chips, and when we make out a check for the food (or pay with a credit card) and take the packages out to our car, we invoke or assume many facets of legal order. To be sure, we do not feel that the legal system, like some sort of Big Brother, is staring at us over our shoulder. But in a sense it is: at us, and at the shopkeeper and his workers. Some branch of law touches every aspect of this ordinary little piece of behavior.

To get to the store, we drove a car or walked, crossing several streets. Traffic law walked or drove with us. Dozens of rules and regulations applied to the conditions and procedures at the factory where the car was assembled—rules about the workforce, and about the car itself, body and engine. Inside the grocery store, there were labels on the cans and packages reflecting more rules and regulations; in the life history of every jar of jam, every tube of toothpaste, rules and regulations are lurking. And, of course, workers in the store, like workers in the auto plant, are covered by federal, state, and local labor regulations.

Indeed, most things we buy—TV sets, mattresses, shoes, whatever—are covered by some body of law, some rules about safety or quality or other aspects of manufacture or use. Most buildings and places of business, including the grocery store itself, have to conform to building codes and to fire and safety regulations. There are rules about standard weights and measures, employee comfort and safety, time and a half for overtime work, Sunday closing laws—the list is endless.

But there is more. When I buy a loaf of bread or a can of soup, I have entered into a contract, whether I realize it or not. If something goes wrong with the deal, the rules of contract law, of the Uniform Commercial Code, or of some branch of commercial law come into play, at least theoretically. The Uniform Commercial Code governs the rules that relate to checks, and a vast body of banking law is relevant to the way these pieces of paper provide credit and payment. Credit-card companies have to comply with many laws as well, and may be subject to rules about how much interest they can charge. If the can of soup is tainted and I get sick, I may have the right to sue the soup company; this will switch me onto still another legal track, the law of products liability, a branch of the law of torts.

This is not to say that we feel law lying on us like a suit of lead. Law is in the atmosphere, invisible and unfelt—often as light as air to the normal touch. (Manufacturers, storekeepers, and bankers, of course, may see things differently; and there are plenty of private citizens who complain about the heavy hand of law.) Moreover, it is wrong to think of law as a tissue of don'ts, that is, as a kind of nagging or dictatorial parent. Much of the law has the purpose—whether successful or not— of making life easier, safer, happier, or better. When the norms do forbid something (or require something from somebody), it is usually for the specific benefit of somebody else. The law might insist that soup companies put labels on their soup. They must tell us exactly what they put inside their soup. This is a burden on the company, but is a benefit (or is supposed to be) for buyers of soup. There are also many ways in which the legal system facilitates, rather than forbids or harasses. It subsidizes; it promotes; it provides easy ways to reach desirable goals. The law about wills or contracts, for example, is basically about ways to do what you want to do, safely and efficiently; it is much less concerned with what not to do or with the punishment or price for disobeying rules. A great deal of law is facilitative in this way. It provides standard ways—routines—for reaching goals. It builds roads for the traffic of society.

Law and legal process are extremely important in our society; that much seems to be obvious. But, as I said in the preface, defining exactly what we mean by law and legal process can be difficult. "Law" is an everyday word, part of the basic vocabulary. But it is a word of many meanings, as slippery as glass, as elusive as a soap bubble. And, as we said, law is a concept, an abstraction, a social construct; it is not some concrete object in the world around us—something we could feel or smell, like a chair or a dog.

As I suggested, to try to get at some sort of working definition, we might start by listening to the way people use words like "law" and see what they are referring to. To begin with, people seem to have in mind the network of rules and regulations that surrounds us. This is clear from such expressions as "breaking the law" and "obeying the law." It is also what the word "law" means in sentences like "It's against the law to drive ninety miles an hour in a school zone." There may be, and certainly are, other shades of meaning, but the idea of rules and regulations is usually at the core. In ordinary speech, then, the word "law" is connected with "laws," that is, with rules and regulations.

Donald Black, in *The Behavior of Law,*[1] puts forward a concise, deceptively simple definition. Law, according to Black, is "governmental social control." By "social control" he means social rules and processes which try to encourage good or useful conduct or discourage bad conduct. There is a law against burglary, and police, judges, and criminal courts try to put teeth into it. All together, they form a pretty obvious example of social control (or at least attempted social control). The whole criminal justice system plainly aims in this direction. For the person in the street, it is perhaps the most familiar, obvious part of the legal system.

But law is more than criminal justice. The rest of the law (what lawyers call civil justice) is actually larger in size, however you measure it, and almost certainly more important. To make Black's definition work, we have to understand "social control" in a broader sense. It must mean the whole network of rules and processes which attach legal consequences to particular bits of behavior.

Take, for example, the ordinary rules of the law of torts. If I drive carelessly or too fast in a parking lot and smash somebody else's fender, there may be very definite legal consequences. Smashing the fender is no crime—I will not go to jail—but I (or my insurance company) may have to pay for the damage. Directly or indirectly, what happens will depend in part on rules of tort law—rules about what happens when one person injures another or damages his property.

These rules may change the way I behave. They certainly affect my pocketbook and the rates of insurance I pay. Hence these rules, too, are part of the system of social control. The rules reward some behavior and punish other behavior (or try to), just as surely as the criminal justice system. They distribute costs and benefits among people, depending on how they behave. Careless drivers have to pay; victims get money.

All law, according to Black, is social control, but for Black (and many others), not all social control is law. Law is *governmental* social control. There are other kinds of social control as well. Teachers use rules (and rewards and punishments) to make children behave; parents use rules (and rewards and punishments) at home. Both teachers and parents also hope to mold behavior for the future. Organized religions, too, are concerned with behavior—with social control. A religion aims to induce its members to live a godly or proper life, as the religion defines it.

But these forms of social control are not governmental: they are not official, not part of the state apparatus. Under Black's definition, then, they are not law. At least we can say that in a country like the United States they are not part of the *official* law. But there are, in fact, two distinct ways to look at law. One way insists, with Black, that law is made up exclusively of official, governmental acts; the other takes a broader approach, and looks at the whole domain of social control.

The main focus of this book is not on "law" so much as on what can be called the legal system. The word "law" often refers only to rules and regulations; but a line can be drawn between the rules and regulations themselves and those structures, institutions, and processes that breathe life into them. This expanded domain is the "legal system."

It is plain that the legal system has more in it than codes of rules, do's and don'ts, regulations and orders. It takes a lot more than that to make a legal system. There are, to begin with, rules *about* rules. There are rules of procedure, and rules that tell us how to tell a rule from a nonrule. To be more concrete, these are rules about jurisdiction, pleadings, judges, courts, voting in legislatures, and the like. A rule that says that no bill becomes a law in New Mexico unless both houses pass it and the governor signs it is a rule about rules. It explains one way to make a legal rule in New Mexico. In a famous book, H. L. A. Hart called these rules about rules "secondary rules"; he called rules about actual behavior "primary rules." The rules against burglarizing the grocery store or against driving at ninety miles an hour to get there would be examples of primary rules. Law, according to Hart, is the union of primary and secondary rules.[2]

In a sense, all rules, including secondary rules, are directives about how to behave. Our example of a secondary rule, for example, is after all a rule about how lawmakers should behave in New Mexico. Both kinds of rule are important, but both are only raw materials, components, parts of a legal system. We could master all the rules and still know very little about the legal system in operation. All we would have is words; and these words—orders, commands, and rules—are blank and empty, unless something happens, unless somebody makes them move, and unless they, in turn, make somebody move or something happen.

This, of course, is not a fresh idea. It is something that everybody knows. People say that a certain law is a "dead letter," while another rule is "in force." Or we use the term "living law." Dead letters are not living law, just as a dead language like Sanskrit or Latin is unlike a language that comes tumbling from the mouths of real people, here and now. Living law is law that is alive in a legal system.

For example, the maximum speed limit on Interstate 280 in California is sixty-five miles per hour. This is a legal rule. But the living law—the actual practice—is much more complicated. The rule itself does not tell us, for one thing, that people can actually drive at seventy, or maybe even seventy-five, without any risk of arrest. Police do not take the speed limit literally.[3] If, on the other hand, somebody barrels down the road at ninety or ninety-five, and a police car is around, its siren will scream and the police will come after the speeder. Each type of situation—whether it is driving a car, buying a house, getting a divorce, or merging two giant corporations—calls forth a particular interaction between the various elements of the legal system. These elements are not just "laws," or even laws and institutions; they also include people and their attitudes and behaviors.

Elements of a Legal System

We now have a preliminary, rough idea of what we mean when we talk about our legal system. There are other ways to analyze this complicated and important piece of the social world. To begin with, the legal system has *structure*. The system is constantly changing, but parts of it change at different speeds, and not every part changes as fast as certain other parts. There are persistent, long-term patterns—aspects of the system that were here yesterday (or even in the last century) and will be around for a long time to come. This is the structure of the legal system—its skeleton or framework, the durable part, the part that gives a kind of shape and definition to the whole.

There is a Supreme Court in this country, made up of nine justices. The Court has been around since the late eighteenth century and is virtually certain to be around in the twenty-first century; its work habits change very slowly. The structure of a legal system consists of elements of this kind: the number and size of courts, their jurisdiction (that is, what kind of cases they hear, and how and why), and modes of appeal from one court to another. Structure also means how the legislature is organized, how many members sit on the Federal Trade Commission, what a president can (legally) do or not do, what procedures the police department follows, and so on. Structure, in a way, is a kind of cross section of the legal system—a kind of still photograph, which freezes the action.

Another aspect of the legal system is its *substance*. By this is meant the actual rules, norms, and behavior patterns of people inside the system. This is, first of all, "the law" in the popular sense of the term—the fact that the speed limit is sixty-five miles an hour on Interstate 280, that burglars can be sent to prison, that "by law" a pickle maker has to list ingredients on the label of the jar.

But it is also, in a way, "substance" that the police arrest drivers doing ninety but not those doing seventy on Interstate 280, or that a burglar without a criminal record gets probation, or that the Food and Drug Administration is easy (or tough) on the pickle industry. These are working patterns of the living law. Substance also means the "product" that people within the legal system manufacture—the decisions they turn out, the new rules they contrive. We know something about the substance of the legal system when we know how many people are arrested for arson in any given year, how many deeds are registered in Alameda County, California, how many sex-discrimination cases are filed in federal court, how many times a year the Environmental Protection Agency complains that a company dumped toxic wastes.

The last paragraph makes it plain that the ideas of substance in this book are not the same as those that, let us say, some lawyers put forward. The stress here is on living law, not just rules in law books. And this brings us to the third component of a legal system, which is, in some ways, the least obvious: the *legal culture*. By this we mean people's attitudes toward law and the legal system—their beliefs, values, ideas, and expectations. In other words, it is that part of the general culture which concerns the legal system. These ideas and opinions are, in a sense, what sets the legal process going. If someone says that Americans are litigious—that is, that Americans go to court at the drop of a hat— he is saying something about legal culture (whether or not what he says is true). We talk about legal culture all the time, without knowing it. If we point out that devout Roman Catholics tend to avoid divorce (because their religion disapproves), that people who live in slums distrust the police, that middle-class people make complaints to government agencies more often than people on welfare, or that the Supreme

Court enjoys high prestige, we are making statements about legal culture.

The legal culture, in other words, is the climate of social thought and social force that determines how law is used, avoided, or abused. Without legal culture, the legal system is inert—a dead fish lying in a basket, not a living fish swimming in its sea.

Another way to visualize the three elements of law is to imagine legal "structure" as a kind of machine. Substance is what the machine manufactures or does. The "legal culture" is whatever or whoever decides to turn the machine on and off and determines how it will be used.

Every society, every country, every community has a legal culture. There are always attitudes and opinions about law. This does not mean, of course, that everybody in a community shares the same ideas. There are many subcultures: white and black, young and old, Catholic, Protestant, Jew, rich and poor, Easterners and Westerners, gangsters and policemen, lawyers, doctors, shoe salesmen, bankers. One particularly important subculture is the legal culture of "insiders," that is, the judges and lawyers who work inside the legal system itself. Since law is their business, their values and attitudes make a good deal of difference to the system. At least this is a plausible suggestion; the exact extent of this influence is a matter of some dispute among scholars.

These three elements in American law—structure, substance, and culture—are the subject of this book. We will take a look at the way the American legal system is organized, at what it does, and at how it does it; and we will be especially conscious of legal culture—ideas and forces outside the law machine that make it stop and go. The three elements can be used to analyze anything the legal system does. Take, for example, the famous death-penalty case *Furman v. Georgia* (1972).[4] In this case, a bare majority of the United States Supreme Court—five judges out of nine—struck down death-penalty laws in all of the states which had them, on constitutional grounds. (Later on, the Court backtracked somewhat; most states reenacted death-penalty laws. This subject will be dealt with in another chapter.)

To understand what happened in *Furman* we must first grasp the structure of the legal system. Otherwise, we will have no idea how the case worked its way up from court to court, nor why the case was in the end decided in Washington, D.C., and not in Georgia, where it started. We will have to know something about federalism, the Constitution, the relationship between courts and legislatures, and many other long-run, long-lasting features of American law.

But this is only the beginning. The case itself takes up no less than 230 pages of print in the official reports—there were seven separate opinions. As we plow through these pages, we are enmeshed in the substance of constitutional law. The case, to begin with, turns in part on whether the death penalty is "cruel and unusual punishment"; if it is, the Eighth Amendment to the Constitution specifically forbids it. There are long discussions in the opinions about what "cruel and unusual" means, what earlier cases have said, and what doctrines and rulings have been woven about this phrase.

But structure and substance together do not explain why the case came up and why it came out as it did. We have to know something about social context—the movement to get rid of capital punishment, who and what was behind the case, what organizations were fighting for and against the death penalty, and why the issue came up when it did—that is, the attitudes, values, and beliefs about the death penalty, law, courts, and so on which explain how the case got started in the first place.

We might be interested, too, in a fourth element, *impact*—that is, what difference the decision made. The Supreme Court spoke; who listened? We know some obvious facts about immediate consequences. For one thing, the men and women on death row never kept their dates with the gas chamber or the electric chair. Their sentences were automatically commuted to long-term imprisonment. There were other impacts, as well, in substance, structure, and legal culture. *Furman* set off a storm of discussion, furious activity in state legislatures, and ultimately a flock of new lawsuits. It may have had more remote (but important) consequences too: on the prestige of the Supreme Court, on the crime rate, on national morality. The more remote the consequences, the harder to know and measure them.

We know surprisingly little, in general, about the impact of decisions, even their immediate impact. It is not the job of courts to find out what happens to their litigants once they leave the courtroom, or what happens to the larger society. But impact is the subject of a small, growing area of research; from time to time the evidence from these studies will be noted or mentioned in this book.

The Functions of the Legal System

But why have a legal system at all? What does it do for society? In other words, what functions does it perform?

One kind of answer has already been given. The legal system is part of the system of *social control*. In the broadest sense, this may be *the* function of the legal system; everything else is, in a way, secondary or subordinate. To put it another way, the legal system is concerned with controlling behavior. It is a kind of official traffic cop. It tells people what to do and not to do, and it backs up its directives with force.

The legal system can do this in a very direct, very literal way. There are traffic cops, after all, who stand on busy corners, waving traffic this way or that, and they are certainly a part of the legal system as we have defined it. The criminal-justice system is probably the most familiar example of law as social control. Here we find some of society's heavy artillery: judges, juries, jails, wardens, police, criminal lawyers. People who break the law, and other "deviants," are chased, caught, and sometimes punished; this is control in the most raw and basic sense.

A second broad function of law is what we can call *dispute settlement*. A dispute, according to Richard L. Abel, is the public assertion of inconsistent claims over something of value.[5] Two people both insist they own the same piece of land. Or a Honda Accord rear-ends a Saturn, and the driver of the Saturn threatens to sue the driver of the Honda. Or the marriage of Mark and Linda Jones breaks up, and they squabble over who gets the house, the child, or the money. These are all disputes in Abel's sense: inconsistent claims to something of value.

Many times, there is some concrete thing (or person) that the parties are arguing about, something you can touch or squeeze or hug—a child, a bundle of money, a house. At other times, the "thing" is more abstract or nebulous: the right to citizenship, a reputation that has been dragged in the mud, damages for pain and suffering, somebody's goodwill or peace of mind. Disputes can be big or little, raucous or moderate. We use the phrase "dispute settlement," generally, when we are talking about putting an end to fairly small-scale, local disagreements between individuals or private businesses. There are, of course, bigger, more basic disagreements in society—disagreements between whole classes or groups. Of this sort might be, for example, clashes between labor and capital, or between regions of the country, or between black and white, or between the young and the old, or between people who want to protect the beaches and people who prefer offshore oil.

It might be a good idea to give these macrodisagreements a name of their own, and call them *conflicts* rather than disputes. In any event, the legal system is as concerned with conflict. as it is with disputes, if not more so. The legal system, in other words, is an agency of conflict resolution as well as an agency of dispute settlement. Courts come immediately to mind in this connection, that is, as the institutions that help most notably to bring conflicts to an end. This they indeed do. But the work of the legislatures is probably, on the whole, more important.

It is Congress and the state legislatures that iron out (if anyone does) most of the bitter battles between employers and labor unions, between businessmen and the Sierra Club, between retired people and the people who pay Social Security taxes. It is in the city council of Chicago, say, that boosters who want new stores and factories and highways bump up against people who want to preserve old mansions and fight for their neighborhoods. In the suburbs, it is town councils and zoning boards that deal with conflict between those who want light industry and shopping centers and "residentialists" who want nothing but one-family houses, green lawns, and rosebushes.

The various functions of law overlap, of course. No single function has a clear and perfect boundary. The line between a dispute and a conflict is woefully indistinct. Other functions of law are even less clearcut. One of these functions is what we might call the redistributive or social engineering function. This refers to the use of law to bring about planned social change imposed from on top, that is, by the government. Social engineering is a very prominent aspect of modern welfare states. The United States levies taxes on people who have money and uses this money to give cash, food stamps, medical benefits, and sometimes cheap housing to the poor and to others who are felt to deserve it. So, too, do all modern Western nations.

Law, then, embodies the planned or "engineered" aspect of social policy—whatever is done deliberately through public choice. It stands opposed to the unplanned market. In the market, the law of supply and demand sets prices. The market decides which products and businesses grow fat and rich and which ones shrivel and die. The market distributes goods and services, benefits and burdens, through a system of prices. It can be compared to a kind of auction in which buyers bid for goods they want; scarce, desirable goods go up in price, while common, less wanted goods go down.

The legal system is in a way a rival scheme for distributing goods and services. It, too, rations scarce commodities. To raise an army during times of war, we could literally buy soldiers; and in the past some countries did exactly that. Today we would never use this system. Mostly, we rely on a volunteer army—using incentives to induce young man (and women) to "join up." This system, along with the use of reserves, probably works well enough in "little" wars (in Grenada or Panama, for example). If a really big war broke out, we would probably get soldiers through a draft, as we did in the Second World War. Congress would pass a law and make rules about who would or must serve in the armed forces. There would be rules and regulations about deferments, city and state quotas, how to handle conscientious objectors, and how to deal with recruits with flat feet or poor eyesight. The market would have little or nothing to do with these rules. If we change the rules, we change the allocation system. In other words, whether we realize it or not, our legal system acts as a way of distributing benefits and burdens: as a giant rationing system, a giant planning system, a giant system of social engineering.

We should not push the term "social engineering" too far. To do so would give too much of an impression that the legal system is constantly at work reforming and improving. Most of the time, legal allocations do exactly the opposite: rather than change things, they act in such a way as to keep, or try to keep, the status quo intact. This function can be called *social maintenance.* The legal system presupposes and enforces structures that keep the machinery going more or less as it has in the past. After all, even the "free market"—even the "invisible hand"—needs law to guarantee the rules of fair play. Even in the most laissez-faire system, the law enforces bargains, creates a money system, and tries to maintain a framework of order and respect for property.

Every society has its own structure, and this structure does not stay put by magic or accident, or even by inertia or the laws of gravity. What makes the structure persist over the years is, first of all, social behavior and social attitudes—customs, culture, traditions, and informal norms. But these, in modern society, do not seem to be enough. Contemporary society needs the muscle and bone of law to stay healthy, even to stay alive. If somebody breaks into my house and refuses to get out, I can call "the law" and get him driven out. If my neighbor owes me $300, I can go to court and collect my money. The law defends my rights, including my property rights. This is the social maintenance function. The criminal law is very much part of this system. After all, the crimes most commonly prosecuted are property crimes—theft, burglary, embezzlement. These are offenses against people who own property. If we punish people who steal things we are at the same time protecting people who own the things that are stolen; hence we are preserving the economic (and social) structure of society.

Obviously, then, the law protects the status quo, and it does so in a very direct and obvious way. This sounds worse, perhaps, than it is. "Status quo" is a phrase usually spoken with a sneer; "protecting the status quo" sounds static, even reactionary. It suggests that law and society are fat and hidebound, and tend to uphold the rights and interests of the privileged against the rights and interests of the poor and the helpless. This is certainly true in large part. But, after all, every society—even a revolutionary society—tries to preserve some parts of its status quo. The revolutionary society tries to preserve and strengthen the revolution. The traditional society tries to preserve and strengthen tradition. Any society has to take steps to preserve itself from forces of disintegration and anarchy. There is no such thing as a total revolutionary—somebody who wants to change everything. Whether it is good or bad to keep up old ways and conserve the general structure of society depends on what the old ways are and which old ways and structures we are talking about.

The central fact of human life is that nobody lives forever. People serve out their little terms of life and die. But societies and institutions go on. A social structure is much more durable than the people who fill its roles. Structure is like a play—*Hamlet,* for example—in which the text carries on from generation to generation but different actors play the parts and new versions, new sets, new costumes appear every once in a while. We know that norms, morals, and customs help bridge generations. We realize that each generation teaches its language and culture to its children, so that the next generation carries on pretty much as its parents did. If we speak English, so will our children, and their children's children, too, even though a newborn baby speaks no language at all and will learn Hausa or Portuguese if that is what is spoken all around it.

Of course, we do have to remember that social roles are not exactly like the role of Hamlet in Shakespeare's play; they are much more subject to change. And social change is taking place today at a fast and furious pace, faster than ever before. Even so, not everything changes at once and in every sphere of life. A man or woman of a century ago who fell asleep like Rip Van Winkle and came to life again today would be amazed by many things: cars, computers, cellular phones, the "sexual revolution." He or she might have trouble adjusting to our world. Yet many other things—clothes, customs, buildings, ways of thought— would be at least vaguely familiar, and some aspects of life would seem exactly the same.

Continuity—and yet change. These are the constants of social life. And the legal system plays a crucial role in promoting both continuity and change. It helps bridge generations, but it also helps direct social change into what people hope will be smooth and constructive channels. For example, there are laws about the inheritance of wealth—about ways to make out a will, about death taxes, about the rights of widows and widowers. We talk about the "dead hand," somewhat ruefully. But without the "dead hand"—without people's right to determine, more or less, what will happen to their money when they die—each generation might have to rebuild its structure from scratch; each generation would have to make up who is rich and who is poor all over again. That might be either good or bad, just or unjust. It would certainly be different. Laws about inheritance and death taxes, as they exist today, practically guarantee a large measure of continuity. Proposals to do away with death taxes, or cut them down to size, float around Congress from time to time. If enacted, such proposals might have a real impact on the distribution of wealth—and of power, prestige, and social status.

All our legal institutions, including courts, legislatures, and agencies, are designed, at least in part, for both continuity and change. They are structured in such a way that changes can take place, but only in a regular, orderly, patterned way. After all, every time Congress sits, every time the Delaware legislature meets in Dover, every time the city council of Omaha goes into session, volumes and volumes of new laws and ordinances come pouring out. Every new law changes something; every law tries to attack some social problem, big or small. Happily, it is an orderly process (most of the time) in this country. Like the rest of the world, America is trying to ride the wild horse of change instead of letting it gallop off in all directions. The legal system is geared up as one important part of the social system, which acts as a kind of safety valve—it prevents too much change, and slows down changes that go too fast; it is a process for limiting volcanic bursts of change. It does not always succeed. Nor should it.

Claims of Right. When we think about social control, we usually have in mind a picture of law and government—of "authorities"—in control of "subjects," the people underneath. Social control is a policeman giving out a ticket for speeding, for example. But we need controls over policemen, too. In our society, there is no horse without a bridle. Nobody—not the mayor of Memphis, not the governor of New York, not the president, not the Supreme Court itself—is supposed to be truly, absolutely supreme. Only law is supreme.

This, to be sure, is theory. Practice is more complicated and considerably less than perfect. Everybody knows that some people in authority abuse their positions. We know about bribery; we know about the petty tyranny of bureaucrats. In 1996, former congressman Dan Rostenkowski, once one of the most powerful men in the country, pleaded guilty to charges of corruption.[6] Probably most abuses never get uncovered, or punished. To correct these evils, there are controls built into the system. Law, in other words, has the further job of keeping an eye on the rulers themselves. This is, in a way, a process of turning social control inside out. (In another way, it is simply a different kind of social control, control exercised over a small but important social subgroup.) Control over controllers is, of course, a basic theme in American government. It is the idea behind checks and balances, and behind the corps of ombudsmen, inspector generals, auditors, and the like, all busily at work. It is also the idea behind "judicial review," the power of courts to decide when other branches of government have overstepped the mark. Courts regularly, and sometimes fearlessly, rebuke or override Congress, administrative agencies, the police, and even the president himself when these have gone beyond what the court feels are the limits of legitimate authority. This is especially true of those limits written into the Constitution or put there by courts in the process of "interpreting" the text.

We also sometimes speak of "claims of right." By this we mean claims of private citizens or of companies against the government. Claims of right help control abuse of power; but most of the time what the claimant wants is relief from some particular mistake of government. There are innumerable examples: pension claims, benefit claims, grievances and complaints about the million and one ways a civil servant in contemporary America can bungle his job. For example—one example out of thousands—a man named James T. Blanks, living in Alabama, who said he was sixty-two years old, applied for old-age benefits. The Department of Health, Education, and Welfare turned him down. According to their notion, he was only sixty, two years short of eligibility. They got this idea from a school census record of Marshall County, Alabama. Blanks countered with a family Bible, federal census records, insurance policies, and affidavits from neighbors and relatives. The HEW people were not impressed; they stuck by their original decision. Blanks went to court. He sued HEW and won his case.[7]

Citizens do not, of course, always win these cases. Probably more often than not, the government wins. In a Pennsylvania case, a state policeman, Joseph McIlvaine, was forced out of his job because (according to the rules) he was too old to serve. This seemed grossly unfair to McIlvaine, and he sued to get back on the force. The Pennsylvania courts turned him down.[8] He tried to get the Supreme Court of the United States to take his case, but this, too, failed.[9]

As we leaf through reported cases, federal and state, we find countless claims of right. They are, perhaps, the tip of an iceberg. Such claims seem to have become more common in recent decades. Why this should be so and whether they bring about effective control of government (or are ineffective or a nuisance) are questions that will be taken up later in this book.

The Common Law and Its Competitors

There is a bewildering variety of legal systems in the world. Every country has its own, and in the United States, each state, too, has its own legal system, which governs the internal affairs of the state, generally speaking; the national (federal) system is imposed on top of that system. A law student usually studies the law of a single country—the one he or she plans to practice in. This is true of the United States too; legal education sticks largely to American law. Our legal education, though, is fairly national-minded; it tends to ignore many of the differences between the laws of the various states. The curriculum and the materials studied are much the same in all law schools, whether they are in Oregon or in Alabama. A student does not go to Harvard Law School to study the law of Massachusetts, or to Vanderbilt to study the law of Tennessee. Nonetheless, the study of law is in a sense quite parochial. Medicine is more or less the same all over the world, and so generally are all the natural and applied sciences: electrical engineering in Uganda is no different, in essence, from electrical engineering as understood in China or the United States. Even the social sciences lay claim to a kind of universality. But law is strictly defined by nationality: it stops at the border. Outside its home base, it has no validity at all.

No two legal systems, then, are exactly alike. Each is specific to its country or its jurisdiction. This does not mean, of course, that every legal system is entirely different from every other legal system. Not at all. When two countries are similar in culture and tradition, their legal systems are likely to be similar as well. No doubt the law of El Salvador is very much like the law of Honduras. The laws of Australia and New Zealand are not that far apart.

We can also clump legal systems together into clusters, or "families"—groups of legal systems that have important traits of structure, substance, or culture in common. The word "family" is used deliberately: in most cases, members of a legal family are in a sense genetically related, that is, they have a common parent or ancestor, or else have borrowed their laws from a common source. English settlers carried English law with them to the American colonies, and to Canada, Australia, New Zealand, Jamaica, Barbados, and the Bahamas. Many countries in the world once were part of the British Empire. These countries are now independent and have distinct legal systems of their own, but they have kept their basic traditions. The legal systems of the English-speaking world have a definite family resemblance. The Spanish brought their law to Latin America. Spanish-speaking countries in that part of the world share many traits and traditions.

The largest, most important family is the so-called civil-law family. Members of this family owe a common debt to a modernized version of Roman law. The ancient Romans were great lawmakers. Their tradition never completely died out in Europe, even after the barbarians overran what was left of the Roman Empire. In the Middle Ages, Roman law, in its classic form, was rediscovered and revived; even today, codes of law in Europe reflect "the influence of Roman law and its medieval revival."[10] Western Europe—France, Germany, Italy, Spain, Portugal, and the Low Countries, among others—is definitely civil-law country. Through Spain and Portugal, the civil law traveled to Latin America. The French brought it to their colonies in Africa. In Canada, the civil law is dominant in the French-speaking province of Quebec. It strongly colors the legal systems of two unlikely outposts, Scotland and Louisiana. It plays a major role, too, in countries like Japan and Turkey, which stand completely outside the historical tradition but borrowed chunks of European civil law in recent times, in hopes of getting modern in a hurry.

Civil-law systems are, generally speaking, "codified" systems: the basic law is set out in codes. These are statutes, or rather superstatutes, enacted by the national parliament, which arrange whole fields of law in an orderly, logical, and comprehensive way. Historically, the most important of the codes was the civil code of France, the so-called Napoleonic Code, which appeared in 1804. It has had a tremendous influence on the form and substance of most later codes. Another influential civil code was Germany's, which dates from the late nineteenth century.

During the Renaissance, European legal scholarship was dazzled by the power and beauty of the rediscovered Roman law, and it profoundly influenced the style and content of legal change in country after country. There was one holdout, however—one nation that managed to resist the "reception" of Roman law. The English were not seduced by the majesty of Rome; they held fast to their native traditions. Many ideas and terms from Roman and European law did, to be sure, creep into English law, but the core of the legal system held firm. This tenacious local system was the so-called common law. It differed and continues to differ in many ways from the legal order in other European countries. For one thing, the common law resisted codification. There never was an English equivalent of the Napoleonic Code. The basic principles of law were not found primarily in acts of Parliament, and least of all in careful, systematic statements of law adopted by legislatures or imposed by decree. The principles were found in case law—in the body of opinions written by judges, and developed by judges in the course of deciding particular cases. The doctrine of "precedent"—the maxim that a judge is bound in some way by what has already been decided—is strictly a common-law doctrine. The common law also has its own peculiar features of substance, structure, and culture—some important and basic, some less so. For example, the jury is a common-law institution. So is the "trust," an arrangement in which a person (or bank) as trustee receives money or property to invest and manage for the benefit of certain beneficiaries.

The common law is no longer confined to a single small country. The English brought it to their colonies, and in most cases it took root and thrived. All common-law countries were once colonies of Great Britain, or, in some cases, colonies of colonies. Roughly speaking, the common law reigns wherever the English language is spoken. This means our own country, for one, and Canada (outside Quebec), Australia, New Zealand, Jamaica, Trinidad, Barbados, and Singapore, among others. Other systems of law contributed bits and pieces here and there—remnants of Spanish-Mexican law poke through the surface in California and Texas—but English law is by far the strongest historical element in our own legal system (Louisiana, as we said, stands off in a corner by itself). England and the United States have been drifting apart, legally speaking, for more than two hundred years, and there are now big chasms between them, but still the relationship between the two legal systems is obvious, instantly recognizable to any lawyer who jets from one country to the other.

The civil-law system was described above as the dominant system in Western Europe. No mention was made of Eastern Europe, which is a rather difficult area for purposes of classification. During the period when the Soviet Union dominated Eastern Europe, some scholars felt that the socialist countries were distinctive enough to make up a separate family of legal systems. Other scholars were not so sure; the Soviet Union and its satellites had close ties with the civil-law systems, and despite the revolutions and one-party rule there were strong resemblances in many details to the legal systems of Western Europe. For this reason, some scholars treated these systems as still part of the family—black sheep, perhaps, or oddball deviants, but family members nonetheless.

Then, quite suddenly, at the end of the 1980s, the Soviet Union disintegrated. Its constituent parts became independent countries—from Latvia and Estonia to Uzbekistan. The countries of Eastern Europe, once under Russian domination, renounced communism and rushed helter-skelter into the arms of a market economy and Western ways of life (more or less). One legal system—the system of the German Democratic Republic—simply expired; the GDR was absorbed into the

German Federal Republic (formerly "West Germany").[11] All of the countries that were formerly part of the Soviet bloc are busily reforming their legal systems, and in the process, they are drawing closer once more to the civil-law world.

"Socialist law" is not, of course, extinct; it survives, for example, in Cuba.[12] The controversy over whether socialist law was and is a separate system or is merely part of the civil-law family may be nothing but a question of words. Obviously, Cuba, which does not recognize private ownership of businesses, and has collectivized agriculture, has a lot in common with the now-defunct systems in Hungary or Poland and less in common with, say, the law of Mexico or Venezuela. In these countries there are private businesses; lawyers work in the private sector and are not employees of the government, as are lawyers in Cuba; the economy is not centrally planned; there is no censorship. Whether these differences mean we have to put Cuba in a separate family is not terribly important. What *is* important is to see how the form of the economy and the structure of society fundamentally alter the resulting legal system.

In general, it is a fairly crude business to assign legal systems to this or that family. There are always troublesome cases at the margin. The Scandinavian countries, for example, do not fit very precisely the technical patterns of law among their European neighbors; some scholars assign them a family of their own. In general, we have to remember that a legal system is not an exercise in history; it is a working system, very much here and now. In essence, it can be looked at as a kind of problem-solving machine, and the problems that face it are the problems of today, not yesterday. Legal tradition may explain some aspects of the shape and style of a system, but history and tradition are probably not as decisive factors as most lawyers (and laymen) think.

For example, Haiti and France are supposed to have very similar legal systems; they are close relatives inside a single family. The Haitian system is derived from that of France. This is certainly true on paper. But is it true when we look at the living law? Until recently, Haiti was a plundered and mismanaged dictatorship. The population was and is desperately poor, almost entirely rural, and largely illiterate. Haiti's suffering people struggle to survive in a wrecked and overpopulated land. France is rich, has a parliamentary system, and is urban and highly industrialized. The two countries may have codes of law on the books that look very similar, but it seems likely that the living law of France has more in common with the law of England than with the law of Haiti, even though the English legal system belongs to a different "family."

This last statement is basically a guess, because there is surprisingly little research about the way legal systems actually work, and what we have is spotty and scattered. Comparing whole legal systems, in operation, is essentially beyond our power. But it simply has to be true that the level of development in a country must have an enormous influence on that country's legal system. If you ever traveled by car in England and France, you noticed (or took for granted) that the traffic rules in the two countries are basically the same, even though the English insist on driving on the "wrong" side of the road. It is probably the case that every country touched by the automotive revolution has traffic rules that have a lot of features in common. Technology is a great lawmaker and a great leveler. The railroad in many ways and in many fields practically rewrote the law books of the United States in the nineteenth century. In this century, the automobile has had almost as big an influence on law. Neither the railroad nor the automobile shows much respect for what family a legal system belongs to.

It is hard to exaggerate the importance of technology in understanding what makes contemporary law tick. Accident law—the heart of the legal field we call torts—is basically the offspring of the nineteenth-century railroad; in the twentieth century, the automobile largely replaced the railroad as a source of accidents, and of accident law. The automobile is responsible for a vast body of rules about roads, traffic, auto safety, buying cars on the installment plan, and so on. Its invention has changed society (and thus the law) in absolutely fundamental ways. We take many of these changes for granted. Could either urban or suburban life go on without cars? Yet the automobile is not something that separates civil-law and common-law countries. It poses the same problems for all of them. It does indeed separate modern systems from older or more primitive systems. And it has a deep impact on the way we live, on where we live, and on the very structure of freedom, our ability to come and go as we think we please.

Only two or three main groups—families—of legal systems have been mentioned thus far. But the civil-law and common-law systems are not the only families of legal systems. Every society has a legal system; thus, many countries have clearly been left out. No mention has been made, for example, of the legal systems of the Far East, or the sacred-law systems of classical India, Israel, and the Islamic countries. Islamic law, in particular, is a living force in the world today. In Saudi Arabia, for example, it has official status, and it has made a dramatic comeback in other Muslim countries, most notably in Iran under the Ayatollah Khomeini and his successors. Africa is the home of dozens and dozens of tribal systems of law. Many of them are extremely interesting; some have been carefully studied; all are under great pressure from Western codes and rules in this age of global economies and instantaneous communication.

This book is about American law, a subject which is daunting in itself; it is impossible to provide much detail about other systems of law. But comparisons and contrasts are always interesting and sometimes enlightening. It is not fashionable anymore to label some systems of law as "primitive" (the word seems too insulting); but it is as plain as day that the law of a tribe of hunters and gatherers, or the law of the nomad empire of Attila or Genghis Khan, has to be different from the law of modern America—or, for that matter, from the law of modern Mongolia. Does it make sense to talk about evolutionary patterns in the history of law—progressions moving inexorably from stage to stage, from lower to higher? In other words, do legal systems evolve in some definite, patterned way, starting from stage A and passing through B and C on the road to D? Are there natural stages and a fixed order of progression?

This is a classic question of legal scholarship. There is no definite answer; some people even deny that the question makes sense. A small band of people with spears and knives has legal needs very different from ours; a feudal system generates one kind of law, big-city America quite another. Changes in social systems and technology necessarily push a legal system toward new burdens and new habits. Classical Roman law did not worry about who has the best claim to custody of a baby born after *in vitro* fertilization, nor about copyrighting software. Legal systems are never static. They change with changing times. In a country like ours, constantly moving, squirming, changing, the law is especially dynamic. We live in a restless world. The rate of change, the kind of change, the effects of change—these are matters of vital interest, and are at the heart of the questions discussed in this book. Whether we call the main lines of growth "evolution" is only a question of words.

2

Law: Formal and Informal

*W*HEN PEOPLE THINK about law or talk about law, what they usually have in mind is the official legal system—that is, the system run by the government, the one we pay taxes to support. Many definitions of law make this concept explicit: Donald Black, as we have said, has defined law as governmental social control.

But there are other ways to define law, and some of these are broader than Black's definition. The legal scholar Lon Fuller once defined law as "the enterprise of subjecting human conduct to the governance of rules."[1] Of course, the government is very much in the business of subjecting behavior to rules (or trying to), but it is not the only entity playing this game. Fuller deliberately framed his definition in such a way that it was not limited to official rules—rules put out by the government. He simply said "rules." If we take his definition at face value, the government has no monopoly on law, in this or any society.

Fuller's definition, in fact, points to quite another way of looking at law. He asks us to look not only at the source of legal process—that is, whether it comes from the government and wears an official badge, so to speak—but also at the process itself. Any organization of any size has rules and tries to enforce them. The bigger the organization, the more rules it is likely to have. Students at university or college do not have to be told that schools make rules and regulations and try to enforce them. These rules and regulations are part of the life all around them. Just as obviously, any business bigger than a mom-and-pop store—and any hospital, prison, or factory—must work with rules: rules about the jobs of employees, about buying equipment, about handling customers and patients, about income and expenses, about bosses and underlings, and so on.

How does a company enforce these rules? It has no official police or courts. But it certainly has sanctions—ways of delivering rewards and punishments. A company cannot hang a worker, whip him, or deport him to a desert island, but it can fire somebody who comes in late all the time, or is drunk on the job, or refuses to follow the rules. At one time, the boss had unlimited power to hire and fire. He was rulemaker, judge, and jury. But in large companies, at least, this is no longer the case—or not to the same extent. The process is much more "legalized" today. In many large companies, there are complicated procedures for handling discipline on the job and for settling grievances. Where the workforce is unionized, the labor contract will often set up and regulate these grievance procedures. Frequently both sides will let a neutral third person—an arbitrator—make final decisions. Many nonunion companies also have some kind of grievance and discipline procedures.

This is not the only way in which a big company resembles a kind of private government, with a private legal system. Not only will a big company have private "courts," it will also have private police. General Motors, for example, had 4,200 plant guards in 1978; this meant that the police force of this company was bigger than the police departments in any except the five largest cities in this country.[2] By 1984, by one estimate, there were 1.1 million security guards, twice as many as the number of police officers.[3] In 1992, it was reported that about 100,000 of these guards toted guns—"more than the combined police forces of the country's 30 largest cities."[4] Security guards wear uniforms and often look like the police who are paid by the state. They often walk regular beats, and they can and do make arrests.

The private police business is growing very fast. But it is not a new phenomenon. The famous Pinkerton National Detective Agency ("the eye that never sleeps") guarded Abraham Lincoln, spied on crooked railroad employees, and supplied scabs to companies whose workers were on strike.[5] Other detective agencies sprang up in the late nineteenth and early twentieth centuries. Companies stung by losses from crime, inside and outside, have turned more and more to private police and private detectives for help. People who live in closed subdivisions in the suburbs also turn to private uniformed guards to give them a sense of security.

In a sense, then, every institution could be said to have a legal system of its own. It would not stretch Fuller's definition very much to claim that even families make law and enforce it. Mother and father lay down rules and make decisions all the time: who does the dishes, when the children can stay out past ten, how much TV they can watch. There are rules big and small—nobody gets more than one slice of cake at a birthday party, chores and toys must be shared, and so on. These rules are, in a sense, part of the "law" inside the family.

There is nothing wrong in defining law to include these rules, and in including in the study of law research on the way fathers and mothers run families. For some purposes such a strategy would be a good idea. But it makes the subject unwieldy. To use the word "law" in this sense swallows up most of human activity and classifies vast areas of behavior as "legal." This may be unnecessary, or downright misleading, if one's aim is to study those processes and institutions that are more conventionally given the title of "law" and "legal order." Nonetheless, it is good to remember that the term "law" can be applied to processes of many kinds, even those that are very informal, very far from the official legal system. What makes them like official law is what Fuller pointed out: they subject behavior to rules.

There are some processes that are both formal and official, in the sense of governmental. This is true, for example, of any law that Congress passes. Other norms are part of the law, but are unwritten, informal—more "custom" than hard law. Here the speed limit provides us with a good everyday example. The formal, official rule sets the limit on Interstate 280 at sixty-five miles an hour. But everybody knows that the "real" rule, the one actually enforced, is closer to seventy-five. In other words, a police officer will not stop you if you are driving sixty-eight miles an hour, even though you are technically breaking the law.

If we turn to *private* law, we also find examples of both formality and informality. Grievance committees in industry sometimes look a lot like courts, may be quite elaborate procedurally, and may even behave like courts. Formal procedures abound in other big institutions. Students cannot be expelled from a university without (if they choose it) some sort of hearing or "trial." In some schools or universities, a student may even have the right to "appeal" from a C grade in a course and get the grade reviewed at a higher level. In case of serious infractions—for example, if a student is accused of cheating on an exam—the student will certainly have the right to some sort of formal process, and may even have the right to bring a lawyer to the hearing. If the student is found "guilty," he or she can probably appeal to a dean or the president of the university. Yet all of this, thus far, is strictly private, at least in private universities. The government plays no part in the process.

This does not mean, of course, that the formal, official legal system had nothing to do with the development of these procedures. Quite the contrary is true. These inside procedures came about, in part, because of outside pressure from court decisions, for example. Indeed, the support of the courts has been a crucial factor in the rise of "due process" in schools. For example, in *Goss v. Lopez,*[6] the United States Supreme Court, the highest court in the land, decided that a high school student could not be suspended from school without some sort of hearing, if the student wanted one. It also does not mean that the results of these disciplinary hearings, even though the "outside" principles are influential, end up in perfect conformity to these "outside" principles, either of procedure or of substance. Colleges have had to deal with matters a lot more sensitive than cheating on exams—date rape, for example, or fraternity hazing, or the fallout from drunken parties on Fraternity Row, including a lot of mistreatment of women. Front-page stories in the *New York Times,* in May 1996, alleged a pattern of excessive leniency, and downright cover-ups, at many universities and colleges.[7]

There are also unofficial courts of various sorts scattered all through the country. Some of these are run by organized religious bodies. Orthodox Jews, for example, can bring disputes to a rabbinical court for settlement. The Catholic Church presides over an elaborate system of canon law. Church courts decide whether a marriage can be annulled, for example. This does not bind the regular secular courts, but it is very important to a devout Catholic, whose religion forbids divorce and who might want to get married again and yet stay within the church's good graces.

Leigh-Wai Doo has described in some detail a quite different kind of court: the Chinese Consolidated Benevolent Association in New England, which handled disputes within the Chinese community. Let us look at one example of this "court" in operation. One busy day in a Chinese restaurant, the chef asked the owner for a raise of $25 a week. The owner said no. The chef then walked off the job. Later, he sent a bill for back wages, plus $25; the owner, for his part, demanded $500 in damages. Neither one paid the other's claim.

Two months went by. The restaurant could not get a good chef, and its business began to suffer. Meanwhile, the chef's "family association" appealed to the Benevolent Association, demanding the back wages and denying that the restaurant had any right to claim damages. The Benevolent Association consulted with the restaurant association and with the family groups; it turned out that the restaurant wanted the chef back at work, and was willing to give him a raise (of $10) if he would change his "unreliable ways." The Benevolent Association then had the "task" of discovering "whether the chef wanted the job back," and, if he did, whether he could be talked into making amends. They "studied the man's character and the best ways of approaching him." After a week of "patient persuasion and stressing that he would not find work if he continued his erratic behavior," the chef agreed.

The Benevolent Association now knew that both sides were willing to settle. It called on them to meet before its board. The reconciliation took about two hours. The chef apologized; the owner rehired him with a $10 raise. They "finalized the settlement by drinking tea together."[8]

Neither a rabbinic court nor the Chinese Consolidated Benevolent Association has the power to back up decisions with force. Such institutions have no way to throw a "litigant" in jail or to squeeze money out of a loser. But they do have moral force, and this may be no small matter. They can bind those people who voluntarily submit to them. By inclination, and also because they are unable to crack the whip, these "courts" lean heavily toward compromise, toward restoring harmony, toward reconciliation and voluntary agreement. In this sense, they are less lawlike than ordinary courts. They are not so very different from the way some judges work "in chambers." And they much resemble courts in simple societies, as anthropologists and others have described them.

These specialized "courts" may also be fairly prone to decay in a society like ours, which is very fragmented and very pluralistic. The old traditions die hard, but they do eventually die. Apparently, the dispute-settlement models described by Leigh-Wai Doo have been losing much of their strength in Chinese-American communities. New waves of immigration—Asian immigration was heavy in the 1980s and 1990s—might, of course, conceivably strengthen them once more.

There are countless other ways in which Americans use law that is unofficial (nonstate) and yet quite formal. Every trade association or occupational group—every big institution of any kind—will make rules and will have some way to enforce them or to settle disputes. Businesses often handle differences through the use of arbitration. Very often, when two businesspeople enter into a contract, they write into it an arbitration provision. This means that if some dispute or problem comes up, the two sides will not go to court (at least not initially), but instead hire an arbitrator—a private citizen, usually skilled and experienced in this work—to settle the dispute. Labor contracts (collective bargains) also typically provide for arbitration. In other words, arguments over what the contract means, or over work rules and the like, will be decided by an arbitrator, someone on whom both management and the union can agree. In some companies and industries, there has been a permanent arbitrator; this was true, for example, of U.S. Steel and the Ford Motor Company. Under other industry contracts, the arbitrator may be chosen case by case. The contract between the Major League Baseball Players' Association and the owners of major league baseball teams, for example, calls for arbitration of salary disputes by a board of three arbitrators.

Arbitration is in some ways a kind of halfway house between official and unofficial law. The arbitrator is, after all, not a professional judge. But his word is usually final, just like a judge's. If a soap company and one of its suppliers agree to arbitrate their disputes, they are going to have to abide by this agreement. The courts will, if pushed, force the losing side to carry out what the arbitrator decided. It is in this sense that arbitration is a kind of mixture of the public and the private.

Just as every institution, down to the family, has the habit and need to make rules, so too is there a general need to find ways and means to enforce the rules; otherwise they are perfectly meaningless. Hence it is no surprise that arbitration and processes like it are so pervasive in society. There is a hunger for ways to settle disputes that the regular courts cannot satisfy, or can satisfy only at too high a price. We can think of the formal courts as fancy French restaurants in a society that also needs pizza and hamburger joints for fast, cheap food.

In California one rather curious system, a hybrid between public and private dispute settlement, has been given the nickname "rent-a-judge." The "rent-a-judge" system is based on an old, rather murky state law, which was rediscovered and put to modern use. In the rent-a-judge system, parties to a dispute sidestep the regular courts; they hire their own judges (actual judges who have retired from the bench). These judges resolve the dispute—privately, but with all the trappings and procedures of a regular trial. The results are treated as binding on both sides. One company, Judicial Arbitration and Mediation Services, is among the largest providers of rent-a-judge services. It did a business in 1991–92 of about $24 million; in 1993 it had 230 judges working out of fourteen offices in three states.[9]

Public and private spheres of law thus interact. They are not totally independent of each other. Students have hearings in universities not because universities decided to grant hearings out of the goodness of their institutional hearts, but in part because they were pressured by court cases on student rights. Arbitration awards, too, as we mentioned, can be enforced in court. The private sphere is also influenced by the public sphere in other ways. Most claims for damages (in automobile accidents, for example) are settled out of court, but the parties bargain "in the shadow of the law."[10] That is, both sides know that there is an operating legal system in the country—that there are rules and doctrines about damage cases—and they or their lawyers have some idea what is likely to happen if they go to court. These ideas enter into their bargaining and influence it, even though the bargaining is strictly private. The relationship between this "shadow" and the out-of-court bargaining process is, to be sure, quite complicated. Divorce lawyers, for example, may manipulate the "shadow," when dealing with their own naive clients, in ways that increase their own power.[11] There is much that we do not know about the way formal law interacts with private behavior.

The discussion so far has isolated four types of law. There is law that is both formal and public (an act of Congress, for example); law that is public (or governmental) but informal (the "real" rules about the speed limit); law that is formal but private (grievance procedures); and law that is both private and informal (rules inside a family). We can also draw a line between legitimate and illegitimate processes. Usually, a system is not illegitimate just because it is informal or private; nor is there anything illegitimate about the formal private systems (like the work of the Chinese Consolidated Benevolent Association or a hearing conducted into cheating allegations at a university).

The informal part of the public system is a more complicated story. Some aspects of it are illegitimate, or downright illegal. It is a basic fact about the American legal system (and the legal systems in other modern countries) that we cannot tell from the way the system is described on paper how it actually operates in life. Sometimes we are perfectly willing to accept a certain shortfall between form and reality. The speed laws can serve as our example once more: it does not seem to trouble us, or the police, that the "real" speed limit on Interstate 280 is not sixty-five, the official figure, but something a bit higher. Most people also feel that rules are made to be bent a little bit, in the interest of common sense or human frailty.

Other situations are not so benign or so readily accepted. Some hover in a kind of twilight zone between the legal and the illegal. Prostitution, for example, is against the law everywhere, except for some counties in Nevada. Yet police and city officials have often closed their eyes to the "social evil," provided certain conditions were met. In many cities, in the past, police would not raid a house of prostitution so long as the house was inside an area of vice, the so-called red-light district. The police sometimes even issued rules to regulate prostitution despite the fact that the business, strictly speaking, was completely illegal. In Chicago, for example, the superintendent of police in 1910 issued a whole sheaf of rules: "No house of ill-fame shall be permitted outside of certain restricted districts, or . . . within two blocks of any school, church, hospital, or public institution, or upon any streetcar line." Prostitutes in Chicago were not supposed to wear transparent dresses, and "houses of ill fame" had to have double doors, not "swinging doors that permit . . . a view of the interior from the street."[12]

Prostitution, in other words, was half inside, half outside the law. It was officially illegal, yet at the same time it was regulated, and by the same legal system that condemned it to illegality. This was not and is not a unique situation. The "real" law about gambling, divorce, abortion, immigration, and many other subjects is quite different from what it is supposed to be, and many aspects of social behavior, like prostitution, are both inside and outside the law at the same time.

There are other forms of "justice" that stand completely outside legality. The justice of underworld gangs, or of organized crime, is of this nature. Gangland justice stays hidden, operating only in certain dark corners of society. But our history is also full of open outbursts of unofficial law, or "popular justice," as it is sometimes called. Perhaps the most famous examples are the so-called vigilante movements.

Vigilantism goes far back in American history. There were examples even in the colonial period—the so-called Regulators of South Carolina appeared on the scene in 1767. But the golden age of the vigilantes was in the West, in the period after 1850. The two San Francisco "Vigilance Committees," both active in the 1850s, were particularly famous in their day; but there were many other vigilante groups, in Montana, Colorado, Nevada, Oregon, and Texas. One scholar counted at least 326 vigilante movements, and if records were more complete, the count would probably rise to about 500. The vigilantes dispensed quick, often bloody "justice" against horse thieves, rustlers, desperadoes, and ne'er-do-wells of one stamp or another. One estimate is that vigilantes shot or hanged some 729 men.[13]

In their day, the vigilantes were often controversial. They were criticized by defenders of orthodox law and order. Still, many people—perhaps a majority—felt that the vigilantes performed a public service; that in the raw, lawless towns of the West, there was no real alternative to vigilante justice. The chief justice of Montana Territory—who might be expected to stick up for law if not order—praised them in 1864 as genuine "tribunals of the people." They were, he felt, an absolute "necessity."

"Popular tribunals"—private systems that rival the official system—come up (we often hear) out of a "vacuum" of power. This usually means that there is some group that feels official law is too weak, or has fallen into the wrong hands. For example, the merchants of Dodge City, Kansas, in 1872, were so concerned about lawlessness that they hired an unofficial marshal, gave him a badge, and set him loose. In 1873, the businessmen formed a vigilance committee, which started its work by killing two men in a dance hall and ordering five more to get out of town. The committee itself later became such a disorderly nuisance that it had to be put down with force.[14]

The vigilantes of history have died out, but even today there are neighborhood associations that call themselves vigilantes (or "neovigilantes"). These groups patrol city streets and keep watch in their neighborhoods, because they feel the "real" police are not doing the job. Richard Maxwell Brown mentions some examples from the 1960s: the Deacons for Defense and Justice (a black organization); the Maccabees of Crown Heights, Brooklyn (largely Jewish); and the North Ward Citizens' Committee of Newark, New Jersey (largely Italian).[15] In 1988, the *New York Times* reported that "hundreds" of neighborhood groups in New York City were joining in a "movement of citizen activism against crack"; the movement "sometimes straddles the line between vigilance and vigilantism."[16] In 1992, a "vigilante Korean security force, wearing white scarves," patrolled the "burned and looted shops of Koreatown" in Los Angeles, after race riots cut a path of destruction through the area.[17]

In the old West, the vigilantes explained and justified themselves in various ways. The job of justification was easiest where people felt "the law" itself was corrupt: where the sheriff, for example, was part of a gang of horse thieves. Other vigilantes—and vigilante-like movements—were concerned primarily with enforcement of the traditional moral code. The so-called White Cap movement started in southern Indiana in 1887; it spread from there to Ohio, New York, and other states as far off as Texas. This was a "movement of violent moral regulation by local masked bands." The White Caps usually punished their victims by whipping; their targets were "wife beaters, drunkards, poor providers, immoral couples and individuals, lazy and shiftless men, and petty neighborhood thieves."[18]

Most of these offenses were not crimes at all, or if they were, the law punished them quite weakly. Throughout the nineteenth century there were outbursts of rioting directed against immorality: in Detroit, for example, between 1855 and 1859, "one bordello after another felt the fury of an angry mob." Seventeen brothels were damaged or destroyed.[19] Similar incidents took place in other cities as well.

"Popular justice," then, took many forms. At one end of the scale, there were self-appointed judges and juries who took some care to imitate regular legal process, even to the extent of holding "trials." At the other end of the scale, popular justice degenerated into blind fury, rioting, lynch law. Some of the most sinister episodes came about where communities (or parts of communities) felt they could not trust "the law" because it was too squeamish, or (from their standpoint) too much committed to rules and procedures.

The notorious Ku Klux Klan arose in the South, after the Civil War; federal troops occupied the southern states, and state governments could not or would not allow whites to terrorize black people openly. The Klan took over the job. In the 1870s, when the federal troops left, white supremacy came to power in most of the southern states. These governments developed other ways to keep black people "in their place," and the Klan went mostly out of business. Some of the methods used to enforce white supremacy were fairly legalistic. For example, poll taxes and literacy tests kept blacks from voting. Other methods, however, were even more savage and violent than the Klan. There was an outbreak of "lynch law" in the 1890s. Hundreds of blacks in the South were hung for breaking the Southern "code"—dragged from prison cells or from their homes and killed by jeering mobs. The Klan cropped up again in the 1920s, and still a third outburst followed in the wake of *Brown v. Board of Education* (1954), when local white custom once again conflicted with firm orders from outside to dismantle segregation in schools and public institutions. This time, however, there was no federal retreat, and the Klan today is a much weaker group, on the fringes of society.

The main line of vigilante history is less bloody and less one-sided than its bastard brother, lynch law. The leaders of the Western vigilante groups were by no means thugs. Indeed, they were often solid citizens. It was the business community that organized vigilantes in Dodge City. Vigilante leaders themselves were, or became, bank presidents, political figures in a couple of cases, even United States senators. Few people today would defend lynch law, but there is a certain yearning for the simplicity and swiftness of "popular justice." There are situations of frustration and rage, mostly over street crime, which lead people to feel that do-it-yourself law and order is justified. There is a good deal of public sympathy for a parent who kills a child-abuser, and there was also a good deal of support for Bernhard Goetz, the "subway vigilante." Goetz shot four black teenagers—one of whom was paralyzed for life— who seemed to Goetz to be threatening him as he rode on the New York subway. Goetz was never convicted of any crime worse than a gun offense,[20] although his most seriously injured victim won a huge jury award in a civil case in 1996.[21] Many popular books and movies glorify the man who "takes the law into his own hands." The phrase is worth thinking about. It asserts—as the vigilantes did—that the private avenger comes not to deny the law but to fulfill it. Whether or not this is the result, or ever was, is another question.

Yet in the long run one of the most important trends in criminal justice has been running in the opposite direction: away from popular justice—away from the layman and toward the professional lawman. In the eighteenth century, there was no organized police force, certainly no FBI, no detectives, no police science. The role and power of the jury (a band of twelve laymen) was as great as it is today, and perhaps greater. The power of the public—of the "mob"—was a fact of life. The word "mob" has a lawless sound, but there was often only a fine line between mob action and public action that was legal, if not downright praiseworthy. The community in general had the right to rise up and catch thieves when the hue and cry was sounded. A magistrate could form a "posse"—that is, a group of able-bodied men, private citizens—to help out the sheriff.[22] This system survived into the American West; the sheriff's posse is familiar to every fan of western movies. The West is, of course, the same terrain where the vigilantes flourished. By the late nineteenth century, Eastern cities all had police forces; law enforcement was professional or, in any event, the job of full-time, paid police and detectives.

Sometimes there are whole governments that technically speaking have no legal basis and are, from a certain standpoint, illegal. History or war is often the ultimate judge. When Grant crushed the armies of the South, he swept away the government and legal system of the Confederacy. Other "governments" have sprung up, sometimes in remote areas, where a vacuum in power and law is perceived. This happened, for example, among the Mormons in Utah, before the organization of territorial government. From the standpoint of the United States, there was no law in effect in Utah. But in fact, the leaders of the Mormon Church exercised tight and effective control over this new community. The "government" in Utah was no different from a legitimate government, in any practical way.

Other examples of mini-governments that are not "official" come closer to the line between legitimacy and illegitimacy. On the American frontier, settlers often formed "claim clubs" to protect their interests in their land against "claim jumpers" (and against each other). In other parts of the country, there were groups of miners who drew up their own codes of "customs." The claim clubs were considered necessary because, strictly speaking, the settlers did not have, in fact, any legally enforceable claims in many situations. They were squatters on public lands. Acts of Congress starting in 1796 provided for the sale of public land in an orderly way. First the land had to be surveyed; when this was done, the president could announce that the land was ready for sale. The tracts would be auctioned off at government land offices. Before the date of the auction, nobody but the government owned the land, and nobody was supposed to settle on it.

This was "the law," but it was flagrantly disobeyed. Thousands of people crowded onto the public domain. They built houses and farms long before the land was officially open for sale. As far as the settlers were concerned, they had a perfect right to the land, which they had earned by their time and their sweat. But legally speaking, they lived in a vacuum. For this reason, they banded together, drew up constitutions and codes to govern their rights, and formed little governments of their own. Their methods were not always sweet and gentle, and their treatment of outsiders was sometimes harsh. But the squatter organizations were yet another example of makeshift law, springing up in the cracks and crevices of the larger society.[23]

The Birth of Formal Law

No legal system in a developed country can be purely formal or informal. It is invariably a mixture of both. Official, government law is generally (though not always) formal: patterned, structured, leaning on the written word and on regular institutions and processes. Nonstate law is usually much less formal, but both the official and the unofficial codes are mixtures of the two. Why is it that some parts of a system of order are highly formal, some parts much less so, and some completely loose and formless?

We can start to answer with a point that may be obvious: historically speaking, the informal comes first. The simplest societies, which probably resemble older human societies more than the urbanized societies, have highly informal legal systems. Formality seems to take over when an informal system no longer works, for one reason or another. In small societies—societies in which most relationships are face-to-face—a formal legal system may not be needed at all. Not many people break the rules. Custom is king. Public opinion—what friends, kinfolk, neighbors think—is a powerful force, a powerful pressure. People do what social norms say they should do, not because they are angels but because their relatives and neighbors can inflict such terrible "punishment." In fact, these societies even dispense with any organized method for applying public force to somebody who breaks the rules. Many simple societies, in other words, do not have courts, judges, or police. They make do without them.

An extreme case is the community on Tristan da Cunha, a lonely, isolated, barren spot of land in the middle of the South Atlantic Ocean. A few hundred people live here, growing potatoes and catching fish. A team of scholars visited the island in the 1930s to study animals, birds—and social life. The social scientists on the team were amazed to see how law-abiding the people were—if we can apply the word "law-abiding" to people living in a place where there is nothing that even looks like law as we know it. Nobody could think of an example of a serious crime—murder, rape, or the like—ever committed on the island. There were none of the trappings of criminal justice—no police, courts, judges, or jails. Nobody needed them.

What made the people of this island such models of good behavior? One idea leaps immediately to mind: the islanders had no choice. They were trapped on their island, with no hope of escape; they were absolutely dependent on each other for social life and support. Life on Tristan da Cunha was totally "transparent"; everyone on the island was exposed, inexorably, to the "Argus-eyed vigilance of the community." Under circumstances like these, informal norms are just too powerful to be disobeyed.[24]

Of course, in a broad sense, there was law on the island, and lots of it. There were norms of behavior, and people followed them; these norms were enforced by real sanctions. Prisons, fines, whippings, and the gallows are not the only ways in which societies punish people. Teasing, shaming, and open disapproval are also methods of punishment. They can be terribly severe, in their own way. It is because they were so strong on Tristan da Cunha that the community never needed courts, policemen, and jails.

There are similar forms of punishment in other small, face-to-face communities. Some are quite familiar from our own legal history. In the American colonial period, Massachusetts Bay and other colonies forced certain offenders to sit in the stocks, where everybody who passed by could see them. Sitting in the stocks was not physically painful, but it exposed a person to public scorn and shame. Samuel Powell, a servant who stole a pair of breeches in Virginia (1638), was ordered to "sitt in the stocks on the next Sabboth day . . . from the beginninge of morninge prayer until the end of the Sermon with a pair of breeches about his necke."[25] Whipping was another common form of punishment. It was painful to the body to be sure, but there was also psychic pain. Whipping was always done in public, before the eyes of the whole community.

But we do not have to go to far-off islands or to the long ago for examples of the process we are describing. It happens every day in our times, too. We see it in schools, in family life, in clubs, in small groups everywhere. The drill sergeant in the army punishes by yelling at the clumsy recruit, exposing him to ridicule. The law school professor in the movie *The Paper Chase* used ridicule and sarcasm to punish students who were unprepared or did not understand the work. School-teachers and parents have a whole repertoire of tricks to invoke shame, guilt, and derision.

But it is also clear that the bigger, the more complex, the more "advanced" the society, the less it can rely on informal sanctions alone. The United States is about as far as one can get from Tristan da Cunha, socially speaking. People in our country live in face-to-face contact with friends and relatives, but at the same time, all of us are in daily contact with people who are strangers to us; we use products and processes made and presented by strangers. We constantly have to deal with people we do not know, on the streets, in the workplace, in banks and hospitals and government offices. The food we eat is packaged in far-away factories; the clothes we wear are woven in distant mills. People we never see manufacture the necessities of our lives, using procedures we do not understand. When we ride in a plane, a train, a taxi, or a bus, we put our lives in the hands of strangers.

These are the facts of life. They have tremendous consequences. As individuals, we have little control over these vital strangers. We open a can of soup and eat it. How can we he sure that the soup is made from good ingredients, that it won't make us sick? Wholesomeness is beyond our control, and certainly beyond our knowledge. Nor can we rely on informal norms or public pressure to guarantee that the soup is not poisonous, that it is nourishing and good. We want something stronger and more reliable than custom, something with independent force. In short, we want law. Hence in complex, interdependent societies, like ours, there arises a sense of need, which generates an enormous appetite for formal controls. But these controls can only come from some kind of organized government, working through rules of law.

As we said, face-to-face life is not gone, despite our dependence on strangers. Even in a big, impersonal society like this one, we have families, we have friends, we have strong personal ties to people and places. Even in this megasociety, we spend much of our lives in tiny groups. The big society is made up of these little molecules of people. Each one of us has some personal zone or sphere, our own island of Tristan da Cunha. Inside our little group, informal norms still rule. But for most of us, there is this vital difference: we see a way to escape from the island. On Tristan da Cunha, the boat came only once a year. For us the boat comes every day, every hour, every minute. To a large extent, we feel we have the chance to change jobs, change cities, change families, if we wish—even, in a sense, to change lives. We may be prisoners to our characters, to our conditions of life, to traditions. But compared to most people in most societies, for us there seem to be many doors of escape.

This means that informal norms stay powerful only when we let them—when we agree that they should remain in full force. Of course, psychological bonds can be, and often are, tremendously powerful. Social norms and the influence of culture are also far stronger than most people realize. To a large extent, we live in invisible cages, unaware of unconscious limitations—unaware how much context and culture determine what we like and what we do. We feel that we are citizens of a "republic of choice," but the reality may be far, far different.[26] Still, in many areas of life, if we *do* stay bound to some corner of society that rules us without "official" sanction, we do so in whole or in part because we want to, collectively—that is, people (or most of them) have consensus about the norms themselves, or at least about who has authority to set standards and make up rules. The Chinese-Americans did not have to abide by the rules of their Benevolent Association. They could escape from that island, so to speak. Increasingly they do tend to escape—particularly the younger generation. If they stay on their island, it is because at some level they want to, or feel compelled to for inner reasons. But when agreement to abide by traditional norms and to submit to (informal) authority breaks down, as happens so often in American society, then formal law will have to step in. Even in face-to-face settings.

We can illustrate the general point by looking at the way law has entered the life of the American schoolhouse. In the past, schools were places where children learned to read and write, to do math, and, in addition, to obey the rules. The rules were for the most part informal; the teacher was in charge of the classroom, the principal in charge of the school, and the school board in charge of the district. In a few rare instances, some parent or student challenged the way schools were run, but these exceptional incidents ended, for the most part, in failure. Until deep into the twentieth century, nobody heard about such things as "dress codes." Everybody knew more or less what children were supposed to wear, how they were supposed to be groomed, and so on. In any event, parents (and children) understood that the teacher ran the classroom; on such matters the teacher's word, or the principal's, was final. There were no written norms, no procedures, no structure of appeals.

This cozy system broke down in the late 1960s. Styles of dress and behavior were changing rapidly. Long hair for boys had become a fashion—and a symbol of rebellion. At least, this is the way some boys regarded long hair, mustaches, and beards. On this point teachers and principals tended to agree: These were symbols of rebellion, and they did not like these symbols. Since informal norms were not working, the schools turned to formality—to dress codes and hair codes. According to the rules in the high school in Williams Bay, Wisconsin—rules which ended up in court—hair had to be "worn so it does not hang below the collar line in the back, over the ears on the side and must be above the eyebrows." In this school, beards, mustaches, and "long sideburns" were also forbidden.[27]

Many other schools had similar rules. But they were not necessarily obeyed. In any number of school districts, high school boys refused to cut their hair and were disciplined, sent home, even expelled from school. There was no longer a consensus about the norms, nor was there any real consensus about authority itself. Most parents and students accepted the rules, but an important minority of parents and students did not. They refused to accept the idea that schools had the right to lay down rules about hairstyle. In a few aggravated instances, parents and students felt deeply enough about the matter to go to court, and schools like the Williams Bay high school found themselves, perhaps to their surprise, forced to defend their dress and hair codes in front of a federal judge. In the federal courts, there were no less than eighty-seven reported cases on hair length alone. The schools faced a dilemma. Agreement was unraveling, and the result was controversy, unpleasantness, disruption.

One way out was to submit; another was the path of formality. The dress codes themselves had been a step in this latter direction. Parents and students would at least know what was expected of them. Schools also developed formal procedures for dealing with disputes about student rights. A whole new field of law developed. Nobody in the nineteenth century had ever heard of "student rights" as a category of litigation, or as a problem for the law and for society. The new procedures spread to other institutions—universities, for example, as we have seen. The general pattern of development was much the same. Once upon a time the professor's word was law in the college classroom. By the 1970s, this was no longer quite so absolute. Now *law* was law. In many universities and colleges, a student had some right to challenge the professor, even with regard to the professor's most personal, most sacrosanct act: the grade given out in the course. Not that many students ever took up this opportunity. But the chance and the procedures were there, if anybody chose to use them. The "legalization" of university life, as we have already seen, later extended to such issues as sexual harassment and student misconduct in general—affairs that were once dealt with summarily or not at all.

We can draw a rather obvious general principle out of this story: informal norms break down in a situation of conflict. Indeed, this proposition is almost tautological, almost like saying A equals A. In a conflict situation, any society (or subsociety) is likely to give up on informal norms—they simply don't work—and turn to a more complicated, more formal system of handling what seems to be the problem. New procedures will spring up. More law will be generated, and law will turn its heavy guns toward higher formality. The innocent days of consensus are over. The teacher in the one-room schoolhouse, ruling the roost, is a ghost out of the past. She has been replaced by professionals, by a massive school bureaucracy, by a dense thicket of regulations and procedures. To a degree, this was inevitable. Sheer size of the system made it so; you can't run a giant retailing operation like Wal-Mart with the same techniques as a mom-and-pop store. Big-city school systems are also far more heterogeneous than they once were—a babel of tongues, a rainbow of races.

These last points give us at least a preliminary solution to a puzzle that runs through this book: why is there so much "law" in this country, so much "procedure," so much "due process," so much "legalization"? Society, like nature, hates a vacuum; and the breakdown of consensus— the decay of authority—*creates* a kind of vacuum, in this big, sprawling, diverse, and open society. Into this vacuum, law (in its formal sense) moves in. Here too is a clue to another puzzle: whether the trends we see will continue in the future, slow down and vanish, or get faster and stronger. Obviously, we have no crystal ball, but at least we have an idea about what to look for in daily life, what barometers to watch, what gauges to read.

3

The Background of American Law

*T*HIS BOOK IS about American law today. But legal systems have a past, a history, a tradition. To understand American law as it is, it is helpful to know where it came from and how it grew to its present shape. This chapter briefly sketches the historical background of our law.[1]

Beginnings: The Colonial Period

The territory which is now the United States was first settled by English-speaking people in the early seventeenth century. Their settlements were scattered along the eastern coast of the country. The Puritans sank their roots into the soil of New England; the Quakers settled in Pennsylvania; English Catholics colonized Maryland. There were also early settlements in what is now Virginia and the Carolinas.

The English were, of course, not alone in the race to plant colonies in the New World. The Spanish and Portuguese dominated what is now Latin America and many of the Caribbean islands. The Spanish flag once flew over Florida. Spain also claimed vast tracts of land in the far western deserts and along the western coast. The Dutch settled in New York, only to be pushed out by the British before 1700. The Dutch language and some bits and pieces of Dutch law lingered on in New York for a while before dying out.

A few traces of Dutch law perhaps spread beyond the borders of New York. The office of district attorney may have originated in the

Dutch-speaking areas. The matter is in some dispute. But no one disputes the survival of rather big chunks of Spanish law, and of civil law generally, among the states carved out of land that was once under Spanish rule. Another survivor, too, must be mentioned: the indigenous law of the native tribes. The people who were here before Columbus had their own systems of law. The interaction between these systems and the law of the conquering settlers has been complex, but among many of the larger groups—the Navajos, for example—tribal law and custom still play a significant role, and there are functioning tribal courts.

Nonetheless, it is true that the main body of American law derives from a single source, the law of England, if it derives from any outside source at all. No other legal system really had a chance to establish itself, just as no language other than English ever really had a chance to set down roots. Through the English, the common-law system—its habits, its traditions, its ways of thinking—crossed the Atlantic and took hold in this country.

Books on legal history often talk about "the" colonial period; but this can be somewhat misleading. After all, more than 150 years went by between the landing of settlers on Plymouth Rock and the outbreak of the Revolution. This is as long a stretch as the span of time between 1847 and 1997—an interval full of tremendous social change. The colonial period was not quite so turbulent and fast-moving, but it was crowded with events and developments, and it was structurally quite complex. For one thing, there were many different colonies—colonies whose identities were as distinct as those of New Hampshire and Georgia. The settlements were strung out like beads along the narrow coastline. Communication among them was poor. Communication with the mother country was even poorer; the immense, trackless, turbulent ocean separated the colonies from England.

This was a fact of vital importance. In theory, the British were in full control of the colonies, and the colonists were subjects of the king. In fact, the London government had only a feeble hold over these far-off children. The British were too far away to be effective tyrants, even when they wanted to be. Also (at least in the beginning) they had no consistent policy of empire, no idea how to govern distant colonies. For much of their history, then, the colonies (or most of them) were virtually independent.

The colonies can be divided into three groups. The northern colonies—Massachusetts, New Hampshire, Connecticut—were, in terms of English law, the most deviant. The middle group of colonies—New York, New Jersey, Pennsylvania, Delaware—stood halfway between north and south, legally as well as geographically. The southern colonies were the most conservative, in law and legal culture; they stuck more closely to English models.

These differences among colonies were not, of course, accidental. Puritan New England and Quaker Pennsylvania struck out on new paths, deliberately, in ways that Virginia and the Carolinas did not. Climate and land conditions were also influential. In the South, mild winters allowed a different kind of agriculture, organized on the plantation system. This made Southern society structurally somewhat closer to British society, ruled as it was by a landed gentry. Black slavery was another striking aspect of Southern life. The first Africans arrived in Virginia and other southern colonies before the middle of the seventeenth century. It is not clear when the legal status of slavery crystallized in Virginia and other colonies, but by 1700 a developed law of black slavery was in place. And by the time of the Revolution, slaves made up as much as 40 percent of Virginia's population.

There were no blacks in England, and there was no such thing as slavery under English law. The law of slavery was an American invention, stitched together out of various sources, powerfully influenced by strong feelings of race, and mixed together with the labor customs of the West Indies and the southern colonies.[2] Slaves were slaves for life, and the children of slave mothers were slaves from birth. There was slavery in the northern colonies, too; in New York, slaves made up over 10 percent of the population. There were slaves even in Massachusetts and New Hampshire. But slavery never dominated the North's labor system, as it did that of the South. New York slaves, for example, mostly "worked not in gangs but as domestic servants."[3]

In the colonies there were also thousands of "indentured servants." Indentured servitude was a kind of temporary slavery. Indentures were written documents—contracts of labor, in a way—which spelled out the terms and conditions of work. An indentured servant signed on to serve his master for some definite period: five to seven years was common. The servant earned no salary. During the term, the master had the right to sell the servant—or, to be more precise, to sell the right to the servant's labor for whatever was left of the term. The servant could not control this process; nor could the servant quit the job. Runaway servants were hunted down just like slaves. But when the period of indenture was up, the servant, unlike a slave, became completely free. Under custom and law, the servant was not supposed to leave the master's service empty-handed; he had the right to "freedom dues." In early Maryland, for example, these consisted of clothes, a hat, an ax, a hoe, three barrels of corn, and (until 1663) fifty acres of land. Later, food, clothing, and money were more typical dues ("Corne, Cloaths and Tolls").[4]

A good deal of research has been done on colonial legal systems. Most of it has concerned the northern colonies, especially Massachusetts. In truth, the legal system of Massachusetts Bay (as the colony was called) is uncommonly interesting. It deviated tremendously from English law, or at least from English law as practiced in the royal courts in London. Massachusetts law, in fact, looks so different from English law that at one point scholars argued among themselves whether it ought to be considered part of the common-law family at all.

By now, this idea seems a bit foolish. Despite some strange habits and language, the law of the colony was firmly rooted in English law and English practice. Some of its peculiarities disappear when we remember that the early colonists were not lawyers and were not members of the English landed gentry. The law they first brought with them was not the law of the great royal courts, which had little to do with the mass of the population; rather it was local law—the customs of their communities.[5] We might call this element "remembered folk law." Naturally, it was different from the strict, official law of the London courts. Nonetheless, the key elements of this law were English, and so was its vocabulary. How could it be otherwise? This was the only law that the settlers knew. Their law, in other words, was a kind of Creole or pidgin form of the common law.

The details of colonial law are complicated and confusing, but its essential nature is easy to grasp. Imagine a group of American college students shipwrecked and marooned on a desert island, forced to build a new society. They will organize some crude sort of government, and they will create something that can be called a legal system. It will be very different from the one they left behind. For one thing, most of the old legal system will be irrelevant. Traffic laws, for example, will not be needed where there is no traffic. On the other hand, the "colonists" will have to make up many new laws—rules about posting sentries on a hill to try to signal passing ships, rules about how to divide fish and clams caught in local waters, and so on. People on the island will reproduce those parts of American law that they remember and that fit their new life and their new community. Ideology will also play a role. It will make a good deal of difference to know who the students were—whether it was a shipload of Young Libertarians that landed on the island, or a shipload of Young Socialists; what part of the country the students came from; what their religion was.

Colonial law was something like a legal system built up by shipwrecked, stranded people. It, too, was made of these three elements:

remembered folk law, new law created because of the brute needs of life in the new country, and legal elements shaped by the settlers' ideologies (Puritans in Massachusetts, for example; or Quakers in Pennsylvania). If we look at the *Laws and Liberties of Massachusetts,* one of the earliest colonial law books (1648), we find dozens of examples of all three elements. We find, to begin with, all sorts of references to juries and judges, to wills and other legal documents, to a system of private property—all of these brought over from England as part of the baggage of custom and memory and taken almost for granted.

On the other hand, life in a raging wilderness demanded arrangements far different from those of Stuart England. There were rules, for example, against selling or giving "to any Indian . . . any . . . gun, or any gun-powder shot or lead . . . or any militarie weapons or armour"—a rule that of course had no counterpart in England. Ideology mattered, too: this was a community dominated by stern men of religion. There were rules against Jesuits, Anabaptists, witches ("any man or woman . . . that . . . hath or consulteth with a familiar spirit" was to be severely punished). There were also laws against heretics (those that "go about to subvert and destroy the Christian Faith and Religion, by broaching or mainteining any damnable heresie"). Blasphemy was a crime. There was certainly nothing remotely like the modern idea of separation of church and state.

Massachusetts law, inevitably, was simpler than the general law of England. It was stripped bare of old technicalities, for the most part; it was streamlined and altered so as to make it much easier to handle. English law in the seventeenth century was a trackless labyrinth of technicality. It had grown slowly over the years, and this slow evolution allowed it to take the form of a dense texture of irrational, overlapping segments—a crazy patchwork that worked tolerably well in practice, but had become so complex that only a handful of lawyers even pretended to understand it completely. Even had the settlers wanted to, they had no way to duplicate this kind of system exactly. A colony is always, in a sense, a fresh start.

In form and substance, then, Massachusetts and other colonies struck out on their own. To take one example, the king's law in England called for primogeniture. That is, if a landowner died without making out a will, all of his land went to his eldest son. Massachusetts, from the word go, discarded this rule. All children shared in the inheritance, though the eldest son got a double share. Most of the other northern colonies (Rhode Island and New York were exceptions) simply abandoned primogeniture, and quite early. It lasted much longer in the southern colonies: in Georgia it was abolished in 1777, in North Carolina in 1784, in Virginia in 1785. It is hard to resist the idea that differences in the way society was structured had a good deal to do with the fate of primogeniture. Only in the South were there large estates or plantations. In New England, topography and soil militated against plantation agriculture; instead, there were small farms and compact settlements, and this favored dividing the land among all the children.[6]

The court system in England was as complicated as the rest of the law, if not more so. Lord Coke, who described the court system as it was in the seventeenth century, needed a whole volume just to list and explain the dozens of separate courts—royal, local, customary, and special courts in mind-numbing numbers—a maze of jurisdictions that litigants (and their lawyers) somehow had to navigate. This system was bad enough in England; it would have been totally ludicrous in the small, poor, struggling settlements along the American coastline. Massachusetts set up a clean, simple structure of courts; so did the other colonies. Court structures tended to be similar, though never identical, in the various groups of colonies. But there were also striking differences. In England, the courts of *equity*—which lacked a jury, and which administered a body of rules quite different from the ordinary courts—had grown up alongside the "common law" courts, and complemented those courts, so that one could not understand English law without in a way adding the two systems together. Massachusetts, however, never developed separate courts of equity; this prominent (if baffling) feature of English law was absent from the colony. South Carolina, on the other hand, had well-developed courts of this type.

In the eighteenth century, legal systems, both North and South, seemed to converge somewhat with English law; that is, they began to look more like their English model. This took place naturally and, for the most part, automatically. To a limited extent, this was because the British forced themselves on their colonies: they came to realize, with a bit of surprise, that they were in charge of an empire and that they might as well run it accordingly. As we all know, these attempts ended in disaster. The British began too late, in a sense. The colonists were used to running their own affairs; and when the English imposed new taxes, set up new courts, and in general behaved as imperialists, they touched off a revolution. As a result, they lost the crown jewel of their empire.

But pressure to conform to English models also came from more natural sources. First of all, whatever their political differences, the colonies had close commercial ties with the mother country. In the middle of the eighteenth century, America was a more sophisticated place than it had been a century before. The population was larger, cities had grown up, and the colonists used and developed legal institutions and doctrines that had been beside the point in the days of little villages along the coast, barely hanging on, isolated, and preoccupied with their own survival. The changeover was particularly marked in commercial law: the merchants, whose ships sailed to England, Jamaica, and ports all over the world, were eager users of up-to-date mercantile law as it was practiced in England and the rest of the European world.

There were also strong cultural ties with England. Lawyers who practiced in the colonies were Englishmen; some had actually gotten their training in England. The legal materials they used were English. Aside from collections of local statutes, the colonies published no native law books to speak of: all the treatises were English, all the published case reports were English. Anybody who wanted to learn about law had to read English books, and these books, of course, told about the English way of law, not the American.[7]

In 1756, William Blackstone's *Commentaries on the Laws of England* first saw the light of day in England. It became a best-seller there, but it was an even greater success on this side of the ocean. Blackstone had a clear, concise style. He wrote his book for English gentlemen—laymen who wanted to know something about their law. Americans laymen and lawyers alike seized eagerly on the book, because it was a handy key to the law of the mother country. An American edition was published in Philadelphia in 1771–72. Blackstone would never have become so popular in this country if there had been a book which was even roughly equivalent, explaining the law in distinctively American terms. No such book ever appeared, or was even thinkable.

The colonial period has been dwelt on in some detail here, first, because it is interesting in itself, and second, because we can use it to explore one of the major questions of this book: how do social conditions mold and determine the legal system of a society or community? If we could adequately answer this question, we would understand our legal system today, and we would also have the key to understanding the legal past.

A Free Nation: American Law
After 1776

In 1776, war broke out and the fragile ties between England and its colonies snapped. The war for independence was successful, but it left the colonies with the problem of finding the right way to glue themselves together once the old connection was gone. They needed to form some kind of federation—a body with a central nervous system, so to speak—but the individual colonies also wished to keep a good deal of autonomy for themselves. After one false start (the Articles of Confederation), the colonies drew up a charter, the Constitution of 1787, which is still the highest law of the land. The Constitution gave the central government much more power than it had had under the Articles of Confederation, but the government was still one of limited powers, within a federal system. Each state stayed sovereign in its own sphere. The United States (that is, the national entity) soon elected a president and went into business. Later it built itself a capital (Washington, D.C.). The national government ran the capital, foreign relations, the army and navy, and the post office. The states continued to run most other public affairs.

The new government faced one early and fundamental question: what should be done with the western lands? The United States owned a huge tract of wilderness. The public domain consisted of hundreds of miles of forest and prairie, stretching all the way to the Mississippi and including what are now the Midwestern and border states, and down through Alabama and Mississippi. The individual colonies, especially Virginia, had claims to most of this land, but these claims were ceded to the federal government between 1781 and 1802.[8]

It was still the case in the 1790s that most of the population lived in settlements strung along the eastern coast. The western lands were in the hands of native peoples, except for a few trappers and small, scattered settlements. Many Americans looked on these areas as lands of the future—lands that would fill up with settlers someday. The basic policy decisions were embodied in the famous Northwest Ordinance (1787). The United States, itself recently part of an empire, decided not to run its lands as a colonial power would. The dependent lands were its children, and like children, they would someday be adults. "Territories" would be carved out of the wilderness. When the population of a territory reached the right size ("five thousand free male inhabitants, of full age"), the territory could elect a "general assembly" to help the appointed governor run the territorial government. And when the population reached "sixty thousand free inhabitants," Congress could admit the territory as a new state, "on an equal footing with the original States, in all respects whatever."

And so it was. The union of states ultimately grew to fifty. In almost every case, the new state passed through a period of territorial government—its childhood, so to speak—before emerging into statehood. In only a few instances—Texas, for example, which began as an independent country—did the states avoid this period of pupilage. And it was not for a full century that the United States came to acquire lands which it did *not* organize on a territorial basis. The booty wrenched away from Spain after the Spanish-American War (1898) included Puerto Rico and the Philippines. These were the first important instances in which the Constitution did not "follow the flag" and in which the United States held colonies in the true imperial sense. It is no coincidence that these were places where most of the people were not white—a factor which also slowed down Hawaii's bid for statehood.

The law of the United States also spread east to west, but not by conquest so much as by natural infection from the original states. New states borrowed heavily from the law of older states. After all, settlers always came from somewhere; except for the immigrants from abroad, the older states were the somewhere. Very often we can explain peculiarities in the law of a new state simply by looking to see where its settlers hailed from. In the old Northwest, the new American arrivals swamped the handful of trappers and villagers who lived in Illinois and elsewhere, spoke French, and carried on their lives in accordance with French legal customs. The old Northwest Territory borrowed pieces and chunks out of the statute books of Pennsylvania, Virginia, and other states. As the population of the Northwest grew, new states were admitted to the Union from the Northwest Territory, starting with Ohio shortly after 1800. When fresh territories were organized—Indiana, Illinois, Wisconsin—the old Northwest Territory split like an amoeba, and its legal system divided like the rest of it.

Everywhere, the wave of American settlers was strong enough to crowd out whatever body of settlers lived under different languages and law. The native tribes were dealt with ruthlessly, and their tribal customs followed them into exile or death. Only in Louisiana was there a settled "foreign" population big enough to make a difference. In Louisiana, Spanish and French traditions were too firmly entrenched to give way without a struggle, and the common law never in fact succeeded in overthrowing the old legal system totally. It was a decisive step when Louisiana adopted its Digest of 1808, modeled after France's Napoleonic Code. Scholars still quarrel over whether French or Spanish law provided more raw material for the Digest. In any event, both of these systems were alien to the common law; they were civil law to the bone.[9]

English did, in time, overwhelm the French language in Louisiana, except in remote bayous; but the French legal tradition had more staying power. In theory at least, Louisiana to this day does not belong to the common-law family, but rather to the civil-law tradition. In some ways, indeed, its law sticks out like a sore thumb. The state is rather proud of its codes and its peculiarities of law and procedure. Whether by now the living law of Louisiana is all that different from the living law of other states is a more difficult question. Louisiana enjoys (or suffers) the same federal tax law as other states, and the same federal regulations. It is protected by the same Bill of Rights. Its lawyers speak English, and the legal culture is open on all sides to massive influence from forty-nine siblings.

Spanish or Mexican tradition strongly colored the law of California, Texas, New Mexico, and other western states carved out of Mexican territory after the brief war of 1848. The civil law was never strong enough to survive as a system in these states, but big chunks were left behind. One famous example is the so-called community-property system (totally unknown to New York or Iowa). In a community-property state, whatever a husband earns when he is married, and whatever property he acquires, will automatically belong half to him and half to his wife, as a general rule; the same is true the other way around. In other words, in these states a married couple is, generally speaking, treated as a unit—a "community"—unless the couple specifically makes some other arrangement. To be sure, in the bad old days, the unit was not a community of equals. The husband ran the show: he had the exclusive right to manage and control the community property.

We must be careful not to make too much of survivals—old anomalies, pieces of law left over from dead or submerged traditions. Social, geographic, and economic conditions were always much stronger influences on law in these western states than the traditions that predated American settlement. Community property did not survive in California because of nostalgia or historical accident; it must have survived because it was a useful and powerful system which seemed to suit the population well. The community-property system has lived on to this day because it has been able to compete with the common law and win a place for itself: it carried on despite, not because of, its Mexican roots. Indeed, in contemporary society, the community-property system seems to fit family life better than the common-law system, and it has tended to expand its domain over time.

A striking example of law generated by local conditions was the law of slavery—an enormous body of rules, statutes, and doctrines built up primarily in the southern states. Black slavery had existed in the North as well, during the colonial period, as we pointed out, but the northern states abolished slavery after the Revolution. The Vermont Constitution of 1777 began the trend; by 1800 the other states in the North had either gotten rid of slavery completely or had "provided for its gradual extinction."[10] From this point on, the line was sharply drawn: there were

slave states in the South and "free" states in the North. A state was
either one or the other, not both or in-between. The law of slavery was
thus confined to the southern and border states.[11]

Slavery was one of the issues that ultimately poisoned relations
between North and South to the point where the country fought what
was then the bloodiest war in human history (1860–65). The war was
fought to "preserve the Union," as far as the North was concerned, but
the question of slavery was at the emotional heart of the conflict. Slavery
was also at the core of the Southern social system. Slaves were capital
assets of enormous value to their owners. In the days before farm
machines, black bodies were the motor force that made plantations productive. Slaves cleaned Southern (white) houses, raised Southern
babies, worked in Southern factories. In many parts of the South, most
of the population was black and enslaved: a white layer of rulers sat on
top of a mass of subordinated blacks.

Slavery was a vital cog in the machinery of Southern society; naturally, then, it was a vital aspect of Southern law. Each slave state had an
elaborate code of laws to govern slavery and slaves. The master had
almost complete control over the lives of the slaves. The slave was a
piece of property. He had to obey his master; and, indeed, it was an
offense for a slave to be "insolent" to a "free white person." Slaves could
not legally marry. They could not own property. They could not come
and go as they pleased: a slave was not to "go from off the plantation
. . . without a certificate of leave in writing from his master." These
provisions come from the North Carolina code of 1854; they are typical
of the codes of slave states in general. Slaves had certain rights, at least
officially; but these rights were hard to enforce, and were mostly on
paper.

Even a freed slave was shackled with many disabilities. The slave
code was also a race code. No black man, slave or free, had the right to
vote or hold office in the South—or in most northern states, for that
matter. If a slave owner set a slave free in North Carolina, as in many
other southern states, the freedman had ninety days to get out of the
state. An ex-slave who stayed on without permission (it was sometimes
granted) was liable to be arrested and sold into slavery once more.

Southern slave law had to concern itself with the massive fact that
slaves were pieces of property. Black people were bought and sold on
the open market, mortgaged by slave owners who were in debt, leased
out by slave owners who had "extra" slaves, left as legacies in the wills
of dying slave owners, seized by a slave owner's creditors when the
owner could not pay his bills.[12] States from Maryland to Arkansas to
Florida built up an elaborate structure of rules and cases—all of it now

extinct—to cope with the details of slave property and the affairs of men and women who owned, bought, sold, or dealt in human flesh.

In one case, for example, decided in Georgia in 1853, a man named Latimer owned a slave whose services he did not need. He auctioned off the right to use the slave for a year. A certain Dr. Thompson, who ran a hotel in Atlanta, was the winning bidder; he paid $91 to get the slave for a year, and he put him to work as a waiter in his hotel. One of the guests came down with smallpox; the slave was ordered to take care of the guest, and the slave came down with smallpox himself. A doctor was called in; he treated the slave and presented a bill, as doctors tend to do. But who was liable for the doctor's bill? Was it the original owner, because it was *his* slave? Or was it Dr. Thompson, who had the right to the slave's services in his hotel? Who should bear the risk? In the end, the Georgia Supreme Court put the burden on Dr. Thompson.[13]

This case was only one of many cases in which slaves figured as part of the property system. This vast body of law was, of course, unknown in the North. The North was concerned with slavery, but as a political and moral issue, and as an issue of federal relations. There was bitter controversy, for example, over the duty of northern states to return runaway slaves to their masters. The various fugitive-slave laws were deeply resented, and at times defied, by the northern states.

Northern states—farm states and commercial states of the seacoast—had their own set of legal and economic issues. These were by no means uniform. In New York at the beginning of the nineteenth century, for example, the courts handled dozens of cases about marine insurance. Kentucky, quite naturally, had very little of this. The states of the old Northwest were much more concerned with public-land law than was Rhode Island. And so it went.

These differences are still very important. Some states are crowded and industrial. (New Jersey is as densely packed with people as Holland.) Farmers, growers, or miners dominate the politics of other states. In the dry western states, the population is light; grazing rights on public land or restrictions on strip mining or on the logging of old-growth timber may be major issues. Southern states still have large black populations, memories of a lost war, and a tradition of conservatism. The Sun Belt, however, is growing and changing fast. The older industrial states—states like Michigan—are struggling to adapt to a world in which the global economy threatens their industrial base. One state, Nevada, is dominated by an unusual industry, gambling.[14] Another state, Hawaii, is tropical, was once a Polynesian kingdom, has a largely Asian population—and a "sovereignty" movement among native Hawaiians—and lives largely off the tourist trade. Demographically, the states vary considerably: Cuban-Americans live, by and large, in southern Florida; California and Texas have huge Chicano populations; California has a growing number of Asians; there are French Canadians in Maine; and so on. The core of the law in all states (Louisiana is something of an exception, as we have seen) is the American version of the English common law. But the pressure of events, the rush of social forces, the needs and demands that come from people and places, from businesses and workers, are the basic forces molding the law at any given time.

In many ways, American law is distinctly and uniquely American. This is a natural and obvious fact. Every country has something unique about its legal system. To take a simple, almost trivial example: by law, we celebrate independence on the Fourth of July, and that day is a national holiday. Other countries celebrate their independence on other days. A legal system is a mosaic of rules, processes, institutions, behaviors, and roles. Every country has its own legal system, and no two are exactly the same, or even close. After all, every country has a unique place in space, its own mix of birds, animals, plants, and insects, its own range of manufactured products and crops, its own political history. The experience of a society, in every aspect, colors its system of law.

American law, then, is unique. But no legal system, contrariwise, is *entirely* different from all the others. Our system has many features and traits it shares with other common-law countries, like England or Australia. Yet the American and English systems are noticeably different—different languages, though closely related: in a way, like German and Dutch, or Spanish and Portuguese. An American lawyer would have trouble practicing law in England (assuming he was entitled to do so); he would need special training—a crash course at the very least. Still, he could probably learn English law pretty quickly; French law, even in translation, would take more doing. The legal differences among American states—say, between Florida and Oregon—big as they are, are of a much lower order than the differences between two common-law countries.

It is not surprising—to go a bit further—that American law also has a lot in common with the law of other modern Western industrial countries. For example, it has an income tax; so does Sweden; so does Japan. Rules about air traffic control, wiretapping, gene-splicing, copyrights for software, and so on can be found in all advanced countries at the end of the twentieth century. Medieval England or France had no such rules and problems. New technology and a global economy tend to make the legal systems of the world "converge," at least to a degree.[15]

America: A Middle-Class Civilization

In the eyes of many nineteenth-century visitors, America was an amazing place. Some of its characteristics which we take for granted struck outsiders as remarkable in the extreme. Compared to European countries, America seemed exceedingly classless. Even before the Revolution, there was more equality of condition in the United States than in European countries, including England. It is important to put this "equality" into perspective. In America, there were rich people and poor people, of course; there was also a large population of black slaves. Free blacks could not vote or hold office. Neither could women. Indeed, married women could not really own property or enter into contracts. When a woman married, her property automatically passed into her husband's clutches. He had total dominion and control. A married woman, legally speaking, was more or less on a par with idiots and babies. These rules were not changed until the middle of the nineteenth century. The pioneer law was passed in Mississippi in 1839; New York enacted important reforms in 1848 and 1860. But bits and pieces of these old "disabilities" (legal inequalities) lingered on in the law much longer.[16] And women did not get the vote until the twentieth century.

On the other hand, it was never the case that a few great families owned all of the land in America, or even most of it. There were large landowners, to be sure, but nothing like the vast estates of the European nobility and gentry. There were no real peasants or serfs in this country. Especially in the North, the land was owned by men and their families; tenancy (renting or sharecropping) was the exception, not the rule. Only in the South, after the slaves were freed, was there a large body of farm workers who lived more like peons or serfs than the free farmers of Iowa or Illinois.[17]

The wide ownership of land was no accident. It was partly a natural development, in a country without an aristocracy, and with an abundance of land available to be settled and farmed. (It has to be stated bluntly, of course, that a good deal of this "abundance" was achieved at the expense of the native peoples who were forced off the land.) Partly, too, diffuse ownership was a matter of deliberate policy. The national government, as we noted, came into possession of millions and millions of acres after the Revolution. The Louisiana Purchase (1804) brought millions more. Yet no one ever intended to keep this land under federal ownership. On the contrary, it was national policy (and felt to be national destiny) to sell the land to the public—to people who would clear away boulders, cut down trees, settle on the land, and grow crops.

This was the basic spirit of public-land law. This body of rules, before the Civil War, was in philosophy completely unlike public-land law today. Today a strong central theme is conservation, preservation—holding on to the land, working it or using it (if at all) in the public interest, for the good of the population as a whole. There are, of course, controversies over public-land policy—between conservationists, for example, and timber and mining interests. But almost nobody proposes flat-out disposition of the public domain. Land law before the Civil War was mostly concerned not with keeping but with getting rid of the land—selling it or giving it away. And when land was sold, it was sold at low prices—a dollar or two an acre, at most.

Public-land law was a maze of rules, and in practice there was a wide gap between theory and reality. There were endless scandals and corruptions at the level of local land offices. Yet, on the whole, the policy worked. True, speculators sometimes got hold of huge tracts of land, but even these speculators never intended to hold on to the land for long. They were wholesalers, not land barons. Their aim was to sell out at a profit. In any case and by whatever path, the land passed out of government hands and wound up in the hands of smallholders—hundreds of thousands of settlers, farmers, and tradesmen. The year 1836 was probably the peak year for land sales. The federal government sold over 20 million acres of land and took in about $25 million. Between 1820 and 1842, some 74 million acres were sold—about as much land as there is in Michigan and Wisconsin combined.[18]

At the same time, the government gave away millions of acres. Some of this land went to state governments; they in turn sold the land, using the money for schools, roads, railways, and so on. In the Revolutionary period, soldiers were given, as part of their pay, pieces of paper that entitled them to bits of the public domain—one hundred acres for a private, five hundred for a colonel. Many of the states, too, granted such military bounties.[19] The so-called Morrill Act (1862) gave every state a gift of public land, to be used to endow higher education. Out of this came such "land-grant" schools as the University of Illinois.

The pressure for cheaper and cheaper land, on easy terms and conditions, was politically almost irresistible. Symbolically, at least, the famous Homestead Act of 1862 was a fitting climax to the trend. This law offered 160 acres of public land, absolutely free, to actual settlers. In fact, the best farmland was already gone by 1862; what was left was mostly in the West and was rocky, arid, or otherwise unsuitable. Still, the law restated, in an especially vivid way, what had always been one goal of land policy.

One theme stands out, then, in the tangled history of American land law: private ownership, and not by a small elite, but by millions of people. There is no General Motors or IBM of American real estate. Large landowners—even the largest—own only a trivial portion of this enormous continent. Legal policy insisted on widespread ownership of land and reinforced the pressure for this ownership. Mass ownership of land, in turn, had incalculable consequences for the legal system. English land law had been a maze of technicalities. Generations of budding lawyers broke their heads over land law; no layman could wander into the maze without getting hopelessly lost. The law was so technical that it could work only in a society where landowners were few, rich, and leisured—a class that could afford skilled lawyers to disentangle legal knots.

American law never had this luxury. To get by at all in a country with millions of landowners, land law had to be revised—stripped clean of its worst technicalities. It had to function for ordinary people who owned small amounts of land, people who could read and write, but were not rich and not legally sophisticated, and who did not and could not know the intricate details of land law. The law also had to fit the needs of a fast-moving, active land market—a market in which tracts of land changed hands almost like shares of stock on a stock exchange.

In England, a single great family might live in one place for centuries, developing deep, sentimental ties to its house, its land, its "estate." The very meaning of land was different in America. Only in the South, with its great plantations, were there estates in the English sense: the "Tara" of *Gone with the Wind* had no analog in Vermont or Illinois. In the North and in the West, men started farms, built them to the point where they could be sold at a profit, and then (very often) sold out and moved on, to start a new farm somewhere else. Even when the owner stayed put, his sons were likely to move on rather than stay on ancestral soil. After all, there was plenty of land—and plenty of opportunity. From the start, Americans were a restless bunch.

Land law was not the only branch of law that needed to sing a fresh tune in the New World. Law never lost all its maddening complexity, but many fields were at least streamlined and refined to the level where they worked in this middle-class society. This was certainly true of commercial law; it was also true of family law and the law of wills and succession at death.

The rise of divorce law is a good, if somewhat complicated, illustration of the way in which law adapted to the social facts of life in the new country.[20] Divorce was rare and expensive in England—until 1857, practically speaking, divorce was available only through an act of Parliament. Divorce was also extremely rare in colonial America. Here, too, divorce was mainly "legislative"; that is, each divorce was a separate law passed by the colonial assembly. In the nineteenth century, divorces began to become more common and also easier to get, especially in the northern states. Many states passed laws that allowed "judicial" divorce—divorce as we know it, divorce in court.

How do we explain this rise in divorce rates and the change in divorce law? Were American families less happy than families in Great Britain? Did they break up more often? Possibly: the rising divorce rate certainly says something about changes in the structure of the American family. But it is also clear that people wanted—demanded—a quick, cheap way to "legalize" their status, that is, an authoritative ruling on whether they were married or unmarried. Why? Because legal status makes a difference to people who have money or who own a farm or a house. For such people (and this category included millions of Americans) it was important to be sure of one's legal status. Divorce and remarriage was the best way to keep titles and claims of ownership clean and distinct: it made sure that one's children were legitimate, that the right wife inherited a husband's property, and so on. A society of landless peasants or paupers can do without formal divorce. Americans could not.

There was also a shortage of legal skill. True, there were plenty of lawyers in the country, but they were not well trained, as English lawyers were, in the old common-law technicalities. American lawyers were known more for cunning and business sense than for legal learning, in any event, the kind of fancy legal work that the English gentry could afford was far too expensive for the ordinary American. And even the great hordes of lawyers in this country would not have been enough to meet the demand if every little land sale, every last will and testament, every promissory note, and so on, were to take large chunks of a lawyer's time. Hence, the constant simplification of the laws and the constant selling of how-to-do-it books—books like *Every Man His Own Lawyer*, which was mentioned in the preface.

A typical example of this literature, if we can call it literature, was *The American Lawyer and Business-Man's Form-Book*, published by Delos W. Beadle in the 1850s and frequently reprinted. It had "forms and instructions" for contracts, chattel mortgages, bills of sale, bills of lading, bonds, drafts, promissory notes, deeds, mortgages, landlord-and-tenant agreements, vessel charters, letters of credit, marriage contracts, trust forms, articles of partnership, and wills, plus interest tables, digests of the laws of the states on various subjects, and all sorts of other material. The book claimed to be "a manual for the guidance of any and every man in business transactions." Its popularity is another sign of the way legal process percolated into the public mind and public needs, in this middle-class society.

Law and the Economy

Another aspect of the American legal system in the period after the Revolution and up to the Civil War follows closely from the aspect just described. We were a nation of economic boosters. We wanted growth, development, gain. One of the prime goals of the legal system was to find ways and means to foster and encourage an increase in the wealth of the country—and the wealth of individuals and families. Law was a tool to develop the country—to foster growth, to make people rich. J. Willard Hurst has used the term "release of energy" to describe the basic function of law in this period. We often hear people say, somewhat loosely, that law is conservative. In the first century of our independence, it would be more accurate to say, along with Professor Hurst, that law was dynamic: people were willing to "put law in action fast and boldly where they saw tangible stakes in improving physical productivity."[21]

What this means, roughly, is that influential people in this country—voters, property owners, merchants—consciously and deliberately used law in all its forms to push for economic growth. They (and the law) respected property rights, of course, but chiefly because property was an agent of dynamic movement. What they valued was not the fat, old, encrusted "estates" of an aristocracy, but the swift, lean, moving assets of a young country on the make. The legal system was pro-business, pro-enterprise. People were willing—even eager—to throw away old rules of law, if they stood in the way of "progress."

This was, for example, the message of the *Charles River Bridge* case.[22] This great case, decided by the Supreme Court in 1837, turned technically on a narrow issue. The Massachusetts legislature had in 1785 granted a charter to a group of men who undertook to build a toll bridge over the Charles River in Boston. They built the bridge, successfully, and collected tolls for many years. Then in 1828 the legislature chartered a rival bridge, the so-called Warren Bridge; this bridge, after it recovered its costs, would be a free bridge, not a toll bridge. The two bridges were extremely close to each other, and it was clear that the free bridge would drive the toll bridge out of business. The owners of the old bridge fought back in court. They claimed the second charter "impaired" the first charter, and that the legislature had no power and no right to destroy their business this way.

The case found its way eventually to the Supreme Court of the United States. The issue was hotly debated, but the majority, speaking through the mouth of the chief justice, Roger Brooke Taney, decided in favor of the Massachusetts legislature and the second, free bridge. The first charter did not explicitly promise, in black and white, that no other competitor would get a bridge charter. Taney refused to read such a promise into the legislative act. That disposed of the claims of the Charles River Bridge.

There were issues of doctrine and precedent in the case, to be sure, but it was also a kind of inkblot test, measuring attitudes toward property and enterprise. To Taney, the real issue was the conflict between old vested rights and the demands of new enterprise—demands of "progress." Faced with such a choice, American law and American judges tended to choose the side of change, progress, growth. This meant the second bridge and not the first.[23]

We often assume that the nineteenth century was an age of laissez-faire, that is, that public policy and public opinion as a whole were dead set against government regulation and against any meddling in business. By modern standards, it is true that governments of the time were incredibly weak. The annual budget of a state like Massachusetts, toward the end of the eighteenth century, was less than a small city might spend today in a day, or than the Pentagon might spend in half an hour. The state government of Massachusetts spent $215,000 in 1794, and more than half of this was interest on state debt.[24] Millions of people today are on the government payroll; in the early years of the republic, there were the merest handful. Salaries cost Massachusetts $54,000 in 1794. Of course, the dollar went a lot farther in the late eighteenth century than at the end of the twentieth, but nonetheless the scale of government was minuscule compared to what it is today.

But it would be wrong to think that government was completely inert, or that the public by and large was made up of people who would be called libertarians today—people who believed, as a matter of ideology, that the government should have no role in the economy (or in much of anything else). Ordinary people were, on the contrary, quite anxious to get government help so long as it benefited them (which should surprise nobody); in particular, they wanted government action that would boost the national economy. Government (federal and state) did its best to promote roads, canals, turnpikes, bridges, and ferries. Later on, there was a positive orgy of support for the building of railroads. Pennsylvania spent more than $100 million—an astronomical sum in those days—on its main canal and railroad system.[25]

Pennsylvania was no exception. Some states used their resources to set up or to strengthen banks; all of them (and the federal government) used land grants to encourage enterprise, especially transportation. After 1850, the federal government gave out huge tracts of land to help get the railroads built. This giveaway was very popular at the time, whatever later generations thought of it. The farmer could not prosper, could not sell his crops, without some way to get them to market. What the typical landowner wanted, in Iowa or Kansas, was simple: good times, good prices for his wheat or corn, and rising land values. Farmers knew that the only way to get rich was to link their farms with markets back east. Only the iron horse could accomplish this. The same middle-class way of life that brought about simpler deed forms and easier divorce lay behind the policy of land grants for railroads and canals.

The Civil War and Beyond

The Civil War (1860–65), bloody and disruptive, was a cataclysmic shock to American society. It is also a convenient dividing point between periods in American legal history. It is a useful marker of the end of the age of "release of energy"—the boom period of building and settlement, the period of western expansion and early railroads, when agriculture ruled the economy. The postwar age became an age of factories and big cities and floods of immigrants from Eastern Europe; an age of technology and industry; an age in which rural America slowly declined. Of course, the Civil War had little or nothing to do with this development; the process had begun before the war, and merely accelerated afterward.

In one regard, of course, the war was a real watershed. It ended slavery, though it certainly did not bring about any golden age for the black men and women who had been slaves. As soon as the war ended, the southern states passed harsh laws—the so-called Black Codes—to preserve as much of the old way of life as they could, to keep blacks in their place, and to grant them as few rights as possible. But the North would have none of this; Northern armies moved in, most of the provisions of the Black Codes were repealed, and three new amendments to the Constitution (the Thirteenth, Fourteenth, and Fifteenth) were rammed down the throats of the South. The Thirteenth Amendment abolished, once and for all, slavery and "involuntary servitude." The Fifteenth Amendment gave blacks the vote: no state could abridge voting rights "on account of race, color, or previous condition of servitude." The Fourteenth Amendment made "all persons" born in the United

States (including blacks, of course) full citizens—state and national. Two other provisions were destined to have a rich, complicated, and ultimately glorious history: the clauses that guaranteed, against the states, the "equal protection" of the laws to everyone, and that forbade the states from depriving any citizen of "life, liberty, or property, without due process of law."

These were, in the end, powerful tools of racial equality, and were probably so intended. But the courts made less benign uses of these clauses in the nineteenth century. During Reconstruction (the late 1860s and the 1870s), blacks and their allies gained quite a bit of political power in the South. But this ended when "white supremacy" governments took over, after the end of Reconstruction. By 1900, few blacks voted in the South; black voters were disenfranchised by a combination of laws, customs, and brute force. The federal government did little or nothing to protect black voters. Only when a strong voting-rights law was enacted, in 1965, did real change come about. By the end of the nineteenth century, moreover, legal segregation was in place. Later in this book, in Chapter 14, we will discuss the law of race relations in more detail.

In the years after the Civil War, government, in one form or another, played more and more of a role in the economy, especially in the northern states. This development was almost inevitable in the new industrial age. Big business confronted a growing labor movement. What could not be resolved around the bargaining table (sometimes because employers refused to bargain) or through strikes on the streets spilled over into courts and legislatures. State legislatures passed hundreds of new laws on issues of industrial society: wages and hours, company stores, union labels, sweatshops, the employment of women and children, and so on. Some of these statutes were struck down by the courts. The courts also evolved new tools—the labor injunction, for example—which made the task of organized labor more difficult. Indeed, some scholars feel that the crushing power of the law was a powerful influence in bending the labor movement in a relatively meek and conservative direction.[26]

In this period, too, regulation of business expanded mightily and (for the first time) on a national scale. This was the age of the Interstate Commerce Act (1887), which set up the Interstate Commerce Commission, the first of the great national administrative agencies that were designed to regulate business. In 1890, Congress passed the Sherman Act. This law, practically speaking, created a new field of law: antitrust law. This is the branch of law that deals with monopolies and other business practices that "restrain trade" and (in theory) harm competition. The ICC is no longer—it was swept into oblivion by a Republican Congress in 1995[27]—but the Sherman Act, in its second century, is still a mighty legal force.

The administrative state has grown steadily since the late nineteenth century; its huge bulk outweighs all the rest of the law today. (We will deal with it in more detail in Chapter 6.) The New Deal, under President Franklin D. Roosevelt, in the 1930s, was the next great watershed in legal life. The Great Depression had wrecked the economy; in one sense the New Deal was simply a response to this desperate crisis. In another sense, the New Deal merely speeded up what was already in the works: an ongoing process in which the scope and extent of government intervention into the economy increased steadily and consistently. During the New Deal, the federal system changed course dramatically. The Second World War followed immediately afterward, and the modern welfare state arose from the ruins left behind by depression and the dramatic needs of contemporary war. Whatever the sources and the motivations, it is clear that law has gradually extended its domain over more and more areas of an increasingly complicated life.

Freedom and Law

In any brief sketch of the way American law has developed, it is easy to ignore (or take for granted) something that struck nineteenth-century visitors to this country with hammerlike force: our amazing level of personal freedom. During most of our history, Americans tended to congratulate themselves on this point. They may have overdone it. Every nationality has a tendency to pat itself on the back; America has been no exception.

In the 1960s, there was a revulsion and a reaction, especially in scholarly writing, against this rose-colored view of American history. Historians pointed out, quite properly, that the story of race relations in this country has been bloody and dismal. They rubbed our faces in some facts many people wanted to forget. They reminded their readers that in the nineteenth century, freedom and justice were most decidedly not for all, legally or socially speaking. The black population did not share equitably in America's freedom and wealth. Women, too, who made up half the population, were legally and socially subordinate.

There are other skeletons in the American closet. The treatment of the native peoples is a sordid and disgraceful story. At best, they were cheated and dispossessed; at worst, slaughtered in cold blood. The Bureau of Indian Affairs never really understood or tried to understand the culture of these "savages," and it pursued a mindless policy of assimilation. The Chinese on the West Coast were subject to legal and social harassment in the late nineteenth century. During the Second World War, Japanese-Americans were shipped off to camps in the desert on trumped-up, hysterical charges. In the first half of the twentieth century, immigration law was racist to the core; Asians were not allowed to enter the country or become citizens, and in California they could not even own land. Toleration stopped short, too, when it confronted (in the nineteenth century) the Mormon minority (the Church of Latter-Day Saints). The Saints were clannish people with strange and offensive beliefs—in polygamy, most notoriously—and they enraged the "moral majority" of their day. The federal government passed harsh laws against the church and followed an active program of persecution. Leaders of the church were thrown into jail; some went underground. The persecution died down only after the church gave up polygamy (1890).[28]

It is a fairly daunting list. And yet, despite it all, the balance in the accounts may be on the side of liberty. A lot depends on whether we look back on our history from the vantage point of *now* (in which case we see clearly all the failings and deficiencies) or from the vantage point of *then.* For much of our history, we were indeed one of the freest, most democratic, most "equal" countries in the world. Where we were bad, other countries were (and are) much worse. America was never utopia, or even close; it has always been a mix of good and bad, plus and minus. It began as an experiment in letting people run their own country. Not all the people—basically, "the people" meant men and meant whites— but far more than held power in England or France or anywhere else. This experiment worked; and in the course of time, it was extended to include more and more of the excluded. But popular democracy also meant that law reflected, and had to reflect, great waves of popular sentiment. It could never stray too far from the mean. It could express ideals, it could express "enlightened" opinion, but it could never be dramatically better or worse than the values of articulate people, and of people who had some (economic) stake in society. That was its weakness, and also its greatest strength.

4

The Structure of American Law: The Courts

*I*N MANY WAYS the courts are the most familiar part of the American legal system. When people think about "the law," they usually have the courts in mind. This is so even though most people do not have much experience with courts and the way they work. A fair number of people every year serve on juries; a substantial number may have dealings in traffic court. Others may go through a divorce or come in contact with probate court. Very few, except for jurors, have seen or been part of a trial in the flesh. As for the higher courts, only lawyers and judges confront them directly. On the other hand, everyone, almost without exception, has watched a trial on TV or in the movies or on the stage.

The American court system is complex. Each state runs its own separate system of courts; no two state systems are exactly alike. The details of court structure can be quite technical, and confusing even to a lawyer. What makes matters even more mixed up is the double system of courts in this country. There is a chain of national (federal) courts, on top of (or besides) the courts of individual states. At least one federal court sits in every state, from Alabama to Wyoming; states with big populations have more than one. A person who lives in Philadelphia, then, is subject to the jurisdiction of two very different courts, the local Pennsylvania court and the local federal court, and can sue or get sued in either one, depending mostly, but not entirely, on what the case is about.

An Outline of Court Structure

The state court system is a logical place to begin, since the over-whelming majority of lawsuits begin and end in these courts. Despite many local complications and technicalities, it is easy to describe the essential shape of the typical court system. We can think of it more or less as a kind of pyramid.

At the bottom, the broadest part of the pyramid, there is a network of lower courts, dotted all over the state and sprinkled about municipal areas. These courts handle the least serious offenses and the smallest claims. They have various names: justice courts, small-claims courts, traffic courts, police courts, municipal courts, mayor's courts. Many of them are somewhat specialized: traffic courts stick to traffic cases; police courts deal only with petty offenses (you cannot sue your landlord or get a divorce in police court); small-claims courts never touch traffic offenses or cases of drunkenness.

These courts are the bargain basement of justice, in a way; their goods are popular and cheap. They tend to be rather informal. Some of them refuse to let lawyers take part. Some permit a jury if one of the parties insists. Others do not allow a jury; if a litigant insists on his right to a jury, the case is transferred to a higher court. On the other hand, the judges in these basement courts are usually quite professional. They are trained in law, which was by no means always the case in the past. The "justice of the peace" in England was usually not a lawyer at all; he was a member of the local gentry who served as a judge. Some states still have laypeople serving on "limited-jurisdiction" courts at the base of the system—men and women who have never gone to law school and never taken the bar exam. But this is by now rather exceptional.

There has been a good deal of debate about the quality of justice in these lower courts. We hear about slapdash procedures, assembly-line justice, and the like. Maureen Mileski studied a lower criminal court in a "middle-sized Eastern city" around 1970. In this court, 72 percent of the cases were handled in one minute or less. In other words, "routine police encounters with citizens in the field last on the average far longer than court encounters."[1] It is not hard to see why this kind of "rough justice" is open to criticism.

Small-claims courts have also taken their lumps. The first such court was established in Cleveland in 1913, as a branch of the municipal court. The idea spread quickly. It was argued that these institutions would serve as the poor man's court, cheap, easy to use, with no lawyers and no legal tricks. In many ways, these courts have been a spectacular success; hundreds of thousands of claims are processed through small-claims courts every year.

Whether they have really supplied justice for the poor is quite a different question. Beginning in the 1960s, some scholars levied serious charges against them. These courts had become only one more example of the way the scales of justice were tilted against the poor. These were not courts for but against the workingman. They were in essence collection mills for businessmen, "courts of the poor" only in the sense that the poor person was dragged before the court and, in an "intimidating atmosphere," forced "to confront a powerful creditor," or a landlord, or the government.[2]

In some states, bad publicity and criticism led to efforts to restore the courts to what was supposed to be their original function. Some states—New York, Oklahoma—barred collection agencies from using small-claims courts. In many places, the clerk will help a litigant fill out forms; some courts even give legal advice to bewildered litigants. Some courts have mediation processes, and this kind of less hurried, less adversarial way of doing small-claims business is apparently more satisfying to litigants.[3] Recent studies have tended to look at small-claims courts in a more favorable light. A survey of twelve urban small claims courts, published in 1993, did find that businesses filed most of the complaints in small-claims courts, but the survey did not feel that these courts were "primarily debt collection agencies for businesses." Most of the cases that were actually *tried*—that is, the contested cases—were brought by individual plaintiffs.[4]

The next level of the pyramid is made up of *courts of general jurisdiction,* the basic trial courts of the community. These are the courts that hear civil cases "worth" more than the ones the basement courts try (that is, more money is at stake). These courts also handle cases of serious crime—not drunkenness or walking on the grass, but burglary, rape, manslaughter, and murder. There are fewer of these courts, but they tend to be more professional than the basement courts. The judges are always lawyers. The atmosphere is more dignified, more solemn. There is more full-time staff.

These trial courts usually have jurisdiction over more people and larger areas than the municipal or police courts. In many states, the basic trial courts come one to a county. (In counties with big populations, the court may be divided into "departments.") There is no uniform name for the basic trial courts of the United States. In some states, they are called circuit courts; in others, district courts. The basic trial court in California, Connecticut, and a few other states is called the superior court. In New York, through an odd quirk of naming, the basic trial court is called the supreme court; the highest court of the state is the court of appeals.

Only a small percentage of the cases that get filed in court ever go to full trial; the vast majority are settled out of court, dropped, compromised, or handled summarily. Still, every year thousands of cases do go the whole route either to trial by jury or to trial in front of the judge alone (the so-called bench trial). In California, for example, in the fiscal year 1991–92, the superior courts disposed of 907,083 cases. Less than 10 percent of these were "contested trials" (72,150), and many of these were bench trials. Only about 1.1 percent actually went to trial by jury; still, this amounted to 10,082 jury trials in the state during that year.[5]

In the contested cases there are, of course, winners and losers. The loser can throw in the towel; and most do. Or the loser can continue the struggle and "appeal." The term "appeal," in ordinary language, means taking a case to a higher court, an *appeal court,* higher up in the pyramid of courts. Typically, the appeal court does not review every aspect of the trial—it does not try the case *de novo,* that is, all over again. But trial *de novo* is not completely unknown. The loser in a petty court, a justice of the peace court, for example, can usually take his case to the next court up; here the trial is likely to be *de novo.* But except for these small cases, it is the rule that a person who appeals will get only limited review from the appeal court. The higher court looks at certain features of the case, certain parts of the record, checking for errors.

Suppose, for example, a man is tried for murder and the jury brings in a guilty verdict. The defendant is almost certain to appeal, but on what basis? The appeal court will not convene a jury, will not hear new evidence, will not even go over the old evidence. Rather, the defendant (actually, his lawyers) will have to find some "error" to complain about, something done wrong at the trial. He might claim that the judge let the jury hear improper or irrelevant evidence, or that the judge gave the wrong instructions to the jury, or that the judge showed prejudice, and so on. The appeal court may take these complaints very seriously. But it will not try to second-guess the jury. It will not rehash the facts. In a civil case, too, findings of fact (generally speaking) will not be reviewed. If a woman sues the driver of a truck that rear-ended her car, and injured her back, and the jury awards her $35,000, this too will not normally be reviewed; only an "error" can lay the basis for appeal.

In a few states with small populations, like South Dakota, the loser in the trial court can appeal directly to the state's top court, usually called the supreme court. In other words, if you count the trial court as the first tier, South Dakota has a "two-tier" system. In a two-tier state, the supreme court will generally hear everybody who wants to appeal; the court does not screen its cases, or pick and choose the best or the most important. It takes them all. In these states, appeal is "as of right."

This works well enough in South Dakota, but it would hardly do in a state like California, which had more than 31 million people in the 1990s and an enormous network of trial courts, all of them churning out decisions. If we let everybody who lost at trial in California appeal "as of right," the supreme court would be totally swamped. It is no surprise, then, that California, like other states with big or middle-sized populations, has developed a "three-tier" system. A layer of intermediate courts stands between the trial courts and the supreme court. Most appeals go to the middle level; and there they end. These middle-layer courts are called courts of appeal in California and in many other states; in some they have another name ("appellate courts" in Illinois, for example).

In three-tier systems, the top court has tremendous discretion; it can usually decide which cases to hear and which to reject. The loser at trial gets one bite of the apple; he or she has the right to appeal at least once within the system. But the loser has, ordinarily, no right to demand a hearing from the *highest* court. That privilege is reserved to those who convince the court their case is somehow important. There are exceptions written into the law in many states. For example, a man or woman sentenced to death may get automatic review in the highest court. That is true in California.[6] But generally speaking, the high court in three-tier states has enormous control over its workload, and this has important consequences for judicial policymaking.[7]

How does the high court, with this freedom and power, decide which cases to take? Obviously, the judges choose what they consider significant cases. (Tastes in what is and what is not significant tend to change over the years.) As population grows, more people clamor to be heard; courts have to be tough and selective or they will drown in an ocean of paper. In 1950, there were 130 petitions for leave to appeal to the Supreme Court of Illinois; in 1978, there were 989, an enormous jump. The court actually decided fewer cases with full opinion in 1978 (195) than in 1950 (253).[8] The demand has continued to increase, and the state supreme court has gotten even pickier. In 1994, there were 1,895 petitions to the Illinois Supreme Court, and only 130 of these were granted.[9] Illinois is a three-tier state. Most people who appealed in 1994 had to be content with the middle tier of courts.

Federal courts are also organized on a three-tier system. They lack the "bargain basement" tier, however. There are no federal small-claims courts or federal justices of the peace, generally speaking. In the states, the bottom federal level is the *district court:* this is the basic federal trial court. The other two tiers, the circuit courts and the United States Supreme Court, confine themselves to appeals, by and large.

This clean, sharp division was not always the way things were. We take for granted today a strict separation between trial courts and appeal courts. The distinction was not firm in the early nineteenth century. High-court judges, state and federal, often did trial work as well. Even the justices of the United States Supreme Court had "circuit duty." Each justice was assigned to a region of the country. Every year the judge traveled to his circuit and tried cases there. This burden on the justices was not lifted until the end of the nineteenth century. In 1891, Congress made this traveling show optional; circuit work then became quite rare. It was totally abolished in the twentieth century.

There are, as of 1997, ninety-four federal district courts. Every state has at least one. In the smaller states, the district consists of the entire state; the larger states have more than one district. San Francisco, for example, is in the Northern District of California; Los Angeles is in the Southern District. There may, of course, be more than one judge to a district (imagine having only one district judge for the whole Los Angeles area!); each case, however, is tried by a single judge, sitting alone.

The next step up is the level of the United States Courts of Appeal, the federal circuit courts. For many years, there were ten of these. Then Congress set up an eleventh, by splitting in two the old Fifth Circuit, which stretched from Florida through Texas and had been growing very fast in population (the new Eleventh Circuit consists of Alabama, Florida, and Georgia); Congress also added a new D.C. Circuit to service Washington, D.C., partly because so many administrative agencies sit in D.C. and make decisions that generate a large number of appeals. Circuit courts of appeal, unlike district courts, are not one-judge courts. The judges sit in panels usually made up of three judges each. The total number of judges (as of 1997) varies from six in the First Circuit (this circuit handles Massachusetts, New Hampshire, Maine, Rhode Island, and Puerto Rico) to two dozen or more in the Ninth Circuit, a legal giant that includes California and eight other states of the West, plus Guam and the Northern Marianas.[10] If a case is important enough, it will be heard not by a panel, but "en banc," that is, by all the judges of the circuit. (In the Ninth Circuit, by way of exception, "en banc" does not mean all the judges, but a sizable number; the full bench here would be unbearably cumbersome.)

For most cases—indeed, the overwhelming majority—the circuit courts are the end of the line. Above them looms the United States Supreme Court, in all its majesty; getting a hearing there is a rare privilege indeed. The Supreme Court sits at the apex of the pyramid of federal courts; it can also hear cases which come out of high state courts, if they raise important federal issues, usually issues under the federal Constitution. The Court has only nine justices, and its workload is heavy. It has to be jealous of its time and effort, and it is. Few of the cases that knock at its door actually get inside. In 1880, 417 cases were filed with the court; in 1974, 3,661; in 1994, 7,132. The Supreme Court heard only a small percentage of these cases; the rest were turned down. In 1974, there were 2,520 petitions to the Court for certiorari from the United States Courts of Appeals alone. (Certiorari is a writ the Supreme Court issues to a lower court, pulling up the case for hearing.) The Court granted 158 of these requests, or a bit over 6 percent.[11] The other applicants went away empty-handed. In 1994, the Supreme Court issued a written opinion in ninety-five cases, decided sixty-five cases "per curiam" or by "memorandum decision" (that is, the Court decided these cases, but brushed them off in a paragraph or two), and denied or dismissed almost seven thousand supplicants.[12] Getting to the Court makes you a member of a very exclusive club of litigants.

The Supreme Court has almost total control of its docket. But like the top state courts, it was not always in such a privileged position. A century ago, its workload included many rather prosaic cases—ordinary contract or property cases appealed from the territories, from the District of Columbia, or from lower federal courts. This is no longer true. Yet even today the Court is not a simon-pure appeal court. The Court hears a few "original" cases—cases which come to the Supreme Court first, without any stops along the way. The Constitution provides for "original" jurisdiction in cases "affecting Ambassadors, other public Ministers and Consuls, and those in which a State shall be a Party."[13] Under this provision the Court might hear (for instance) a boundary dispute between two states. An example of an original case before the Supreme Court was the long-drawn-out wrangle among Arizona, California, and other states over how much water each state could draw from the Colorado River and its tributaries.[14]

Some states give their high courts "original" jurisdiction over cases of various types. In Nebraska, for example, the supreme court has authority to issue certain extraordinary writs, and to have original jurisdiction "in cases relating to the revenue," in "civil cases in which the state shall be a party," and in "election contests involving state officers other than members of the Legislature."[15]

The structure of courts, state and federal, has been described here in a simple, rather idealized way. In many states, there are oddities or extra wrinkles. Court structure can be very complicated; the farther back in history one goes, the more confused the situation gets. A number of states have tried to reform their court systems, to make them more streamlined, more rational. Arthur T. Vanderbilt (1888–1957), chief justice of New Jersey after 1947, led a notable and successful fight to reform the judicial system in his state, which was woefully out-of-date. But many states have preserved a flock of specialized courts, hangovers from the past.

These courts come in various shapes and forms. Georgia, for example, has separate probate courts which administer affairs relating to wills and estates of the dead. (These same matters, in California, are dealt with by branches of the superior court, that is, the ordinary, general court.) Delaware has the distinction of preserving a very ancient tradition: separate courts of chancery, which decide cases of "equity." This was once a common pattern, but the other states have long since merged "law" and "equity" into a single system of courts; New York joined the two together in 1848. In some states, there are separate juvenile or family courts, distinct from the regular courts. Massachusetts has a Land Court Department in its trial-court system to hear cases of foreclosure, eviction, land titles, and other matters of housing and real estate. Michigan and New York have a "court of claims," for claims against the state. Texas has a separate court of criminal appeals, distinct from the supreme court. Oklahoma has a court of tax review; Nebraska has a workers' compensation court. We have already mentioned municipal, traffic, and small-claims courts. Even in the federal system, there is a special court for custom and patent appeals, a court of claims, and a tax court (not technically a court at all, but in practical terms exactly that).[16] In the planning of court systems, there is a tension between simplicity and flexibility on the one hand and functional specialization (which has its points, too) on the other.

The Judges

Judges in America are overwhelmingly lawyers—members of the bar. The only exceptions are a few justices of the peace and the like, in a handful of states. They are the last survivors of what was once a mighty tribe of lay judges. Basically, then, all judges are lawyers. But only a tiny percentage of lawyers are, or ever become, judges. Who are they, and where do they come from?

In civil-law countries, like Italy and France, judging is a career of its own. Judges are civil servants, separated by training and experience at an early stage from the practicing bar. A person who wants to be a judge will typically take a competitive examination right out of law school (or after some period of practical training). Those who pass the exams become judges. They will probably stay judges for the rest of their careers. Beginners start out as beginner judges; successful judges rise to higher and better courts. Usually the sitting judge has never practiced law and never will.[17]

The situation in the United States could hardly be more different. American judges are lawyers, plain and simple. Usually, they are lawyers who are, or have been, politicians, or at the least have been politically active. One survey of judges in the United States Courts of Appeals, for example, in the 1960s, found that about four out of five had been "political activists" at some point in their careers.[18] The situation is the same on state courts, perhaps more so. Judges are usually faithful party members; a seat on the bench is their reward for political service. They are also supposed to be good lawyers and to have the stuff of good judges; whether this is actually taken into account depends on where they are, who does the choosing, and so on.

The political nature of judgeships is underscored by the fact that in most states judges are elected, not appointed. They run for office on a regular slate, and in many states they have to attach party labels to themselves—that is, they run as Democrats or Republicans. This idea of electing judges would strike many Europeans as very peculiar, as odd as if we elected doctors or police officers or government chemists. But the elective principle goes back rather far in United States history. It was, of course, unknown in the colonial period; it began to take hold soon after independence and became a marked trend in the first half of the nineteenth century. Lower-court judges were elected in Vermont from 1777 on, and in Georgia from 1812. Mississippi decided in 1832 to elect all its judges; New York followed in 1846.

Why elect judges? Essentially, the election of judges is based on the same theory that justifies electing governors or members of Congress: it is to make them responsive to the public. Precisely because judges come from political backgrounds, because they do not resemble the cold civil servants of France or Italy, some kind of public control seemed necessary. But the election system did not work out quite as expected. For one thing, few elections were actually contested in most of the states. Elections tended to be bland and colorless. Sitting judges rarely lost, regardless of party. There were, to be sure, some notable exceptions. The chief justice of Illinois, Charles B. Lawrence, went down to defeat in 1873.

The elective principle was never universal. There have always been a few states in which the governor appoints the judges, sometimes with legislative approval. Massachusetts never adopted the elective system, for example. But the main exception is and has been the federal system. The president, under the Constitution, appoints the justices of the United States Supreme Court "by and with the Advice and Consent of the Senate."[19] The president appoints all other federal judges, also with senatorial consent. This has been the system since 1789. The Senate plays an influential role. The custom of "senatorial courtesy" gives a senator a loud voice in choosing those federal judges who will sit in the senator's state. The president does not always get his way. Richard Nixon was rebuffed twice in his appointments to the Supreme Court; more recently, a Democratic Senate turned thumbs down on President Reagan's nomination of Robert Bork (1987). The appointment of Clarence Thomas, by President Bush in 1991, led to a particularly raucous fight. A president, of whatever party, cannot assume that the Senate will bend supinely to his will.

Once appointed and confirmed, a federal judge has no time limit, no term of office. The judge serves "during good Behavior," as the Constitution puts it. What this means is that federal judges have their jobs for life, or at least until they step down voluntarily. The only way under the Constitution to get rid of a sitting federal judge is to impeach the judge for "Treason, Bribery, or other high Crimes and Misdemeanors." This is rare and difficult. A senile or a drunken judge—or an outright lunatic—has, in theory, the right to sit tight on the bench until he or she is carried off feet first. Obviously, this system has its drawbacks, but it is supposed to guarantee that judges will be independent, nonpartisan, free from the immediate pressures of politics. This is worth the price of an occasional dodderer or misfit. Most observers of court history seem to agree.

Of course, the power to name the judges in the first place is no small power. The president will try to appoint men and women who agree with his policies. This is especially true for appointments to the Supreme Court. Still, once in office, a judge can thumb his nose at the president and the president's program; there is no recourse, no way to fire the judge, no effective sanction. Dwight Eisenhower came to regret that he appointed Earl Warren as chief justice; he joined a long line of presidents who felt betrayed by men they put on the bench. And, of course, judges, if they have longevity—and many do—may serve twenty or thirty years or more, until long after the president who appointed them leaves office or is dead and gone. Chief Justice Rehnquist, the senior justice at this writing (1997), was appointed by Richard Nixon and has served more than twenty years on the Court.

A growing number of states have begun to back off from the pure elective principle. In the twentieth century, some states have adopted the so-called Missouri plan. Under this scheme the governor appoints judges, but his choice is restricted. A commission made up of lawyers and citizens draws up a list of names and gives it to the governor. The governor must choose from the list. The judge serves until the next election, then runs for reelection on his or her record. That is, the judge does not run against anybody; the public is simply asked to vote yes or no. Since you cannot fight somebody with nobody, the sitting judges almost never lose. The very controversial chief justice of California, Rose Bird, and two other associate justices, were removed in 1987, after a bitter and noisy campaign against them. This California ruckus remains rather exceptional, however.

Why do sitting judges so rarely lose, even in states that do not have a plan like the Missouri plan? Judicial elections are usually low-key affairs. It is hard to campaign against a sitting judge. An upstart who tries to defeat a judge already in office has to walk a narrow line. The candidate, unlike candidates for Congress or the statehouse, really cannot make any promises. It is not quite right, after all, to express an opinion about situations that might come before the court. Sitting judges will sanctimoniously hide under the mantle of the law; they will not defend their decisions, but claim rather that they were just doing their duty, just deciding according to "the law," and letting the chips fall where they may. About all a frustrated candidate can say is that he or she can do it all better. Meanwhile, voters on the whole neither know much about these elections and the candidates nor seem to care.

Yet there are signs the process is becoming a bit more political. Between 1916 and 1973, there had never been a real contest in New York for the office of chief judge of the court of appeals (the highest court in the state). Candidates had "always been anointed in amiable cross-endorsements by Republicans and Democrats."[20] In 1973, Jacob Fuchsberg contested the election of Charles Breitel, a brash move that offended the organized bar. Breitel, the logical candidate, was already sitting on the court of appeals. He beat Fuchsberg, but in 1974 Fuchsberg tried again. This time he won a seat on the court as an associate justice. Both campaigns were tough and bitter. They generated a lot of publicity. This brought the office more into the public eye, which may or may not be a good thing in the long run. The California elections, in which a hurricane of voter disapproval sent Chief Justice Bird out of office, also focused attention on judgeships; judges are now, perhaps, more vulnerable politically than they were before. Two Florida justices, Leander Shaw (1990), and Rosemary Barkett (1992), were the target of

campaigns because of their support of abortion rights and their decisions expanding the rights of criminal defendants. Both justices kept
their seats, but with reduced majorities.[21]

Still, judicial elections are not likely to become as partisan as elections for governor or members of the state assembly. There is a deep
feeling that judges, somehow and in some sense, must stand outside the
hurly-burly of ordinary politics. Even elected judges are less beholden
to voters and to political leaders than other elected officials. And nobody
but the voters—not the governor, not the legislature—can get rid of
them at all so long as they avoid gross misbehavior or incompetence.
Judges are supposed to be independent, and to a surprising degree they
are.

This does not mean that judges operate outside public opinion, outside social forces, or free from the constraints of society. That would be
impossible, and undesirable. It does mean that the regime does not
dominate the bench, as it does, alas, in totalitarian countries. A judge in
mainland China who decided an important case against the wishes of
the government, who acquitted a dissident, or who ordered the regime
to grant more civil rights would lose his job and find himself with a one-
way ticket to Sinkiang province, or worse. This simply does not happen
in America. The government loses dozens of important cases each year;
the regime swallows hard, but takes its medicine.

The Work of the Courts: Procedure and Substance

Trial Courts. The organization of court systems has now been briefly
sketched. But what do trial courts actually do, and how do they do it?
It is, of course, not easy to generalize. Each state has its own codes of
procedure, its own rules on how to start lawsuits, how to run them, and
how to finish. Each state is free in theory to think up its own special
procedures. In fact, state procedural systems have a lot in common. For
one thing, the Federal Rules of Civil Procedure have been an alluring
model. The federal rules were originally adopted in 1938. More than
half the states have adopted them for local use. Moreover, all states
(except Louisiana) are part of the common-law tradition, and they are
all part of the same society (this time including Louisiana).

The common-law tradition of trial procedure puts heavy stress on
"orality." Common-law courts prefer the spoken word to the written
document. Not that courts are averse to pieces of paper. Indeed, they
are swimming in it: in many cases, boxes and boxes of "exhibits," deposi-
tions, and documents of all sorts are introduced into evidence. (A depo-
sition, essentially, is the statement of a witness, reduced to writing; it is

used, for example, to get testimony from people who are too feeble, too sick, or too far away to come to the courtroom in person.) Documents are quite indispensable in a great many trials. But still, the spoken word is the heart of the common-law trial, testimony fresh from the mouths of living, breathing witnesses, who stand or sit in plain view in the courtroom and are examined and cross-examined by the lawyers. The system is so familiar, so ingrained, that we take it completely for granted; Americans find it astonishing to learn that there are other ways of running trials, that there are systems in which, basically, judges proceed by shuffling papers and documents and the jury is quite unknown.

Then, too, ours is a so-called adversary system. This means that the parties (and their lawyers) control the case. They plan the strategy; they dig up the evidence; they present it in court. The two sides battle it out mainly by putting witnesses on the stand and asking questions. Lawyers (or teams of lawyers) are the chief actors in the courtroom drama. The judge sits on the bench, more or less in the role of an umpire. He or she sees to it that both sides obey the rules of the game. The judge goes no further. If there is a jury, the judge does not usually decide the big question of who wins and who loses. That is the jury's job. The judge keeps the trial going, and "instructs" the jury, that is, tells the jurors what rules of law have a bearing on the case. Unless the case is so lopsided that there is nothing for a jury to decide, the decision is left to the jury; the judge has to accept its verdict, whether or not he or she likes it or agrees with it. Harry Kalven and Hans Zeisel, who carried out a major study of jury trials in criminal cases, published in 1966, claimed that judge and jury tended to agree in most cases; judges would have come to a different conclusion, had the choice been theirs, in about one case out of four.[22] In this study, juries were found to be more lenient than judges, but later studies have come to the opposite conclusion.[23]

The adversary system is very familiar to Americans. Not everybody knows it by name or could describe it, but everybody recognizes it from books, movies, and TV. The adversary system is the system that creates courtroom drama, with lawyers parading their skills to an eager jury. It is Perry Mason and other detectives of fiction. It is Paul Newman in *The Verdict*. It is *L.A. Law* and *Court TV* and the O. J. Simpson trial. We take this method for granted.

But of course it is not the only way to run a trial. Civil-law countries, for example, do not use the adversary system. Their systems are inquisitorial. In France or Germany or Brazil, judges play a much greater role in building and deciding a case than they do in common-law countries: they investigate the facts, they put the evidence together, they try to get to the bottom of the affair. Historically, civil-law systems have not used juries, and lawyers are not as dominant a presence in the courtroom as they are in common-law countries.

The two systems, adversary and inquisitorial, seem as different as day and night. There has been endless debate about which one is better. It is no surprise that common-law lawyers prefer their own way of conducting trials. The very word "inquisitorial" leaves a bad taste in the mouth of people who speak English. Our lawyers tend to feel that the adversary system is the only fair way to run a trial, the only way to give each party a proper shake. Justice and truth will win out nearly all of the time if we let each side argue, compete, cross-examine.

European lawyers naturally take a different point of view. To them, the adversary system is primitive and often unfair. Adversary trials, they feel, degenerate into battles carried on by lawyers who are too clever by half; the truth gets smothered in the process. Their system emphasizes the work of honest professionals—judges, in short. It is more efficient, more impartial, more rational; and certainly (in their eyes) more just.

In fact, the adversary system is much less adversarial than most people think, and the inquisitorial system is less inquisitorial. An American judge is not always neutral and helpless. The judge can dominate the trial in both obvious and subtle ways. Some specialized courts (family courts, for example) have gotten far away from the adversary system: the judges have tremendous leeway. In some specialized courts, lawyers rarely or never show their faces. In fact, the power of the judge in courts that deal with family or related matters has been subject to a good deal of criticism, and some courts (juvenile courts, for example) have gotten more "legal" (that is, adversarial) in recent years.

Still more important is the fact that most cases never go to trial at all: they are settled out of court. What counts, then, is what happens outside the courtroom, in the corridors, in the lawyers' offices, and in the chambers of the judge. The high drama of the O. J. Simpson case is the exception, not the rule. Most criminal cases get decided by the process of plea bargaining, as we shall see. The same is true of civil cases—the overwhelming majority never see the inside of a courtroom. In civil-law countries, too, it may well be that most disputes avoid the courts, in favor of settlement, arbitration, or mediation. For this and other reasons, some scholars feel that the differences between the two systems are not as great as they appear to be, or that the two systems, in the more developed countries at least, are tending to converge.

A Note on Equity. A short detour is in order here to explain one of the curious features of the history of Anglo-American law—a feature which, somewhat surprisingly, still has meaning today. Medieval England, which incubated the common law, also produced another system, almost entirely different, with its own courts, its own rules, its own procedures. These were the courts of the chancellor, the courts of "chancery." The rules and procedures of chancery made up the system called equity.

The origins of equity are shadowy.[24] In the Middle Ages, the chancellor was one of the king's highest officers. He had important administrative duties; he was also a clergyman, could read and write, and was in charge of the "writs" that set lawsuits in motion. Sometimes he also heard complaints about this or that instance of injustice, and, as the king's representative, he occasionally exercised his power to bend the rules of law a bit, to right some wrong or prevent some injustice from happening. By the sixteenth and seventeenth centuries, equity had developed into a kind of full-blown rival to the common law. It was not just a difference of rules; the whole flavor of the system was different. The chancellor had never been immersed in the common law; if anything, it was church law (canon law) that he knew and that influenced him. Canon law was continental—civil law, in other words. Hence, procedure in equity looked a lot more like European law than like common law. For example, proceedings were written, not oral, and courts of chancery had no juries.

In many ways, equity was less rigid than the common law. This was even true of some of its procedures. In other ways, the two systems dovetailed. Only equity, for example, ever granted an "injunction," that is, an order to a defendant to stop doing something wrong (or start doing something right). Common-law courts had no way of issuing such an order. On the other hand, the common-law courts could award money damages; equity courts could not. The English system of justice was essentially made up of law plus equity. Each one was, in itself, somewhat defective; together they made up a more satisfactory whole.

An example might make this clear. Suppose my grievance is the behavior of my next-door neighbor. He is running a business on his property. From my standpoint, the business is a nuisance. Foul odors and smoke pour out onto my property; my garden is getting ruined; noise keeps me up at night; the value of my property is certainly impaired. If I go to an ordinary court, a court of "law," I can get money damages to make up for the harm my neighbor has done to me. But the court of "law" will not and cannot order him to stop. If he persists, I will have to go into court over and over again, each time collecting damages for harm done in the past.

To put a stop to this nuisance once and for all, I will have to find my remedy in "equity." There, in the chancery court, the judge, usually called a chancellor, can issue an injunction ordering my neighbor to stop his unlawful practices or suffer the consequences. So far, so good; but if I had gone to equity first, and asked for an injunction and money damages for harm already done to me, the chancellor would have politely turned down my claim for damages. For that, one has to go to "law."

Obviously, as this example shows, there is something clumsy about a dual system of this sort. It is certainly not ideal to have two separate systems, run by two separate structures of courts. Often in past times a litigant needed both to get justice. Law and equity coexisted in the United States, somewhat uneasily, until the nineteenth century. In that period, most of the states reformed their systems of procedure and merged law and equity into one. From that time on, the same courts administered both systems, and many distinctions between the two were abolished. Nonetheless, the old double system left fossil traces behind. It can still be important to know if a case would have been "law" or "equity." For one thing, as we said, equity had no jury. If a case was historically "equity," then even today there is generally no right to a jury.

Settled Out of Court. Systems of procedure and ways of managing trials are important to the American legal system. But, as we pointed out, most cases that people file never actually go to trial. They fall by the wayside far earlier. In the lowest courts, creditors file thousands and thousands of claims to collect small debts, to repossess cars, television sets, suites of furniture; landlords file for thousands of evictions; and so on. In the overwhelming majority of the instances, defendants never show up, never defend themselves in any way. Plaintiff wins "by default." (If defendants owe the money and have no real excuse for not paying, why *should* they show up?) Most of us have paid for parking tickets by sending money to traffic court in the form of "bail." Since we never show up for the trial of this dastardly crime, we forfeit the "bail." This is what everybody expects: the forfeiture of "bail" is just a way to collect a fine, thinly disguised with a different name, and with no muss or fuss.

The examples in the last paragraph are all small cases, petty matters—in the eyes of the law, at any rate. The situation in regular trial courts is not much different. Thousands and thousands of couples file for divorce; all but a few suits are uncontested. Thousands and thousands of estates go smoothly through probate without a will contest or serious dispute. Most criminal trials, even for serious offenses, do not go to trial: the defendants "cop a plea," that is, they plead guilty as part of a plea bargain. Thousands and thousands of accident cases are filed every year; only a tiny percentage go to trial. In San Mateo County, California, in the 1970s, about 5 percent of the personal-injury cases filed got to the jury stage. Even in federal court, only 8.7 percent of all civil cases filed in 1974 went to trial.[25] In California, as noted, almost nine cases out of ten in superior court ended without any trial, in 1980–81. In Maryland, in the fiscal year 1992–93, there were 139,267 civil cases filed in the trial courts of general jurisdiction. But of this mass of cases, only 1.1 percent ever made it as far as a jury trial; another 5.5 percent were tried before a judge, and all the rest dropped out or were terminated in other ways.[26]

Most issues, in fact, never even reach the stage of filing. An elaborate study of disputes and dispute settlement points up this fact. The study surveyed selected households in South Carolina, Pennsylvania, Wisconsin, New Mexico, and California to see what legal "grievances" people had and what became of them. The authors found that for every thousand grievances in tort, mostly personal injury matters, only 201 "disputes" emerged, and only thirty-eight of these disputes ever got to the stage where somebody filed a complaint in court.[27] Most of these thirty-eight, moreover, will not go to the jury; they will get filtered out or settled before reaching that point. Thus only a third or so of 1 percent of all grievances go the whole route.

Yet this is supposed to be a litigious society. The fact is that courts play the role of decision-maker in only a tiny percentage of grievance situations. Few contentious situations actually hatch and grow into regular trials. The survival rate is like that of the thousands of eggs that fish, frogs, and insects lay: out of each batch only a few survive.

What happens, then, to the other grievances? Why do so few potential cases ever get as far as filing suit? Why do so few reach the goal line? The general answer is simple: trials are risky and expensive. Usually, both sides would be better off settling, and so settle they do. In auto-accident cases, it makes sense for an insurance company to pay off the claim if the settlement amount is less than what a court case would cost and what the company would probably lose at the trial. Similarly, it makes sense for a victim to settle, even for less than he or she would probably win at a trial. There is always the risk of losing. And the trial itself and the lawyers will cost money, win or lose, in most types of cases.[28] For smallish claims, trying to settle almost always makes sense.

This means that the "real" law of contracts, or landlord-tenant disputes, or auto accidents is not to be learned simply by studying trials and cases. The real law of auto accidents, for example, is the law of insurance adjusters, lawyers' negotiations, and the like, as well as the law of the courtroom. Of course, when a woman hit by a car settles with the driver's company we cannot assume that the law did not influence the outcome. The insurance company and the woman's lawyer are well aware of the state of the law. Hanging over their heads as they dicker are their guesses about the law and about the way a trial will actually come out if they get that far. These guesses affect the terms of their agreement. The parties bargain and reach settlement on their own, but they bargain "in the shadow of the law," to use the pungent phrase mentioned in Chapter 2.[29]

The Business of the Courts

Exactly what kinds of cases do courts handle? What is the business of the courts? We know surprisingly little in any systematic way about this subject. Judicial statistics are a sorry mess, generally speaking. Each state handles its own statistics; some are better than others; in all cases, it is hard to compare across state lines. Legal scholars have not done much to fill in the gaps. There are only a handful of studies that have tried to get a grip on the flow of business through general trial courts; petty courts are even more obscure.

You may find this surprising. After all, courts hardly work in secret. They deal with the public every day; ordinary people come in contact with them. These people no doubt form impressions about what courts do. Judges, lawyers, and court clerks have their impressions, too. But it is one thing to have impressions; to have a sound, systematic grasp of the facts is another thing. After all, we see other people every day, we look at them, we talk and interact with them; but without a census, we would never know exactly how many people live in this country, where they live, who they are, and so on. We would have impressions, of course, but impressions can be very, very wrong.

Bad as they are, published statistics on the work of the courts are a good place to start. They give some idea of the workload of courts. In California, the superior courts are the trial courts of general jurisdiction. In 1994, there were 789 judges serving on these courts. In 1993–94, plaintiffs filed 729,372 complaints in these courts. Of these, 83,721 were classified as "personal injury, death and property damage"; more than half of these (49,523) were under the heading "motor vehicle." There were 166,927 so-called family-law cases; these were primarily divorce cases (or "dissolution of marriage")—marriage accidents, as it were. There were 81,000 cases under the general heading of probate and guardianship—estates of people who had died, and affairs of minors and incompetents. All this was on the civil side. Superior courts in the same year also heard 154,666 criminal cases (felonies) and dealt with 63,711 cases of juvenile delinquency.[30]

Each state, of course, has its own quirks of jurisdiction, as well as its own way of counting and classifying cases. In some states, for example, separate courts would deal with probate or juvenile matters. In the rather oddly named New York Supreme Court (which is the basic trial court and not at all supreme), there were 335,987 new civil matters in 1993. More than half of the caseload was made up of tort cases: 25 percent of the load consisted of "motor vehicle torts," 4 percent were medical malpractice cases, and 28 percent were classified as "other" torts.[31] "Domestic relations" cases are another large category (mostly divorce actions); in Michigan, for example, there were 53,600 of these in 1992, along with thousands of related matters (child support, for example). Slightly less than half of the rest of the "civil filings" in the state of Michigan were tort actions (28,820), and half of these, again, arose out of automobile accidents.[32] Everywhere, in terms of sheer bulk, auto accidents, divorce, and probate loom very large on the dockets.

These numbers of cases are impressive. The numbers filed in petty courts, however, are almost astronomical. There were, it is estimated, 52 million traffic cases filed in the various traffic courts of the states in 1994. But here the trend is not up but down: traffic cases are 15 percent lower than they were in 1984. This is because of a trend to take petty traffic matters (parking, for example) out of the courts and let the bureaucracy deal with them. The numbers, however, are still impressive; and there were, in 1994, over 8 million small civil cases in the petty courts, along with 9.4 million (petty) criminal matters and 1.2 million "domestic" matters.[33] These figures give at least some idea of the tremendous number of petty cases that come up every day in the lowest courts. They are the plankton in the ocean of law.

What the numbers do not tell us, for whatever level of courts, is how much time and effort cases of particular types take up. Often the states count the number of cases filed, not the number that go to trial (which, as we know, is a much smaller figure). Uncontested divorces, for example, puff up the figures enormously, especially in these days of no-fault divorce. But most of these cases are short, snappy, routine. One big trial may gobble up more energy and manpower in court than hundreds of these cut-and-dried affairs. The bare statistics do not give us much feel for the court as a living organism.

We get a better idea from the (rare) studies of courts in actual operation. These confirm that much of what courts do is utterly routine. The uncontested, no-fault divorce is the perfect example. Often there is, or was, a real dispute. A marriage is on the rocks. He and she might argue about property, who gets the house or the car, how the bank accounts should be divided, or about custody of the kids or visiting rights. For most people, these problems are ironed out long before any papers hit the courtrooms—in any event, long before the case reaches His or Her Honor, the judge. The parties themselves work these matters out, often with the help of lawyers. They, the parties and the lawyers, are the ones who decide the case.

The studies all agree on this point. The courts do a lot of routine administrative work; they rubber-stamp uncontested judgments and out-of-court decisions in a high percentage of the cases. Wayne McIntosh did a study of the work of the St. Louis Circuit Court, a trial court of general jurisdiction, from 1820 into the 1970s. His study documents the dominance of voluntary dismissals and uncontested judgments. For the first hundred years of the study about one case out of four ended in a "contested hearing or trial," but after 1925, the "average skirted downward into the 15 percent range." In other words, rather less than one case out of five in the 1970s called for any real judging.[34] Thousands of cases are handled every day in court that a clerk could dispatch, or a well-made machine; as we noted, some states, in recent years, have tried to get petty traffic cases out of the courtroom and into the offices of clerks.

If there are so many routine cases, then can we say that courts have abandoned their historic function of handling "disputes"? Yes and no; the evidence is conflicting. What is clear is that certain kinds of ordinary dispute have tended to drop out of court. In 1994, in forty-five urban courts, less than 4 percent of the civil filings went to trial—1.5 percent to "bench trial" (judge alone), 1.8 percent to a jury.[35] Only a minority of extraordinary cases are still there in court, getting the full treatment; indeed, these extraordinary cases may be becoming a bit more common. Balanced against those who think the courts are doing too little—those who think they are abdicating their function, or neglecting the legal interests of the poor and the middle class—are those (more numerous, probably) who think they are doing too much, upsetting too many applecarts, meddling in too many affairs.

Appellate Courts. The work of appellate courts is, in a way, less obscure than the work of trial courts. High courts publish their opinions; their output is thus an open book. Moreover, these opinions are what students study in law school; they are the raw materials that lawyers often work with in deciding the state of the law. Also, it is the high courts that make headlines (if any courts do). No court in the world sits in the spotlight as much as the Supreme Court of the United States.

Despite this, the general public has only the vaguest idea what the Supreme Court does, day in and day out. Most people know chiefly about a few sensational cases. They probably know that the Supreme Court struck down state abortion laws; educated people almost certainly know that the Court ordered schools to desegregate. Almost certainly, they have never read any Supreme Court opinions (they might be dismayed to find out how wordy the justices are). People know only a little bit about the Court, and many of them probably have as much wrong information as right. (They know even less about what state high courts do.) There is, to be sure, a certain hunger for information (or gossip). *The Brethren,* by Bob Woodward and Scott Armstrong (1979), promised a look "inside the Supreme Court"; it was a runaway best-seller.

So much for the layman. Lawyers, on the other hand, know a great deal about certain aspects of appellate courts, but lawyers, too, have great gaps in their knowledge. Not many lawyers ever appear in front of an appeal court. Even the lawyers that do have not systematically studied the work flow in appellate courts (why should they?); they have at most some vague impressions about the state of the docket.

One lawyerly impression is that over the years the United States Supreme Court has been hearing more and more big, important cases, has gotten enmeshed more and more in controversy, and has handled more and more hot potatoes. This impression may well correspond to the facts. The Supreme Court has gradually gained, as we noted, almost total control over the cases it takes and rejects—a process that began in the nineteenth century, but was only completed in the twentieth. It has used its power to get rid of dull, ordinary cases. Not every Supreme Court case makes the headlines, but every case is by some standard important and is worth at least a paragraph or two in the *New York Times.*

This was not true in the late nineteenth century. The Supreme Court in our day would never deign to take *most* of the cases reported in Volume 105 of the *United States Reports* (covering October Term, 1881). In one of these cases, the Court had to decide whether a method of packing cooked meats for transport was novel enough to deserve a patent. (The meat was to be cooked at 212 degrees Fahrenheit, and "while yet warm," pressed into a box or case "with sufficient force to remove the air and all superfluous moisture, and make the meat form a solid cake"). The Court said no.[36] There were cases about public lands; what the customs tax should be on snuff and on white linen laces; whether a railroad was liable to a passenger who committed suicide in a fit of despondency six months after a railroad accident; whether a commodore in the navy who traveled under government orders to Rio de Janeiro, but in a foreign ship, was entitled to mileage at eight cents a mile. Cases of these types have totally disappeared from the workload of the Supreme Court.

State supreme courts have traveled a somewhat similar road. Many of them now have almost as much control of their dockets as the United States Supreme Court. A statistical study of the workload of sixteen state supreme courts by Robert A. Kagan and associates, covering the period between 1870 and 1970, revealed dramatic changes in court business over time. The typical case in 1870 in the Supreme Court of North Carolina or California would be either a property case (a dispute, say, over who owned some tract of land) or a commercial case (whether a buyer, for example, had a good excuse for refusing to accept a carload of lumber). Many of these cases involved debt (for example, an action by a creditor to collect on a promissory note). In the period 1870–1900, 33.6 percent of the cases in these sixteen courts fell under the heading "debt and contract" and 21.4 percent fell under the heading "real property."

A more recent period (1940–70) showed quite a different picture. Debt-and-contract cases had shrunk to 15 percent, property cases to 10.9 percent. One big winner was "public law," up from 12.4 percent to 19.4 percent. These were cases on taxation, on regulation of business, on government abuse of authority. Criminal cases had risen from 10.7 percent to 18.2 percent, torts cases from 9.6 percent to 22.3 percent. Some of these trends were clearly accelerating; by 1970, criminal appeals had grabbed an amazing 28 percent share of the business of state supreme courts. Free counsel in criminal cases helps explain this great bulge of cases. The rise in torts cases is also not wholly unexpected. It reflects the great boom (if that is the word) in industrial accidents, followed by an even greater harvest of auto accidents, products-liability cases, and such newfangled fads as medical malpractice.[37] Of course, more accidents does not necessarily mean more accident cases; many people feel there has also been a rise in claims-consciousness. But this is a matter of some dispute.[38]

We must remember that the Kagan study looked only at the top courts in the sixteen states that constituted its sample of states. Many of the big states, California, for example, now have three layers of courts, not two. Some of the cases disappearing at the top are common at the middle level. It seems clear, though, that something is happening even in smaller, two-tier states, like South Dakota. They are following the same road, though a bit more slowly and with less control of their destinies. The study tells us, at least, what kinds of dispute top courts consider important enough to spend time on; to a certain extent, we also learn something about the demand for the top court's time.

The trends are not inconsistent with what seems to be happening at the trial-court level. Here, too, it is the ordinary case that gets squeezed out. Everyday business cases (contracts, property), which have become less common at the high-court level, and the simpler family cases (estates of the dead) are also dropping off at the trial-court level, or else, as in divorce, filings may be high, but actual trials are uncommon. On the other hand, cases in which individuals or groups confront the government seem to be increasing in number. This category includes criminal cases. Most criminal cases get plea-bargained out, but of those that "stay the course," more will be hard-fought and more will get appealed than would have been true a century ago.

There seems also to be growth in some categories of unusual or extraordinary cases—the tough cases, cases about society's dirtiest linen and hottest potatoes, the deepest, most sensitive, most poignant issues of the day. This is certainly true in the federal courts, and true to a lesser extent in state courts. Many people, from high-court judges on down, wonder why some of these cases are in court at all. They illustrate something mysterious and fundamental about American society and its legal system. In the United States, social issues often dress themselves up in legal costume and muscle their way into court. There are few countries in the world where abortion policy is decided, in the first instance, by judges. In few countries would courts draw the boundary lines of school districts or demand wholesale reform in state mental-health facilities. Yet these things happen in the United States.

A movement is going on which is bringing these issues into court, which expands the very idea of what should or can be dealt with through law and litigation, and which causes "law" to seep into nooks and corners where it never penetrated before. Nobody has quite found the right name for this movement or trend. We can call aspects of it judicialization, legalization, constitutionalization, the due-process revolution, or something similar. Whatever its name, it is certainly a significant trend. Courtlike procedures and habits extend their tentacles throughout government, big institutions, and society in general. Courts themselves have become final arbiters of many social issues, not just individual disputes.

How Courts Decide Cases

We have looked at the kinds of cases courts hear, the way they are handled, and the numbers that get filtered out along the way. Who wins and who loses in the cases that do get decided? And *how* are these cases decided? What factors tilt verdicts and decisions one way or the other?

Formally, it is easy to describe the process. In a trial court, the lawyers on each side present evidence and make arguments. Then the jury, if there is one, retires behind closed doors, talks things over, votes, and brings in a verdict. The jury deliberates in secret and never gives out reasons for what it does. (Individual members sometimes talk to reporters after the verdict is in, when the case is newsworthy—for example, after the celebrated trial of O. J. Simpson, in 1995.) Generally speaking, the mind of the jury is a closed book. However, research has opened the book somewhat. We know, for example, that the thought processes of juries do not result in decisions that are radically different from what judges would decide; that juries do pay attention to what the judge tells them; that they generally try to live up to their expected role.[39]

Juries, however, are the voice of the community; and the "community" may be prejudiced or ignorant. Historically, juries in the white South were notoriously prone to act unfairly toward blacks. How much race and gender prejudice remains in jury decision-making is a much debated subject. Historically, too, there have been many examples of what is called jury "lawlessness"—willful refusal to follow the law. "Lawless" or "nullifying" juries have refused to convict bootleggers or drunken drivers or poachers or even rapists, and even when the defendants were clearly guilty. A jury will behave "lawlessly" when it reflects norms outside the official norms of the law. This sort of jury lawlessness undoubtedly exists, but perhaps on a more modest scale than at times in the past.[40]

Judges and jurists deplore jury lawlessness, but not everybody agrees that jury nullification is always a bad thing. There is even an organization—the Fully Informed Jury Association (FIJA), formed in 1989—which lobbies for "laws protecting the right of nullification." FIJA gathers together some strange bedfellows, right-wing and left-wing, united in their hatred of certain laws—marijuana laws, tax laws, mandatory-helmet laws, for example—and eager to authorize juries to disregard these laws.[41]

What about the higher courts? Appeals courts do not run trials, but they hear oral arguments, receive "briefs," confer, decide, and write opinions. (A brief is a lawyer's formal argument, putting before the judge one side's version of the law and facts. Many of them are anything but brief.) The opinions pour out of the presses every year, volume after volume. Every state publishes opinions from its highest court, and many states (New York, California, and others) publish opinions from middle-level courts as well. Pennsylvania even publishes some trial-court opinions. A good law library has literally thousands of these volumes of reports, and more of them tumble off the press every year. There are over five hundred bound volumes for the United States Supreme Court alone. Opinions of the lower federal courts fill over a thousand volumes; there are many times that number for state courts. Inside these volumes are millions of words, all, in a way, telling the world how the court decided its cases.

The typical written opinion follows a fairly standard format. The opinion sets out the facts, states what the issues are, looks at past cases (if any) on the same subject, looks at statutes (if any) which have a bearing on the matter, and discusses the relevance of these "authorities." The court will announce certain legal principles which it (or courts in earlier cases) squeezed out of precedents or statutes. It applies, or tries to apply these principles to the facts of the case and comes up with an answer to whatever question or riddle is posed. This, then, is the decision. It either agrees with the results of the lower court (in which case the decision below is "affirmed") or it disagrees (in which case the decision below is reversed). Many cases are "reversed and remanded," that is, sent back down to the lower court, with orders to do it over again, and this time get it right.

Usually, the decision of an appeal court is unanimous—that is, all the judges agree with the decision. Less often, one or more of the judges has a different view of the matter, and there will be a "dissent." Courts almost always have an odd number of judges (five in Idaho; nine in the United States Supreme Court). The majority wins. If there is no majority (if a judge is sick or absent or disqualified and the rest split evenly), the lower court's decision will stand. Once in a while, a judge who agrees with the majority as far as its result is concerned will nonetheless quibble about the reasons. Such a judge can write a special opinion, called a "concurrence."

In some courts, dissent is quite common; in others it is rare. Certain kinds of cases are dissent-prone; others are not. The percentage of cases with dissents has been rising over time. In the study of sixteen state supreme courts, it was found that all but 8.7 percent of reported cases in the period 1870–1900 were unanimous. The nonunanimous cases rose to 15 percent in the period 1940–70. In the latest decade that the study covered, 1960–70, the rate had risen still more, to more than 16 percent.

These were the aggregate figures. Variations from court to court were striking. About 98 percent of the cases decided by the highest court of West Virginia were unanimous in the 1960s, but only about 56 percent of such cases in Michigan. In some courts, there seems to be a tradition of squelching dissent. Other courts place less value on presenting a united front. In some states, the dissent rate fluctuates, for no apparent reason. In Arizona, the dissent rate was 17.77 percent in 1917 and a big fat zero in 1921. In 1989, the rate was 6.81 percent; the next year, 1990, it jumped to 14.65 percent.[42] The overall trend, however, is clear. High courts take and decide fewer cases than they did a century ago, but the ones they take are more controversial, and this in itself probably generates a rising dissent rate.[43]

Dissents are often more personal and less legalistic than majority opinions, but in essence they rehash the same sorts of legal arguments. Dissents, however, make the point that in many cases there are no "right" legal answers—or at any rate, the right answers are not self-evident, even to a judge. Most close scholars of the legal process have their doubts about whether "the law" is ever that clear and knowable, even in unanimous decisions. After all, few appeals are "frivolous" (that is, totally hopeless, or without any merit whatsoever). There is at least *some* sort of argument, for both sides, in almost every case.

In general, scholars who study courts are a fairly skeptical lot. They read the written opinions, as they must, but they take them with a grain of salt. They certainly do not think that written opinions give an accurate picture of what goes on in the minds of the judges. They are suspicious of the power of dry legal arguments. They find it hard to believe that these arguments really persuade the judges, really move them to choose one side over the other.

But if not, what does? And is the elaborate facade of legal reasoning nothing but window dressing? An immense effort has gone into the study of judicial decision-making, trying to smoke out the governing factors and paint a realistic picture of the process. It is not an easy job. Nobody can read minds, few papers, notes, or diaries of judges are available, and judges rarely tattle on themselves. They are shy creatures, who dislike public attention. They want obscurity, and they generally get it. The United States Supreme Court is a special case. Its decisions can hardly avoid the limelight. Yet its actual work goes on behind a velvet curtain of secrecy. Some judges even destroy their legal papers. Enough remains to shed some light on the process, but there are many gaps.

As one author put it, journalists who cover the Supreme Court are like those assigned "to report on the Pope." The justices issue "infallible statements," draw their authority from a "mystical higher source," and conceal their status as human beings "in flowing robes." The justices also "have life tenure, which implies a license to thumb their noses at the news media."[44]

The air of mystery is probably one reason for the astounding success of Woodward and Armstrong's *The Brethren,* the 1979 "exposé" of the court. The book was based in part on gossip leaked from the justices' clerks. It titillated the public with its claim to tear aside the veil of secrecy. In the introduction, the authors described the court as an institution working "in absolute secrecy." No other institution has "so completely controlled the way it is viewed by the public." The public seemed quite eager to read this collection of tidbits about the justices, their habits, their likes and dislikes, their internal bickering, their opinions about each other, and the little inside dramas that led to this or that famous decision.

The Brethren was hardly a systematic study. Some scholars, however, have tried to study judicial behavior in a more rigorous way. Much of the effort has gone into dissecting the work of the United States Supreme Court; much less has been done on the work of state courts or lower federal courts. The overall questions are the same: Can we find some factors which explain why judges decide the way they do? Does it matter whether a judge is a Republican or a Democrat? Whether the judge's family was rich or poor? Whether he or she is Protestant or Catholic? How much can we learn by exploring judges' attitudes or values? How much would we learn if we could give the judges personality tests?

The results are not terribly exciting. One study of the Supreme Court of Michigan found that Democrats were more likely than Republicans to favor "claims of the unemployed and the injured."[45] No great surprises here. On the whole the studies do not tell us much that is new or startling or enlightening. The background or the personality of judges apparently does not carry us very far in explaining why they vote the way they do. Does gender make a difference, now that we have women judges? Recent studies say yes, but perhaps not *much* of a difference, and only in certain types of case.[46] Perhaps the measures used in the studies are too crude. In any event, the research has not reaped much of a harvest.[47] Much more sophisticated research and better theories are needed.[48]

Trial-court research has been disappointing, too. Many scholars suspect that judges, consciously or not, are prejudiced against blacks or poor people, or that white-collar criminals are treated better (or worse) than street criminals, or that courts are more lenient (or harsher) toward women defendants. There have been many, many studies—hundreds of them, in fact—on such issues. What is surprising is how little has been proved one way or another. Do blacks charged with a crime in the United States today (yesterday may be different) get a worse shake— more convictions, tougher sentences—than whites facing the same sort of charge? It turns out that this question is devilishly hard to answer, because of problems with data and because there are so many variables.[49] The jury is still out, so to speak, on this general subject.[50]

The meager harvest from these lines of research has led some scholars to try a different tack. Have we been too skeptical about the effect of the law itself on decisions? Perhaps judges honestly try to live up to what is expected of them. Perhaps they really try to play their part. Society has cast them in the role of judge, and they try to follow the script. In other words, the job description, the black robes, the tradition, may be as important in explaining judicial behavior as are childhood background or training or social class. As far as appellate courts are concerned, there is also the doctrine of precedent, that is, the idea that courts are supposed to follow past cases, indeed, are "bound" by them. Despite our skepticism, is it possible that this is what judges are really trying to do? It at least sounds plausible. But the idea that the law itself is the decisive variable still waits for more rigorous tests.

The conceptual and methodological issues are quite complex. A study by Ilene H. Nagel analyzed decisions on whether to grant bail or not in about 5,600 criminal cases from a borough of New York City, 1974–75. The study seemed to confirm that "formal law" was a significant factor in the "decision calculus" of the courts. It was not the only factor, but it was extremely significant. "Bias" on the part of judges played a lesser role. But Nagel also points out what many studies gloss over: the law itself often embodies a flexible, shifting standard. Judges are allowed by law to take many factors into account. Thus the distinction between legal and extralegal factors has been much overdrawn and overemphasized: "the complexities of law have often been ignored, and the extralegal category has been narrowly and selectively defined." Understanding how courts work will take continued study and greater sophistication in design.[51]

A few scholars have stressed what we might call the "structural" element in decisions.[52] High-court cases are decided by groups of judges, not by one judge sitting alone. The Supreme Court, as we mentioned, is made up of nine justices. California's top court has seven. The middle-level federal courts usually deliberate in panels of three. Typically, there will be some sort of process for assigning cases to particular judges, who then draft an opinion. To build a majority, a judge may have to make some sort of "deal," concessions to other judges who more or less agree with him. He may have to tone down certain language, or change the emphasis, and so on.

This process was one of the Supreme Court "secrets" that *The Brethren* so breathlessly revealed. No political scientist or court watcher was much surprised, of course. This inside dope was old news to them. This fact does say something about structure: a single judge, sitting alone, does not have to shade his views to construct a majority. Such a judge is, however, worried about the structure on top—the appeal court. No judge likes to be reversed. It is also obvious that upper courts need and want the cooperation of lower courts, which, after all, apply the doctrines and rules that upper courts lay down. Some high courts may make concessions or frame rules with the lower courts in mind.

There has been surprisingly little work on still another factor: the influence of outside social forces. One reason is that research tends to focus on differences among judges. The studies ask why Judge A and Judge B seem to disagree in their voting. This means concentrating on cases in which at least one judge dissented. But it might be just as interesting and important to note the ways in which Judge A and Judge B think alike, to see how all judges change their tune in the course of time, under the pressure of social change.

For example, all judges (or almost all) today have attitudes about race relations, powers of government, civil liberties, and the like that are light-years away from the attitudes of almost all the judges who worked and wrote a century ago. If you brought back to life a nine-teenth-century judge, he would be dumbfounded to learn about the state of civil-rights law today. He would even be amazed at what has happened in tort law, how far the courts have gone in making companies pay for damages caused by badly designed products, such as defective cold cream, soup, medicine, and automobiles. The wheels of doctrine have turned many times, in response to changes in the world outside the courtroom. True, some judges today stand on the right side of the political spectrum, while others stand on the left. But the point around which they revolve, the point from which they deviate, right or left, is determined by social forces, by the national agenda—in short, by the way things are today.

If we look at the long run, at major trends, the law seems like so much putty in the hands of the larger society. Probably there was not one judge in the nineteenth century who thought the death penalty was unconstitutional. Some were for it, some against it; nobody imagined that it violated the Eighth Amendment of the Constitution or any other amendment, for that matter. Today, some judges think it does. The Supreme Court, as we will see, went around and around on this question, and ended up upholding the death penalty—as most state court judges have done as well. But even these judges would agree that a serious legal question was posed. This was not true a hundred years ago.

Similarly, most nineteenth-century judges saw nothing wrong, legally speaking, with segregation of the races. Today, not a single federal judge thinks it acceptable (or is willing to admit it). That abortion and gay rights were constitutional issues was quite unthinkable. If anybody suggested to John Marshall or his associates, or to Thomas Jefferson himself, that the right to free speech included the right to sell picture books showing naked people making love, they would have thought that person crazy. The world has changed since then; judges' ideas have changed accordingly—even though they do not all agree. And of course the law has changed with them.

Social change, in short, drags doctrine along. Judges live in society, and their way of thinking shifts, consciously or unconsciously, as things happen in the world all around them. Often they are hardly aware of what is going on. If you ask judges what they do and how they decide cases, they are still likely to tell a rather old-fashioned tale. They will say that they search conscientiously for the law, and that they are guided by existing law. Many of them (not all) deny that they take social policy into account. Yes, they have values and beliefs and opinions, but they try to suppress them when they do their judging. This general pattern emerges from the few interview studies of judges. There is variation among judges (and courts), but on the whole, the typical judge is quite conservative in what he or she says about the job. In a study by Henry A. Glick, for example, Louisiana judges, almost to a person, expressed the opinion that "nonlegal factors" played no role in a judge's decision-making.[53]

There is no reason to accuse the judges of Louisiana of hypocrisy. No doubt they meant what they said. Judges do try to play the "legal" role, though probably not in every case. Some cases seem minor or unimportant; they are interesting only to lawyers, or not even to them. When a case of this kind comes up, the judge may have no strong feelings one way or the other. The judge (or a clerk) "looks up the law," figures out which way old cases point, and goes with the flow of past doctrine.

Even these cases, of course, may not be as cut-and-dried as one might think. As every law student comes to know, the law is often cloudy, ambiguous, uncertain. What the judge sees as the law is, in many cases, a little like a social inkblot test. The judge sees the case through his or her personal lenses. In these cases, the law is not in the books; it is inside the judge's head.

A small but important batch of cases fall into quite a different and distinctive group. These cases cut much closer to the bone. They have massive importance, massive consequences. Here social currents swirl all about, filling the courtroom with their sound and motion, and these currents affect judges whether they know it or not. In other words, we can think of decision-making as a kind of two-stage process. The first stage is the judge's decision whether to play the law game or not. The second stage is the actual decision.

At both stages, attitudes, values, and social forces are crucial. After all, these are what determine whether the judge sees a question as boring or exciting, important or trivial, technical or nontechnical, socially and politically sensitive or solely as "legal." The judges, to be sure, may not be aware at all of this two-stage process. They may feel that they are strictly bound by the law, and nine times out of ten they are quite sure that "looking for the law" is exactly what they are doing. But the two-stage process explains a mystery—how it is that social forces seem to have a powerful influence on the way the cases come out, yet at the same time judges say (and feel) that they simply "follow the law."

Glick's study found that most high-court judges do not think of themselves as policymakers or as lawmakers. They are old-fashioned in their attitudes about judging. But not all of them: some have a more sophisticated notion. This was true, for example, of the judges in New Jersey. Their minds were much more open to policy issues, which frankly played a role (they felt) in decisions. There is some evidence—it is rather indirect—that high-court judges in general are moving in this direction. We can call this attitude legal realism. "Legal realism" is the name of a school of legal thought which flourished most notably in the 1930s. The realists argued that judges were much more independent than they admitted; they sneered at the idea that the way to decide cases was by logical deduction from preexisting cases and rules. Judges in our system make law; they create new policy. In fact, they cannot help doing so in certain cases. A realist judge would be a judge who is aware of outside and inside pressures, aware of the way they affect the judge's work. Such judges would be sensitive to the impact of their decisions—that is, their social consequences—and would be willing to take these into account.

How do we know that legal realism is a genuine force, that judges are gradually converting to this faith? Some crude measures can be found by looking at the style of judicial opinions. This is definitely changing over time. For one thing, opinions are getting longer; dissents have become more common. Interesting changes are taking place, too, in citation patterns. When a court writes an opinion, it typically sprinkles citations about in the text. These are the "authorities" that justify its decision.

Mostly, the "authorities" are cases, prior decisions on the same legal points. The court will also cite any laws (statutes) on the books that have a bearing on the case, or cite the Constitution if that is in issue. In a small but growing percentage of cases, the court reaches out a little bit further. In California, for example, the citation of law reviews (scholarly journals, mostly published by university law schools) doubled between 1950 and 1970. In 1960–70, about 35 percent of the opinions written by New Jersey's highest court cited law reviews; the California figure was about 26 percent. (In such states as Alabama and Kansas, however, only 2 or 3 percent of the opinions cited law reviews.) A few cases even cited newspapers or studies by social scientists. In a study of federal circuit courts in 1989, researchers found that these courts cited law journals in about 10 percent of their opinions; the Supreme Court cites scholarly articles far more frequently.[54]

It is likely that the trend toward citing "authorities" outside the narrow band of cases and statutes will continue. Typhoon winds of social change rage about the courts; the problems that high courts face perhaps become more and more massive and intractable. As a result, some judges reach, however gingerly and delicately, for outside help. Changes in judicial culture help to smooth this path.[55]

Most research on judicial decision-making has focused on high courts, and especially on the United States Supreme Court. This is certainly no surprise. The Supreme Court is unique in our system. The state high courts are also of obvious importance. After all, they make and unmake common law. The lower courts suffer from scholarly neglect.

This is a pity. The lower courts may be undramatic, but that does not mean they are unimportant. The day-to-day work of lower courts, even traffic courts and small-claims courts, has a tremendous effect on the lives of ordinary people. In the long run, these courts have a tremendous effect on the life of society, as well. It was in the lower courts that the collusive or friendly divorce developed, long before anybody thought of a no-fault system. In the lower courts, creditors repossess thousands and thousands of pianos, automobiles, TV sets, suites of furniture. These courts foreclose mortgages, evict tenants, hear claims for wages. In all these cases, they act as the agents of a bustling, growing, rampant economy, for better or for worse.

That is not all. They also process hundreds of thousands of wills, they naturalize foreigners, they let people change their names, they put their stamp on the adoption of children, they appoint conservators for old people with Alzheimer's disease, they approve accounts of guardians and trustees. They smooth over (or aggravate) unnumbered disputes between families or neighbors. They punish millions of drunks, millions of speeders, millions who disturb the peace. They register far-reaching changes in social and economic life. They take part, in other words, in a series of events, utterly trivial looked at one at a time, but of volcanic importance in the mass. Fresh research may someday clarify how much they have meant, and still mean, to this country.

5

The Structure of American Law:
Statutes and Statute Makers

*C*OURTS ARE PROBABLY the best-known legal institution in our society, except perhaps for the police. But they are not necessarily the most powerful. One classical and durable legal theory has always insisted that courts have no right or power to make new law. They can only "find" law, or at best apply old law to new situations. It is the legislatures that have the right to make law, boldly and openly. Indeed, this is their job: they "pass laws." Yet when students study legal process in this country, they focus almost entirely on the courts (including the way in which courts *do* make law, despite the theory). Legal education more or less neglects legislative bodies—Congress, state legislatures, city councils. It also neglects the administrative agencies.

Yet the legislative branch is a tremendous presence in society and in the legal system. It is part of the bulk and body of Leviathan. There are vast numbers of lawmaking bodies, all up and down the land. As with the courts, we can imagine them arranged in a kind of pyramid. At the base of the pyramid, in the typical state, are the lawmaking organs of local government. In the 1990s, according to one authority, there were about five thousand local bodies with some lawmaking or rulemaking power in California alone. These included city councils, county boards, boards of supervisors, and thousands of special-purpose bodies. At the time there were fifty-eight counties in California (San Francisco was specially classified as a "city-county") and 448 cities. There were 980 school districts and 3,440 special districts (in charge of parks, sewers, bridges, mosquito abatement, and so on).[1]

One could quibble about whether these were all really legislative bodies, but they all had one thing in common: it was part of their business to establish general rules. This is, of course, obvious for legislatures, which churn out "laws" or "statutes"; towns and cities produce "ordinances." Park districts, transit authorities, sewer districts, and so on also make rules which are binding inside their own small orbits of power.

The state legislature sits at the top of the pyramid in California. It is made up of two houses, a senate and an assembly. Every state has a legislature, and in every state except Nebraska the legislature is bicameral, like California's—that is, there are two houses, an upper and a lower. California is divided into legislative "districts," which elect senators and assemblymen. At one time, senators were elected more or less on a county basis. One man represented the millions of people in Los Angeles County; at the same time, a few thousand voters in the high Sierra counties had a senator all to themselves. The United States Supreme Court put an end to this; it declared most forms of "malapportionment" illegal, in a series of cases that began with *Baker v. Carr.*[2] Today, all senatorial districts in California are more or less equal in population.

Legislative bodies in California have been described as forming a kind of pyramid, like the courts. The analogy is somewhat misleading. In some ways, the organization is very much looser: there is no such thing as an "appeal" from the city of Fresno, California, to the legislature, or from Yolo County to the legislature, or from the city of Hollister, California, to the county of San Benito. A citizen can, of course, complain that a city or town has overstepped its legal powers. But this complaint need not go to the legislature, and normally would not. It would most likely go to the courts.

Still, in another respect, legislative control over cities, counties, and towns goes far beyond the control which a high court exercises over lower courts. The legislature is in theory totally supreme. It can completely change the laws about towns and counties. It can shift boundary lines or add new counties. It can charter cities, amend charters, or take charters away. It could even abolish some local governments. In practice, the legislature stays out of most local affairs. But the state capital does have the last word; it is politics, not legal structure, that protects cities and counties from massive change from above.

We live, of course, in a federal system. There is a national legislature, too: the Congress. It, too, is divided into an upper house (the Senate) and a lower house (the House of Representatives). The House is elected on a population basis, but every state is entitled to at least one representative, no matter how tiny its population. There are 435 members, or roughly one for every 600,000 people. There are one hundred senators; each state has two, regardless of the size of the state or its population. California, with over 31 million people, has two senators; so do states with less than a million people, like Wyoming, Alaska, and Vermont. This scheme was written into the Constitution, and it is immune to *Baker v. Carr.*

The legislative system, like the rest of our legal structure, is influenced by federalism and, more significantly, by the American habit of decentralization. Voters take it for granted that the people they elect represent localities and local interests. We do not elect senators or congressmen "at large." The representatives in Congress must please the people in their districts, or they will find themselves out of a job. Also, in the states, and in most cities, each lawmaker is elected from a particular district, and must be a resident of that district.

This is not the case in England, for example; a member of Parliament from East London need not live there at all. The American system struck James Bryce (who wrote a classic description of American government in the late nineteenth century) as plainly deficient. It meant that "inferior" men would inevitably sit in Congress: "There are many parts of the country which do not grow statesmen, where nobody . . . is to be found above a moderate level of political capacity," he felt. It was his opinion that men of "marked ability and zeal" were "produced chiefly in the great cities of the older States."[3] This sounds snobbish and wrong to American ears—the two presidential candidates in 1996, President Clinton and Senator Dole, both came from small towns in small states (Arkansas and Kansas); both, whatever else one might say about them, were men of "marked ability and zeal." Still, Bryce had a kind of point. The system tends to send men and women to Congress (and to state capitals like Albany and Sacramento and to city halls) who lack the "big picture"; they think first and last of the wants and needs of their own little districts. Indeed, they have to.

It is easy to think of legislatures and courts as alternative lawmakers, or even as rivals. In some ways they are. But in our tradition, legislatures do many things that courts cannot do at all, or do only poorly. Legislatures can impose taxes and can spend money, which courts cannot really do, at least not directly. Courts respond to particular cases, in which John Smith sues Mary Jones, or the Acme Toothpick Company sues the city of Little Rock. In making a decision, an appeal court may lay down a general rule; but even so, the rule is supposed to be limited to the class of cases which *Smith v. Jones* represents.

Of course, it is anybody's guess how broad that category is. But in theory, anything that goes beyond the case is "dictum" (incidental talk) and is not binding on later courts. Whatever the theory, courts do act with caution most of the time. They do not presume to lay down minute, specific, detailed regulations. When a court hears a zoning case that turns on whether a gas station can be lawfully opened for business on the corner of Oak and Elm, the court may think the whole zoning ordinance or plan badly needs redoing, but it will not assume it has the right or the power to redo it on its own. Nor do courts change the speed limit or adjust parking fines; they do not generate systems of traffic rules or propose a list of chemical additives that can safely be used to make chicken soup yellow. Courts, in general, do not evolve quantitative measures. That is left to the legislature. In the opinion of some critics, courts have strayed far from their classic preserves and are meddling in affairs that should not concern them, but the basic line between courts and legislative bodies still, in general, holds fast.

The Legislative Output

The sheer volume of work done by legislatures, in the mass, is growing by leaps and bounds. This fact seems crystal-clear, though there are few systematic studies of legislative output and even fewer on the output of city councils and other similar bodies. In the mid-1990s, 6,550 bills were introduced into the California legislature in its biennial session.[4] The typical statute book of a typical state, in the mid-nineteenth century, consisted of one fat volume; in other words, all the statutes in force in, say, Michigan or Indiana were gathered together in a single thick book. Today, the collected statutes of any state, even a small state, will be ten or twenty times that size.

The reasons are not difficult to find. This is a complex society, and governing it calls for many detailed rules. (Consider, for example, how much law is on the books because of, or about, the automobile—traffic rules, speed limits, driver's licenses, and so on.) And just as courts have occasionally fudged the borders between their work and that of legislatures, so too have legislatures encroached on what was historically the turf of common-law courts. For example, there was a vast body of law (and litigation) on industrial accidents in the nineteenth century; the courts created and developed almost all of the rules. Around the time of the First World War, the states began to pass workers' compensation laws, which covered most of this field and basically changed the rules of the game.[5]

The change was, of course, not just a matter of taste. The courts had developed rules which were for the most part vague and general.

The new statutes were precise and detailed. For example, in the Idaho statute (passed in 1917), a worker who lost his "great toe at the proximal joint" in a work accident would receive 55 percent of his average weekly wage (but not more than $12 a week) for fifteen weeks. It is exactly this kind of precision that goes beyond the traditional power of courts. At any rate, though an immense body of case law on workers' compensation has accumulated in the last eighty years or so, the basic scheme operates in a routine and administrative way, under ground rules and schedules set up by the legislature. Even court cases on the subject use the statute as their starting point.

Codes and Uniform Laws

The common-law system is inherently messy; to understand what the law is, one must (in theory) rummage about in volume after volume of published cases. Judge-made law in the United States, with its fifty states, is especially ragged, nonuniform, inconsistent. A code—a statute—setting out the rules of law is much neater and more concise. Perhaps it is fairer too, since it may make clear, in advance, exactly what the law is, exactly what rules a citizen has to follow. As the English philosopher Jeremy Bentham pointed out in the early nineteenth century, common-law judges made law "as a man makes laws for his dog. When your dog does anything you want to break him of, you wait till he does it, and then you beat him for it."[6] Civil-law systems, with their clean, logical codes, at least *seem* much more rational, more organized, than the common law.

In the nineteenth century, some jurists in the United States, too, were intrigued by the idea of codifying the law—taking excess power away from judges and setting out the basic rules of law in modern codes. The idea is associated above all with David Dudley Field, a New York lawyer (1805–94). Field drafted or supervised a whole series of codes. The most successful was the Code of Civil Procedure. New York adopted this code in 1848. It merged law and equity into a single system and in other ways, too, simplified and modernized pleading and process in court. But New York turned down Field's other codes, which dealt with substance. These codes, orphaned in New York, found homes in some of the western states—states like California and Montana. Even in these states, lawyers were not trained in habits of reverence for statutes; the attitude of judges and lawyers toward the civil code of California is far different from the attitude of French judges and lawyers toward *their* civil code.

At the end of the nineteenth century, another strong but quite different codification movement arose. This movement focused on commercial law. The United States had entered the age of railroads, telephones, telegraph, interstate business. Goods and labor moved freely across state lines; laws did not. A company that did business in many states or that sold its goods in many states had to try somehow to comply with a whole host of slightly different laws.

The uniform-laws movement was the brainchild of law professors, jurists, and bar groups, but it succeeded, no doubt, because the the business community felt a need for it. In 1892, a Conference of Commissioners on Uniform State Laws was founded. The commissioners were appointed by the governors of the states. The first "uniform" law suggested by the conference was the Negotiable Instruments Law (1896), dealing with checks, bills of exchange, and promissory notes. It was quite successful; every state eventually adopted it. The Uniform Sales Act (1906) won thirty-four adoptions. The commissioners continued their labors and drafted many other laws, some of which also proved popular. The Uniform Simultaneous Death Act is one example. This statute dealt with the mess that results when, for example, husband and wife die together in a common wreck and their estates are entangled with each other. Most states adopted this uniform act.

But no state is forced to enact a "uniform" law, and in practice the laws may not be quite so uniform as they may look in print. Interpretations sometimes vary from state to state, and local amendments are always possible. Undaunted, scholars in the 1940s and 1950s proceeded with a complex task: drafting (and selling) a whole commercial code. The leader was Karl Llewellyn, one of the country's foremost legal scholars. The Uniform Commercial Code, divided into ten divisions ("Articles"), goes over ground covered by at least half a dozen older laws. It replaces the Negotiable Instruments Law, the Sales Act, and others of the older "uniform" laws.

The code got off to a rocky start and met with considerable sales resistance. Massachusetts and Pennsylvania adopted it, however, and finally, after intensive efforts, it took off everywhere. Louisiana is now the main holdout, although it too has been influenced in some critical regards by the code. Still, each state is formally free (if it wishes) to repeal or change the code. The code is a good example of how it is possible to come close to legal unity in this enormous country, simply through state cooperation and parallelism. But obviously this sort of uniformity can never be as stable and complete as the uniformity that comes from a single central government.

Statutes: Form and Content

It is hard to generalize about the form or content of statutes. A statute can be about any subject that law touches on, which means, in practice, anything. The form, too, is infinitely various. Usually we think of statutes as being general directives, unlike decisions, which apply to particular cases. It is a statute that makes burglary a crime and fixes a range of punishment, but whether Joe Doakes, a particular burglar, goes to jail is a decision made by judges, juries, and others, not by a legislature.

But even the statement that statutes are general is only partly right. Not all statutes are directives that apply to whole classes of cases. Congress, for example, still passes many so-called private laws, which may apply to a single person. Private Law 103-6 of the 105th Congress (1994) provided that "Orlando Wayne Naraysingh shall be classified as a child under section 101(b) (1) (E) of the Immigration and Nationality Act for purposes of a . . . visa petition filed . . . by his adoptive parent." Private Law 102-8 of the 102nd Congress (1992) directed the secretary of the treasury to pay to Craig A. Klein, of Jacksonville, Florida, "the sum of $8,947 for damages incurred as a result of the search and seizure of his sailboat, 'Pegotty,' by the United States Customs Service."[7]

Private laws were once common in state legislatures, too: states used them to charter corporations, to settle minor property disputes, to straighten out administrative messes, and even to grant divorces. In 1850, for example, the Alabama legislature passed a law changing the name of Matthew Robinson McClung to Matthew McClung Robinson.[8] Another private law allowed a certain John B. Moore ("who has been engaged in practicing medicine nine years . . . and is considered skillful and useful") to continue as a doctor, even though he had no license.[9] But private acts came to demand too much legislative time, and were open to corruption besides. After the Civil War, state constitutions began to outlaw the practice. The Illinois constitution of 1870 forbade "local or special laws" and provided that "in all . . . cases where a general law can be made applicable, no special law shall be enacted."[10]

The output of Congress or a state legislature, in any session, consists of dozens and dozens of statutes. Some are long, complicated, and important; some are short and succinct; some may change a comma or two or make some trivial amendment to an older law. Some statutes lay down broad principles which courts or agencies will have to flesh out and interpret; other laws contain detailed regulations, dotting every *i* and crossing every *t*.

The Internal Revenue Code (the federal tax law) is probably the most complicated law (or system of laws) in the United States. Some of its provisions are broad and general; other parts of the code go into incredible detail. It is also almost totally unreadable—a dark, impenetrable jungle of jargon and bewildering cross-references, which only specialists dare tackle, and even they have plenty of trouble. Here is a small sample of its deathless prose. This is from Section 170 of the code, a long and involute section about income-tax deductions for gifts to charity. One part of this section puts a limit on corporate gifts to charity; in any year, the limit is 10 percent of the corporation's net income. What if a corporation gives more? Here is the crystal-clear answer:

> Any contribution made by a corporation in a taxable year . . . in excess of the amount deductible for such year . . . shall be deductible for each of the 5 succeeding taxable years in order of time, but only to the extent of the lesser of the two following amounts: (i) the excess of the maximum amount deductible for such succeeding taxable year under subsection (b) (2) over the sum of the contributions made in such year plus the aggregate of the excess contributions which were made in taxable years before the contribution year and which are deductible under this subparagraph for such succeeding taxable year; or (ii) in the case of the first succeeding taxable year, the amount of such excess contribution, and in the case of the second, third, fourth, or fifth succeeding taxable year, the portion of such excess contribution not deductible under this subparagraph for any taxable year intervening between the contribution year and such succeeding taxable year.[11]

At the other end of the spectrum are laws which delegate broad authority to the president or some agency, or which speak in very vague, general terms. The famous Sherman Act, passed by Congress in 1890, is the fountainhead of federal antitrust law—the branch of law that deals with monopoly and restraints on trade. The Sherman Act is only a page or so long. One key provision simply outlaws "every contract, combination . . . or conspiracy in restraint of trade"; another provides that everyone who "shall monopolize or attempt to monopolize" any part of interstate commerce is guilty of a misdemeanor. Obviously, this leaves many questions unanswered. What *is* a monopoly? What does it mean to "restrain" trade? If a company controls 56 percent of the market in lead pencils, is it "monopolizing" this market? Anyway, does the pencil business constitute a "market"?

The act is not very specific, to say the least. Nor does it set up any special agency or body to run the fight against "trusts" and to decide how the law should be interpreted and enforced. In this regard, the Sherman Act is quite different from other regulatory statutes, particularly later ones. But the law which created the Federal Communications Commission is also marvelously vague. The commission has power to license radio and television stations; the only standard mentioned in the law is "public convenience, interest, or necessity."[12] This means nothing much in itself, but at least we know that the commission will be in charge. It will put some flesh on the bare bones of the statute. It would have been nice if Congress had given the commission some guidance; Congress chose not to.

As far as the Sherman Act is concerned, policy is set by the attorney general, the Justice Department, and the lower courts. They have the job of deciding what to consider a violation, whom to prosecute, whom to let alone. The attorney general and the Justice Department make these decisions in the first instance; the federal courts accept or reject the government's line. More than one hundred years have gone by since the Sherman Act was passed; a huge body of law has accumulated. Without the statute, this body of law would not exist, yet its exact shape owes relatively little to the precise (or imprecise) words of the statute.

Why should Congress give away so much power? Why should it delegate its authority to other agencies? Much of the development makes sense simply in terms of the scope of government. Congress is made up of only so many men and women, and there are only so many hours in the day. Congress has neither the time nor the know-how to handle every detail that modern law requires. For example, Congress decided, in the Pure Food Law of 1906, to forbid the manufacture and sale of adulterated food. This is the general principle. But it is the Food and Drug Administration that makes specific choices. The FDA, not Congress, decides how much butterfat must be in ice cream before you can call it proper ice cream, and what chemicals can or cannot be used to make cucumbers green and shiny in the stores. It is the FDA that hires chemists and doctors and puts them to work on this problem. Deciding questions about butterfat and additives is the agency's job. Congress has other things to do.

This is not the only reason for delegation. Delegation is also a form of delay, a way of dodging or compromising an issue. In the background of the Sherman Act, in the late nineteenth century, was a tremendous public uproar over the issue of "trusts." The trusts were huge industrial combines; the biggest of all was the Standard Oil empire of John D. Rockefeller, which controlled virtually the entire industry. Congress had to do something to calm the public, which was thoroughly aroused. But it did not quite know what to do, and big business, of course, was a powerful political force on the other side. Congress responded to these conflicting pressures by passing a broad, sweeping act, marvelously vague. This sent a soothing message to the public: we have taken action against the trusts. At the same time, the act set up no real machinery for carrying out the policies it so broadly expressed. In this way, Congress dodged the long-term issue and passed the buck to the executive branch and the courts.[13]

Every important law or ordinance, whether passed by Congress or by a state legislature or city council, is its own special blend of specific detail and broad, vague principle. Some, of course, leave out the detail altogether; some leave out the big, broad brushstrokes. Still others mix them together. Ohio—to take one example out of thousands—has a food, drug, and cosmetic law which prohibits the sale of "adulterated" food. What does the word "adulterated" mean? There is a long chain of definitions. Some are quite general: food is adulterated if any "valuable constituent" has been "omitted." But the statute also gets down to minute detail: candy is adulterated if it has "any alcohol or nonnutritive article or substance except harmless coloring, harmless flavoring, harmless resinous glaze not in excess of four-tenths of one per cent," and so on.[14]

Why are statutes written one way or the other? Who makes these decisions and why? The mixture of detail or nondetail depends in each case on the history and politics of the particular law. Beyond this, it is hard to say anything more definite, except to point out that "historical accident" has almost nothing to do with the matter, nor is it a mere question of the techniques of draftsmanship. Legislatures do not pass laws as academic exercises or out of whim, but because somebody is pushing them; the social forces that lie behind any particular statute explain its form as well as its substance.

Statutes and Their Interpretation

A statute is, of course, a kind of command. Legislatures pass them, but they are not in the business of enforcement or interpretation. These jobs are left for others to do. Every statute, then, has a double message. In the first place, the statute delivers to the public (or some part of it) a statement of do's or don'ts, or rights and privileges. In the second place, the statute also contains a message to some legal authority, giving instructions about carrying out the law. The second message may be, and often is, implicit; the statute does not necessarily say it in so many words.

For example, the Indiana penal code (Section 35-42-5-1) provides that if a person intentionally takes "property from another person" with force or threat of force, the crime called robbery has been committed.

A convicted robber can be sent to prison. This section of the penal code is, first of all, a message to the general public, warning people (if they need the warning) that robbery is forbidden and can be punished. At the same time, the statute is a message to district attorneys, police officers, judges, jurors, prison wardens, and a whole host of other officials, authorizing them to do their job with regard to robbers. None of these officials are mentioned explicitly, in this particular law. Other Indiana laws deal with the structure of the criminal justice system, and the code section on robbery implies and assumes these other provisions. If we want to know whether the robbery statute "works" or not, we have to examine the impact of both of its messages. Is it getting through to robbers and potential robbers? And is it also getting through to law-enforcement officials? Are they doing their job of enforcement? These two impact questions are not, of course, unrelated to each other.

This is a simple example, because the robbery statute is itself relatively simple. The wording is not particularly difficult. A street holdup is an obvious case of robbery. There may be borderline situations, but the main thrust of the law is clear to anyone who reads it. Moreover, the layman does not have to read it. People do not go around studying the text of the penal code; in this case, they *know* that robbery is a crime. The penal code itself rests on well-known, basic norms of American culture. The other branch of the message is also fairly clear. Dealing with robbers is part of the normal, ordinary work of police, judges, prison people, and so on.

Many of the thousands of statutes in the typical statute book are much more problematic, as far as their meaning is concerned: they are ambiguous, or confused, or novel, or very complicated, or extremely vague. We have seen some examples: the Internal Revenue Code is an example of enormous complexity, the Sherman Act an example of great vagueness. Even "clear" statutes run into problems of interpretation. Life is full of surprises, and situations often come up that do not quite fit the statute—but then again perhaps they really do. In other words, there are constant problems about what a statute actually says, how to interpret it if there are two conflicting meanings, and what to do when we are not sure that it covers some special situation.

Who decides what a law really means? A lawyer would say, almost automatically, that the courts do. In a difficult case, it is true, courts have the last word in deciding on the meaning of a law. When Congress enacted Title VII of the Civil Rights Act of 1964, did the legislators mean only to get rid of discrimination against black people and other minorities, or was it their plan to sweep the law clean of any race discrimination, however "benign"? Could a white person claim the protection of the civil-rights laws? The background was ambiguous, and the words of the statute were no help in the toughest cases. The Supreme Court had to decide, in the end, what to do about "reverse discrimination." In one notable case decided in 1979—*United Steelworkers v. Weber*[15]—the Court confronted the issue head-on. The union had entered into a collective bargain with Kaiser Aluminum to reserve for blacks half of all new openings in craft-training programs. A white worker complained. In a split decision, the Court upheld the plan and ruled that the Civil Rights Act did not forbid this arrangement.

This was an instance of "interpretation"—in theory, at least, a search for a meaning that is already *in* the statute. It is, in theory, not a question of the justices' values, ideas, beliefs or preferences. This theory seems naive, to say the least. The Court that decided *Weber* was much more open to "benign" discrimination than the Court in the 1990s; backlash and political change had had its impact on the appointment process, and a (narrow) majority of the Court, in a 1995 decision, expressed the view that *all* "race-based action," at least by "state and local governments," was deeply suspect, and almost certainly unconstitutional.[16] That this attitude, and others, affects "interpretation" (of statutes or constitutional texts) seems undeniable.

In a real sense, then, when courts "interpret" the statutes, they are actually making law. A law that has not been authoritatively interpreted—that has never come under the gimlet eye of the judges—is, in a sense, incomplete, inchoate; its meaning is clouded. Many lawyers would nod their heads in agreement at this last statement. But we have to be careful not to let the point distort our picture of the legal process at work. Of the thousands of laws and amendments to laws that pour out of legislative chambers every year, only a tiny (though important) minority ever go to court for interpretation. The rest are "interpreted" (if at all) by other people. All the people who handle the law in any way, including the police, officials of the Social Security Administration, yes, and members of the general public, interpret the law, whether they know it or not. Lawyers play a key role in this process. Take, for example, the murky provision of the Internal Revenue Code about deductions for charity, which we quoted before. This message is much too complicated, much too "legal," for the general public. Somebody else has to receive the message, digest it, store it up, and feed it out in an easier form. This is the tax lawyers' job.

The lawyers do not do it alone. In their offices, they gather material from law-book companies, commercial tax services, trade associations, and so on, which help keep them current. Similarly, there are people working for any big company or any big institution (a university, a hospital) who have the job of sifting through the piles of matter that flow into the institution, all the laws, rules, and regulations that affect what they do. These staff people, too, digest law and store it in a form that their organizations can use. They, too, interpret the law.

The statutes that courts interpret, of course, are not a random selection of all statutes. Courts decide *cases,* so these statutes are involved in some controversy that has ended up in court. The issues raised tend to be the most hotly controverted. This is probably why they got to the court in the first place. How does a court decide what a statute means? Courts have been working with statutes for centuries. They have built up a body of doctrine on "construction" (interpretation) of statutes. They have, in other words, generated rules—or, more realistically, guidelines, rules of thumb—about the interpretation of laws. Some of these rules are in the form of "maxims" or "canons of construction"— slogans or sayings that sum up guidelines of interpretation in a pithy sentence or two.

There is, for example, one maxim to the effect that penal laws should be "strictly construed." This means that when a law makes behavior criminal, courts should interpret the law quite narrowly. They should stick as close as they can to the literal meaning of the words. They should avoid any interpretation that would apply the law to conduct which is not clearly, unmistakably covered by the text of the law. Otherwise, we might punish people without giving them fair warning in advance that their behavior is a crime.

Put this way, the idea is just and sensible. In practice, the notion can easily be carried too far. In one famous case,[17] decided in 1931, the United States Supreme Court had to construe the National Motor Vehicle Theft Act of 1919. The law defined a motor vehicle as an "automobile, automobile truck . . . motor cycle, or any other self-propelled vehicle not designed for running on rails." Congress made it a crime to cross state lines in such a vehicle "knowing the same to have been stolen." Defendant McBoyle flew a stolen airplane from Illinois to Oklahoma. Had McBoyle violated the law of 1919? An airplane is a vehicle, it has a motor, and it definitely does not run on rails. But the Supreme Court set McBoyle free. A penal law must give "fair warning," in "language that the common world will understand." The statute here was couched in words that would "evoke in the common mind only the picture of vehicles moving on land." It would not be fair (said the court) to extend this law to airplanes. McBoyle went unpunished, and Congress amended the law in 1945 to include aircraft.[18]

If this strikes you as farfetched, you are not alone. Did McBoyle really think it was no crime to steal an airplane? Presumably he did not know it was a *federal* crime; but did he know there was a federal law about taking "vehicles" (*whatever* that meant) across state lines? Not all courts are such sticklers, and there are some state laws that tell them explicitly not to be. For example, Section 4 of the California penal code states baldly that California does not follow the common-law rule requiring penal statutes to be "strictly construed." All criminal laws are rather to be interpreted "according to the fair import of their terms, with a view to effect its objects and to promote justice."

According to another famous maxim, statutes in "derogation of the common law" must also be strictly construed. This does not have a very precise meaning, but it expresses an interesting bias. The bias is this: courts should look suspiciously at changes in law that come from legislatures instead of from the courts themselves. Historically, many courts indeed took a rather narrow, illiberal view of statutes. They looked on them as (in a sense) alien intruders, disturbing the beauty and symmetry of common law. This general habit of courts helps explain the rather peculiar style of American (and English) statutes. Many of these statutes are incredibly verbose, piling synonym on top of synonym. Here is a typical example:

> All promises, agreements, notes, bills, bonds or other contracts, mortgages, or other securities, when the whole or part of the consideration thereof is for money or other valuable thing won or lost, laid, staked, or betted at or upon a game of any kind, or upon a horse race or cockfights, sport or pastime, or on a wager, or for the repayment of money lent or advanced at the time of a game, play, or wager, for the purpose of being laid, betted, staked or laid, betted, staked or wagered, are void.

This language comes from an Ohio statute, and all it means is that gambling contracts are void (that is, a court will not lift a finger to help either party collect or enforce them).[19] Its essential meaning can be expressed in four words; about a dozen more might help to explain it a bit further. The code uses more than eighty separate words, all part of a single very long and difficult sentence. The drafters wrote as if they had to cover every possible crack or gap in meaning—as if the text were a small, leaky boat in a storm on a hostile sea. These precautions, these synonyms, these long legalisms, were presumably there to prevent courts from punching holes in the statute or changing little holes into big ones.

There are many other maxims or canons of interpretation. Some states list them as official and make them part of the statute books. Even when this is done, it is questionable whether the maxims are very effective, whether they are anything other than convenient excuses for courts to do more or less what they want to in the way of interpretation. Karl Llewellyn, in a well-known essay, pointed out that most maxims have their countermaxims; these act more or less as escape hatches, so that a court can ignore whichever of the two it wishes and use its opposite instead. For example, according to one maxim, courts should interpret statutes in such a way as to give sense to every word or clause in the text. On the other hand, a court can (by another maxim) reject as "surplusage" words that are "inadvertently inserted" or "repugnant" to the rest of the statute. The two maxims seem rather inconsistent.[20]

Systematic information is lacking about the ways courts handle statutes in practice. Probably a great deal depends on the attitudes of judges toward the actual subject matter covered by the statute. Even the maxims make distinctions—for example, the maxim that criminal laws should be narrowly construed; there is no equivalent for laws about contracts or torts. In any event, courts do their "interpreting" within certain rather definite limits. They can twist and pull a little, but they can hardly construe "black" to mean "white" or "up" to mean "down." The words of a statute are not putty; they are more like a rubber sheet that gives a little here and there but cannot totally change shape. To "interpret" in such a way as to turn black into white or night into day would violate the boundaries of judicial tradition and upset the judges' own sense of their legitimate role.

As we said, "interpreting" a statute is not something a court decides to do on its own; it takes a case to do this, and that means at least *some* measure of controversy or dispute. It is also not true that a statute has no real meaning unless and until a court tells us what it is. As we pointed out, most statutes are not interpreted by courts at all. Nonetheless, they may have a real operative meaning; the people who carry them out or who come under them grasp this meaning, and act accordingly.

When a statute *does* come before a court, to be interpreted, is there a right way and a wrong way to do the job? One obvious "right" way is to search, honestly, for the "true" or "real" meaning of the text. But does such a thing really exist? Often, to be sure, there is a literal meaning, but sometimes this makes no sense or leads to absurd results. Perhaps, then, the meaning of a statute has something to do with its purpose, with what the members of the legislature had in mind, or the reason why the statute was passed in the first place. This actually carries us only a little bit further. Legislative intent is a slippery concept. First of all, no one can actually read the minds of the legislators; second, there are too many minds to read—435 in the House of Representatives alone. Neither in theory nor in practice is it easy to find out the actual purpose or intention of a law.

Indeed, for most legislative minds there may be nothing to read, even if we could get somehow inside the heads of members of Congress. Many members have never even looked at the bills they vote on; others may have only a faint idea of what was in them. Some vote out of party loyalty, others to do a favor to another legislator. Even those members who take an active part in writing some particular law, or arguing for it, or pushing it along, might have among them quite different, conflicting notions of the purpose and sense of the law.

Of course, in a doubtful case, the interpreter can make an honest search for the purpose and sense. He or she might begin by asking what prompted the legislature to act. There might be important clues in what is called "legislative history." This term refers essentially to material, outside of the actual text, which could shed light on what the text might mean. We would certainly want to consider the events or situations which led to the introduction or drafting of the bill. We could also take a look at the various drafts and how they changed as the bill snaked its way through Congress; we can read committee reports and debates on and off the floor of the legislature; we can consider the words of experts and advocates who appeared before Congressional committees—everything, in short, that happened up to the point where the president or the governor signed the bill into law.

In England, courts traditionally refused to pay attention to legislative history; they insisted on looking only at the text. However, in the 1990s, the high British courts have begun, rather gingerly, to permit use of parliamentary material in some situations—for example, where legislation is "ambiguous or obscure, or leads to an absurdity."[21]

American doctrine has been much more receptive. Some judges have argued that background is important only when the text is ambiguous: if the law has a "plain meaning" there is no reason to rummage around in the windy expanses of the *Congressional Record,* and so on. But the plain-meaning rule has long since been officially discarded, and it is now standard practice to use legislative history to interpret statutes. Take, for example, *United Steelworkers v. Weber,* the 1979 case on "benign" discrimination we have already cited. Here a white worker challenged an affirmative-action program for black workers; he claimed this was a form of race discrimination against whites. Justice Brennan, in his opinion, quoted extensively from the *Congressional Record* to drive home his points about the meaning of Title VII of the 1964 Civil Rights Act. Not to be outdone, the dissent of Justice Rehnquist quoted even more extensively, to make the very opposite point. In this case, as in so many, legislative history hardly leads to a single right answer.

Though state legislative history is often fairly skimpy, Congress spews forth reams and reams of paper. In many cases, the trouble is that there is entirely too much history. There may be so many versions, drafts, debates, reports, messages, and so on that a judge can find some material to support *any* interpretive position. The *Weber* case is a good example. But this is no real argument against the use of legislative history. As Professor Kenneth Davis has put it, that would be "a little like saying that we should not drill for oil because much of the drilling ends with dry holes. The important fact is that some of the drilling yields oil."[22]

Nonetheless, the use of legislative history has not gone unchallenged—by some legal scholars, and by a few judges, including Justice Scalia of the United States Supreme Court. Scalia, in a case decided in 1993, excoriated the use of legislative history as "likely to confuse rather than to clarify"; he quoted a judge who compared the use of legislative history to "entering a crowded cocktail party and looking over the heads of the guests for one's friends."[23] Yet in that very year, and indeed in subsequent years, members of the Court poked around in legislative materials in virtually every case that involved a federal statute.

Legislative Decision-Making

Just as there is a body of literature on decision-making in the courts, so there is a body of literature on the way legislatures make decisions. This literature is concerned, among other things, with the effect of public opinion (in general) on the legislative process, and (in particular) with the role of lobbyists and organized interest groups. The literature is rich and complex, and cannot be summed up in any single, simple formula. A few points stand out:

First, most scholars agree that legislators, at least to some degree, behave in response to their constituents. They tend to do what the voters in their districts want, or at least those voters who write letters, donate money, or otherwise try to exert some pull. Legislators do not simply follow their own inner values. Of course, ideals and convictions are important to legislators; but a member of congress or the state assembly knows that it could be fatal to get too far out of touch with the voters' wishes; the member could be thrown out of office at the next election.

Second, what legislatures do reflects the social force exerted; in other words, we can explain output (legislation) through input (social pressure). The man or woman in the legislature is a medium, a conduit, not an independent force. There is, however, a good deal of controversy about the source of the pressure. Who is it that exerts the force? Moderates (and conservatives) tend to stress the "pluralism" of American political life. They do not claim that everybody in the country has an equal say, but they stress how many groups and how many interests get some response from the lawmakers. There is a good deal of popular rule, in other words. Legislators listen to many voices, demanding many different ends and means. The groups have to deal with each other, inside and outside the legislature; they have to bargain and compromise; no single group ever gets its way entirely. The very form of the government reinforces this system: there is no "single center of sovereign power"; rather, there are "multiple centers of power, none of which is or can be wholly sovereign."[24]

But many scholars reject this image. They feel that it paints too rosy a picture. These critics argue that the rich and the powerful are, in practice, the only serious influences on major decisions; they are the only ones who can afford lobbyists, the only ones who can mount a real campaign to get results in Congress or a state legislature. Besides, campaigns themselves have become very expensive. Candidates cannot survive without heaps of money to buy television time, to conduct polls, to print leaflets, to hire managers and staff, and so on. Only big interests have the financial power to make important contributions; this gives them a say in elections and in the behavior of legislators which the average person can never hope to have. The poor, the minorities, the unpopular are shut out of the process. So are such "diffuse" interests as those of consumers and pedestrians.

The word "lobbyist" has, if not a sinister, at least a distasteful ring. Since 1946, Congress has required all lobbyists to register. Lobbyists are those who, for money, try to influence passage or defeat of legislation. The lobbyist must disclose who he or she represents, and also reveal a good deal of financial information.[25] Literally thousands of lobbyists have registered under this law.

Lobbyists claim, with some justice, that they do not deserve their shady reputation. Of course there have been corrupt lobbyists—lobbyists who used pressure or bribery to get their way. But in general lobbying is a vital part of the democratic process. Lobbyists mobilize public support or opposition to bills; they keep legislators informed of what is going on at the grass-roots level (or other levels). The Sierra Club has lobbyists; so do the National Rifle Association, the Japanese government, and Harvard University. In fact, like so many facets of law and government, lobbying is a complex phenomenon; it is neither all good nor all bad, and it is, in any event, deeply ingrained in the American tradition. Still, we do not have to demonize lobbying, or discount its value, to wonder about the role of money and power in the legislative process.

Studies of the legislative process emphasize the fact that votes on bills are not isolated acts. A legislature is an institution, a system; its members know each other, and they must learn to live and work with their colleagues. Congress is not "an anonymous group of men and women who occasionally meet to pass legislation"; on the contrary, it is a continuing body, with "an elaborate formal and informal structure, traditions, norms, and agreed-upon practices."[26] The same is true of state legislatures.

This means, for example, that to understand the legislative process, we have to understand the committee structure, seniority, the party system, and so on. We have to understand the structure of legislatures, and how it affects the work of the body. The Senate, for example, is usually a slower, more sedate, less ideological body than the House of Representatives, and structure must account for this difference.

We must also realize that members do not deal with each single bill in isolation. Rather, they "deal" with each other; they trade votes, in subtle and not-so-subtle ways. There is a lot of open "logrolling," especially in regard to "pork-barrel" bills—legislation about construction projects, irrigation works, dams, harbor improvements, research centers, and the like, to be located in local districts. That is, legislator A agrees to vote for a dam in B's district, because B will vote for the harbor improvement in A's district. More subtle, and more important, is what has been called "implicit" logrolling; vote trading which is less blatant, less open, but still part of the process of "getting along."[27] A legislator is always aware of other legislators (and of the president or governor) and is generally willing to accommodate others in exchange for goodwill or a helping hand, or at least a friendly hearing, on his or her issues. There are, of course, limits to how far a legislator can "deal." Legislators must be careful not to deal themselves out of office.

One would expect, then, in the light of all this, that any complex statute would turn out in the end to be some sort of compromise. It comes about after an intricate game of give-and-take in which legislators, nudged constantly at the elbow by constituents, play power poker with each other. Almost any big bill could serve as an example. Any important law touching on, say, health-care reform will surely reflect in various ways the influence of doctors, hospitals, and insurance companies, as well as the public at large. The Sherman Act reflected both the outcry of the public and the defensive maneuvers of big business. How much weight each interest has had is of course in each instance the important question. It is not always easy to tell.

There is a middle view, then, between the exaggerated pluralist position and the extremists on the other side. The legislative process is neither as good at accommodating everybody as some have thought, nor as elitist and undemocratic as the worst of the cynics has described it. Rather, it is rough, complex, and imperfect. It also changes over time. African-Americans and consumers have, for example, a much greater chance to win the ear of legislators than they did some fifty years ago.

In general, legislative lawmaking needs a good deal more research. We particularly need to know a lot more about the bottom layers of decision-making. Most of the research we have puts the searchlight on Congress, although a certain amount does deal with state legislatures. We are much more in the dark about city councils, zoning boards, and school districts. The city council of Memphis, Tennessee, or the school board of Bangor, Maine, may not seem very important to the rest of the country, but the work of these local agencies, taken all together, is absolutely fundamental, and worthy of careful study.

6

The Structure of American Law:
Executing Policy

*T*HE ADMINISTRATIVE SECTOR is in many ways the fastest-growing part of the legal system, the cutting edge. This is the domain whose body and bones are made up of hundreds of boards, agencies, authorities, committees, commissions, and the like, poking their fingers into every aspect of modern life. The public is in constant contact with it. Yet it is also, on the whole, the most obscure branch of government. When a citizen applies for a document or a service, it may seem to him (as Herbert Jacob has put it) that the request "drops down a dark chute and emerges untouched by a visible hand."[1]

Though in many ways obscure, this domain is also a domain under attack. Deregulation is one of the catchwords of the day; the Reagan administration won power in 1980 as the sworn enemy of "bureaucrats," and this was also a powerful theme of the Republican Congress that was elected in 1994. Both parties obviously feel that there is political hay to be made in attacking "big government"; and what makes government big is not the legislature, not the courts, but the administrative apparatus.

A good deal of the political noise is, in all honesty, simply that: noise. In fact, no one seriously thinks the end is near for administrative law and administrative government. Even the most zealous cutter and chopper hopes at most to slice an inch or two off its tremendous bulk; miles and miles will remain.

It is easy to reel off examples of administrative agencies or administrative tribunals. But it is hard to come up with an exact definition of the administrative sector. Indeed, the best definition, sloppy as it seems, may be a negative one: the administrative sector is everything left over in law and government if we take away the courts and legislative bodies, the president, and all the governors, mayors, and county supervisors (along with their immediate staffs), the police, and agencies concerned with national defense. The residue—everything else in the legal system concerned with rules and policy and with making rules and policy stick—is the administrative sector.

This residue comprises an enormous body of men and women and an enormous apparatus. Here we have the Food and Drug Administration, the Securities and Exchange Commission, the Federal Trade Commission, the Federal Power Commission, the Social Security Administration, the Environmental Protection Agency, and dozens of other important administrative agencies, bureaus, and commissions, with headquarters in Washington and branches strewn about the country. Many of these agencies have counterparts in the states; many do not.

On the other hand, the states have many agencies which have no real federal (national) equivalent. Among these are most occupational licensing boards. These obscure bodies (housed, perhaps, in small offices in the state capital) run exams, make rules, and give out licenses to doctors, nurses, plumbers, watchmakers, barbers, clinical psychologists, and midwives, among others.

These boards are by no means unimportant, if we take them all together. Some trades and professions (doctors, for example) are universally subject to licensing rules. There is a common core of licensing functions in all states, along with some local variations and additions. Tennessee has a state board of accountancy, a state board of examiners for architects and engineers, and boards for barbers, cosmetologists, funeral directors and embalmers, general contractors, real-estate brokers, landscape architects, land surveyors, auctioneers, collection agencies, pest-control operators, "rental location agents," "private investigators," fire-alarm contractors, and "polygraph examiners," not to mention members of the healing and helping professions, doctors, nurses, veterinarians, psychologists, speech pathologists, dentists, chiropractors, hearing-aid dispensers, optometrists, osteopaths, and pharmacists, as well as "massage therapists," who manipulate "the soft tissues of the body with the intention of positively affecting the health and well-being of the client."[2]

Administrative bodies are found on the local level, too—for example, boards of zoning appeals. These decide such decisions as whether Mr. and Mrs. Smith can open a restaurant on Elm Street, or whether

Elm Street must stay residential. This is not a question of earthshaking importance, but it means a lot to the Smiths and to their next-door neighbors. On the local level, there are also park commissioners, port authorities, bridge commissions, and tax assessors; there are sewer districts and agencies charged with mosquito control. And most important, perhaps, there are local boards that run the schools.

Do all these agencies and bodies, from the top to the bottom of the pyramid, have anything in common? They share, on the whole, a curious combination of dependence and independence. It takes an act of Congress, a law of some state legislature, or a municipal ordinance to bring them into life. Their "parents" can also put them to death, simply by repealing the law or ordinance. It is a well-known fact that this does not happen very often. Once born, they cling stubbornly to life, and their parents oblige. Still, history is littered with fossils of extinct agencies. The Office of Price Administration, for example, had almost dictatorial power during the Second World War, fixing prices, wages, and rents. It is only history now. The Interstate Commerce Commission, regulator of railroads, lasted over a century; Congress put it out of its misery in 1995.

In many agencies, there is a curious mixture of powers. On the one hand, they act like legislatures; that is, they make up rules and regulations. The Food and Drug Administration, for example, decides what chemicals can be added to food. It also has a staff and inspectors to enforce its rules. It can also act like a court. That is, if a food company complains about some ruling or decision of the FDA, the agency can hold a hearing, sift the evidence, and come to a reasoned decision. Thus, in 1995, the FDA decided, after extensive agency evaluation, that "an aminopeptidase enzyme derived from *Lactococcus lactis*," employed "in the manufacturing of cheddar cheese," was safe for use.[3] A few weeks later, the Department of Transportation proposed a rule that would require the company that made Airbus Models A 320-231 to modify "the firewall of each engine."[4] Many agencies even publish reports. Volume after volume of decisions of the National Labor Relations Board, for example, sit on the shelves of law libraries. These contain accounts of NLRB decisions, which are often as important as the decisions of courts.

Some scholars and politicians are dismayed by the rapid development of the administrative state. They look on it as a kind of cancerous growth. Yet the fact that the administrative state is massive and pervasive must mean that there is some massive, pervasive social demand at the root of it. And there obviously is: the demand for continuous, systematic, planned attention to certain social problems and concerns. The rest of government has a short, spasmodic attention span. Congress lurches from crisis to crisis, the courts from case to case. Only the Securities and Exchange Commission doggedly keeps after the stock exchanges, reviews financial reports, and so on. Only the FDA monitors drug companies. Only the FCC lives in the world of TV networks, day in and day out.

American government mirrors what goes on in the community at large, to a greater or lesser degree. Planning and system in government grew up alongside of planning and system in business. Big business had to control and coordinate its various subsidiaries, divisions, and units. It tried to do this through formal rules. Workers punched time clocks and followed instructions; modern labor law "legitimized, while it regulated, patterns of workplace order and command relationships."[5] The administrative state is the public, official form of a pervasive private reality.

How the Leviathan Grew: A Brief Sketch

It is hard to think of a more striking change in government and the legal system over the last century or so than the rise of the administrative agency. The administrative state has grown enormously in scale and scope. Administrative agencies as such are as old as the nation. There were administrators and agencies of government when George Washington was president. The post office was a major branch of government then, and it is still a big operation today. Each cabinet office in the federal government was and is an administrative agency of its own. The same was and is true in the states.

Today, there are millions of jobholders in the civil service. The federal workforce in the days of George Washington, on the other hand, was a tiny handful of men. The staff of Pickering, Washington's postmaster general, consisted of one assistant and one clerk. They took care of all the agency's business.[6] In general, administrative process in the early days of the republic was weak and inefficient. Most of the action, of course, was at the level of the states. But the states, too, had tiny budgets and tiny staffs.

One of the biggest responsibilities of the federal government in the nineteenth century was managing and selling public land. The General Land Office in Washington presided over an empire of land—millions and millions of acres. It supervised dozens of local land offices. Public land was supposed to be disposed of in an orderly way. First, the land was to be surveyed and mapped. Then the president had the power to declare the land ready for sale. At that point, it would be auctioned off to settlers and buyers. But local offices were poorly run, on the whole, and badly staffed. Congress was always stingy with expense money. One surveyor complained in 1831 that he did not even have decent storage space for his papers: roaches and crickets had "free access"; mice made "beds out of old field notes . . . papers are thrown into old boxes and put out of the way: the roof leaks . . . and injures the books and papers."[7]

The states did at least as poor a job with their own lands. There was no tradition of a trained civil service, and government was usually weaker than its greedy subjects. The land office was a primitive operation, a far cry indeed from, say, the Internal Revenue Service today, which commands an army of lawyers, accountants, and agents and banks of computers, and has vast powers of audit and enforcement.

From the dawn of American history, regulating business was one of the jobs of the administrators. Even the early colonists were eager to have quality control of important goods. Under the *Laws and Liberties of Massachusetts* (1648), the selectmen of Boston and other towns that shipped pipe staves abroad were empowered to name two men from each town, "skilfull in that commoditie," to act as "viewers of pipe-staves." All pipe staves for export had to pass before the watchful eyes of these viewers, who could reject staves that were "not merchantable" because of "worm-holes" or were poor in size and quality. For example, staves had to be four and a half feet long, three inches and a half "on bredth . . . without sap," and "in thickness three quarters of an inch"; they also had to be hewed "well and even."

In the eighteenth and nineteenth centuries, cities of any size had somewhat similar laws for the inspection of basic commodities (butter, coal, bread). A Connecticut law of 1822 provided for local inspection of a huge array of products: beef, pork, butter, lard, fish, hay, flour and cornmeal, lumber, barrels for fish, sawed shingles, potash and pearl ash, and "onions put up in bunches."[8] Local government also levied taxes, laid out roads and kept them in repair, and issued licenses to taverns, inns, and gristmills. Each township or county also had its "overseers of the poor." These local citizens administered the "poor laws," the primitive welfare system of the day. They raised local taxes and spent the money on relief for the sick and the destitute, though in a bare-bones and minimal way. Since every additional "pauper" took money from local pockets, towns looked with a jaundiced eye on poor people who moved in from outside. Instead of being greeted by the Welcome Wagon, newcomers could be warned to get out of town; if they did not listen, they could be "removed"—dumped bodily across the township line.

Cities, counties, and towns performed other important administrative tasks. Education was one of them: running the local school system.

Until recently, the federal government left education pretty much alone, financially and otherwise. Even centralized state control developed slowly. The schools were doggedly local affairs. Police, and law and order generally, were traditionally given over to local administration. In the nineteenth century, as the economy expanded, so did state administrative law. There were commissions to regulate banking, state lands, canals, bridges, and insurance companies. Connecticut in the 1840s had a commission of three ("annually appointed by the general assembly") to visit and check every bank in the state.[9] Insurance regulation was a particular concern of the states. States regulated many aspects of the insurance contract and the insurance business; the work was often handed over to an administrative body, the insurance commission.[10]

Cities and states welcomed the first railroads with open arms. But from about the 1850s on, control of the railroads became an important policy issue. The New England states set up the earliest railroad commissions, in the 1860s. Connecticut, for example, gave a three-man commission power to inspect the state's railroads, though mostly to check on safety and repair of equipment. The commission had limited enforcement power and no jurisdiction whatsoever over freight rates and passenger fares.[11]

The next wave of railroad commissions, in the 1870s, was far more potent. The most noted of these commissions were in Midwestern states. They were the product of the so-called Granger movement; farmers and shippers lashed out in anger and frustration, accusing the railroads of abuse of power, of crude profiteering. The Granger commissions of Wisconsin, Illinois, and Iowa were far from toothless. The Illinois Railroad and Warehouse Commission, for example, had broad authority over railroads and grain elevators in the state. Besides general inspection power, the commission had power to enforce state laws, which included actual regulation of rates. Indeed, one law set a maximum charge for storing grain—two cents a bushel per month—and another law, aimed at the railroads, outlawed rate discrimination.[12]

The Granger laws were fairly radical for their day—so railroads and warehousemen thought. Business challenged the Granger laws in court, charging that they were unconstitutional. The famous case of *Munn v. Illinois*[13] reviewed the right of the state to regulate grain elevators. Under Illinois law, grain elevators had to procure a license to do business, and the law fixed prices for storing and handling grain. The Supreme Court turned back the challenge and refused to strike down the law. Regulation, even price-fixing, was acceptable, as long as the regulated business was "affected with a public interest." That is, a business with a crucial or vital place in the social or economic scheme could not claim immunity from public intervention. The principle of *Munn* was broad enough to cover most forms of administrative regulation.

The Interstate Commerce Commission Act (1887)[14] was a landmark in the history of administrative regulation. Indeed, this was a landmark in American history generally. The original law created a federal (national) commission, the Interstate Commerce Commission, to regulate railroads. The statute laid down the general rule that all freight rates and passenger charges had to be "reasonable and just." It outlawed rebates, kickbacks, price discrimination, and other practices that had kindled the anger of farmers and shippers.

What stimulated the federal government to enter the field of railroad regulation? State regulation of railroads had generally failed. At first, railroads were small, local lines linking two towns, rarely crossing state boundaries. New Jersey, for example, chartered a "Belvedere and Water Gap Railroad Company" in 1851;[15] New Hampshire incorporated a "Concord and Portsmouth Railroad" in 1855.[16] But gradually, local railroads merged and consolidated, big sharks swallowed up little fish, and the railroad barons strung together large interstate networks. A few names, like "Atchison, Topeka, and Santa Fe" (later called the Sante Fe Railway) remained for many years to remind us of the older stage. At any rate, the individual states had neither the legal nor the political muscle to control these giant railroads. They had become a national concern.

The commerce clause of the Constitution gave Congress power to regulate commerce "among" the states. This was taken to mean power over interstate movements of vehicles and goods. The Supreme Court had for many years emphasized the negative aspect of the commerce clause: the commerce clause prevented states from impeding the flow of commerce across state lines. Now came the positive side: the power of the national government to regulate commerce itself. The ICC act was not the federal debut in regulation or in the administrative business, but it was a major step in a fateful direction.

Some historians feel that we have tended to look at the ICC through the wrong end of the telescope. They claim it was in fact not an attempt to tame the railroads, not a reform law passed in the public interest. Rather, the railroads benefited from the law. The ICC put a lid on competition; its regulatory actions were a protective cocoon for existing railroads. It guaranteed friendly guidance from a sympathetic agency, decent profits, and orderly markets for all.[17]

Some parts of this thesis are quite plausible, though it no doubt goes too far. Laws like the ICC Act cannot be totally one-sided. Railroads had a powerful voice in Congress; so did farmers and shippers, in the aggregate. Both groups influenced the law. The ICC Act, as is typical, was some kind of compromise. Each side gained something, and lost something, too. This much is clear. The farmers and shippers gained some measure of control over rates and practices. The railroads gained order and protection. Administrative regulation, in general, strikes a compromise between battling interest groups. The results are almost never all one-way. The hard question is to assess who won the most, and why. Often, "compromise," which implies a certain rationality, is not the right word: the interplay of forces and interests produces a monster—a misshapen, irrational mess, with something for everybody, to be sure, but no coherence, no consistency, no underlying sense. Indeed, the ICC act may well have fallen into that category.[18]

In any event, the ICC Act foreshadowed the rise of the administrative state at the federal level. In the twentieth century, the pace accelerated.[19] The Food and Drug Administration dates from 1906; the Federal Trade Commission Act, which was supposed to put teeth into antitrust law, was created in 1914. The New Deal of President Franklin D. Roosevelt, in the 1930s, was the next great watershed. Congress established a flock of new and powerful agencies. Some reflected twentieth-century technology, for example, the Federal Communications Commission (1934), which controlled "communications by wire and radio," later adding television. Others came out of the social changes and reforms of the New Deal, for example, the Securities and Exchange Commission, which regulates stock exchanges and the sale of stocks and bonds by corporations; the National Labor Relations Board, with its powers over collective bargaining; and the Social Security Administration—a major federal incursion into a field (welfare) that had once been strictly local.

The New Deal is in many ways still with us. And presidencies since Roosevelt's only added to the stock of agencies. Under Lyndon Johnson (1964), the Office of Economic Opportunity was created to run the "War on Poverty." The War on Poverty is dead now, but many of the Johnson programs, like Medicare and Medicaid, remain, and are administered by vast bureaucracies. The Equal Employment Opportunity Commission (EEOC) was created in 1964 to enforce the new civil-rights laws.[20] OSHA (dealing with occupational safety), ERISA (pension and retirement plans), and EPA (environmental protection) are other recent examples of "alphabet-soup" agencies. Eugene Bardach and Robert Kagan describe the legislation of the 1960s and 1970s as a "quantum leap" in federal action to protect public safety. They mention not only OSHA (1970), but also the Water Pollution Control Act (1972) and the Surface Mining Control and Reclamation Act (1977).[21]

Meanwhile, administrative agencies have multiplied like rabbits on the state level, too. The occupational licensing boards mentioned earlier are all state agencies; the great rush to enact licensing laws began in the 1890s. The states have their own laws on corporate securities ("blue-sky laws"), and they are in control of many areas of life (zoning is one) that the federal government leaves almost entirely alone. Some state regulatory agencies have tremendous significance: the Texas Railroad Commission, despite its name, controls the oil and gas industry in Texas; it has power to stop the production of oil "in excess of . . . reasonable market demand," which gives it fantastic economic leverage.[22]

The result is a huge melange of boards and agencies, on every level of government. In 1994, a Republican Congress, with Newt Gingrich as speaker of the House of Representatives, roared into office with promises to cut the bureaucracy back and turn many functions back to the states—promises that Presidents Reagan and Bush had made before him. So far (1997), the troops have hardly made a dent in Leviathan. "Deregulation" has had some notable successes in the last decades—air fares and bank interest are two prominent examples—and the ICC has been eliminated. But the core of the bureaucratic state remains largely intact.

A Typology of Administrative Bodies

There are so many agencies, their work is so various, and they operate in such different ways that it is almost a hopeless task to try to describe them in general terms. One useful way to classify them is by subject matter. Thus, some agencies are concerned with regulation of business and labor (NLRB, SEC), others with welfare (for example, the Social Security Administration), still others with public resources (for example, the Bureau of Public Lands). Again, some regulating agencies regulate single industries (airlines, banks), others regulate business in general (SEC, OSHA).

Another important way to distinguish among agencies is to look at their structure. Some agencies are "independent," others are not. An agency is legally independent if it is not attached to an executive department. Independence means the executive cannot control the work of the agency. The president appoints National Labor Relations Board members; once they are installed in office, he is not their "boss," and they do not have to obey his commands. The Social Security Administration, on the other hand, is part of the Department of Health and Human Services. The administrator makes policy, but the secretary of HHS is the boss and can overrule the administrator, or even fire him, and so can the boss's boss, the president of the United States.

We can also draw a distinction between "friendly" and "hostile" boards and agencies, if we remember not to take these terms too literally. "Friendly" boards and agencies are manned by the very people the board or agency is supposed to regulate. The Federal Aviation Administration is not "friendly," in this sense. This agency is part of the Department of Transportation. It has an administrator and a deputy administrator. By law, neither may have "a pecuniary interest in, or own stock or bonds of, an aeronautical enterprise."[23] The state boards that license druggists, plumbers, or optometrists are a different story. Druggists, plumbers, or optometrists control these boards and fill all or most of their seats. For example, the state board of optometry in California consists of nine members, appointed by the governor. There are to be three laymen ("public" members), but the other six must be registered, practicing optometrists.[24]

There are good historical reasons for the difference between the two types of agency. Licensing of plumbers was probably the plumbers' own idea. They wanted to keep out amateurs, enhance their own prestige, control the work, and hold prices steady and stable. These are mostly economic goals, not very different from some of the goals of labor unions or of workers generally. But not all occupations are able to band together and form an effective union. Against whom could druggists, doctors, or plumbers call a strike? Whom could they ask for a raise? They can best achieve results by forming trade groups and by persuading the legislature to license their occupation, vesting in a board of practitioners the power to decide who gets licenses, and how and why. This puts control of membership and work conditions firmly in friendly hands.

At least part of the thrust to regulate railroads, on the other hand, was "hostile." It came from shippers and merchants who feared the railroads, who thought railroads had far too much power for the good of the country. Of course, there is more to the story of railroad regulation than that. Many concessions were made to the railroads as the ICC Act journeyed through Congress, and the results, as we noted, were fairly incoherent. But the hostile element remained part of the package. This is true of economic regulation in general.

Whatever the origin of railroad regulation, or regulation of public utilities, airlines, and so on, what happens in practice? Whom do the commissions serve? One popular theory is that the regulated industry tends to "capture" the agency and bend it to suit industry purposes.[25] The ICC became the creature of the railroads early in its career; television networks allegedly took over the FCC. The puppets shove aside the puppet master and make him dance on their strings.

Often there is some truth to these charges. For one thing, regulators have to live with their subjects. They learn to see things through their subjects' eyes. Also, commissioners are supposed to regulate businesses, not kill them. A gas or electric company applies to a state power commission for a rate increase. It presents facts and figures about rising costs: coal, oil, and labor are all more expensive. If the commission accepts the facts and figures, it will grant the increase, more often than not. The commission, after all, is responsible for the health of the industry. The gas and electric companies are privately owned and must show a profit. Then, too, some commissioners come from the industry they regulate, and many expect to go back there when their terms are up. They are reluctant to be tough and unyielding. Historically, the public or consumer interest has been weak, diffuse. Who, after all, speaks up for John and Jane Q. Public, day in and day out, at the agency? In many cases, nobody. Yet lobbyists and lawyers for industry have always been there, pressing their cases. Only in recent years has a strong, even strident consumer lobby emerged.

There is some empirical evidence in support of the "capture" idea. For example, David Serber[26] studied California's department of insurance and the way it handled consumer complaints in 1969. He paints a depressing picture. The department leaned overboard to accommodate insurance companies; consumers who made noise were treated as cranks by the staff; the staff systematically disfavored women, blacks, lower-class people, and anybody who seemed "inarticulate or angry."

This was a small state agency, and the data came from 1969. Is the situation changing? There are signs that it is. The consumer movement is stronger than it was in 1969. External controls over administrative agencies are also more vigorous.

The Republic administrations of Reagan and Bush, and the Republican Congress elected in 1994, have all emphasized the opposite problem, as we noted: red tape, bureaucracy, oppression of citizens, interference with business and (as a result) severe harm to the economy. They can certainly find evidence to support their claims; "regulatory unreasonableness" is a problem in many areas of the administrative state.[27] Probably the truth (as so often) lies somewhere in the calm quiet between the shouting on all sides of the controversy: the administrative state is doing both too much and too little; is dispensing both justice and injustice.

A lot also depends on *what* the agency is, whom it regulates or services, and how. The Internal Revenue Service, a state department of motor vehicles, an agency dealing with abused children, the antitrust division of the Justice Department—these are all different, with their own internal cultures, their own ways of handling clientele.

Control of Administrative Behavior

Administrative process is everywhere in the modern world. It is the fastest-growing part of the law, yet in some ways the least visible. Administrators have a great deal of power. Even some lowly clerk at the bottom of the ladder can at times exercise considerable authority. To someone who wants a pension or a dog license or a zoning variance, or to a company that wants to float bonds or build a new plant, the power of administrators seems boundless, almost out of control. One of the biggest issues in administrative law is, how tightly should agencies be kept in check? Who will watch the watchmen? Who will do the job, and how?

Administrative agencies are subject to both inside and outside control. Inside control is control built into the structure of an agency. Higher officials supervise lower officials. Inspectors and auditors monitor the working bureaucrats. Reports, spot checks, reviews, and internal audits prevent corruption or sloppy work. At least one hopes so. Outside control begins with the governing law. Controls and limits are written into the text of the law for each specific agency. Thus, the Federal Trade Commission has power to prevent or stop "unfair" methods of competition, but the FTC Act also specifically gives businesses whose methods are challenged the right to appear and fight, with lawyers, at formal hearings.[28] There are also more general controls. The Administrative Procedure Act, first passed in 1946, applies pretty much across the board. It sets down rules of procedure that all agencies must follow. For example, under the APA, an agency must publish "descriptions of its central and field organization"; and it must make public its rules of procedure and inform the public where people can pick up necessary forms. All this appears in the *Federal Register.* The agency must also make public its rules and regulations, and it has to give notice when and if it intends to change these rules. The *Federal Register*—in the first nine months of 1996, it ran to over 45,000 pages—is hardly the six-o'clock news, but at least it is accessible to lawyers and specialists who know what to look for. Agencies have to spread on the *Register* the gist of any of their new rules, and they must give the public a chance to object or to make comments in writing.

Congress, with its statute-writing power, is the most obvious outside control over federal agencies. Congress passes the laws that make the agencies; it can repeal those laws and kill its creatures. It can give them

new marching orders any time it wishes. Congress (after intensive lobbying from industry) told the Consumer Product Safety Commission in
1981 to lower safety standards for power lawn mowers. The commission
has no choice but to obey.[29] Congress has the ultimate power: the power
to destroy an agency altogether. As we saw, it got rid of the ICC in 1995.

Some controls are inside the agencies but outside the regular chain
of command. It is possible to give controllers or inspectors great independence, even though technically they belong to the organization they
seek to control. The army and navy have inspectors general. So do many
governmental agencies. The Inspector General Act of 1978 created
such offices in cabinet departments and in some agencies (EPA, for
example).[30] The IG is authorized, among other things, to "receive and
investigate" complaints about waste or abuse. The IG is supposed to
keep secret the identity of whistle-blowers.

This form of control is based in part on the concept of the "ombudsman." The word, if not the idea, comes from Scandinavia. Many private
institutions—Stanford University, for example—have set up such posts
for themselves. The ombudsman is an official who is independent and
is supposedly independent-minded; he or she hears complaints from
employees or others and tries to deal with them somehow. Presumably
the ombudsman has no ax to grind and makes fair and impartial recom-
mendations. How much actual power an ombudsman has depends on
the particular institution.

Congress has attempted, too, to guarantee that the agencies deal
fairly with people who complain. The employees of agencies who decide
"cases" brought by outsiders are much more independent than they
once were. They are now (since 1978) called "administrative-law
judges," and the point of calling them by this name is to emphasize that
they are supposed to do justice, not slavishly follow what their superiors
in the agency want. As of March 1996, there were 1,333 administrative-
law judges in the federal system. This number, however, has been fairly
static, and there has been a kind of backward trend—the growth of
"non-ALJ adjudicators," who are "sprouting faster than tulips in Holland" and numbered (in 1996) more than three thousand. The agencies
have come to prefer hearing officers who are "easier to manage, and
who can be procured at bargain rates" (ALJ's are very well paid).[31]
Nonetheless, the *idea* behind the corps of administrative law judges is,
basically, alive and kicking.

Judicial review is perhaps the best-known form of outside control
of administrative agencies. Most of what is called administrative law, as
taught in law schools, is really the law of judicial review. Suppose a
company is dissatisfied with some decision an agency makes—a drug

company wants to market a diet pill, and the FDA has refused approval. The company first has to "exhaust" procedures or appeals inside the agency—in a big, complex agency there will be a regular pyramid of hearings and appeals. If all else fails, the company has one more chance: it can try its luck in court. Almost all the statutes setting up administrative agencies provide for or imply the right of courts to review decisions the agency makes. The Administrative Procedure Act itself provides for review, and the Supreme Court has held that a right to review is implied unless Congress firmly and explicitly says otherwise. This happens from time to time. Congress declared that certain decisions of the Veterans Administration (now a cabinet-level department) were absolutely "final and conclusive." No court had "power . . . to review any such decision."[32] This, however, is a highly unusual situation.

Getting a court to review a decision of the FDA or the NLRB or the SEC is not a simple matter; one does not just snap one's fingers and file a complaint. Many roadblocks stand in the way. To begin with, there are procedural problems. One is the concept of "standing." Not everybody can complain about what an agency does. To have standing (the right to complain) usually means the complainant must show a financial stake—the drug company blocked by the FDA is an obvious example. But if the Department of the Interior decides to let Hilton Hotels build a lodge in Yellowstone Park, can I complain in court (or in the agency) because I backpack and birdwatch in Yellowstone? Probably not; I have no standing. Using or liking or enjoying Yellowstone is not enough. Rules of standing are complicated; as they broaden or narrow, the scope of judicial review broadens and narrows in turn. For a while, federal courts applied quite liberal rules about standing; they were willing to stretch a point to allow groups that represented "the public" to intervene in decisions, even though they had no financial stake. This opened the door to conservation groups that opposed power plants, and to church groups or just plain viewers who complained about the policies of some TV station.[33] In the 1980s and 1990s, the courts tightened up somewhat; as one judge, Richard Posner, put it in 1991, plaintiffs would be "tripping over each other on the way to the courthouse if everyone remotely injured by a violation of law could sue to redress it."[34]

Also, the scope of judicial review is narrow. Courts do not second-guess the agencies. If the FDA decides a drug does not work and takes it off the market, the manufacturer can try to persuade a court to overturn the decision. But as a general rule the court will not rehash the evidence; it will not ask whether the drug works or not. On that point, the court will consider itself bound by what the agency decided. After all, it is the agency that has expert knowledge; it is the agency that has on its payroll chemists, engineers, economists, and whatnot. The court will mainly check the agency's procedures. Did FDA follow the Administrative Procedure Act? Did the FDA do what Congress told it to do, and in the right way, according to the governing statute? Was its decision supported by *some* evidence? If the answer to these questions is yes, the court will, almost certainly, refuse to overturn the agency's decision.

All well and good; but in fact the line between procedure and substance, between decisions of "law" and decisions of "fact," is quite fuzzy, and some courts have been known to review agency work in a bold and assertive way. Before the New Deal, courts were on the whole hostile to administrative agencies; they scrutinized their work rather carefully, some would say too carefully. During the New Deal, the Supreme Court reflected this hostility in a number of notable instances. The Court did not want Congress to "delegate" its essential powers to agencies. Perhaps the most notorious New Deal decision was *Schechter Poultry Corp. v. United States.*[35] Here the court declared the National Industrial Recovery Act unconstitutional and knocked out one of the keystones of Roosevelt's program.

Schechter and similar cases raised storms of protest. In the long run, President Roosevelt won his point. The old, conservative judges resigned; the president appointed new ones more in tune with his views. The Court lost most of its taste for savaging administrative agencies. After the New Deal period, a long honeymoon set in for the agencies. Courts were reluctant to intrude into administrative decisions except in extreme cases. They refused to interfere if what the agencies had done was in the least bit defensible procedurally and had any shred of evidence to back them up.

That honeymoon seems to have ended in the 1970s. Then came a generation of diminished deference. Individuals and groups on the outside are more active than before in fighting the agencies in court, and the courts themselves are taking a more active role in controlling administrative behavior. A Washington lawyer, in 1974, spoke for most lawyers when he talked of a "strong impression" that judicial review was tougher than before; the courts fancied themselves "as watchdogs at least comparable to the stature of the agencies."[36] Most observers would agree. But the facts are rather hard to come by.

In 1984, in *Chevron, U.S.A., Inc. v. Natural Resources Defense Council,*[37] the Supreme Court told courts to respect the way agencies interpret the law; agency interpretations on doubtful points were to be upheld, unless they flatly contradicted what Congress had plainly said. This was understood by commentators to mean a regime of more respect for agency determinations and less vigorous judicial review. And, in fact, a study of the work of the courts, published in 1990, does show that federal courts *usually* side with the agencies—about three times out of four, in fact.[38]

But judicial review remains a powerful tool. How much impact it has, on any particular agency, is a tough (and largely unanswered) question. Why, despite *Chevron,* is it likely that judicial review retains its power? Courts are sensitive to what goes on in the outside world. The public generally has lost some of its faith in administrative process. Administrative process, of course, is here to stay; but more and more people think of it as a necessary evil at best. Administrative process is "red tape," "bureaucracy," "Big Brother"; it is waste, fat, inefficiency. Politicians of both parties find it convenient to run against "bureaucracy." The movement to "deregulate" has been mentioned. There is an urge to turn back the clock, to reverse the trend toward more and more state control of economic life. Perhaps these attitudes make a difference in the way courts approach the work of the agencies.

The movement toward deregulation has not so far made a major impact on the scope of regulation. But it does represent a reaction against government that has wider meaning. The Republican Congress of 1994, like the Reagan and Bush administrations before it, was determined to shrink the size of government, cut hundreds of pages out of the *Federal Register,* and stop the flood of rules and regulations. These aims seem to be politically popular. The Democrats rather feebly protested, and ended up saying simply that they could shrink the government better and in a less extreme way. Shrinking the government is, of course, easier said than done.

Judicial review is expensive and time-consuming. Only a big drug company has the money to attack an FDA ruling. But in the last decades, new actors have entered the stage, representing new groups— consumers, for example. Of course, no single consumer has the time, money, or skill to battle against the giant agencies or lock horns with the great corporations. But when consumers band together, the story is quite different. Where would environmental law be without the pressure of groups such as the Sierra Club, or the Natural Resources Defense Council (which took part in the *Chevron* case)? Particularly important are the "public interest" law firms, organized to fight legal battles on behalf of consumers. There are only a few of these firms, but they make a big splash in the courts.

Again, a change in public attitude lies behind this trend. Consumers band together because there is a consumer movement; that is, some consumers feel angry at business or government and want to take action to make their weight felt. Recently there has been much discussion about whether agencies are responsive enough to the public. This is a tricky subject. Often when people complain about unresponsive agencies they mean that the agency does not respond to *them*. But an agency may ignore group A because of pressure from group B, which is pulling in the opposite direction. In such a case, we can easily, but mistakenly, imagine that the agency is performing poorly because of technical, structural, bureaucratic reasons. The agency in fact *is* responsive; what is wrong (from our standpoint) is its pattern of response. Technical reform will not cure the problem. What is needed is political reform, giving group A more power, or exerting pressure on our own (if that is what we want).

On the other hand, there really does seem to be something about a bureaucracy that slows down its actions and toughens its outer skin. After all, the whole point of making agencies independent is to free them from short-run political pressures and control. If we make jobs "civil-service" jobs instead of patronage jobs, we loosen the grip of politicians and "special interests." But this can work all too well. When we regularize promotion and tenure, when we make internal controls stronger than external controls, we run the risk of distorting the incentives of those who staff the bureaucracies. Individual creativity is discouraged and downgraded; outstanding performance becomes risky. Timid, bureaucratic minds dominate the agency. Those who stick to the rules and never get in trouble are rewarded. Policy change becomes almost impossible.

Bureaucracy is at the heart of modern law and government. A vast civil service grinds away in thousands of tiny offices, churning out rules and applying them. To many people, it seems like a troop of blind army ants, mindless and implacable, following rules the way ants follow instinct. The work of life, to be sure, could not go on, in contemporary society, without this corps of ants. There is the charge that the bureaucracy squeezes vital juices out of the economy and commits, day in and day out, nagging, petty acts of tyranny. Is there some way to give the modern state a human face? Is effective, efficient, and fair government possible? Can we make regulation "responsive"?[39] All sorts of reforms have tried to supply an answer. It is not easy to judge their ultimate success, but there seems little doubt that some of the worst forms of abuse have been brought at least partially under control. What is easy to forget is the *benefit* side of the administrative state. Many people insist they want government "off the people's backs," which means rolling back the bureaucracy. Yet, if a plane crashes, they are likely to complain with shrill voices that the government was not strict *enough* with regulation and inspection. If there is a flood, a fire, an earthquake, they want rapid response from federal emergency agencies. They want service in all sorts of ways, and they want it fast. Among the fundamental rights of the citizen is the right to hold contradictory opinions at once.

7

Federalism and American Legal Culture

ONE OBVIOUS, STRIKING fact about the American legal system is that it is organized on a *federal* basis. A federal system is a government and legal system in which the central, national government shares power with states, provinces, or sections, each of which is to some degree sovereign in its own right. There are quite a few countries in the world organized on a federal system. One of the best examples is Canada, our northern neighbor. Australia is also a federal state. So is Switzerland. So is Germany. The now defunct Soviet Union was supposed to be a federation, made up of individual "republics" (Russia itself, Armenia, Estonia, and so on). Each Soviet republic, in theory, even had the right to secede. In fact, Moscow called the tune, and when it relaxed its iron rule, the union disintegrated, and the individual "socialist republics" all became independent states. The European Union—formerly the European Economic Community—is an interesting hybrid. The *general* government is relatively weak, and the individual countries (France, Italy, Germany, Austria, Denmark, Portugal, and the rest) retain their seats in the United Nations, their ambassadors, and all the trappings of sovereignty—and a great deal of control over their domestic law and politics. But this may change over time; indeed, the central government of the EU—the bureaucracy in Brussels and the courts— is already more powerful than many people ever expected.

The United States is a federal country that takes its federalism, on the whole, quite seriously. The national government sits in Washington, but the fifty states are hardly empty shadows. The states have their own governments and their own capitals, and within their spheres they are supposed to be "sovereign," that is, in full control. In many ways, they echo the structural patterns of the federal government. They all have constitutions—and these are, very often, quite different from the federal Constitution. They have legislatures, with two houses in every state but one. Each state has a chief executive, the governor. Each has its own court system, as we have seen. Each has a cabinet, an executive staff, and a flock of administrative agencies. Of course, the states are sovereign or independent within certain limits. The national (federal) government is more powerful, employs vastly more men and women, and taxes and spends much more. It is only Washington that sends out and receives ambassadors, coins money, owns guided missiles and aircraft carriers, and tries to "fine-tune" the economy through control of the money supply. On the other hand, the federal government does not as a general rule arrest speeders, grant divorces, or probate wills; it does not pass zoning ordinances or run school districts; it does not foreclose mortgages, repossess television sets, or put people on trial for robbing gas stations. It does not do most of the ordinary, workaday jobs of the law.

Federalism, as it has evolved in this country, is a complex and interesting system. It is also a good example of the interaction between structure and culture, within our system of laws.

Federalism: The Formal Plan

The basic story of the American Constitution is well known. After the Revolutionary War, the former colonies became independent states. They set up a central government, under the Articles of Confederation. This central government was relatively weak; real power stayed in the states. Many people considered the experiment a failure: there was fear of anarchy as the separate states began to squabble in an unruly way, unrestrained by a strong central authority.

The Americans (or many of them) resolved to try again. A convention was called and a new plan drafted: the Constitution of 1787. It gave more power to the central government. It is still an open question exactly how much power the framers intended to give to the national government. Clearly, the men who wrote the Constitution intended to provide some muscle for the national government, but they also intended to keep a strong role for the states. They proposed a more or less clear-cut division between the two levels of sovereignty, spelling out what the general government could do and what was left to the states. Some powers, of course, would have to be shared. Many details of the division were left rather obscure.

The center had power over war and foreign relations; it had power to levy taxes, run a postal system, and coin money. It also had some smaller powers important to the legal system—power to lay down "uniform" rules for naturalization and "uniform laws on the subject of bankruptcies"; also power to grant patents and copyrights.

The Constitution also set up a separate court system for the central government. At its head was a (federal) Supreme Court, along with "such inferior courts as the Congress may from time to time ordain and establish" (Article IV, Section 1). These courts would have jurisdiction over questions of federal law. They would handle admiralty cases as well. Admiralty cases were maritime cases—cases about affairs on the high seas or about the business of ocean commerce. In England, these cases went before a special court, the court of admiralty; in America, the powers of this court were given to the federal courts. The national courts also had jurisdiction to decide cases "between Citizens of different States." This is the so-called diversity jurisdiction. The idea here was that the federal courts would provide an impartial forum, free of state jealousies, rivalry, and chauvinism. The federal courts, unlike state courts, would not show bias against "outsiders," people from other states.

The Constitution also listed some sovereign acts specifically forbidden to the states. They were not to coin money or levy any taxes on imports or exports (except "what may be absolutely necessary for executing . . . inspection Laws"). Commerce was to pass freely from state to state, without barriers or costs. The states were also shut out of foreign affairs; they were not to "enter into any Treaty, Alliance, or Confederation" or any "Agreement or Compact . . . with a foreign Power." They were not to wage war, except with Congressional consent. Relations with the outside world were the province of the central government.

There was a good deal of opposition to the proposed Constitution at the time, but in the end it was ratified nonetheless. The hope was that the central government would be strong enough to keep the country from disintegrating into little quarreling baronies—strong enough for that, but no more. The states had control of their domestic affairs, and of everything not specifically granted to the central government. That reserve, most people thought, was a vast and important domain.

Federalism: History and Culture

Federalism, of course, is much more than a formal plan. It is also a tradition, and it is an important facet of our legal culture. In fact, federalism as a structure would be meaningless or empty unless federalism were also part of the culture. To understand federalism in this country, how it grew and how it changed, it will not do simply to tell how the constitutional plan has altered over time. Indeed these changes (on paper) are fairly small. The Constitution of 1787 is still very much with us. It has gone past its two hundredth birthday, yet it has been amended only sixteen times since 1800. By now, it is by far the oldest written constitution still in force anywhere. There are countries with much longer histories, but most of them (like France) have suffered constitutional upheaval time and time again. There is no American Third Reich or Fifth Republic. There is still the first and only American republic. The Civil War was, to be sure, a major constitutional crisis, but even then, the Constitution survived (though at tremendous cost in blood).

But in what sense has the Constitution "lasted" or "endured" for two centuries or more? The words are the same, but the music? Can a plan set up in 1787, in the horse-and-buggy age, when men wore powdered wigs, and before the Industrial Revolution got going, really suit the world as it enters the twenty-first century? Probably this is not the right question. Obviously, in many ways, the Constitution, as it was understood in 1787, cannot possibly fit the world of today, but the constitutional *system* has evolved over the years. The reality of federalism has drastically altered in the process, and the culture of federalism along with it.

This is precisely what we would expect. Massive social and economic changes have taken place in the last two centuries. Technology has altered the world. In 1787, communication between the center and the periphery was tortuously slow. A message from New Hampshire to Georgia took days or weeks. Today, telephones, telegraph, radio and television, jet airplanes, computers, satellite communication, all make it possible for the first time to govern a continent from a single nerve center. The power of Washington, D.C., in the twentieth century would be unthinkable without these innovations. Swift means of travel and communication have created mass markets across the country and stimulated the consumer economy. The American population is restless and mobile. People ceaselessly cross state lines, by train, plane, and car, looking for new jobs, visiting relatives, searching for sunshine and scenery, and so on. If there is to be any control over the national economy, it will have to come from the center.

Social change, culture (attitudes), and legal structure are bound together in so many ways that we cannot ever really disentangle them. None of the three basic elements of law—structure, substance, and culture—has meaning without the others. Federalism is a structural fact. It also generates substance (rules about state and national powers).

These in turn influence the legal culture. At the same time, it is the legal culture (what people think and believe) that makes federalism a living part of law, a structure with meaning. And the legal culture is not static. It changes along with society.

Federalism in the first half of the nineteenth century was a far cry from federalism today. The national government was a tiny dot on the legal map. Washington, D.C., was a miserable village, with muddy roads, appalling summer heat, and few permanent inhabitants. The federal government was pathetically small by modern standards. The Department of the Treasury in 1801, which "far overtopped any other administrative agency," contained more than half the civilians who worked for the federal government. It had seventy-eight employees in its central office, and 1,615 in the field.[1] In 1829, the whole body of federal employees in Washington, "from the lowliest clerk, messenger, and page boy to the President," and including congressmen and senators, was 625.[2]

In short, the central government was small and, in many ways, insignificant. It played second fiddle to the states. The states probably loomed much larger in people's lives than the federal government. People thought of themselves as citizens of Virginia or Pennsylvania first, as Americans second. The national legal system was like the tiny brain of a giant dinosaur. There was not much in the way of a central nervous system. The weakness and remoteness of the federal government became even more pronounced as one traveled west. In the early nineteenth century, people in a state like Kentucky, separated by mountains from the eastern seaboard, saw little use for a central government and were rather bitter about its revenue laws (which they largely ignored). But we should not exaggerate the point. Mary Tachau has studied the federal courts in Kentucky during this period; she found in these courts a surprising level of strength and activity.[3] Still, in most respects the state government was the heart of public life, the national government distant and irrelevant.

In one regard, the West was more national-minded in the later nineteenth century, though for a rather special reason. Local culture and local tradition were thinner in the West than in the East and in the South. The population of the West was a migrant population. People in Idaho or Oregon had no roots there; there was no state patriotism of the Virginia type. Americans were rolling stones. What could devotion to Montana, or love for Montana culture and tradition, mean in 1890, when most people who lived there had literally just arrived? Even today, state "patriotism" varies greatly from state to state, depending on cultural tradition. There is tremendous local pride, almost nationalism, in parts of New England and the South. In California or Arizona most people are raw newcomers who came for sunshine or jobs, or are at best the children of newcomers. The idea of a California "patriot" is absurd in a way that the idea of a fanatical Texan is not.

American legal culture is local in another sense. Judges and lawyers are locals. There is no national career line for judges. State judges cannot cross the border and still be judges: once a Delaware judge, always a Delaware judge. There is no way to transfer to Pennsylvania. Even federal judges tend to be locals: the district judge in North Dakota is a resident of North Dakota. The lower bench is even more parochial: judges of Aroostook County, Maine, will stay there, unless promoted; they will not take up court in Kennebec County. (In some states, however, the chief justice or a court administrator can shift judges around temporarily, to clear up backlogs.) Lawyers also tend to be local. A lawyer who practices in Memphis, Tennessee, will not take cases in Louisville, Kentucky. While many large law firms tend to have several branch offices (a rather recent phenomenon), most lawyers within the firm will practice primarily at one of the offices; they will not, ordinarily, leave "home."

It is true that major law schools claim to be "national"; they draw students from all over the country and ignore the law of the state they sit in. Only a handful of Yale's students will practice in Connecticut, even though the school is in New Haven. Yale students will learn very little about Connecticut law in the classroom; they will study the common law as a general system, along with some aspects of national (federal) law. Students will argue about cases under the federal Constitution. The constitution of Connecticut will probably never get mentioned.

On the other hand, fresh-minted lawyers are great travelers. In an earlier day, they flocked to new settlements out west. Today, many will leave home for New York or Washington or other centers of practice, or for places like Seattle and Denver that appeal to them. Still, most of these fledgling lawyers will not wander very long. Once the tumbleweed days are past, they take root in one place and stay there. Each state admits lawyers to its own bar only; some states once admitted lawyers county by county. A Georgia lawyer is a layman as far as Oregon is concerned. A lawyer who moves to a new state does not automatically get "reciprocity." He or she may have to take the bar exam over again, like the rawest recruit. In general, then, lawyers are pretty much bound to one jurisdiction, just as the judges are.

This state of affairs makes American legal culture somewhat parochial; it tends to keep alive aspects of local legal culture. This point was vividly illustrated by a study of delay and congestion in trial courts.[4] The researchers wanted to find out why cases, once filed, had to wait so long for trial in some cities, while in others there were only short delays, or no delays at all. In other words, some courts were slow, some were fast, but why? The scholars started out with hunches about the reasons, but none of these, surprisingly, panned out, either in civil or criminal cases: "Neither court size, nor trial rate nor judicial case load, nor use of settlement conferences, differentiates faster from slower courts."[5] Then what does? The scholars fell back on what they called local legal culture: "informal court system attitudes, concerns and practices." Judges and other courtroom hands had old, deep-seated habits and ideas. How fast cases were handled differed from city to city, but judges and lawyers knew only what went on in their own bailiwick. What happened someplace else never came to their attention. Thus, local legal culture was slow-moving, a kind of legal molasses. Fads like the hula hoop or disco dancing or wearing baseball caps backward race across the country; local legal culture barely crawls.

In some ways, then, courts and lawyers in different communities are sealed off from each other. But we must not carry the point too far. The federal court system is fairly uniform, and it enforces national policy. Federal courts follow local law in "diversity" cases; but the Federal Rules of Civil Procedure (and of Criminal Procedure) govern courtroom behavior and the local rules of procedure (if different) do not. Nor do federal courts bow down to local opinion and local prejudice, in matters on which Washington (or the national Constitution) has spoken. This became dramatically clear after the *Brown* decision in 1954. Some federal judges were segregationists and resisted the Supreme Court decision as much as they could; others, however, acted with great honor and courage and refused to defer to local norms.[6] As a whole, the federal lower courts were much more willing than the state courts to carry out civil-rights policy in an honest, consistent way.

Except at the federal level, the country is not *legally* unified, at least in matters of detail. But it is definitely unified in economic life. There is also a common language, and the culture has a certain commonality, from coast to coast. There are strong regional differences, of course, but TV and rapid travel and the Internet and internal migration are tending to level these off as time goes on.

The economic unity of the country is especially basic. People and products stream across state borders. There is no legal way for one state to keep out the goods of other states. The Constitution expressly forbids it. Vermont cannot put import taxes on New Hampshire goods. Colorado cannot exclude the products of Utah. At most, a state can stop rotten fruit and sick cows at its borders. Beyond this, it cannot go.

Nor does a state have power to keep out unwanted people, any more than unwanted goods. Oregon has no right to chase migrants from Ohio away. At one time, states were able to keep out "paupers" (or try to), but the Supreme Court put an end to this practice years ago.[7] No state, said the court, can "isolate itself from difficulties common to all . . . by restraining the transportation of persons and property across its borders." According to the Constitution itself, if a criminal escapes into another state, that state has to extradite him, that is, he must be "delivered up," on demand of the governor, to the "State having Jurisdiction of the Crime."[8]

The Constitution also provided for the return of fugitive slaves, although it included them rather delicately in a more general phrase: persons "held to Service or Labour." They were to be "delivered up on Claim of the Party to whom such Service or Labour may be due."[9] Congress accordingly passed a number of fugitive-slave laws to put this provision into effect. These were controversial laws, wildly unpopular in parts of the North. Attempts at "slave catching" in the North sometimes led to outright defiance, or even bloodshed. No issue put a greater strain on federalism than this one.[10] Slavery and race pitted state against state, region against region. The Civil War by no means ended the conflict.

Slavery put a strain on federalism because, under the constitutional scheme, states are required to recognize, and give effect to, the laws of other states. This meant, for example, that states with tough divorce laws had to recognize (by and large) divorces in the easy states. In 1996, the *chance* that Hawaii would recognize same-sex marriages led to a kind of moral panic on the mainland. Would other states have to recognize these marriages? Congress quickly passed a law to prevent just this result.[11]

The gay-marriage controversy represents a kind of cultural protectionism. The states have not always been free from the more ordinary type of protectionism—economic protectionism. That is, they have often tried to wriggle out of the constitutional plan, passing laws to benefit their own residents at the expense of people in other states. Some cities and states in the nineteenth century tried to tax to death out-of-state peddlers or put special burdens on "foreign" corporations (that is, corporations from other states). A Virginia law of 1866, for example, required agents of "foreign" insurance companies to get licenses; the companies had to deposit bonds with the treasurer of the state. The Supreme Court upheld the law,[12] partly on the grounds that "issuing a policy of insurance is not a transaction of commerce"; insurance policies were not "commodities to be shipped or forwarded from one State to another." Thus they were not "interstate commerce," which Congress might regulate, but were off limits to the states. In the twentieth century, however, the Supreme Court vastly expanded its definition of "commerce," and protectionist measures have on the whole done poorly in the courts. They have failed economically as well. American borders are as weak as pieces of string.

These borders are meaningless in other ways, too. They are never great cultural divides, as is sometimes the case in Europe. Every single state (except Hawaii, a collection of islands) has a straight line somewhere on its borders. Western states are mostly lines on a map: Wyoming and Colorado are rectangles, plain and simple. Rivers separate Wisconsin and Minnesota, Kentucky and Ohio, Missouri and Illinois, but even these natural boundaries do not divide one civilization or language from another. North Dakota and South Dakota are separate states, but not separate cultures. They do have different criminal codes, divorce laws, and tort laws, and somewhat different systems of procedures. Some differences in legal structure and in the culture of lawyers and judges do tend to persist over time. But in many ways these differences are not terribly important, except to lawyers. In any event, they are not closely meshed with differences in economy or society in the two Dakotas.

Legal differences between the states, then, tend to be rather minor, on the whole. This is, after all, a single country. The state laws are like dialects of a single language. (Louisiana is in some ways an exception.) A man with a strong Boston accent can tell a Southerner a mile away, but the two of them can still talk easily to each other. The border with Canada means much more, legally speaking, than does the straight line between North and South Dakota; and the border with Mexico is legally very wide and very deep, much wider and deeper than the Rio Grande and much, much harder to cross.

Federalism and the "Market" for Laws

The central fact of American federalism is worth repeating: the United States is by and large an economic union, by and large a social union, but not a legal union, or at least not completely. State laws are, or can be, rather similar, but this is, first, because the states choose to harmonize their laws, and, second, because conditions in the states are fairly similar. A state is free to be different (if it wishes), within its zone. But since the 1860s, the central government has gotten stronger and stronger, and there has been a steady, marked change in relations between states and the federal government. It is obvious why this took place. Changes in technology and socioeconomic structure paved the way. In the age of e-mail, cyberspace, satellite communication, and jumbo jets, the country is a single entity to an extent undreamed of in 1787.

When all is said and done, however, the states still maintain a substantial reservoir of power. This makes possible what we might call a "market" for laws. The states vie with each other for "customers," by passing competing laws. And one state can frustrate the policy of others by offering for sale (so to speak) a cheaper, better, or simply different brand of law.

Nevada is, in a way, an extreme example.[13] Nevada is a large but barren state, mostly mountain and desert. It was admitted to the union in 1864. There is some mining in Nevada and some cattle here and there munch at sparse grasses, but basically there is not much to do for a living in the state. The population in 1900 had fallen to about 42,000. Still, this wilderness of sagebrush and ghost towns had one great ace in the hole: it was a sovereign state, like all the others. It had a governor and a legislature. It had the power to pass whatever laws it wanted. This was a kind of natural resource, just as much as silver or gold.

Specifically, Nevada could compete with its neighbors, especially California, the giant to the west, by passing laws that California did not have and that the majority in California did not seem to want. Nevada could legalize behavior that was illegal in California. Hence Nevada, either deliberately or by happy accident, stumbled into its present role. First, it became a divorce mill, as early as the 1920s. This was not a new idea. There had been divorce mills—places where divorce was quick and easy to get—in other states in the nineteenth century: Indiana, the Dakotas. Those divorce mills eventually collapsed under the weight of moral indignation.[14] Moral indignation has never been big in Nevada.

Nevada is also the motherland of legal gambling in the United States. Today, gambling and its spin-offs are by far the largest industries in the state.[15] Thousands and thousands of pleasure seekers from California fly or drive there across the Mojave Desert. Jets bring hundreds of thousands to Reno and Las Vegas, from all over the country and abroad. Nevada allows its counties (except Clark County, where Las Vegas is located) to legalize houses of prostitution. No other state has gone this far (not, at any rate, officially). Nevada also competes for the marriage business. It requires less time and fewer formalities than California, and it allows anyone over sixteen to get married with parental consent. Many California couples, of all ages, who want to elope, get in a car and hightail it for the Nevada border. They bring along their wallets, and the newlyweds pump still more money into Nevada's economy.

Nevada is only one blatant example of how the "market" works. Delaware is another case in point. This tiny state, clinging by its fingertips to the base of Pennsylvania, is the "home" of thousands of corporations, including great corporate giants. All sorts of companies are chartered in Delaware without any real connection to the state; it would not be the least bit surprising to find that (say) a Denver bus company was actually a Delaware corporation. Why is the state so popular? The answer is no secret: around the turn of the century, Delaware deliberately passed lenient corporation laws. This attracted companies like bees to honey. They set up "headquarters" in downtown Wilmington, Delaware, for the most part—tiny cubbyholes where the company could receive mail. (The real head offices were elsewhere.) Many of these companies are there to this day. Their taxes, low as they are, are a boon to the Delaware economy.

We can note another consequence of the national "market" in laws. Well into the twentieth century, the divorce law of New York State was unusually stringent. Basically, adultery was the sole ground for divorce. Year after year, there was pressure to loosen up these laws, to bring them in line with the divorce laws of other states. There was also strong pressure on the opposing side, some of it on religious grounds, from the Catholic Church and its faithful, or from Protestants who feared the results of easy divorce. Probably New York could hold out so long was precisely because there was an escape hatch in Nevada, at least for those with money enough for the trip. In other words, New York stumbled into a kind of rough compromise. The strict divorce laws remained on the books, making their moral statement. But the shoe did not pinch too hard: rich New Yorkers went to Reno and got their divorces anyway. Needless to say, this arrangement was not completely satisfying, especially for people without much money. Nevertheless it lasted for generations.

In other words, the legal "market" has both advantages and disadvantages. On the one hand, a state can forge ahead of its neighbors: it can act, as Justice Louis Brandeis once put it, as a "laboratory" of social reform. On the other hand, conservative states, for their part, can retard economic changes. This was what happened in labor law, for example, before the New Deal. Organized labor gained political power in the northern industrial states, and these states passed the first tough child-labor laws. Southern states had no such laws on their books, or if they did, they enforced them fitfully. The northern states were afraid of runaway factories; they were worried that textile mills and other plants would pack up and go south, where wages were low and where children could work in the mills. In general, the southern states did not adopt the welfare and labor statutes that became standard in the North and West, or accepted them much more slowly. Since capital and labor could easily flow from North to South, the federal system was a drag on reform. Or so it seemed to Northern liberals.

It was a frustrating situation. The southern states nullified the effectiveness of the labor laws of northern states, in much the same way that Nevada made a mockery of New York's divorce laws. The remedy had to be on a national level, that is, through federal law. Congress obliged. It passed a statute in 1916 which prohibited the interstate shipment of goods made in factories that used child labor. But a conservative Supreme Court, in *Hammer v. Dagenhart*,[16] declared the law invalid. Congress, said the Court, had no power to pass such a law. The case set off a storm of protest. There were attempts to get around *Hammer v. Dagenhart* through the taxing power or through constitutional amendment. For one reason or another, these measures failed. Effective control of child labor, on a national scale, was achieved only during the New Deal period, in the 1930s.

Child labor was a controversial subject, but in other parts of the law, which were more "lawyerly" and less politically visible, there were more successful movements to come to grips with the problem of legal disunity. The best examples of "success" were in commercial law, in the uniform-laws movement, described in Chapter 5. The success of some of these laws, and in particular the Uniform Commercial Code, means that commercial law has at last become in essence a national legal subject.

Federalism in Recent Times

The "market" effects we have talked about are still with us, as the example of Nevada shows. But their influence has gone down considerably, because the role of the central government has gone up and up. Federal control of economy and society is pervasive; traditional ideas of states' rights have come to impede the power of Washington less and less. The Constitution did not give the federal government much regulatory control, on the surface. It doled out power in teaspoons. The central government could regulate commerce "with foreign Nations, and among the several States, and with the Indian Tribes" (Article I, Section 8). "Among the several States" was assumed to mean commerce that flowed across state lines. But interstate commerce was the exception, not the rule, in the early nineteenth century. Commerce was mostly local trade.

In addition, Congress (before the ICC Act) showed little inclination to regulate even interstate commerce, and the Supreme Court up until the New Deal tended to take a narrow view of Congressional power— not narrow enough to please extreme "state's righters," but certainly narrow from the modern standpoint. For example, in *United States v. E. C. Knight Co.* (1895),[17] a Sherman Act case, the government had moved to break up the so-called Sugar Trust. The American Sugar Refining Company had already gobbled up most of the country's sugar refineries and had just gotten its grip on four more, which would give it 98 percent of all sugar-refining capacity in the country.

This certainly looked like a monopoly under the Sherman Act, but the Supreme Court decided against the government. Congress had power over "commerce," and the Sugar Trust was engaged in manufacture, not commerce. Of course, a monopoly of manufacture necessarily affected commerce, but the court brushed this point aside.

This narrow view of the commerce clause and of federal power over national affairs is now almost completely discarded. The federal government in fact exercises vast control over the economy, and the legal barriers implied in the limitation of Congressional power to regulate "interstate commerce" are by now almost meaningless. Interstate commerce is the dominant form of commerce, and both Congress and the Court have reduced the effect of the interstate commerce clause to a thin, thin wisp of its former self. This process began in earnest in the 1930s, and it has gone very far indeed.

For example, the Civil Rights Act of 1964 outlawed race discrimination in stores, restaurants, hotels, and other public places. Where did Congress get power to tell some tiny snack bar, some Southern greasy spoon, that it had no right to exclude black customers? A prior "public accommodations" law, of 1875 (passed after the Civil War), was thrown out by the Supreme Court; under the Fourteenth Amendment, said the Court, only *state* discrimination was outlawed, not private acts of discrimination.[18] Congress chose to solve the problem by resting its power on the commerce clause. Any restaurant that served interstate travelers fell under the act; so too if the "food which it serves . . . has moved in commerce." If the soup cans on the shelf, or the meat in a roast beef sandwich, or the box of Rice Krispies, had ever crossed state lines, then the restaurant came under the terms of the Civil Rights Act.

This line of argument was (perhaps) logically flimsy, but it was ethically powerful. The nineteenth century, or even the early twentieth century, would have found the argument absurd. The modern Supreme Court bought the argument eagerly and swallowed it whole. The case was *Katzenbach v. McClung.*[19] In this case, a place called Ollie's Barbe-

cue, in Birmingham, Alabama, made legal history; it was the subject of
the test case in which the Supreme Court gave its endorsement to the
"public accommodations" aspect of the Civil Rights Act of 1964. This
case only underscores the fact that the commerce clause hardly seemed
like a serious restraint on Congress any longer. When it came to enforcing national policy on an issue as sensitive as civil rights, the courts
would impose no restraint.

It was something of a surprise, then, when the commerce clause
corpse, in 1995, seemed to twitch and show signs of new life. The
Supreme Court struck down the "Gun-Free School Zones Act," which
made it a federal offense to "possess a firearm" in a school zone. To say
that this had anything to do with interstate commerce was too much of
a stretch for the Court. Even so, this was the decision of a bare majority
of the Court—four justices vigorously dissented.[20]

The commerce clause, in any event, is far from dead in its negative
sense. It still operates as a limit on what the *states* can do. States are
not allowed to discriminate against the goods of other states. California
cannot bar Florida oranges. And state regulations that "burden" interstate commerce unduly, for instance, a weird rule about mudflaps on
trucks, or restrictions on the length of interstate trains as they run
through the state from outside, have been struck down by the courts.[21]
In a landmark case in 1951, the Supreme Court reviewed an ordinance
of Madison, Wisconsin. The city banned all supposedly pasteurized milk
unless it was processed and bottled at "an approved pasteurization plant
within a radius of five miles from the central square of Madison." An
Illinois milk company challenged the law. The Court struck down the
ordinance. The concept of "preferential trade areas" was "destructive
of the very purpose of the Commerce Clause." The ordinance put a
"discriminatory burden on interstate commerce"; hence it had to go.[22]
And in 1992 the Court struck down an Oklahoma statute that forced
utilities in Oklahoma, if they used coal, to burn a certain proportion of
coal mined in Oklahoma.[23]

This is a difficult, technical area of law. The courts have been struggling to find some reasonable middle ground. The states should have
some right to run their own affairs, make their own policy. But the
national economy comes first. Where is the line to be drawn? Can New
Jersey prevent landfill companies from dumping in the state "solid or
liquid waste which originated or was collected outside" New Jersey?
The Supreme Court said no.[24] Yet the Supreme Court allowed Maine
to ban out-of-state baitfish, mentioning the danger of "possible . . . para-
sites and nonnative species."[25] In another case, Montana charged its
residents $30 for a license to hunt elk and other animals; outsiders had

to pay $225. Was this a violation of the Constitution? No, said the Court; it was a reasonable way to preserve a "finite resource."[26] The line-drawing process continues.

Today, the federal government is a vast taxing machine, sucking up billions upon billions of dollars to support its great enterprises and to feed its millions of mouths. The tax money goes primarily for three main objects: welfare entitlements (such as Social Security and Medicare), defense, and interest on the national debt. The armed forces of a super-power, in this dangerous world—even after the end of the Cold War—are obscenely expensive. Only the federal government can afford them; only the federal government is a player in world affairs. Arkansas has no atom bomb, no ambassadors, no say in international politics. But international politics is a matter of life and death, and so is international trade. These facts feed federal power and cut down the relative importance of the states.

Since the New Deal of the 1930s, more and more areas of American law, government, and life have crossed an invisible line from state responsibility into the federal domain. Before the New Deal, welfare law was as local as local could be. It was hardly even centralized at the state level; townships, cities, and counties ran the show. The Great Depression wrecked local finance. Social Security moved in. Today, the federal government is the dominant partner in old-age pensions, unemployment relief, Medicare, and most other social programs. Even the welfare "reforms" of 1996, turning *some* of the responsibility back to the states, leave untouched a massive federal presence.

Education, too, was once exclusively the affair of local school boards, with some degree of state supervision. In any event, the federal government had no say in the matter. In 1950, Congress passed a law granting money to "impacted" school districts. These were districts with special "financial burdens" because of some federal activity (an army base with heaps of kids, for example).[27] In 1965 came a dramatic change, the Elementary and Secondary Education Act.[28] This provided money for school districts generally, whether impacted or not. From that point on, federal money and federal rules, about bilingual education, race segregation, handicapped children, and so on, began to transform the law and practice of educational administration. The Department of Education is now a cabinet post, spending billions and overseeing dozens of programs. Noises have been made from time to time about abolishing the department, but there seems little chance that the federal role is about to evaporate. Quite the contrary.

At one time, too, nothing was more solidly local, more exclusively under state and city control, than criminal justice. The local police took care of murder, robbery, and rape, and gambling and drunkenness, too. There were only a few federal crimes (smuggling, illegal immigration) in the nineteenth century; the federal government did not even have its own prisons before 1891. It boarded its few prisoners in state prisons.[29] Today, crime itself has gone interstate in many respects. Federal crimes became more significant in the twentieth century, because of laws against driving stolen cars across state lines; and laws against drugs, draft evasion, and income-tax fraud. There is a powerful Federal Bureau of Investigation; the federal government even plays some role in financing local crime-fighting. The Law Enforcement Assistance Act (1965) and the Omnibus Crime Control and Safe Streets Act (1968)[30] pumped money into state and local governments. The 1968 act stated that crime was "essentially a local problem," but that the high incidence of crime was a threat to the "peace, security, and general welfare of the nation." This justified a program of federal support for local law enforcement.

For the last generation or so, crime and criminal justice have been major *political* issues; consequently, they have vaulted into the spotlight in federal elections. Abraham Lincoln and Theodore Roosevelt did not have crime policies. But modern presidents must. Presidents Reagan, Bush, and Clinton have all tried to show that they are truly tough on crime—and this means legislation. In the 1990s, it seems clear that no major program of government is completely "local" anymore—especially if it is politically hot; and this remains true despite all the talk about turning matters back to the states.

The federal government, then, has become a colossus. Yet the old balance is not completely dead. Federalism still has some hold on legal culture. There is an intense ideology favoring government close to home. The Constitution tried to build a system of "checks and balances." Executive, legislature, and judiciary would control and monitor each other. State governments would balance the federal government; the federal government would keep states in control.

All this was part of the original plan. The founders distrusted unbridled power. They rejected the divine right of kings or kinglike rulers. They preferred a kind of warlord system, that is, a government made up of little pieces, of small fiefdoms, without overall plan or direction. Even in the nuclear age there is something to be said for the plan. Much battered by history, it has not given up the ghost. The Republican Congress of 1994 zoomed into office vowing to reverse the trend and give government back to the states. They appealed to a nostalgia for an older federalism, a federalism tilted more strongly away from the center.

Whether this "new federalism" will be a major trend, or a tiny chirping in the night, remains to be seen. There may be some shifting here and there, but in an age of *national* economies (not to mention international ones), instant communication, and rapid transport across state lines, the federal government seems, on the whole, here to stay.

8

Inside the Black Box:
The Substance of Law

*T*HE STRUCTURE OF LAW, the court system, legal procedures, legal history, the place of law in society—all of these are important subjects. But at the core of the legal system are its actual operating rules, the substance of law. What behavior does the system try to control? How well does it do it? How does the law influence behavior? What conduct does it encourage or discourage? These are key questions in any society.

The legal system affects our lives every day. This is especially true when we take a broad view of law, defining it as all public social control. The system is of awesome bulk, and it touches on many matters, big and small, as the tale of the trip to the grocery in Chapter 1 made clear. The law also operates on many levels. Imagine yourself living in Omaha, Nebraska. You are, of course, a citizen of the United States of America. You are under the Constitution of the United States, under its protection and also constrained by the kind of government it sets up. As an American, you are under the wing, or the thumb, of the federal statutes. The unannotated version of the federal statutes, 1994 edition, ran to twenty-six volumes of text, averaging more than a thousand pages per volume. True, most of this mass of material has nothing to do with you or your life, directly or indirectly. Still, a surprising amount of it *may* have an impact on you or your family, sometimes (or often) in ways you are totally unconscious of. You may, for example, neither know nor care about the law of patents. But inventions that were patented under patent laws, from telephones to computers to safety pins, most definitely matter to you. You run into the banking laws every time you go to the bank or use an ATM. We could multiply examples endlessly.

The federal statutes are only a start. There are also more than five hundred volumes of Supreme Court cases and well over a thousand volumes of decisions of lower federal courts. Here even less of the contents concerns most of us personally, but in this great mass of words there are undoubtedly decisions (on war and peace, on the economy, on abortion or affirmative action) that do affect millions of people, every day. Then there are the federal regulations, volume after volume, and decisions of administrative agencies and tribunals on food and drug matters, the income tax, labor law, civil rights, stock markets. It is literally impossible to count these.

Yet this is only federal law. You are also under the jurisdiction of Nebraska. It, too, has a legal system. The Revised Statutes of Nebraska fill a good-sized shelf. A supplement, published in 1995 and covering only changes in the law of Nebraska since 1990, ran to two volumes and 1,754 pages. There are also the reported cases of the Nebraska supreme court (several big shelves), and the rules, regulations, and decisions of state agencies. We are not yet done: there is the City of Omaha, too, with its ordinances and its local rules, regulations, and decisions, about schools, about traffic, about local sanitation, about where you can build a house and where you cannot, and so on.

All this amazing mass of material has to be organized in some way. Otherwise, nobody could teach law in law school and lawyers could not navigate their way through the mess. It is perfectly clear that no lawyer can ever hope to "know the law." Every lawyer knows some of it, of course, and a specialist lawyer knows some of it well and precisely. But even the most learned lawyer is ignorant about most of our law. What lawyers do know (or should know) is the *limits* of what they know. They also know how to "look up law," and how to deal with law once it is found.

The written laws, in other words, are like entries in a gigantic English dictionary. Most people know some of the words, the easy, everyday words. Specialists know the words that belong to their specialties (biologists know biology words, gourmets know food words, soccer players know soccer words). The same is more or less true of the law. People in general know the easy words (judge, jury, contract, mortgage, murder). They also know some simple rules. Lawyers know a lot more: they know the basic principles, the stuff everyone learns in law school. Specialists know their fields—tax law, for example. But the tax expert may know little or nothing about food and drug law or admiralty law or the law of prisoners' rights.

We have been talking about the visible, written parts of the law. But lawyers are not just people who look up law. Many lawyers operate day after day without looking anything up in a book, or even in a computer database. They have experience; they have gone through the ordinary processes a hundred times before. They have closed dozens of house deals, or probated dozens of estates, or handled a hundred divorces, or filled out countless tax returns. They also know how the legal system actually works in their towns. They know whom to see, what to do, what forms to fill out, when to wait quietly and when to move swiftly and soon. Their practical knowledge is a vital part of their skills, as vital as "knowing the law."

Classifying Law

The Romans were probably the first people to address the problem of reducing law to a system. Long before the Romans, of course, societies had laws and codes of law. But as far as we know, early peoples like the Babylonians and the Hittites did not write treatises about law or try to organize legal knowledge in some systematic way. The Romans did. They organized and classified their laws, and they did so in a way that has proved useful—or at least historically persistent—ever since.

Classical Roman law, for example, drew a line between the "law of persons" and the "law of things." William Blackstone, whose *Commentaries on the Laws of England* tried to sum up English law for a lay audience in the middle of the eighteenth century, used the same distinction, and it is also found in many basic civil codes in Europe and Latin America. In Louisiana, too, the first part (Book I) of the civil code is called "Of Persons" and includes (among other things) rules about marriage, divorce, and minor children. Book II is called "Things and the Different Modifications of Ownership"; it is basically about property law.

Civil-law scholars (mostly European) have always been interested in classifying law. They have searched for some rational and systematic way to break law down into subjects or parts. The common law has shown a lot less zest for this task. Of course, over the years, the common law has expanded, reaching an uncomfortable size. As this happened, scholars in England tried to take it apart and put it together in some handy way, restating the whole in convenient form. Blackstone was one of these scholars. He borrowed his arrangement, essentially, from civil-law scholars. As we have noted, his *Commentaries* were wildly successful, especially in this country. There were many "American" editions, that is, versions of Blackstone with special notes on American sources and the differences between English and American practice.

After independence, American jurists tried their hand at the Blackstone game, this time with respect to American law. The most notable effort along these lines was James Kent's *Commentaries on American Law,* first published between 1827 and 1830. This work, in four volumes, was arranged more or less like Blackstone's *Commentaries.* It, too, ran into many editions.

Blackstone was a good popularizer but not much of a legal philosopher, at least not by European standards. Still, his book was far more systematic than most of the earlier attempts, in England, to cope with the common law as a whole. The "abridgments" of the law were another method of trying to restate the basic rules of the common law. The word "abridgment" might seem a bit ironic, since some of the abridgments were many volumes long. They were arranged as crudely as possible: alphabetically, by topic.

This idea, too, carried over into America. Nathan Dane put together an *Abridgment of American Law* in the early nineteenth century, with the same general organization (or nonorganization). Huge, alphabetical legal encyclopedias, used as reference books, continued to be produced into contemporary times. One of these is *Corpus Juris,* which (along with its continuation, *Corpus Juris Secundum*) tries to cover the whole of American case law. *Corpus Juris* is arranged alphabetically, by topic, like a dictionary or encyclopedia; so are many digests of state or multistate law. The second edition of *American Jurisprudence,* one of the major digests, currently runs to eighty-three volumes; the first volume begins with "Abandoned Property," the last volume ends with "Zoning and Planning." Contemporary lawyers also have at their fingertips electronic systems for searching the law. A lawyer's office is still conventionally lined with sturdy rows of impressive-looking books; but more and more lawyers (and their assistants) can be found at the computer keyboard, reading screens and printouts rather than books.

An alphabetical arrangement means that the arranger has no overall theory for joining the pieces together. But the arranger must still find a way to carve the huge carcass of the law into segments or pieces. Otherwise, one could not even list things alphabetically. Like flour or sugar, law has to be packaged in boxes or sacks before one can handle it. Conventionally, there are dozens and dozens of such packages, to be found in the encyclopedias, but most of the categories (like "Abandoned Property") are of minor importance. A few categories are of major significance; they constitute big, basic subdivisions of law. These chunks of subject matter are often the names of basic courses taught in American law schools. A few of these big subdivisions will be mentioned here, and briefly described.

Contracts. Contracts is the body of law that by and large concerns voluntary agreements. Most people understand more or less what it means to enter into a contract. They realize that a contract is a bargain or agreement between two people (or more) to do some work, to buy or sell goods, to put up a building or tear one down, or to perform countless other activities, which one person or company promises to do in exchange for a counterpromise (usually a promise to pay money). Anytime you buy a newspaper, or a car, or even a can of soup, you are technically making a "contract."

Well over a century ago (1861), the great English jurist Sir Henry Maine published a book called *Ancient Law.* In a famous passage, Maine tried to describe how the law had evolved over the years in "progressive" (that is, modernizing) societies. In such societies, Maine argued, the law moved "from status to contract." What he meant was that legal relations in modern societies do not depend primarily on birth or caste; they depend on voluntary agreements. Elizabeth II is queen of England because of an accident of birth, but it is not an accident of birth that I may be making monthly payments on a used yellow Plymouth; it is because I agreed to buy the car, on my own, as an adult, and quite willingly.

In this sense, a regime of contract is fundamental to modern society. The whole economy—indeed, the whole social system—rests on this basis. But a regime of contract, a system of contract, that is, an economy organized around voluntary agreements, governed mainly by the market, is not the same as the law of contracts as conventionally defined and taught in law schools. The law of contracts deals with only certain aspects of the market, and with certain kinds of agreement.

In legal terms, a contract is a promise (or set of promises) that the law protects and enforces. If I promise to deliver a carload of lumber and the buyer promises to pay me a certain price, and I do not deliver the lumber, I have "breached" my contract. The buyer can sue me for damages, if the buyer chooses.

To make a valid contract, generally speaking, we need at least two parties; both have to have legal "capacity." A small child or an idiot cannot legally enter into a contract. One side must make an "offer"; the other side must "accept" it. "Offer" and "acceptance" are ordinary English words, but they have specialized, technical meanings in law. A department store ad which announces an "offer" of a sewing machine for sale at a low price, as a "Thursday-Only Special," is probably not making a legal offer. For one thing, there is no actual promise to sell the sewing machines. If, for example, the public gobbles up the stock, the store (probably) cannot be forced to sell cheap sewing machines to disappointed customers.[1] An "offer" which is the starting point for a contract, however, has to be a real promise. An "acceptance" is a promise which follows an "offer."

"Offer" and "acceptance" are promises, then, and they must be supported by a mysterious substance called "consideration." This is an intricate legal concept, hard to define in a sentence or two. The underlying idea, however, is fairly simple. Each party to a contract makes his or her promise "in consideration" of something which the other one promises. If I offer to sell my old car for $2,000, and the buyer accepts (promising to pay $2,000), the "consideration" on each side is clear. But if I promise to give my daughter a bushel of stock certificates because I love her, there is no "consideration" for my promise; she contributes nothing in return. (Love, alas, does not count in the law of contracts.) Here, if I fail to deliver (or die before I get a chance to), she has no right to sue me or my estate and claim the stock certificates.

There are, of course, many other issues in the law of contracts. Samuel Williston's treatise on contract law, the leader in the field for many years, lumbers through volume after volume. There is, however, some question whether all this lore matters very much in the world of affairs. In a classic article, Stewart Macaulay explored the behavior of businessmen in Wisconsin. He found that many of them tended to avoid or sidestep (formal) contract law and contract doctrine. They especially shied away from suing each other, even when they had a good case, according to formal law. The reason was not at all mysterious. The businessmen depended on each other; they lived and worked in networks of continuing relationships. A manufacturer might buy paper clips, pens, and office supplies from the same dealer, year in and year out. Suing at the drop of the hat, or arguing excessively, or sticking up for abstract "rights," was disruptive; it tended to rip apart these valuable relationships. Also, there were norms, practices, and conceptions of honor and fairness that businessmen customarily followed. These were more subtle, more complicated, than the formal norms of the lawyers.[2]

"Contracts" is a standard first-year course in every law school. Yet it is probably a less important part of the living law than other fields which build on contract law or contract ideas. One of these fields is commercial law. This is the branch of law that concerns the buying and selling of goods, especially sales for credit and on the installment plan; it also deals with checks, promissory notes, and other "negotiable instruments." Another related field is the law of bankruptcy and creditors' rights. A bankrupt business or individual goes through a process that wipes the slate clean and allows the bankrupt to begin again. Even more important, the bankruptcy process is designed to ensure fairness to all of the creditors. It tries to avoid a dog-eat-dog struggle over the assets of wrecked businesses and failed debtors. Bankruptcy law is a federal concern and is administered in the federal courts. Another rapidly growing field is the law of consumer protection. Still other fields concern themselves with special kinds of contract, for example contracts of insurance. Insurance contracts, like the insurance business, are quite heavily regulated and subject to distinctive rules.

Torts. Tort law is usually defined as the law of "civil wrongs," and it is hard to give a more exact definition. I commit a tort if I hit somebody accidentally but carelessly with my elbow or my car; if I falsely call someone a thief or put this accusation in writing (slander and libel); if I have somebody maliciously arrested, or invade somebody's privacy, or trespass on someone's land without permission.

This is a more or less ragtag collection of behaviors, which have little in common except that they are all defined as wrong and do not grow out of a contractual relationship between victim and "tortfeasor." They are also "civil" wrongs, which means they are not crimes (at least not necessarily). If I wander onto somebody's land by mistake and trample on something valuable, I may have to pay, but I have not committed a crime and I will not go to jail. It is not a crime for me to back out of a parking space and dent somebody else's fender, unless I did it willfully and recklessly. But of course I have to pay. There are torts that are also crimes, especially if the behavior is reckless or malicious. The ordinary tort is not.

A tort is conduct which causes injury and does not measure up to some standard which society has set. Everything listed in the last paragraph is a tort, but some torts are more important than other torts. The heart of tort law is the action for personal injury, a claim against a person or company for hurting the claimant's body in some way. Probably 95 percent of all tort claims are for personal injury. Auto accidents, nowadays, are responsible for a hefty share of these. Formerly, railroad and work accidents were the most prolific sources of tort cases. Indeed, the law of torts was insignificant before the railroad age of the nineteenth century, and no wonder. This branch of law deals above all with the wrenching, grinding effects of machines on human bodies. It belongs to the world of factories, railroads, and mines—in other words, the world of the Industrial Revolution.

Basically, then, the railroad created the law of torts. Not a single treatise on the law of torts was published before 1850, either in England or in the United States. Early tort cases often came up out of railroad accidents. Nicholas Farwell, who worked for the Boston and Worcester

Railroad, had his hand smashed in a switchyard accident, sued the railroad, and got nothing; but *Farwell v. Boston & Worcester Rr. Corp.* made legal history.[3] In this case, the chief justice of Massachusetts, Lemuel Shaw, announced an American version of what came to be known as the "fellow-servant rule." Under this rule, an employee could not sue his company for work injuries if the accident was caused by the carelessness of a coworker (a fellow servant). This was, of course, the usual situation in a factory or mine or on the railroad. Hence the rule protected employers against almost all claims of injured workmen.[4]

Despite the rule, industrial accidents in which workers like Farwell were mangled by machines were a fertile source of tort cases in the nineteenth century.[5] In the twentieth century, the fellow-servant rule was abolished; an administrative system, workers' compensation, replaced it. Each state has a workers' compensation law. Under these laws, generally speaking, *all* work accidents are compensated, no matter who is or is not at fault, but the amounts of recovery are limited. In the twentieth century, too, the auto accident came to occupy center stage in the world of torts. Lately, two subfields of the law of torts have grown rapidly: medical malpractice and products liability (injuries caused by defective foods, toys, appliances, drugs, or other commodities). A study of jury trials in Cook County, Illinois (Chicago and its suburbs), between 1960 and 1979 documents how auto accidents dominate in the lower courts. Of the civil jury trials in that period, 65.5 percent were auto-accident cases. Products liability cases rose from 2.3 percent to 5.8 percent at the end of the period; medical malpractice rose from 1.4 percent of the load to 3.5 percent.[6]

These last two categories, however, create an uproar in society out of all proportion to their numbers; the rise in medical malpractice cases generated a sense of crisis in the profession and led to all sorts of efforts to put a ceiling on how much plaintiffs could recover from doctors and hospitals. These efforts were successful in many states. "Tort reform," including limitations on recoveries, is still an important political issue in the 1990s. In fact, however, plaintiffs do not do particularly well in medical malpractice cases, at least those cases that go to a jury. A careful study of malpractice cases in North Carolina between 1984 and 1990 found that plaintiffs lost the vast majority of these cases; the median recovery was a piddling $36,500, and million-dollar recoveries, despite all the noise in the media, were as rare as hen's teeth.[7]

A fundamental concept of tort law is "negligence." This means, roughly, carelessness. Basically, if somebody causes me harm I can sue for damages only if that person was negligent. The person I sue has to be at fault. If the person was as careful as he or she should have been (as careful as the imaginary "reasonable person," the yardstick for measuring negligence), then I cannot recover for my injury.

Thousands of cases have turned on what does or does not amount to negligence. In the twentieth century, the concept has gone into something of a decline, especially in products-liability cases. More and more, courts impose "strict liability," that is, a victim can recover even if there was no negligence and if the manufacturer was as careful as is humanly possible. If a company makes jars of pickles and has good quality control, it can still happen that one jar out of a million is bad, slips through the net, and makes someone sick. The company has not been negligent, in nineteenth-century terms. But modern cases insist, on the whole, that the company must pay.

The Law of Property. The old common law was preeminently the law of real property, and the distinction between "real property" and "personal property" was a crucial one in the law. Generally speaking, real property means real estate—land and whatever buildings are on it. But it also includes such things as growing crops. Everything else— money, stocks and bonds, jewelry, cars, carloads of lumber, IOUs, bank deposits—is personal property. We all have a stake in real estate, since we all live somewhere, and we work, study, and travel somewhere, too. Everyone is a renter or an owner, or lives with renters or owners, or, at worst, camps out or squats in a place that somebody owns. But for most of us, personal property means more than real estate. It seems odd, then, that as far as the law is concerned the word "property" means primarily real property; personal property is of minor importance.

Actually, personal property is legally a minor field precisely *because* personal property has become so important. There is no single, special field of law devoted to personal property. Personal property is what contract law, commercial law, and bankruptcy law—yes, and torts, too— are all about. But there are so many special rules about real estate that it makes sense to treat "property" as a separate field of law.

Which it is. It is both separate and fairly fundamental. Real-estate practice, too, is a significant branch of law practice. But historically considered, real-property law is a mere shadow of its former self. One of the major developments in our system, if you take the long view, is the relative decline of real-property law. In medieval England, to say that land law was the law of the land would be only a slight exaggeration. When Blackstone published his *Commentaries* midway through the eighteenth century, one whole volume (a quarter of his space) was devoted to land law. A modern Blackstone would shrink the topic to a fraction of this bulk, 5 or 10 percent, at most, of the total law.

Medieval England lived under a feudal system. Power and jurisdiction, the cornerstones of wealth and position in society, were based on land and land alone. The "lord" was a person who held an estate, a person with ownership, mastery, control over land. A person without land was a person with no real stake in affairs of state. The common law, as the royal law courts expounded it, had little to say to men and women without land, who were the overwhelming majority of the English population. Even in this country, at one time, only persons who had interests in land were entitled to vote or hold office. Under the New York constitution of 1777, for example, only men who owned "freeholds" worth £100 or more, free and clear of debt, were entitled to vote for state senators (Article X).[8] All this, of course, has long since ended. Today, land is only one form of wealth. A great and powerful family is one that controls mighty enterprises, rather than one that rules vast estates.

Property law still covers a rich and varied group of subjects. To begin with, it asks: What does it mean to "own" land? How can I get title to land and how can I dispose of it, legally? There are issues about deeds, joint ownership, and land records and registration; and problems of land finance, including rules about mortgages and foreclosures. There is the law of "nuisance," which restricts me from using my land in such a way as to hurt my neighbors, pouring smoke or sending bad smells onto their land, for example. There is also the law of "easements" and the exotic law of "covenants" (especially those that "run with the land"): these deal with rights a person might have in a neighbor's land, rights to drive a car up a neighbor's driveway, to walk across a neighbor's lawn, or to keep a neighbor from taking in boarders. These are not rights of ownership; rather they are "servitudes"—restrictions or exceptions to the rights of a landowner, in favor of other people, or the public in general.

The common law was ingenious in carving up rights to land into various complex segments called "estates." These could be either time segments or space segments. A "life estate" (my right to live in a certain house, for example, until I die) is a time segment; so is a three-year lease of a farm or apartment house. Space segments include air rights (the right to build on top of certain property) and mineral rights (the right to dig underneath it). Nowadays, the condominium is also popular; I can own a slice of some building, even if my slice is thirty stories above the ground. The common law was also quite ingenious in devising forms of common or joint ownership, with subtle technical differences between them.

There are also all sorts of "future interests" known to the common law. Suppose I leave my house to my sister for life, and then to any of her children who might be alive when she dies. The children have a future interest; that is, the time they will get the house is postponed to some far-off date. But the future event is certain to happen, and thus the future interest can have value and reality now, while my sister is very much alive. The law of future interests developed in a most gnarled and complicated way. Its intricacies drove generations of law students to quiet despair.

Another important, and fairly new, branch of property law is the law of "land-use controls." It deals with the limits imposed on what people can do with their property. This was an issue in the law of nuisance, but modern controls go far beyond this. Zoning is a familiar type of land-use restriction. Zoning ordinances date from about the time of the First World War; they are now almost universal in cities and villages. Zoning ordinances divide towns into zones designated for different uses. If my neighborhood is "zoned" residential, I cannot build a factory or run a restaurant on my property. If the zone is restricted to single-family dwellings, I cannot even run a rooming house or rent out apartments.

The Law of Succession. This field, the law of wills and trusts, is closely related to property law as such. It is the branch of law which, essentially, considers how property gets passed along from one generation to the next. The United States is firmly wedded to the system of private property. Property is allocated among individual owners, by and large; this is generally the practice in modern, industrial societies, unlike more traditional societies, where land may be "owned" in common or by clans, families, or tribes. We tend to have title to our land and homes outright, along with whatever else we possess, from rings and wristwatches to stocks and bonds and money in the bank. Since it is a fundamental rule (alas) that we all die in the end and take nothing with us (the pharaohs tried and presumably failed), this property must somehow move on at our death.

One way to make this happen is to execute a will. You, the owner, will decide, for the most part, what should become of your worldly goods when you die. This is the principle of "freedom of testation." You decide, but you must do it in a certain way. If you forget to make a will (or botch the job of drawing it up), you have died "intestate," and the state will distribute the property for you according to a fixed scheme set out in the statute books. Intestate property passes to the heirs at law— the nearest surviving relatives. If you leave behind a large enough estate, the government takes a bite of it, too, in the form of death taxes.

A will is a formal document. It must be made out just right, and in most states it needs two witnesses. In about half the states, mostly in the West and South, you can also execute a will without witnesses, the so-called holographic will. A man or woman who wants to make out a holographic will has to write it entirely by hand; typing is not allowed. (Nobody will do this for a long, complicated will; hence holographs, though common, are mostly short, do-it-yourself documents.) If you have a valid will, you can disinherit any blood relatives you choose. A parent can, with a stroke of the pen, cut off his or her children without a penny (except in Louisiana; and minor children may have some rights to support, during the probate period). A husband or wife cannot be cut off so easily. The surviving spouse has a claim to a share of the estate, and though many angry spouses have tried, it is not at all easy to find a way around the law and disinherit a marriage partner completely.

"Trusts" are arrangements which, in essence, transfer property to a trustee (often a bank), to invest and to manage. The trustees usually are required to pay the income to one or more "beneficiaries," who are quite passive; they sit back and collect the money. Trusts are gifts, and rich people use them as part of a general estate plan, their scheme for orderly disposition of their property. Many trusts are "testamentary," that is, part of a plan contained in a will. Others are set up long before death, but even these generally have death and death taxes in mind. The law of trusts goes together with the law of wills, both in law school and in the lawyer's office; both are aspects of "estate planning." Lawyers who specialize in this branch of practice get paid for their skill in finding the best, cheapest, and most effective way to carry out the wishes of their clients, at the same time avoiding the buzzards of taxation as much as possible.

Estate planning is basically law for the rich. Most people do not have enough "estate" to need the fanciest tricks of the trade. Adults who have money or property do need wills, but many people do not bother with them. In Cuyahoga County, Ohio, whose main city is Cleveland, a study in 1964–65 found that almost a third of the estates probably lacked wills.[9] The percentage of "intestacy" was probably higher in the general population; a lot of people who die leave so little money that the family does not bother with probate. For 1980 in Los Angeles, it has been estimated that about 15 percent of the men who died and 23 percent of the women left wills that went through probate.[10]

Sociolegal scholars have paid relatively little attention to the law of succession. This is unfortunate. It is a crucial branch of law, as vital to social continuity as DNA is to survival of the species. Since all of us eventually die, society must reproduce itself every generation, not only biologically, but also socially and structurally. The basic techniques are far from mysterious. Social norms and structures get transmitted from generation to generation through education, child-rearing, and other processes that mold the new generation in the shape of the old one. But the inheritance of property also plays a crucial part. Without the laws of succession, there would be no such things as "old money," aristocracy, or "good families." Each generation would start over, and social structure would be fundamentally altered—perhaps for the better, perhaps not. In any event, life would be different, in a revolutionary way. Even the socialist countries allowed some inheritance of property. And the middle class, too, has a stake in the law of succession. The law permits money to flow across time, and specifies how this is to be done. Without succession, there would be no heirlooms, no old family homes, no gifts left to grandchildren for college. There might be less family quarreling as well.

Perhaps just as important as the rights of inheritance are the limits on inheritance. There are complicated rules about estate taxes (the taxes charged by the federal government on estates of the dead). The larger estates are, the more taxes they pay, but there are important escape valves. One of these is the unlimited right to give to charity, tax-free. Without this right, the great charitable foundations would not exist. Other rules limit dynasties of wealth in their duration. No trust—no arrangement tying up money over generations—can last forever (charities are exempt from this rule). The limiting rule is called the rule against perpetuities. Its details are of daunting complexity, but the upshot is to restrict the dead hand to something less than a century at the absolute limit.

Family Law. One branch of family law borders on the law of succession. Most people, after all, leave their money to relatives, or give it away to family during their lifetime. Family law is concerned with marital property, including the community-property systems of California and other western states. What rights does a husband or wife have in the money or income of the spouse? This field also concerns marriage and divorce, child custody, and children's rights.

Family structure is changing rapidly, and family law changes with it. Divorce, for example, was once rare and difficult to get. Indeed, in the early nineteenth century some states granted divorces only through special acts of the legislature;[11] one state, South Carolina, simply allowed no divorce at all. Even in "easy" states, divorce was based on the so-called fault system. A married person who wanted a divorce had to go to court and prove some "grounds" for divorce. Divorce was available only to "innocent" parties, whose spouses were guilty of adultery, desertion, cruelty, habitual drunkenness, or whatever else was on the statutory list. Some states were much stricter than others. In New York, one of the strict states, adultery was, practically speaking, the only grounds for divorce.[12]

The nineteenth century moaned and groaned about rising divorce rates; in retrospect the rates seem ridiculously small. Only in the twentieth century has divorce become an everyday affair. But for at least a hundred years—since the 1870s or so—most divorces have been consensual. That is, the courtroom proceedings were a mere ritual, a sham; there was no real contest. The alleged grounds of divorce were often faked. Courts knew all this, but they closed their eyes to reality and let the system run its course. There was a heavy, rising demand for divorce, while the stigma attached to divorce steadily weakened.

Beginning in 1970, state after state has adopted a so-called no-fault system. There is no longer any need to prove grounds for divorce—or indeed to prove anything. All that is required, essentially, is the fact that the honeymoon is over—that the marriage has broken down irretrievably. Divorce is now legally as well as socially routine. It is not even called divorce anymore in California; the new (official) name is "dissolution of marriage."

Easy divorce does not mean easier problems for family law. Indeed, changes in family structure, which lie behind the divorce explosion, brought certain dilemmas closer to the surface. Custody disputes are if anything more common and acrimonious than in the days before no-fault divorce. The basic legal principle is that the child's best interests come first, but in the modern world that does not carry us very far. We can no longer assume, as we once did, that "best interests" almost always means mother. Joint custody is one of many new ideas which the system is trying out, to cope with problems of the children of divorce.

The family and "family values" are important political and social issues. The issues inevitably spill over into family *law.* Controversy over same-sex marriage, custody for gay or lesbian parents, rights of surrogate mothers, womb mothers, and the like, do not produce a mass of cases, but the few that do arise are of uncommon interest and importance.

The Law of Business Associations. The corporation is the dominant form of business enterprise today, the dominant employer, the dominant force in the economy. It is also the main concern of the law of business associations. Corporations take many forms, but they have in common limited liability and a division of function between the owners of shares and the actual managers of the company (unless the managers themselves own the shares). Corporations are legal entities. They are "persons" in the eyes of the law, and can sue and be sued in their own names. Limited liability means that shareholders cannot lose more than the value of their shares, no matter how many debts the corporation accumulates. Shareholders, in other words, are not personally liable for the corporation's debts.

At the time of the Revolution, and for several generations afterward, setting up a corporation was not easy. The incorporators had to follow a long, laborious route. Corporations were chartered one by one; each charter was a special law passed by the state legislature. Most of these early corporations held "franchises": they were little monopolies, with the right to build a bridge over some particular river or a railroad between this town and that. It seemed only right to deal with them case by case. The law was also quite strict about their powers. They were not allowed to move one step beyond what their charters specifically authorized.

Today, corporation law is entirely different. Basically, it is much more permissive. Anybody who wants to form a corporation fills out a form or two and pays a state fee ($900 in California, as of 1997), and that is that. Corporations, generally speaking, last forever and can do whatever they wish, provided it is not downright illegal. Courts will generally uphold the business judgment of management. Tricky questions still arise, to be sure, about the rights of shareholders and about the duty of officers toward their companies, creditors, and others. There is also a significant measure of federal control. The Securities and Exchange Commission monitors the issue of public securities—stocks and bonds offered to the public. SEC rules are designed to promote honest disclosure of financial facts. They are meant to prevent the kinds of fraud and chicanery that were once all too common among the gaudy wheelers and dealers of Wall Street.

The corporation is not the only form of business association. Most law firms, for example, are partnerships. The rights and duties of partners, in relation to each other and to third parties, raise many legal problems. The law of "agency," too, is closely linked to the law of business associations. This is the branch of law that deals with principals and agents. If a pedestrian is hit by a truck that belongs to Acme Toothpick, Inc., the pedestrian will almost certainly sue the company (the "principal") even though the actual tort was committed by the driver (the "agent"). Can the pedestrian sue the truck driver instead? Yes, but the company has more money and is a better target. And the company is liable for the acts of its agents. This is the doctrine of *respondeat superior*—"let the superior [principal] answer," or, in cruder language, "make the boss pay."

This much seems clear. But it assumes the driver was actually on company business. This is usually but not always the case. Suppose the driver had borrowed the truck to go to a ball game. The driver is off on a "frolic," as the law quaintly puts it. Is the company still liable? In other words, if you hire people to work for you, exactly how much responsibility will you have for the various things your agents might do? The law of agency explores this and similar questions.

Public Law

European legal scholars make much of the distinction between "public" and "private" law. The distinction goes back to classical Roman law. Private law concerned the rights and interests of individuals; public law concerned the Roman state. From this standpoint, most fields we have discussed in this chapter fall under the heading of private law. A divorce case is *Smith v. Smith*, between husband and wife; tort cases are mostly between person and person, or person and insurance company; most disputes over title to land are also "private." But when the government brought a huge lawsuit trying to break IBM up into smaller parts (the Reagan administration finally abandoned the suit), this was definitely public law.

Theorists in common-law systems make much less of the distinction between public and private law. And, as many scholars have pointed out, the distinction seems less and less relevant as time goes on. There are few, if any, fields today that are purely "private." Government is a silent—or noisy—partner in every branch of law, to a greater or lesser degree. Land law is essentially private, but zoning is public. Tort law is private, but dozens of statutes on safety regulation and the like affect the course of private lawsuits. And so it goes.

Lawyers' work, too, shifts more and more from the private to the public side. There is, for example, taxation, a bloated monster of a field. The federal government spends hundreds of billions of dollars every year; so do the states and the cities, in the aggregate. The money has to be wrung out of taxpayers. Taxpayers wriggle and resist. As a consequence, tax law may well be the single largest field of law, in terms of effort, dollars involved, and the sheer bulk of statutes and regulations, however one measures it. It is also a field of awesome technicality. The Internal Revenue Code, the key to all of Uncle Sam's billions, is the longest, most difficult statute in the whole federal armory, as we have seen.

Taxation is one among many great fields of public law. There is antitrust law, concerned with monopolies and restraint of trade. There is regulation of business in general—public utility law, and such specialties as food and drug law, maritime law, and immigration and naturalization law. Public law also includes bankruptcy and consumer-protection law and most of the rules and structures that bear on labor relations. Most of the work that most lawyers do—especially the lawyers who practice in big-city firms—is "corporate law," that is, law relevant to the giant businesses that dominate the economy. Much of this work, perhaps most of it, is "public law." The growth of public law is bound up with the rise of the administrative state. All through this book, we have seen examples of public law at work. Constitutional law and civil liberties are two key fields in this large area, and they merit fuller discussion in a chapter of their own.

9

Crimes and Punishments

*F*OR THE LAYMAN, the criminal side of the legal system is in many ways the most familiar aspect of American law. In fact, when you mention law or the legal system to people, what springs most naturally into their minds is criminal justice and its cast of characters and settings—police, courtrooms, juries, trials, prisons and jails, the gas chamber. The drama of the trial has fascinated people for centuries. Crime and punishment are front-page news, and are the subject of hundreds of plays, movies, and books. There is a great novel called *The Trial* and another called *Crime and Punishment*. No novel worth reading is called *Antitrust Suit* or *The Shopping-Center Lease*.

Criminal justice is a vast, complex system. It is, in essence, that part of the legal system which, first of all, marks off certain behavior as wrong or "criminal"; second, takes steps to control or prevent that behavior by threats of punishment; and third, if prevention fails, tries to catch and to punish the wrongdoer. Some aspects of the system are exceedingly familiar; others are obscure and much misunderstood.

To begin with, we can ask, what is a crime? Every country, and in the United States every state, has its own special list of forbidden behaviors. The list is part of an elaborate statute which is usually called the penal code. The code lists types of conduct which it declares illegal and defines as "crimes"; it also sets out punishments. The federal government has its own code, which is fairly specialized. It does not cover most ordinary crimes (the states, not the federal government, punish murder, arson, drunk driving, and the like). The national government punishes violations of federal laws, like smuggling or tax fraud. The District of Columbia has its own criminal code, much like that of the states. Some acts can be both federal and state crimes—this is true, for example, of many drug offenses.

Some crimes are in the penal codes of every state: murder, manslaughter, robbery, burglary, rape, arson, and so on. Others are less universal. The Georgia code makes it a crime "to be a peeping Tom" or to invade a person's privacy with acts "of a similar nature."[1] The Georgia code also deals with the sale of obscene literature, shooting guns on Sunday, illegal use of credit cards, necrophilia ("any sexual act with a dead human body"),[2] sale of Molotov cocktails, and dozens of other offenses. The list of crimes is not exactly the same in any two states.

What is criminal in one society need not be criminal in another. It was a serious offense in the former Soviet Union to speculate in foreign currencies. In our country, on the other hand, the same act may be done by currency dealers as part of their quite respectable business. For medieval Mongolians, it was a crime to urinate into water or ashes. Americans would find this offensive in some circumstances, but hardly a crime. Definitions also vary with time and circumstances. It was once illegal to own gold ingots in this country. This is no longer the case. During the Second World War, wages and prices were frozen and it was a crime to charge more than the "ceiling" price. There are no such restrictions today.

Are there some acts which are crimes universally, that is, which every society defines as criminal? Yes and no. It would be hard to think of a society that did not forbid murder—that is, the wrongful killing of another human being. But each society has its own definition of murder. Not every intentional killing is murder. A soldier can lawfully kill during wartime; citizens are allowed to kill in self-defense. Infanticide is murder in the United States, but abortion is not, although there are certainly many people who would like to forbid abortion by law. In some societies, it is not murder to kill for revenge or to get rid of someone who has brought dishonor on the family. There have been societies in which it was not a crime to kill baby girls or to dispose of old people who had outlived their usefulness.

Many crimes listed in the penal code are acts which shock the conscience. Murder is a prime example. But different societies have different consciences, as the last paragraph shows. And not every listing in a penal code carries the same moral freight. The codes are motley collections. There are many regulatory or economic offenses which are unknown to most people; most of us will never run up against them because they affect small groups or particular occupations, like druggists or taxi drivers or used-car salesmen. Other acts (shooting deer out of season, picking rare orchids, overtime parking) are well known, but do not shock the conscience as, say, murder does. These are crimes only because the state so defines them; murder would be (in a sense) a crime even if the laws against it ceased to exist. It is a crime, in other words, in people's minds and hearts.

The great, classic crimes are part of the social code, whatever their status in the legal code. The average person *knows* these are crimes. People have a rough working knowledge of what constitutes murder, even though they do not understand a lot of fine distinctions and technicalities which are part of the body of criminal law. Cold-blooded killing is murder, we know, although few of us can tell the difference between first-degree and second-degree murder, or what "malice" means in a state where this is part of the definition of murder, or what level of insanity excuses an act of killing.

Punishment, too, is variable. It depends mostly on how serious the crime. Seriousness is not inherent in the criminal conduct; it is a social judgment. Legally speaking, serious crimes are called felonies; less serious crimes are called misdemeanors. The exact line between them is a matter of legal definition. In California, a felony is a crime which can be punished by death or by "imprisonment in the state prison."[3] All other crimes—which carry fines, or a stint in a county jail—are misdemeanors, except for some petty acts (traffic violations, breaches of ordinances) which are called infractions. Infractions carry less of a punishment than crimes and have less of a stigma. A history of parking tickets is not a criminal record.

Functions of Criminal Justice

Why do we have criminal justice? What functions does it serve? The short and obvious answer is that this is the system that guarantees law and order. Criminal justice substitutes for private violence and vengeance; instead of "taking the law into their own hands," communities turn to specialized people and agencies who do the job for them.

Every society has deviant behavior; every society has people who behave in ways which society (or its leaders) cannot tolerate. In small, isolated societies, there are no specialists or specialized agencies (like the police) to enforce social norms. The anthropologist E. A. Hoebel has described the system of handling deviance among the peoples of the far North. The Eskimo groups he wrote about had no police, no judges, no obvious courts. But when someone stepped out of line, some member of the community, more or less self-appointed, could punish on behalf of the community, perhaps even killing the "criminal."[4]

Clearly, this system would not work in a complex society like ours. Criminal justice is supposed to take the problem of dealing with violence and other forms of deviance out of the hands of private citizens and concentrate it in the hands of the government. This is justified as a way to protect the great mass of people against the bad and the strong. It also makes revenge, blood feuds, and lynching illegal. But it is also an obvious opening for oppression and tyranny, for the so-called police state: if the state has a monopoly of violence it may misuse or overuse it. History, alas, is full of examples. Not all of them are to be found in far-off places. Abuse begins at home.

Outlawing private violence is not an either-or affair; it is the product of a long evolution, a process, and it is even now not complete. There are those who defend or romanticize a certain amount of private vengeance; it is amazing how often this crops up in movies and on TV, and in heroes played by, say, Clint Eastwood. But private citizens and laypeople do not have much of an official role in criminal justice in modern societies; the task is more and more given over to officials—to professionals in the field.

The most obvious function of criminal justice, however, is control of dangerous behavior—dangerous, of course, as the particular society sees it. Another function is to set out and enforce a moral code. Prostitution is a crime, but why? It is not physically dangerous in the sense that murder is; unlike burglary, it does not threaten the property system or take away people's hard-earned goods and money; it does not violate the sanctity of the home. Indeed, some people think prostitution should be stricken from the roster of crimes, because it is not dangerous to life, health, or property. Yet many other people want to keep it on the books as a crime. Some of these people might emphasize the harm done to the women themselves. Others—probably the majority—would insist that prostitution is morally offensive, and one business of criminal justice is to announce and enforce rules of morality. The penal code is full of crimes whose main point is ethical: they offend the moral interests or tastes of some fraction of the public.

Criminal justice is also concerned with order and discipline. It is not dangerous or immoral to park overtime on a busy street or to go through a red light when no traffic is coming. It is neither dangerous nor immoral in the classical sense to hunt deer out of season or to catch a fish that is too big or too small. The word "order" implies a kind of rationing system. There are not enough deer or fish to go around. There are not enough parking spaces for everybody. We need rules to prevent overuse.

Rules of order are common in our society. For example, a public library may have rules against talking. Talking is a harmless activity; if there were only one or two people in the library, probably no one would care if the users had a nice conversation. But to keep order the library feels it has to restrict this harmless activity—in other words, ration it or forbid it altogether. The legal system provides this kind of order, for space on the streets and other scarce commodities, and the criminal justice system enforces it. Breaches of order are punished, not so drastically as more serious crimes—the gas chamber or long jail terms would be out of place—but punished nonetheless.

The word "discipline" applies to a special kind of order. We "discipline" behavior when it violates rules of order that have some flavor or nuance of immorality or danger. Rules against public drunkenness are a good example; for many years this was the commonest "crime" of all, the one most frequently punished in many places.[5] Another crime against discipline is disturbing the peace. The line between dangerous behavior and undisciplined behavior is, of course, very fuzzy, and disturbances of the peace can range from drunken singing on the sidewalk to something close to a riot.

Perhaps all these functions can be summed up in a single formula, and fitted into one huge macrofunction. They are all concerned with keeping society on an even keel, protecting its structure, and safeguarding its boundaries. Stealing is a crime, and if it is punished, a special service is rendered to people who have property worth stealing. Criminal justice protects the property system and the value system; it is the watchdog of the house, guarding the furniture, the pictures on the wall, and the peace and contentment of the residents.

Criminal justice, then, is vital to any social system. It is essential to welfare capitalism, but it is also a pillar of socialism in Cuba, of Muslim fundamentalism in Iran and Saudi Arabia. Whatever the system, criminal justice supports it. The law supported apartheid in South Africa, and it supports the dismantling of apartheid today. Law buttressed Hilter's vicious and murderous regime, and it supports democracy in Finland or Holland. This chameleon-like quality does not mean that criminal justice (or law) is by nature conservative, that is, inherently an enemy of change. In fact, patterns of power and wealth change constantly in the United States, through tax laws, for example, or through other forms of legislation. Many of these changes are slight, but they are changes nonetheless. The legal system is not against all change; rather, it tries to control the process. It stamps some methods of altering structure and rules as fair and legitimate—for example, those that come about through acts of Congress or court decisions. It outlaws all others—riots and revolutions, or the robbing of banks. Criminal justice is the strong arm of the law, its main weapon against these outlaw methods.

In our modern welfare state, criminal justice has a special role in enforcing rules about the economy. Many "economic crimes" are best looked on not as dangerous or repulsive acts, but as activity subject to rules of rationing or of order. Thus, in Rhode Island, it is an offense to catch lobsters without a license or to take a lobster less than three and three-sixteenths inches long, "measured from the rear of the eye socket along a line parallel to the center line of the body shell to the rear end of the carapace."[6] There are countless other examples, in state and federal laws. But why make these technical regulations part of the criminal process? One reason is that criminal justice is *public* justice; it requires *public* litigation. The plaintiff is the people or the commonwealth or "the state"; the state sets the process in motion and the state pays the bills.

This makes criminal justice useful in situations in which private citizens do not have financial stakes high enough to encourage private enforcement. If a butcher runs a crooked scale and cheats every customer a nickel or two per pound of meat, no customer would sue, even in small-claims court, for the money lost on three pounds of hamburger, or a two-pound steak. But if using crooked scales is made a crime, the state can prosecute and control this offense, presumably for the benefit of all of the customers at once.

Types of Crime

There are a number of conventional ways to classify crimes. One is to ask what interests have been injured by the crime. Thus we speak of crimes against the person and crimes against property. Crimes against the person contain an element of force, of physical contact: murder, manslaughter, rape, kidnapping, robbery, assault. Crimes against property include the various forms of stealthy stealing (burglary, theft, shoplifting, embezzlement), plus various frauds, extortion, forgery, receiving stolen property, etc. Property crimes also include arson, a serious, dangerous crime. There are also crimes against public order, or against the administration of justice. These include disorderly conduct, prison escape, rioting, resisting arrest, and perjury.

We also speak of crimes against morality. Examples are gambling, drunkenness, prostitution, and drug abuse. The law also forbids various kinds of "unnatural" or immoral sexual behavior: incest, for example. "Sodomy" and "bestiality" are crimes in some states and not in others. Sexual contact with children is quite generally proscribed.

We can also speak of "regulatory" crimes: adulterating food, criminal monopoly, price-fixing, dishonest weights and measures, dumping toxic wastes, and so on. There are many regulatory crimes, and the numbers are increasing. They are a product of the administrative state, of a sense of social interdependence, and of a desire to protect public health and safety. There is a newfound interest in conservation, too—in the beauty of the country and in the preservation of the national heritage; hence laws against littering, against killing bald eagles, against tearing down historic houses. There are also regulations of billboards and other forms of outdoor advertising. Each state has its own special interests to protect. Florida, for example, with its tropical coastline, has a total ban on the taking of sea turtles' eggs, and an elaborate statute protects the manatee, a lovable but endangered creature which is the official "state marine mammal."[7]

Among serious crimes (felonies), property crimes clearly predominate; they account for more arrests than all other categories. In 1993, police nationwide reported some 2,400,000 arrests for "serious crimes." "Larceny" and "theft" accounted for more than half; burglary added 338,000 more, motor-vehicle theft another 169,000. There were 20,000 homicides, 33,000 rapes, and 154,000 arrests for robbery. Among "nonserious" crimes, which produced over 9,000,000 arrests, "driving under the influence" was the leader—over 1,200,000 arrests. Liquor-law violations and drunkenness produced another million; "drug-abuse violations" close to a million. Prostitution accounted for only 89,000 arrests, sex offenses (other than rape) another 88,000.[8]

Arrests, of course, do not tell us how many crimes were reported to the police or how many were actually committed. We can learn some of this from "victim" studies, which ask people if they have ever been victims of crime, whether or not they reported the crime to authorities. The figures are somewhat alarming. In 1993, people surveyed claimed they reported only 34 percent of the rapes, 40 percent of the assaults, 48.9 percent of the burlgaries, and 27 percent of the purse-snatching and pickpocket incidents.[9]

Arrests also vary because of policy decisions. The police arrest any murderer or burglar they get their hands on, but not every speeder, gambler, or public drunk. Arrests for crimes against morality or public order may rise and fall more dramatically than arrests for murder or burglary. In many cities, the police normally ignore, or wink at, gambling, prostitution, pot smoking, and certain other offenses. Then suddenly some scandal rocks the town and makes big headlines; a crackdown follows because of the public outcry, and the arrest rate for the crime zooms—at least for a time.

Crimes against morality or public order make more of a splash in arrest records, if we look at arrests for petty offenses (misdemeanors). In San Francisco, in 1989–90, for example, out of about 61,000 arrests, there were fewer than a hundred for homicide, and only 1,495 burglary arrests; but there were 10,653 arrests for drunkenness, 2,874 arrests of "drunken drivers," 244 arrests for gambling, 1,537 arrests for prostitution, and 892 arrests for "malicious mischief."[10]

Almost all of us accept without question the idea of punishing crimes against the person, and there is not much controversy about burglary or theft. Crimes against morality are another story. These are much more sensitive to ebbs and flows of public opinion, to shifts in the moral climate. This is why arrest rates zig and zag so radically, especially for laws against "victimless crimes." Many people argue it is wrong to punish acts simply because they are "immoral." Morality is "not the law's business," as the title of a book by Gilbert Geis puts it (1972). There is a movement to wipe most of these laws off the books, to decriminalize adultery, fornication, and "unnatural" sex, at least between consenting adults. Many states have already done so. Some people would go further and legalize gambling, prostitution, or the use of drugs like marijuana or cocaine. Many people resist this movement, of course, and oppose decriminalization. Taboos against gambling seem to have broken down greatly—there are state lotteries in many states, and casinos are springing up like weeds. But the "war on drugs" continues unabated in the 1990s.

We sometimes hear people talk about the "Puritan heritage" of the country. This heritage gets blamed for what some people feel is an unhealthy tendency to meddle in private lives and punish people if they choose styles of living outside the mainstream. In fact, the history of victimless-crime law is not a simple line of descent from the colonial past. It is rather a story with surprising twists and turns.[11]

The Puritan colonies, in the seventeenth century, were in fact very much concerned about crimes against morality. No crime in Massachusetts Bay was punished more frequently than fornication. Thus we read, for example, that in Salem, Massachusetts, in 1655 the court ordered Cornelius Hulett to be "whipped ten stripes on some lecture day in seasonable weather, for fornication with Elizabeth Due."[12] These were small, gossipy communities; the clergy held leadership roles; and in general, law made little or no distinction between sin and crime. Hulett was only one of hundreds who were whipped, fined, put in the stocks, or forced to marry because of the "crime" of fornication.

If we leap forward to the nineteenth century, we get a different picture. Laws against fornication and adultery were still on the books.

But there seemed to be little appetite for enforcement. In some states, the crimes were redefined: in Indiana, for example, adultery was against the law only if it was "open and notorious." In other words, adultery could not be punished unless the adulterers flaunted themselves before the public. The law was much less concerned with secret sin. Vice was tolerated if it kept in its place. In every large American city, there were red-light districts. Prostitution was illegal in all of these cities, but it was "tacitly tolerated" and "relatively undisturbed" so long as it stayed put in the districts. Despite sporadic outbursts of morality and occasional riots, brothels were "almost as much a part of social life as the cocktail lounge is today."[13]

The situation changed rather dramatically, beginning in the late nineteenth century. There was a new birth of interest in outlawing and punishing victimless crime. In 1873, Congress passed the so-called Comstock Law, which made it a federal crime to mail any "obscene, lewd, or lascivious" book, or "any article or thing . . . for the prevention of conception." In 1895, Congress prohibited the interstate sale of lottery tickets. In 1907, Arkansas passed a law making it a crime to manufacture, sell, or give away "any cigarettes or cigarette wrappers or papers to any person."[14]

There was more to come. The famous Mann Act (1910)[15] made it a federal offense to transport any woman across state lines "for the purpose of prostitution or debauchery, or for any other immoral purpose." Under the Harrison Act (1914)[16] it was illegal to buy or sell narcotics, except with a doctor's prescription. For the first time, practically speaking, the law made outlaws out of drug addicts. The climax of the purity movement came just after the First World War: the Eighteenth Amendment to the Constitution (1919) launched the "noble experiment" of Prohibition. This was the end point of a long struggle for temperance. Congress sent the amendment to the states in November 1917; Nebraska, the thirty-seventh state, ratified it in January 1919, putting it over the top. National Prohibition actually began in January 1920. The Eighteenth Amendment and the supporting laws slapped a total ban on the "manufacture, sale, or transportation of intoxicating liquors" in the United States. Congress also passed a strong federal law (the Volstead Act, 1919) to enforce prohibition.[17]

It is one thing, of course, to pass a law and quite another to enforce it. The troubles of Prohibition are legendary, and most historians consider it a dismal failure. It certainly did not get rid of alcohol, although there is a good deal of dispute about its actual impact. There was clearly a lot of evasion, corruption, and scandal. After a decade or so of conflict and misery, the country got rid of it, in the Twenty-first Amendment

(1933). Another failure (in the long run) was the red-light abatement movement, which flourished around the time of the First World War. This was a campaign by reformers and moralists to get rid of vice and prostitution once and for all. Tough new laws were passed, and armies of the righteous closed down the Barbary Coast in San Francisco, Storyville in New Orleans, and other notorious vice districts, at least temporarily. (Sin had a way of popping back, in the end.)

The movement had just about run its course by the 1930s; a strong reaction set in. In recent years, the pendulum has swung in the opposite direction. Many states have taken the criminal label off fornication and adultery. A few states have all but given up the fight against marijuana. Many states have stopped punishing homosexual acts among consenting adults. The struggle for legitimization continues. But opposition is also strong and highly motivated, particularly in the conservative South.

It is far from obvious what lies behind all these movements and countermovements. They begin in the dark and mysterious world of social attitudes. If we knew what brought on the "sexual revolution," we would understand more about the legal reaction, too. Many people feel that loose laws on personal behavior weaken family life, endanger public morality, and threaten the very health of society. This may or may not be true. But again, even if it is true, it is probably a mistake to blame the laws—or to assume that tightening up the laws will bring about a renaissance of sound morality. The legal system plays a part, to be sure, in the moral constitution of society, but it is a secondary, symbolic, and derivative role. The laws are symptoms; they are not the disease. Law responds to social movements, to forces that come and go, to deep rhythms and great powers that lie outside of the system itself.

The Criminal Process

So far we have talked mostly about laws on the statute books. Let us turn now to the criminal process, and take a look at the life cycle of a typical felony case, in California.[18] We begin, of course, with the crime itself, a burglary, let us say. Somebody climbs through a window into a house in Atherton, California, and steals jewelry, silver, and hi-fi equipment. The people who live in the house come home and find to their horror that somebody has broken in. They call the police.

All too often, alas, this is nearly the end of the story. Most break-ins are never solved; no arrests are made; the goods are never recovered. In 1971 in New York City, victims reported 501,951 felonies to the police; in four cases out of five, nothing more happened. The police made 100,739 felony arrests. Some of the people arrested were charged with more than one reported felony. Still, the police were able to "clear" by arrest only 111,824 of these half million felonies.[19] The situation has hardly improved since the 1970s. In 1993, only 44.2 percent of the violent crimes were "cleared by arrest," and a mere 17.4 percent of the property crimes; 65.6 percent of the murders led to an arrest, but only 13.1 percent of the burglaries.[20]

Our householders, let us assume, are among the lucky few. The police take notes, go off, and lo and behold, in due course they find a suspect and arrest him. The police now "book" the suspect, that is, they record the charges, photograph the man, and take his fingerprints. He goes before a magistrate (a judge), who tells him about his rights. This judge may also set bail, and may arrange for a "public defender," who will act as the suspect's lawyer. Sometimes the suspect will hire his own lawyer, if he has the money to do so.

The district attorney's office will make the next move. The staff will have to decide whether the case is strong enough to act on. Is there enough evidence to make prosecution worthwhile? If not, the case must be dropped. Let us suppose the DA thinks he can get a conviction. Before the man can be brought to trial, there is one more major hurdle. This is the "preliminary examination."

The preliminary examination is a kind of pretrial trial. It starts when the prosecutor files an "information," that is, formal charges. These proceedings, too, take place before a "magistrate," usually a municipal-court or police-court judge. There is no jury. Magistrates hear what the prosecution has to say. They do not decide whether the accused is actually guilty. The magistrate has three choices: to dismiss the charges and let the accused go free (if the prosecution seems to have no case); to knock the case down to a misdemeanor; or to decide that the state does have enough of a case so that it pays to go on to a full-scale trial. To do this, the case must be transferred to another court, a court that tries felonies. In California this would be the superior court.

In some states, this "information" method is not used. Screening is done by a different body, the grand jury. The grand jury is made up of laymen who are picked at random, like the members of an ordinary jury. The number of grand jurors varies. Texas law calls for not less than fifteen or more than twenty.[21] Grand jurors serve for a limited time. Prosecutors show their stuff to the grand jury, and ask for "indictments" against the accused. The grand jury decides whether to indict or not to indict. If it indicts, the case will go forward for felony trial. This alternative method (by way of the grand jury) is on the books in California, too, but the "information" method is much more common and is much preferred.

The prisoner's fate will be finally decided in superior court. The judge may, of course, dismiss the matter there, too, either on his or her own accord or because the prosecution decides not to press charges. The defendant can plead guilty and end the matter that way. His lawyer can file any one of a number of "motions" on points of law. The lawyer can, for instance, file a motion to suppress certain evidence, on the grounds that the state gathered it illegally. This motion usually fails; nonetheless, it is an irritant to those who would like the system to get tougher. Under the "victim's bill of rights" in California, adopted in 1982, "relevant evidence" is not to be "excluded in any criminal proceeding."[22]

Most felony cases do not get this far. Only a small minority actually go to trial. The rest fall by the wayside. Data from 1987–88 from a variety of places show a high rate of "attrition" in felony arrests. Out of one hundred arrests, only three will actually end up in trial; fifty-two will plead guilty. The rest will be rejected at initial screening or dismissed by the prosecutor or judge (six will be referred to "diversion programs" or other courts).[23]

Trials, then, are a relative rarity. Yet trials are the most dramatic and familiar way of deciding on innocence or guilt; they are what people see on *Court TV,* and what they see in dozens of movies. Not all trials, incidentally, go on before a jury. Defendants can waive their right to a jury. The judge will then handle the whole case. This is called a bench trial. If the defendant does not choose this route, the court proceeds to pick a jury.

A jury usually consists of twelve men and women chosen from the community. Twelve is the traditional and almost sacred number, but a few states (Arizona, for example) allow less in *some* serious cases, and most states allow for smaller juries—often six—for petty cases.[24] Jurors are supposed to be totally impartial. Lawyers on either side will question prospective jurors, and the lawyer can "challenge," that is, demand dismissal, if a juror seems unsuitable for one reason or another—a man is the defendant's brother-in-law, for example, or a woman says her mind is made up. (In some states, the judge conducts the question period.) A certain number of prospects, too, can be "peremptorily" challenged, that is, for no legal reason at all. A defendant's lawyer may have a hunch that this sour-faced, mean-looking man would be deadly for the defendant; the lawyer can get the man excused, using one of the defendant's precious stock of peremptory challenges. In Minnesota, for example, a defendant charged with an offense "punishable by life imprisonment" is entitled to fifteen of these challenges; the state can have nine. In all other cases, defendant can have five, the state three.[25] But these peremptory challenges cannot be used as a tool of race discrimination—as a way to get rid of black (or white) jurors systematically.[26]

Once the jury is chosen, the trial can begin. Both sides present their cases, usually through lawyers. They cross-examine each other's witnesses. The judge is supposed to see to it that the trial runs smoothly and correctly. The judge makes rulings on points of law and decides any questions that come up on questions of evidence. A police officer may want to testify, for example, about something the officer heard a witness say. If the defendant objects, claiming that this testimony is "hearsay," the judge will decide which side is right.

At the end of the case, the judge "instructs" the jury. That is, the judge recites the legal rules that are supposed to guide the jury in reaching its decision. Unfortunately, such instructions usually do not instruct very well. In past times—in the early nineteenth century, for example—judges gave the jury real explanations, in everyday language, about the relevant rules of law. Today, judges simply shovel out to the jury a mess of canned, stereotyped formulas, written in dense legalese. Legally speaking, these instructions are quite accurate; whether the jurors can make head or tail of them is much more doubtful. Curiously enough, in many states the judge will refuse to explain them any better even if the jury begs and pleads.[27]

In any event, the case now goes to the jury, and for the first time the jurors are truly in the driver's seat. They retire from the courtroom and deliberate in private. Generally speaking, a jury verdict in a criminal case *has* to be unanimous (in Oregon and Oklahoma, this rule has been weakened, but only for misdemeanors).[28] Sometimes a jury "hangs," that is, the members absolutely fail to agree. When this deadlock happens, the trial is at an end; the prosecution will either have to start over again from scratch with a brand-new trial or give up completely. In Kalven and Zeisel's major study of jury behavior, it was found that juries, overall, hang about 5 percent of the time. They acquit roughly a third of the defendants and convict the rest.[29] More recent figures suggest somewhat higher conviction rates: 84 percent in federal courts in 1990, and (in figures for the 1970s, at least), about three out of four in a sample of state courts. Kalven and Zeisel thought juries were more lenient than judges; the more recent figures suggest that perhaps this is no longer so. But the matter remains in some doubt.[30]

How the jury goes about deciding is mostly a secret. Some jurors have been willing to talk about what happened in the jury room, in high-profile cases like that of O. J. Simpson (1995). Social scientists have studied the process with various techniques. One is to look at experimental juries—panels of laypeople who are asked to decide hypothetical cases. There are obvious drawbacks to research that uses make-believe cases. But they do have one powerful advantage: researchers can manipulate variables one at a time, for scientific purposes. This cannot be done with the messy materials of real life.

Some of the research findings are of uncommon interest. They shed light, for example, on the hung jury. If only one juror holds out for conviction or acquittal, the jury does not end up hung. The sole dissenter—the "minority of one"—has a "lonely and unattractive" role. The other eleven are almost sure to convert him or her to their side. (In the movie *Twelve Angry Men,* a lone holdout ultimately brought the rest of the jury around; this is exceedingly rare in real life.) Support from even one other juror, however, makes a big difference to the holdout.[31]

Legally, the power of the jury is clear. If it finds the defendant not guilty, the defendant goes free. The jury decision is final. No matter how wrong or how foolish this seems, there is no appeal. If the jury convicts, the judge sets a date for sentencing. A convicted defendant can also try to appeal on the grounds of error at the trial. Generally speaking, "error" means legal error; it is not enough to say the jury must have been wrong, or failed to do justice, or acted stupidly. An appeal court does not try the case over again, or redecide issues of fact.

The more serious the case, the more likely that the defendant will appeal. Practically everybody sentenced to death will appeal—indeed, the case *must* be reviewed; in every state, an appeal is automatic whenever a death penalty is imposed. But overall only a small minority of losing defendants go on to a higher court. The rest give up and take their medicine.

Plea Bargaining and the Guilty Plea

It is a striking fact that trials, as described above and as the public knows them, are not the usual way a defendant's fate is decided. Most men and women behind bars did not get there because a jury put them there. They got there because they pleaded guilty. Overwhelmingly, this is the case. For the year 1992, only 4 percent of the men and women convicted of felonies got to that unhappy destination by way of jury trial. Another 4 percent were convicted at a bench trial, and 92 percent pleaded guilty.[32]

How does this happen? Why do defendants give up and call themselves guilty? Sometimes, no doubt, they do so out of shame, hopelessness, or remorse. But mostly the guilty plea is part of a "deal"—part of the practice called "plea bargaining" or "copping a plea." The prosecutor agrees to press for a lighter sentence, or to drop some charges, or to give the defendant a break in some other way; this is in exchange for a guilty plea, which avoids trial by jury. Plea bargaining has pushed the jury trial into a small corner of the criminal process. The big cases, the headline cases, still go before a jury: the trial of Patricia Hearst, or John Hinckley, who tried to kill President Reagan, or a celebrity defendant like O. J. Simpson. Ordinary cases, like the case of our house burglar, are unlikely to go to a jury. And the jury's role has been steadily shrinking over the years.

Plea bargaining is controversial. Some people defend it. Most people arrested, they say, are guilty anyway. Why bother with a trial? Why waste public money? Plea bargaining is a compromise: both sides give a little, get a little. Trials take time; there is always the chance of some slipup. It is best (for both sides) to avoid it.

On the other hand, many people feel that plea bargaining is a disgrace. "Law-and-order" people think it shows too much softness toward defendants. Dangerous criminals cop a plea and slip through the nets. Others argue that the process is unfair to defendants who are innocent, or who might have a good defense, if they only had a chance to show it. One study claimed that up to one-third of the people who plead guilty would be acquitted if they went to trial.[33]

This is a startling conclusion. But it does not mean that these people were in fact innocent of the crime, only that they had a legal excuse or that the evidence was weak. In any event, plea bargaining (so the argument goes) makes a mockery of criminal process. It certainly does not fit our image of due process or our picture of the adversary system. In general, as Herbert Jacob has put it, in the criminal-justice system today "the most important decisions are made in private—either in the prosecutor's office or in the judge's chambers."[34] Justice consists in the main of deals by lawyers in the back rooms or the courthouse corridors.

It is no surprise, then, that demands for reform have come from all sides. It has also been proposed, for example, that plea bargaining should come out of the closet; that it should take place more openly, with the judge participating all along.[35] Some prosecutors have tried to end plea bargaining. In Wayne County, Michigan, the prosecutor ordered his staff not to bargain in any case where the defendant used a gun. The attorney general of Alaska, in 1975, banned the practice of plea bargaining entirely. The voters of California, in a 1982 initiative ("Proposition Eight"), adopted a "victim's bill of rights" which, among other things, restricted plea bargaining. In California, the "three-strikes-and-you're-out" law (1994), which imposed extremely long sentences for three-time felony losers, specifically provided that "[p]rior felony convictions shall not be used in plea bargaining."[36]

But do these reforms actually work? Milton Heumann and Colin Loftin studied the Wayne County experiment. Did it really curb plea bargaining in Detroit? Their answer was, "Sort of." Plea bargaining in the literal sense was cut back. But "other mechanisms came into play" which were, they felt, "functional equivalents" of plea bargaining. Through a "mix" of techniques, the system "managed to digest" the new policies without really changing its ways.[37] The California restrictions of 1982 did not put a serious crimp in the practice. And the total ban in Alaska? As of 1990, a study showed that "limited forms of the practice" had "returned to most areas of the state."[38]

Why did this happen? Then again, why do we have plea bargaining in the first place? To many people the answer is simple. They assume that plea bargaining is a recent innovation and that it is a response to crowded conditions in urban courts. They connect plea bargaining with a deterioration in criminal justice over the last thirty years or so. Actually, plea bargaining is not as recent as most people think it is, and it is not found only in crowded urban courts.

In fact, there was never a golden age of full, fair trials. True, in 1800 or 1850 most defendants charged with serious crime did go before a jury. But trials were short, routine, cut-and-dried. Historical research on this point is skimpy, but consistent. John Langbein found these slap-dash trials in eighteenth-century England; another study confirmed this with a bit of research in the late-nineteenth-century records of Leon County, Florida (Tallahassee is the county seat). The average trial there took about half an hour. Case after case paraded before the jury. Few defendants had lawyers. Justice was careless and swift.[39]

In other words, hasty, routine processing did not begin with plea bargaining at all. Plea bargaining changes the style and the place. Quick, rough justice has moved from the jury box and the courtroom, to the corridors of the courthouse, to judges' chambers, to the offices of lawyers.

Plea bargaining itself goes back more than a century. One study found it, for example, in Alameda County, California, in the 1880s.[40] Judges in the county even talked about the way they gave "credit" for guilty pleas. Plea bargaining was not as pervasive as it is now—not even close to it—but it was by no means rare.

There is plea bargaining in England, too, apparently, but in other systems of law, on the continent of Europe, there is nothing exactly like it. Plea bargaining depends on a central feature of our system: the guilty plea. In some legal systems, there is no such plea. Of course, a defendant can confess his crimes, and a confession is powerful evidence of guilt. But, at least in theory, the state must still prove its case. Our system is different. The guilty plea is accepted as truth; except in very rare cases, it puts an end to the proceedings. Once a defendant pleads guilty, the trial is over. There is nothing left but sentencing.

The guilty plea, too, goes back many years. In 1839, in New York State, one out of every four criminal cases ended with a guilty plea. By the middle of the century, there were guilty pleas in half the cases. In Alameda County, one out of three felony defendants pleaded guilty as charged in the decade 1900–1910. In the 1920s, guilty pleas accounted for 88 out of 100 convictions in New York City, 85 out of 100 in Chicago, 70 out of 100 in Dallas, and 79 out of 100 in Des Moines, Iowa.[41] It has kept its dominance ever since. In short, we can trace a steady, marked decline in trial by jury from the early nineteenth century on.

The Professionalization of Criminal Justice

Why is trial by jury declining? This is, in part, only one aspect of a larger, long-term trend—the professionalization of criminal justice. If we could go back in time two centuries and watch criminal justice at work, we would be struck by how much it was dominated by laypeople, amateurs. There were no public prosecutors in England. If somebody robbed a storekeeper, the storekeeper himself had to prosecute. There was nothing like the modern district attorney. If the storekeeper did nothing, the case simply vanished. There were also no defense attorneys; and the jury, of course, was a panel of amateurs.

In the United States, unlike England, there was a public prosecutor, the district attorney, from colonial times on. But even this was usually a part-time job; private prosecution was quite common well into the nineteenth century. Police science as we know it did not exist in colonial times and in the early republic. Indeed, neither did the police. The first police force, in the modern sense, was established in London, England, in 1829. New York City had a police force by 1845. Even so, the New York patrolman was "essentially an amateur . . . little more than an ordinary citizen delegated with legal power."[42] It was not until the twentieth century that police forces became truly professional, that is, specially trained for their work.[43]

Today the criminal-justice system is awash in professionals: public defenders, probation officers, social workers, detectives. Criminal justice makes use of "science" in the most literal sense: ballistics authorities, pathologists working for the coroner's office, fingerprint experts, experts on DNA. In short, the center of gravity has moved dramatically away from a system controlled by laypeople to a system controlled and dominated by experts and full-timers of various sorts. The decline of the jury (and the grand jury, too) is part of this general development. Plea bargaining, then, is merely the modern, professional version of routine processing. It is the same process, in essence, as the slapdash trials of Leon County, Florida, in the nineteenth century, but under new and professional management.

Punishments and Corrections

Conviction by judge or jury is not, of course, the end of the line. The defendant now faces sentencing. In many ways, this phase of the process is more important to the defendant than what went before. Most defendants, after all, plead guilty. Their only question is, what will my punishment be?

Generally speaking, the law vests great power and discretion in the judge. The judge has many options and much leeway. Some defendants will pay a fine and some will get "probation," a kind of conditional freedom; this will be especially true of first offenders. A lot depends, of course, on what the crime is. "I'm a first offender, give me a chance" is not an argument that works in a murder case; 95 percent of convicted murderers go to prison or jail. For convicted burglars, the figure is 75 percent; for those convicted of larceny, only 65 percent.[44] These figures are for 1988. In the atmosphere of "toughness" that has prevailed since the 1980s, more and more states are prescribing mandatory minimum sentences for certain crimes—drug offenses, or crimes in which the accused uses a gun.

We are used to thinking of prison or jail as the basic punishment for serious crime. Yet before the nineteenth century, imprisonment was rarely used for punishing criminals. Jails were for people who could not pay their debts, or for people waiting for trial who were not out on bail for one reason or another. In colonial Massachusetts, criminals were whipped, fined, put in the stocks, branded with a hot iron, and in especially serious cases banished or hanged. This was true in England, too. The mother country made heavier use of the gallows, and also "transported" convicts to the colonies. Australia began as a penal colony.

The modern prison or penitentiary was a nineteenth-century invention (if "invention" is the right word). The United States was among its social pioneers. An early example was the "penitentiary house" at the Walnut Street prison in Philadelphia, with sixteen little cells for solitary confinement. The classic penitentiaries of this period, the first third of the nineteenth century, were Cherry Hill in Philadelphia and Auburn and Sing Sing in New York State. These were huge, forbidding structures with thick outer walls and strong cells with iron bars.

In these dour prisons, convicts lived one to a cell. They lived in a world of total silence, and in an isolation broken only by hard labor. During the entire term in prison, and this could be years, not a word was supposed to be spoken. Life in this quiet tomb was completely regimented; each day was exactly like the next, every prisoner getting up at the same time as all others, going to bed at the same time, wearing the same uniform, eating the same food. It was in theory a kind of radical surgery, meant to separate the prisoner totally from the corruption and rot of society. The iron discipline of prison would give the prisoner a chance to repent and to learn new habits of life.[45]

In its classical form, the penitentiary system did not last very long. The "Big House" remained, architecturally speaking; we recognize it clearly in dozens of Hollywood prison movies and from such living museums as San Quentin. By the time of the Civil War, there were clear signs that the "silent" system would have to be abandoned. For one thing, it would not work unless prisoners were housed one to a cell. But this was expensive, and the legislatures were far too stingy to provide for solitary confinement for everybody.

When the silent system disappeared, so did the theory that isolation and regimentation at hard labor would cure criminals of their habits. The late nineteenth century turned to new schemes of reform: parole, probation, the indeterminate sentence. These were geared toward dividing convicts into two classes, the hopeless incorrigibles and those who could be saved and returned to society; the aim of penal practice was to sift out the savable ones and severely punish the others. New York began to experiment with the indeterminate sentence in the 1870s. In its developed form, it rested on a simple idea: the judge would no longer fix the defendant's sentence. Rather, he would prescribe some minimum (one year, as a rule). In prison, the convict would be carefully observed, graded and marked like a schoolchild. If he behaved and showed the right character, he would earn a light sentence and early release. If not, he would rot in prison. Some people, so the theory went, should never be released. That would be as senseless as letting loose "people suffering from leprosy."[46]

The indeterminate sentence spread rapidly among the states. Along with it went the parole system, a program to let promising convicts out early, under supervision. Probation was another reform. It gave convicted criminals (especially first offenders) a chance to escape prison altogether. Probation, too, was (at least in theory) a kind of supervised freedom at the end of a rather taut string: one wrong move, and the criminal justice system would jerk its end of the string and the probationer would land in jail. Still another innovation was a special court for young people, called the juvenile court. The first true court of this kind was established for Cook County, Illinois, in 1899. By 1945, every state had juvenile courts.

These reforms had one trait in common: they were relatively professionalized. They also vested great discretion in parole boards or juvenile judges or probation officers. These reforms also shifted emphasis from the offense to the offender. Decisions were highly subjective, and varied from case to case, from defendant to defendant. Probation officers, for example, were not bound by narrow, legal rules of evidence. They were allowed to investigate the whole background and character of the defendants. Early probation reports in California show graphically what kind of evidence a probation officer might gather. One 1907 report, about a sixteen-year-old boy, solemnly announces that he smoked about ten cigarettes a day, masturbated, had been to a house of prostitution three times, and read magazines; however, he had no library card.[47] This information was all legally irrelevant, but it could mean the difference between freedom and iron bars.

Still, probation was in many ways a reform, a step toward leniency. In operation, it no doubt often worked in an unfair and arbitrary way. But it kept some people out of prison and saved their lives or their souls. Partly because it was so subjective, so discretionary, a reaction has set in in recent years. Decisions of parole boards, too, have been criticized as far too random, too personal, for a system of justice and due process.

Even more important has been the reaction from the law-and-order side. The rampaging crime rate frightens and outrages people, as it should; fear of crime focuses attention on any part of the system that can be accused (however unfairly) of "coddling criminals." The indeterminate sentence rested on a kind of faith in rehabilitation. At least some prisoners would benefit from prison: prison experience would reform them. Rightly or wrongly, hardly anybody believes this anymore—certainly hardly anybody in the general public.

In the 1980s and 1990s, crime became perhaps the number one domestic issue. The demand now was for tougher and tougher measures. Few political figures can or do resist. But "tough" means long, flat sentences. California, among other states, has gotten rid of the indeterminate sentence. Parole, too, is under attack: Maine has abolished its parole board, and so has Illinois. As we noted, some states have tried to impose mandatory sentences for certain crimes. California, and other states, adopted "three-strikes" laws in the 1990s; under California's law, a third "serious" felony brings about a mandatory long, harsh sentence. Minnesota pioneered a program of "sentencing guideliness," to promote uniformity in sentences and to cut down the discretion of judges. Federal guidelines went into effect in 1987.[48]

Like programs to abolish plea bargaining, these changes in law never quite work out as advertised or hoped. Many judges are uncomfortable with the rigidity (and inhumanity) of some of the harsher mandatory laws; it is not just a question of protecting their turf, although that might be a factor with some. The prisons are bulging. It is doubtful, though, that all this activity really makes a dent in the crime rate; rates of homicide and the like did seem to pause for breath in the 1990s, but it is far from clear why this happened.

And what about the death penalty? This is the most controversial, gaudiest, most extreme form of punishment. Not every state has it— Minnesota, Wisconsin, and Michigan, for example, do not—and of those that do, some use it only rarely. We will deal with this king of "corrections" in Chapter 11.

Class, Race, Power, and Criminal Justice

The criminal justice system is where law most openly shows its teeth. Here are the clubs and handcuffs of the police, the cells and walls of San Quentin, the gas chamber and the electric chair; here is the jailhouse and the riot squad. The police constitute the armed forces of civil authority. The police have tear gas and guns. They are the sworn enemies of crime and disorder. But they can also pound their fists on dissenters, or oppress the weak and powerless. History, alas, makes it clear that society can and does use power for evil ends. The police state is all too real, in many parts of the world.

What about the United States? Does criminal justice treat people fairly? Does it fall more heavily on the poor and the powerless, on black people and other minorities? Does it reflect the values of men rather than women, to the detriment of women? It seems clear that there are biases in the system; many of them are more or less covert. As to race, the days of lynch mobs are, happily, over. But if race prejudice is present in society as a whole, why would we expect criminal justice to be free of this curse?

Many studies have tried to measure bias in the system, with some degree of rigor. As noted in Chapter 4, the results are surprisingly inconclusive. One study reviewed more than seventy research projects that had tried to ferret out race prejudice in the sentencing process alone. Some of these studies came to the conclusion that there was race prejudice; some came to the opposite conclusion. Does that mean that the case is not proved? There are surely individual judges, however, who betray bias against race.[49] But what of the system as a whole?

Bias may come in many forms. There can be bias in the rules themselves. Rules may be tilted in favor of (say) landlords and not tenants, or in favor of the state and not defendants. This bias would affect outcomes even if judges, police, and prosecutors applied the rules fairly and evenly. Or the rules might classify as criminal certain patterns of behavior that are more common in some communities than others. Or crime may be more of a temptation among people who are poor, downtrodden, despised, and shut off from legitimate opportunity. If we look only at the way the rules are applied, the system might seem quite fair, fairer than it really is.

These considerations are not just theory. The "war on drugs" weighs much more heavily on black users and dealers than on whites. More black users and dealers are arrested, proportionately, than white users and dealers. Crack cocaine—associated with blacks—is treated in the law much more harshly than powder cocaine; and in 1991–92, more than 91 percent of all federal crack defendants were black.[50] As a result, thousands of blacks are jailed, and for longer terms than whites; the bias is in the law itself.

Bias can also work more subtly, and at an early point in the process. Suppose the manager of a boutique catches a well-dressed white woman in the act of stealing a hat. He may quietly take back the hat and show the woman out the door with a warning, rather politely. Later he finds a black teenager shoplifting. This time he delivers the teenager straight to the police. If this happened consistently, throughout the city, arrest figures would suggest that most shoplifters were black. That, of course, would be misleading. The police themselves might have a double standard as between rich and poor, black and white, in deciding whether to book a person or let him go.

That something is wrong, and that race is a factor, is obvious on the surface from the most elementary statistics. About 7 percent of the black male population is in prison; the figure for white men is about 1 percent. Black men in prison in 1995 outnumbered white men—about 735,200 black men, approximately 10,000 more than whites. (Blacks are about 12 percent of the American population.) In fact, in Georgia in 1995, 24 percent of the young black men of the state were under the jurisdiction of the criminal justice system—almost 9 percent in prison or jail, another 15 percent or so either on probation or on parole.[51] In other places, the figures are even worse.

How much of this appalling situation is the bitter fruit of discrimination, direct or indirect? Undoubtedly, although there is a great deal of bias in enforcement and in the norms, African-Americans do seem responsible for more than their share of crimes, including violent crimes. Why is this so? African-Americans are weaker than whites in economic and political power; they have higher rates of unemployment. But as Austin Turk has pointed out, "powerlessness does not explain very much. Women have less power in this society than men, yet women make a very feeble showing at crime."[52] Indeed, in 1979, women were only 4 percent of the country's prisoners. By the end of 1993, the proportion had risen slightly—to something over 5 percent.[53] Crime is definitely not an equal-opportunity activity.

Indeed, women's complaints were of a different nature: that the system tended to ignore them as *victims*—making light of domestic violence, and treating them unfairly as victims of rape and sexual harassment. In response to these complaints, the laws have been overhauled in major ways in the last two decades; police departments are more sensitive to domestic violence, and make more arrests. And the law of rape has been substantially recast.[54]

The huge disproportion between the experiences of blacks and whites in regard to criminal justice is another matter. It is a brute fact, and a disturbing one. Moreover, black and white perceptions of criminal justice are radically different. Most blacks feel that the police, and the criminal-justice system in general, are incurably racist. Blacks feel they know this from their own personal experience. They can also read about it in the newspapers and see it on TV. The Rodney King incident reinforced these beliefs. King was a black motorist stopped by policemen in Los Angeles, in 1991; the police proceeded to beat him unmercifully. By chance, a resident of a nearby house captured the incident on video. Even though the policemen had been caught red-handed, an all-white jury, in April 1992, acquitted them, touching off a wild riot in Los Angeles.[55] As the country moves toward a policy of more and more prisons and tougher and tougher sentences, the impact on minorities can only grow, and the disaffection of these communities is likely to increase.

The Rights Revolution

We hear a lot today about the "rights revolution," about tenderness toward criminal defendants, about the way courts "coddle" criminals, about due process of law. How much of this is real and how much is talk? When we ask whether trials are basically fair, we must remember that most people accused of crime never go to trial. Their rights are decided in other ways, often through plea bargaining. For those who do go to trial, how much concern does the law show for defendants' rights?

And how does this solicitude compare with times past?

The basic rights of defendants are, of course, quite old. The Bill of Rights—attached to the federal Constitution more than two hundred years ago—is a kind of minicode of criminal procedure. It prohibits cruel and unusual punishment, unreasonable searches and seizures, and excessive bail. It guarantees trial by jury and the writ of habeas corpus (a protection against illegal imprisonment). Compared to justice in other countries, and especially in the dictatorships, American criminal justice is a shining example, and always has been.

But no country is perfect, or even close to it. The Bill of Rights is, after all, only a bunch of words—an expression of a goal, an ideal. Actual practice fell and falls far short. There is much to be ashamed of in our national past. There is, in particular, a sorry record of police brutality and unfair prosecution of unpopular defendants—by no means ended, as the Rodney King incident shows.[56] There is also a history of lynch law, and a deep, dark stain of racist justice, especially in the South. The vigilantes were not as admirable as some people think—they were sometimes little better than a lynch mob themselves. People outside the mainstream have usually found little protection from criminal justice—quite the opposite. Moreover, the system has often cut corners, dealing with people accused of crime in a slapdash, indifferent way. Sometimes, at least, corner-cutting ends up convicting the innocent. Prisons have often been citadels of cruelty and rape, in which the weak are terrorized both by the prison authorities and by the more vicious prisoners.

But the past is dead. What is the current situation, and in what direction are we going? The *formal* rights of criminal defendants have expanded enormously, especially since the 1950s, with the Supreme Court under Earl Warren leading the way. In *Miranda v. Arizona,*[57] the Supreme Court addressed the question of the rights of people arrested by police. The police must inform the suspect of his constitutional rights, including his right to say nothing. If this warning is not given, the court can refuse to allow the defendant's words to be used as evidence. It has become a standard practice for police to give the "Miranda warning" to anyone picked up for a serious crime.

Does *Miranda* make much difference? Maybe the police simply mumble a verbal formula, or find other ways to browbeat the people they arrest.[58] Perhaps. But *Miranda* was only one of a whole series of decisions by the Warren Court (and like-minded state courts); the net effect of the cases as a whole may be far greater than the effect of any single decision. Police and prosecutors may have to be more sensitive to due process than in the past, before courts (and civil-rights organizations) were constantly looking over their shoulders. In *Gideon v. Wainwright*,[59] the Supreme Court took another bold step. In this case, out of Florida, the Court decided that a person accused of a felony has a right to a lawyer. If there is no money to hire one, the state must provide one, and pay the bill. This case, at least, did have an effect, if not on the system in general, then on thousands of lives and thousands of cases.

The criminal justice system is headline news, and the subject of great controversy. Crime (especially crime in the streets) is a terrible social problem. At the same time, the "rights revolution"—the expansion of due process, and a heightened public consciousness of right—is an established fact. People who speak for the poor, for black people, and for other racial minorities complain bitterly about the behavior of police, prisons, and the rest of the system. The system, in other words, is under attack from both the right and the left, from those who think it is too soft and those who think it is too hard. At the moment, the hard-liners are definitely in the saddle. Both parties—and the majority of the public—want a tighter, tougher system.

In some regards, however, there is no going back. The "due process" camp won many victories, in and out of court, and these victories are hard to reverse. But in other areas, there have been both reform and reaction. Bail law is one example. A person who is arrested and charged with a crime does not always sit in jail until his case comes up; he is often released "on bail," that is, after he puts up some money as security. He forfeits the bail if he does not show up for trial. The Eighth Amendment forbids "excessive bail," but even a fairly modest amount of bail looks excessive to somebody poor or unemployed. Bail makes a tremendous difference to the outcome of cases. People out on bail can prepare their defense better; they can also go about their daily lives. A person in jail is suffering a kind of punishment, even if he is found innocent in the end. He loses freedom, and he might also lose his job. Hence, reformers proposed letting people go free before trial, on their word of honor, if they seemed like good risks. People with ties to the community are not likely to skip out on the court. Release of this kind was promoted by the Manhattan Bail Project of the 1960s, a project funded by the Vera Foundation. Congress passed a Bail Reform Act in 1966 for the federal courts; other states developed their own versions.[60] But bail reform, too, became a prisoner of the search for toughness. In the 1980s, new bail "reform" laws were passed, this time not so much to help poor defendants as to protect the public from the release of defendants who were potentially dangerous.[61]

The prisoners' rights movement is also worth mentioning. It led to the establishment of grievance procedures in prisons and helped curb some of the worst abuses of the prison system. Starting in the 1960s, a dramatic series of cases, brought by and on behalf of prisoners, have led to decisions which have expanded the scope of due process within prisons and declared illegal some of the most shocking aberrations from humane penal policy.[62]

But reforms have a depressing tendency to dribble out into nothing. Malcolm Feeley reviewed the evidence on the impact of bail reform, sentence reform, and "pretrial diversion," that is, the plan to siphon off certain defendants before trial (for example, those with mental problems or alcohol problems) by referring them to more appropriate social agencies. He found that planned changes or reforms accomplished very little. Of course, important changes do occur in the criminal-justice system, but they usually emerge quietly, in unanticipated ways, or because of changes going on in society at large.[63]

In truth, the criminal-justice system is hard to deal with, in either direction. This is the message of Feeley's book. He looked at hard-line reforms as well as soft-line reforms. New York, under Governor Nelson Rockefeller, passed a Draconian drug law, meant to put pushers in jail. This law (and others like it) had, on the whole, as little effect as the softhearted laws. There was "little measurable deterrent effect on narcotics use"; the law was "astronomically expensive to administer, and it led to harsh sentences for marginal offenders." In 1979, the law was repealed.[64] Failure has also been the experience, by and large, of perennial attempts to put teeth into laws against drunk driving. Experiments in tougher enforcement sometimes work, as experiments, but the system soon lapses back into its old ways.[65] The California "three-strikes" law, adopted with such fanfare in the 1990s, was almost immediately assailed as a costly failure, for all sorts of reasons.[66]

We can compare the criminal-justice system to a leaky garden hose, full of holes. If you try to turn up the pressure at one end, the extra water simply squirts out of holes in the middle. In many ways, the criminal-justice system is just such a leaky hose.

Is it really a *system* at all? The word "system" suggests some sort of rational organization, some sort of overall coordination. Criminal justice is a pseudosystem at best. Nobody is really in charge. Everybody can frustrate the work of everybody else. The legislature can pass laws, but cannot enforce them. The police can arrest people, but they have no way to guarantee prosecution. The prosecutor can prosecute, but cannot be sure the court will convict. The judge can sentence people, but cannot keep them in prison. The jury can disregard the judge; the judge can disregard the jury. And so it goes. The system, in short, is "decentralized, fragmented, made up of bits and pieces." It is "like some . . .

primitive beast, with primeval power to regenerate; snip off a leg, an arm, an organ here and there . . . , the missing part simply grows back. No brain is in control, no central nervous system."[67] For better or for worse, this is the system as it is.

10

Constitutional Law and Civil Liberties

*N*O ONE CAN write about or discuss the American legal system seriously without taking account of a document whose two hundredth birthday has come and gone: the American Constitution. The Constitution dates from 1787, which probably makes it the oldest written constitution still in force. It is certainly the most legally active. It is not, of course, quite the same document it was in 1787. The Constitution has been amended twenty-six times; some of the amendments (the First and the Fourteenth, for example) have been extraordinarily important. But when we consider how the world has changed since 1787, twenty-six amendments do not seem like a lot. Twelve of these had been added to the Constitution by 1804; there have been only fourteen since.

A note of caution. When we talk about the influence or effect of the Constitution, we must remember that the Constitution in itself is only a piece of paper. There is no magic in words and phrases. It is not the American Constitution that is powerful, but the American constitutional *system*. It is a system made up, first, of public attitudes toward the Constitution, and second, of behavior patterns and institutions that have grown up around the Constitution. The Constitution itself, important as it is, well crafted as it is, could not and cannot account for the constitutional system, for the living law of the American Constitution.

The experience of other countries proves this point. Dozens of countries have written constitutions, but some of these are little more than bad jokes played on the public. For example, the 1982 constitution of the People's Republic of China is full of glittering, noble phrases. It promises "freedom of speech, of the press, of assembly, of association, of procession and of demonstration" (Article 35). These promises, of course, have very little to do with living law or the structure of power in China. In this regard, the Chinese constitution has plenty of company. On the other hand, the British have no written constitution, no firm "guarantees" of liberty. Parliament in theory is utterly supreme, more powerful on paper than the Chinese state. Yet Britain is a pretty democratic place, and the rule of law is healthier there than in many countries with beautiful constitutions.

Whatever the situation elsewhere, constitutional government is a strong force to be reckoned with in the United States. It is part of the fabric of American life. The American Constitution is living law because it is enforced; Article 35 of the Chinese constitution is not. The United States Constitution is made into living law through a variety of means. There is, very notably, enforcement through the courts, by means of "judicial review." This refers to the power of the courts to decide if laws and acts of the other branches of government, or of the state and local governments, are valid or not, constitutionally speaking, and to reduce these acts to zero if they fail the test. The courts are not the only guardians of the constitutional system, but they are a powerful and important one. Indeed, when people talk about "constitutional law," they usually mean doctrines and understandings that courts have invented, developed, and spread.

These doctrines and understandings may be rooted in the text of the Constitution (and in theory they must be). But the Founding Fathers would hardly recognize these doctrines and understandings today. As we asked in an earlier chapter, what would Jefferson say if he were told that today "freedom of speech" seems to mean that magazines can print pictures of naked people making love? What would he make of the argument that "privacy," including the right to an abortion, is guaranteed by the Constitution? Or that the commerce clause allows Washington to tell farmers how many peanuts they can grow?

The Constitution, in short, is what the judges say it is, as Chief Justice Charles Evans Hughes once bluntly put it. What they say is said in the context of actual cases. Actual cases arise out of real disputes between real litigants. They are always a product of their times. They reflect the social issues of the day; hence, realistically, it is these issues that are the immediate sources, or incentives, for the creation of constitutional law.

This is a basic fact of our constitutional system. It is important not to stress judges and courts unduly. Constitutional behavior is more than judicial behavior. Constitutional law begins outside the courtroom: it begins with claims of constitutional right. Also, there are traditions of behavior and understanding, quite independent of judges and courts. The First Amendment guarantees freedom of speech; so do all the state constitutions. Yet the Supreme Court did not decide an important free-speech case until *Schenck v. United States* (1919).[1] Schenck was convicted of violating the 1917 Espionage Act during the First World War. Schenck was an opponent of the war; he mailed a document out to draftees, attacking the war and the draft.

By then, the First Amendment was over a century old. Yet the federal courts had said almost nothing about the meaning and limits of freedom of speech. During those years, the federal government took many actions which would be considered gross violations of our speech rights today. On the other hand, there was never general censorship of the press during peacetime. Wide-open political debate was always possible, on a scale that few other countries achieve even today. Freedom of speech, then, was part of our basic tradition. That tradition, however, is not immutable; it changes at the margins, and, at times, in its very core. The essential point is this: constitutionalism is more behavior than theory, in every period of history.

But one should look at theory, too. The place to begin is with the Constitution itself. Its basic idea is simple. The Constitution is the supreme law of the land. It is the highest authority. No person and no branch of government—not the president, not Congress, certainly not the police officer on the beat—has the right to set the Constitution aside; its words and its rules are law.

In the early republic, the powers and role of the courts—treated only briefly in the constitution itself—were far from settled. In the famous case of *Marbury v. Madison* (1803),[2] the great chief justice John Marshall first exercised the mighty power of judicial review to strike down an act passed by the United States Congress. The issue was a technical one: did the Supreme Court have the authority to issue a certain kind of legal writ, called a mandamus, against the secretary of state? An act of Congress gave it the authority; but the Constitution (as Marshall read it) restricted the Supreme Court to appeals, except for a few narrow, specific exceptions. Thus the act of Congress conflicted with the Constitution, and Marshall boldly set it aside. Many of Marshall's critics attacked this decision as a naked assertion of power, and one that was not justified by anything in the text. But the case—and the principle—held firm.

Judicial review is not, of course, solely a federal power. The state courts exercise it, too; each state, after all, has its own constitution. State legislatures, not to mention city hall and the various state agencies, must conform to the state constitution—and the constitution of Nebraska (to paraphrase Hughes) is what the Supreme Court of Nebraska says it is. The power of judicial review, state and federal, is now so deeply ingrained in our system that it is hard to imagine our legal world without it.

Nonetheless, judicial review is still subject to debate. For one thing, it is "countermajoritarian." That is to say, nobody elects the Supreme Court. The voters elect congressmen, senators, presidents to govern them. Why should the Court overturn what the public decides, through its representatives? True, the Constitution is the highest law of the land. But it is really naive to claim that the Supreme Court only "interprets" the text, that is, that it does nothing more than ask what the document means or what it meant to the people who wrote it. The Court goes far beyond anything that can reasonably be called "interpretation." The Court invents and expands constitutional doctrine, and some of this doctrine is connected to the text by gossamer threads, if at all.

Hence the Supreme Court, and courts generally, have immense power in this society. Some scholars—and many political figures—are wary of this power. They want more "restraint." They want the court to confine itself to what the Constitution "actually means." But this is easier said than done. What *does* the constitution "mean"? Is it even possible to detect a "meaning" for these ancient words? And must the meaning be the same now as it was in 1787? The world has changed enormously since then. Should the Constitution stay the same?

Hundreds of books, articles, essays, statements, manifestos, and judicial opinions have wrestled with the problem of judicial review, and how to justify it in a democratic society. One strong position is that the Court has a duty to give meaning to the constitutional *system,* in particular to enforce basic human rights, and especially the rights of minorities. As far as the text is concerned, those who take this position prefer, of course, to ground the Court's work in the text. But they insist that the text itself allows us to depart from the text, paradoxical as that might sound. The Constitution is a living, evolving document, they say. And it was intended to be such. Its words express principles, not rigid rules.

The point is to prevent the "tyranny of the majority." Majority rule, the argument goes, is a good idea in general, but there is nothing absolute about it. The majority is not always right. Freedom is a value which everybody ought to enjoy, whether the voters think so or not. The rights of minorities are especially important, they would add, in a country like the United States, where people of different races, religions, nationalities, lifestyles, and political beliefs all have to live together. We cannot allow a majority to squash the rights of people the majority does not like, or does not agree with. The Supreme Court must insist that these rights are respected. That is what the constitutional system means.

There is no question that the Court, in large part, agrees with this view—or at least *behaves* as if it did. Indeed, minority rights are one of the great themes of constitutional history. In case after case, issues have turned on the claims of some member of a despised minority, or the litigant was a person who held hateful opinions or was weak, deviant, or powerless. In *Yick Wo v. Hopkins*,[3] a Chinese laundryman in San Francisco made legal history; in *Gideon v. Wainwright*,[4] it was a middle-aged, drunken no-good; in *Terminiello v. Chicago*,[5] a rabid racist and anti-Semite. Through the cases parade an amazing battalion of underdogs: outcasts, the downtrodden, or those who are just plain different— Jehovah's Witnesses, sharecroppers, pornographers, rabble-rousers, "reds," and born-again troublemakers.

Some scholars also look to the Court as the only place in this society where we can expect cool, rational, high-minded debate on controversial issues. Some of these are issues so hotly disputed that they threaten to tear us apart. The Court and the Court alone is strong enough and independent enough to tackle these issues. The justices have life tenure. They draw their paychecks no matter who is president, no matter who controls Congress, no matter what the Gallup Poll reports about public opinion. Laurence Tribe, championing the court and its work, put it this way: "By debating our deepest differences in the shared language of constitutional rights and responsibilities, and in the terms of an enacted constitutional *text,* we create the possibility of persuasion and even moral education in our national life," looking not toward a "permanent reconciliation of conflicting impulses but toward a judicially modulated unending struggle."[6]

This may be more than a trifle overstated or romanticized. The Court is certainly aware of political feeling—indeed, in many ways, it is political to the core. It has done more than its share of backpedaling, and it has certainly been known to give way to sentiments we would now label as prejudice. Its overall record on civil liberties is far from perfect—some would argue that, on balance, and if we put to one side a few famous and atypical cases, the Court's record on resisting popular hysteria is rather poor. To take just one example, it meekly ratified sending Japanese-Americans to concentration camps during the Second World War.[7]

There is no need, then, to romanticize the Court or to put it on a pedestal. But all in all, it does remain a strongly independent body, and its sensitivity to enlightened opinion is not to be sneezed at. In our times, many people feel that social justice, overall, gets a far better shake—or at least a far more sympathetic *hearing*—in the marble halls of the Court than in the back rooms of political life.

It is possible, then, to justify the astonishing power of courts, even in a democratic society. The power is not random or willful; the Supreme Court (and the other courts) are nothing if not careful and responsible. They consider a wide range of factors—including narrowly legal ones. The debate over the role of the courts goes on, as it has since *Marbury v. Madison.* It will continue. Meanwhile, the Court does its work, and the country, by and large—with a few egregious exceptions—tends to accept the results.

Another point is worth making: there is a big difference between long-run and short-run values. The Constitution tried to set up a plan for the long haul. Short-run pressures pour in every day, on Congress, the president, and the rest of the government. This tempts them to hasty actions which they may live to regret. Public opinion, too, is excitable, volatile. The Constitution (fiercely guarded by the courts) can cancel or prevent mistakes of the moment; we may all be better off in the end when we are forced (by the courts) to resist short-term temptation.

An analogy may be helpful. Two friends set out for a party on New Year's Eve. One of them, as he knows, has a drinking problem. He gives his friend the keys to the car, and says: "Don't let me drive if I get drunk, no matter what." At the party, he drinks too much—just as he feared. Drunk, he demands the keys. But the promise was "constitutional"; even though he begs, coaxes, and pleads, the friend refuses to give up the keys. The drunken man is angry, disappointed. He complains loudly that his friend is unfair. After all, it is his car; they are his keys. But in the cool, pearly light of morning, he will be glad his friend refused him and stuck to his guns.

The Constitution and the courts that give it meaning are, of course, the keepers of the keys.

Stepchildren of Research: The State Constitutions

If you study constitutional law or constitutional history in college or law school, you study the federal Constitution and the way courts interpret it. Yet every one of the states has its own constitution, too. State constitutions are significant documents in their own right. They are the highest law within each particular state. State courts have the last word, by and large, on questions of state constitutional law. The California constitution affects the rights and duties of more than thirty million residents; this makes the California Supreme Court, prime interpreter of the California constitution, an important institution indeed. The same can be said for the Court of Appeals of New York—or, for that matter, the Supreme Court of Wyoming.

State constitutions are by no means pale imitations of the federal Constitution. Of course, the states have been influenced by the Constitution of 1787. For example, they all have bills of rights, patterned more or less on the federal Bill of Rights. This is, in a way, repayment of an ancient debt; the federal Bill of Rights drew heavily on some of the early state constitutions, for example, Virginia's. Since 1787, the federal Constitution has been a powerful model for the states. But the state constitutions differ greatly from each other and from the federal Constitution, both in structure and in detail.

There are many provisions in state constitutions that have no counterpart in the federal document. Many states, in the second half of the nineteenth century, enacted special restrictions on the power of their legislatures. Some legislatures had been, alas, quite corrupt and richly deserved distrust. Maryland, in 1851, took away the legislative power to grant divorces, set up lotteries, spend money for canals and railroads, and go into debt by more than $100,000.[8] Many states outlawed "local or special laws" or "private" laws. (Congress still has this power; as we saw, it can, and does, pass laws that apply to only a single person, place, or event.)

Many states also put constitutional limits on the *form* of laws. One common provision provides that no law should cover more than one "subject"; this subject has to be "expressed in the title."[9] The point is to keep a crafty senator or assemblyman from slipping some pet provision into a bill and getting it by the senate or assembly unawares. Whether a statute covers more than one topic is a fairly subjective judgment. Hence this provision gave the judiciary another meat ax to butcher legislation.[10] The clause, in state constitutions, has been a fertile source of litigation. It has no equivalent in the federal Constitution.

State constitutions have generally had more tangled histories than the federal Constitution. The federal Constitution has been, on the whole, a model of stability. It has been amended, but never overthrown—though the Civil War, of course, was a major crisis for the constitutional system. Only a few of the states (Wisconsin is one) have made do with a single constitution. Louisiana, at the other extreme, has had nine or ten, depending on how one counts. The Louisiana constitution of 1864 was replaced in 1868; the constitution of 1868 was replaced in 1879; this one lasted only until 1898. The 1898 version had 326 articles; it fixed the governor's salary at $5,000 and had twenty-eight separate provisions that dealt with the government of New Orleans.

This was a classic case of constitutional bloat. It was a far cry from the federal model, in which the document sets out the core framework of government, lists basic principles and rights, and then leaves it at that. Constitutions like Louisiana's of 1898 are actually a kind of super-statute. No wonder that these constitutions are continually tinkered with or replaced. These detailed constitutions are terribly brittle. The federal Constitution, broad and sweeping, bends with the wind and does not break.

Amendments

The Constitution is the highest law of the land, but it can be amended. Under Article V, Congress can propose amendments, which go into effect when "ratified by the Legislatures of three fourths of the several States." This is the method which up to now has been followed every time. There is an alternate way, which starts out with a constitutional convention; it has never been used. In either case, the amendment process is tough and slow; many proposals never succeed. The Equal Rights Amendment (favored by women's groups) sailed through Congress and won the approval of more than thirty legislatures, but finally died in 1982, a victim of backlash and recalcitrance. Congress has come close on occasion to passing a proposed balanced-budget amendment—for example, in 1995—but this, like most suggestions, never made it out the door of Congress.

The states, too, have methods of amending their constitutions. A speciality of a few states, notably California, is the "initiative." This is the power of voters themselves to propose and pass statutes—and also to amend the state constitution.[11] Amending the constitution is almost a way of life in California. In every general election, the California voter finds on the ballot one or more "propositions" to amend the constitution. It takes a big effort to get a proposition onto the ballot. The organizers have to collect voter signatures totaling at least 8 percent of the votes for all candidates in the most recent election for governor. But obviously it *can* be done, since proposed amendments do make it to the ballot. Some are trivial, some significant. "Proposition Thirteen"[12] in California cut property taxes to the bone and shook up the whole system of state finance. Each general election brings a new crop of proposed constitutional amendments, to be voted on by the public. In the November 1996 general election in California, Proposition 209 proposed to amend the California constitution to prohibit affirmative action (it won); Proposition 218, another proposed amendment to the constitution, was aimed at limiting the authority of local government to raise taxes without voter consent. In other states, too, this form of direct amendment seems to be a growth business. In this same 1996 election, Colorado voters were invited to add a "parental-rights" amendment to their constitution, declaring that parents had the "natural, essential and inalienable right to direct and control the upbringing, education, values, and discipline of their children." Although the language sounds harmless, this too turned into a bruising left-right struggle, and the voters, in the end, turned it down.

The Flowering of Judicial Review

Marbury v. Madison,[13] John Marshall's great decision, is a convenient starting point for talking about judicial review. After *Marbury,* despite grumbling in state courts and among Thomas Jefferson's followers, judicial review won general, if gradual, acceptance. It became a swift and mighty sword in the hands of the courts.

But at first the sword almost grew rusty from disuse. It was more than fifty years until the Supreme Court clearly struck down a piece of federal legislation. This was the infamous *Dred Scott* case (1857).[14] The Court, in an opinion written by Chief Justice Roger B. Taney, held (among other things) that the Missouri Compromise (adopted by Congress over thirty years before) was unconstitutional.[15] The case also held that black people could not be citizens of the United States. Taney's views on slavery, race, and territorial politics, as expressed in *Dred Scott,* were totally obnoxious to antislavery forces in the North. No decision in the Court's long history has been so thoroughly vilified, then and now.

During the long latency period between *Marbury* and *Dred Scott,* judicial review was not completely dormant. The Court did use its power, from time to time, to void *state* statutes. Article I, Section 10(1) of the Constitution provides: "No State shall . . . pass any . . . Law impairing the Obligation of Contracts." This clause was intended to prevent states from going too far in protecting debtors against creditors, especially during times of economic crisis.

The Supreme Court read the clause very broadly. In *Fletcher v. Peck,*[16] the Court applied the clause to land grants. Georgia's legislature in 1794–95 transferred huge tracts of so-called Yazoo lands to speculators, for a low price. Some of the legislators took bribes. Later the voters turned the rascals out of office. The next legislature tried to undo the land grant, declaring it null and void. By this time, a good deal of the land had passed into the hands of new investors who were not part of the original deal; many of them lived out of state. The Supreme Court labeled the original grant a contract and refused to let Georgia wriggle out of the deal. In *Dartmouth College v. Woodward,*[17] the Court went even further. It held that a legislature could not tinker retroactively with the charter of a corporation (charters were issued, at the time, in the form of statutes). The Court also decided some contract-clause cases more strictly concerned with debtor relief; here, too, it sometimes boldly overturned the policy of individual states. Contract-clause cases were among the most critical constitutional cases decided before the Civil War. There were also scattered cases on the scope of state and federal power over interstate commerce, and, more generally, on the relationship between the two spheres of government. The issues have an antique flavor: runaway slaves; toll bridges and turnpikes; control of the newfangled steamboats, puffing their way in the waters between New York and New Jersey. But the problems of mapping the jagged boundaries between state power and the federal government are with us yet.

After the Civil War, the triumphant North pushed through three amendments to the Constitution, the Thirteenth, Fourteenth, and Fifteenth. The Thirteenth Amendment abolished slavery and "involuntary servitude," except as punishment for crime. Under the Fifteenth Amendment, the right to vote could not be "denied or abridged" by reason of "race, color, or previous condition of servitude." The Fourteenth Amendment (1868) undid the *Dred Scott* case and made a citizen out of anyone born or naturalized in this country. It forbade states from depriving anyone of "life, liberty, or property, without due process of law." States were also not to "deny" to anyone "within [their] jurisdiction" "the equal protection of the laws." Nine-tenths of modern constitutional law seems to have burst forth like a rocket from the two pregnant phrases "due process" and "equal protection." A massive social revolution would ultimately hang on them, or be made to hang.

The Civil War was itself a source of change. A weak, part-time government, idling in the swampy village of Washington, was forced to mobilize itself and run a great war. The war destroyed slavery and ruined the economy of the South. In the North, an agricultural society, with a few mills and factories scattered about like raisins in a cake, swiftly became the center of an industrial society in the postwar period—a society of mines, railroads, manufacturing plants, and rapid communication. The very basis of social life inevitably altered. The war had not brought this on, of course, but perhaps it speeded up the process. And a dramatic new age of judicial review began.

As late as the 1860s, the Supreme Court decided only four or five constitutional cases on average each year; by 1890, it was deciding about twenty-four.[18] Under Chief Justice Fuller, the Court declared five federal acts unconstitutional in a single decade (1889–99), together with thirty-four state laws and four municipal ordinances.

This great expansion of judicial review in the late nineteenth century pivoted on the due-process clause. Doctrines sprang out of these few words like rabbits from a magician's hat. The draftsmen of the Fourteenth Amendment were almost certainly thinking only of procedure when they used the words "due process." They were thinking of fair trials in courts of law. But by the turn of the century, the phrase had come to mean something quite different, and vastly greater. As the Court saw it, an "unreasonable" or "arbitrary" law amounted to a deprivation of due process. Only the justices, of course, could say what was unreasonable or arbitrary. Too great an infringement of "liberty of contract," for example, violated the Constitution. Out of such bricks, the Court built a structure which, in effect, made rugged free enterprise part of the constitutional scheme.

Not, of course, consistently; and not without loud voices from left and center crying out against the Court's work. In some notorious instances, the Court used "substantive due process" to tear the guts out of popular laws—laws passed to give labor more power against capital. The high-water mark, perhaps, was *Lochner v. New York,*[19] decided in 1905, a case which has "come to represent the transgressions of an ostensibly activist judiciary."[20] The issue was a New York statute regulating bakeries. Among other things, it restricted the long, killing hours some bakers worked. Under the statute, no one could be "required or permitted" to work in a bakery more than sixty hours a week, or more than ten hours in a day.

The Supreme Court struck down the law. The majority—as Justice John Marshall Harlan pointed out in his dissent—brushed aside evidence of subhuman work conditions: how bakers suffered from flour dust in their lungs; how "long hours of toil" produced "rheumatism, cramps, and swollen legs"; evidence that bakers were "palefaced," had delicate health, and "seldom" lived past fifty. Oliver Wendell Holmes, Jr., also dissented; to him, the majority rested its case "upon an economic theory which a large part of the country does not entertain." This was the theory of pure free enterprise. Holmes himself was personally sympathetic to this theory, but he did not wish to raise it to the level of constitutional principle. To the majority, however (speaking through Justice Rufus Peckham), none of this mattered. The health arguments were a sham. The statute was fatally flawed. It interfered with "the freedom of master and employee to contract with each other." A regulation of "hours of labor" of this kind violated the Fourteenth Amendment.

Some state supreme courts (Illinois's, for one) were even more

active, constitutionally, than the Supreme Court, and along the same
lines of doctrine. Labor and social-welfare laws seemed to fall like ten-
pins at the turn of the century. But it is hard to measure the actual
impact of *Lochner* and its fellow travelers. Most statutes, in fact, survived constitutional challenge. Many were never tested at all. On the
other hand, we can never know what statutes did not pass—or passed in
weakened form—because legislators in Illinois or Tennessee or Rhode
Island were afraid the courts would strike them down. Perhaps, too, the
opposite sometimes happened: a legislature passed a "radical" law to
please some constituents, hoping deep down that the court would kill it
and take the legislators off the hook.

One thing is clear: challenges to the validity of laws were common
from the 1880s on, and had not been common before. They became, in
effect, part of the life cycle of important laws. There was no turning
back. Judicial review did not weaken in the twentieth century; quite the
opposite. It grew, first of all, in terms of sheer volume: more statutes
reviewed; more statutes struck down; new doctrines, some of them very
bold, very sweeping. In a single year (1915), the Supreme Court voided
twenty-two state statutes.[21] The pace continued. An active, intrusive
Supreme Court became a permanent part of the landscape.

What it is active *about* has also changed, and dramatically. In the
Great Depression of the 1930s and during Franklin D. Roosevelt's New
Deal, the country shifted to the left. Power flowed from the exhausted
cities and states to Washington. The Supreme Court at first refused to
get the message. In a series of cases, the Court nullified key New Deal
statutes. For example, in *Schechter Poultry Corp. v. United States*,[22] the
court swept off the books the National Industrial Recovery Act of 1933,
a crucial piece of New Deal legislation.

Once more there was great anger in the country—and in the White
House, too. Roosevelt hit on a plan: he would "pack" the Court
(increase its size) by appointing new justices—men more to his liking,
who would neutralize the "nine old men" who then sat on the Court.
Under the plan, the president was authorized to appoint one new justice
for every sitting justice who was seventy years old or more. There were
six of these justices in 1937. But for once, FDR's political sense had
failed him; the Court-packing plan was attacked from all sides as a
threat to the independence of the justices and to the whole American
system. The plan was hastily abandoned and died on the vine.[23]

But in the end, Roosevelt won his war against the Court. He was
elected president four times, and the "nine old men" simply could not
outlast him. He got his Court without packing it; the Supreme Court
after 1937 submitted—at first, rather meekly and reluctantly—to the

expansion of national power and the New Deal's experiments in big government. Congress and state legislators could do as they liked with the economy; the Court would not say no. The later justices, President Roosevelt's men, eagerly embraced the new line of doctrine.

A clear expression of the Court's new attitude was the case of *Williamson v. Lee Optical.*[24] William O. Douglas, one of Roosevelt's appointed judges, wrote the opinion. The state of Oklahoma had passed a law regulating the eyeglass business. No one was allowed to make or to fit eyeglasses except a licensed optometrist or ophthalmologist, or without having a prescription from one of these. The law was supposed to protect the public, and it had some vague connection with health, but these were rather skimpy grounds. The real motives seemed basically anticompetitive: opticians ("artisans qualified to grind lenses, fill prescriptions, and fit frames") were the target of the law, and it hurt them badly in their business. The Supreme Court as it was in 1900 might have gone over the law with a fine comb and could well have struck it down. The Court of 1955, on the other hand, was not of a mind to interfere. Douglas brushed aside all objections to the act. Let Oklahoma do what it wants: "The day is gone," he said, when the Court made use of "due process" to "strike down . . . laws, regulatory of business . . . because they may be unwise."

Williamson is still the law of the land, and the Court, so far, has not gone back on it, in spirit or letter. The Court takes a hands-off approach to laws that regulate business—generally speaking. But the energy saved, as it were, simply flowed into other fields of action, into the so-called social issues: race relations (especially after *Brown v. Board of Education,* in 1954); the rights of criminal defendants; civil liberties in general; sex discrimination; and a motley collection of cases on what we can call, for want of a better term, personal lifestyle.

Here the Court has been active indeed. It has hacked away at dozens of old taboos. Laws against contraception and abortion were declared unconstitutional.[25] *Furman v. Georgia,*[26] decided in 1972, struck down all existing death-penalty laws, although four years later the Court approved of a new set of such laws—somewhat carefully tailored to meet the Court's objections. Decisions in all of these areas have been in the highest degree controversial. Has the Court gone too fast, too far? Many scholars, and citizens, think so. Others defend the Court. The noisy debate goes on.

Probably it is the conservative wing of the country that finds the Court most offensive. William French Smith, President Reagan's first attorney general, complained in 1981 that the Court had "overstepped the proper bounds." It had made up "fundamental rights" out of thin air, "the right to marry, the right to procreate, the right of interstate travel, and the right of sexual privacy." These rights were highly "subjective"; the Court drained power from Congress and state legislatures and drew this power to itself.[27] Others, of course, disagreed with Smith. They approved of the results, and of the methods too. At any rate, Presidents Reagan and Bush used their appointment power to try to redress the balance. The Court became noticeably more conservative. In President Clinton's first term, however, two relatively liberal justices were appointed. In the mid-1990s, the Court was badly splintered—and where it is headed remains unpredictable. So far, the judicial revolution that began in the New Deal era remains mostly in place.

The mechanics of that "revolution" are easily described. Almost all of the bold new cases rested, however precariously, on the two great phrases of the Fourteenth Amendment: "due process" and "equal protection." Modern constitutional law balances on these few words, like an elephant standing on a dime. The Court treats these phrases as wonderfully prismatic. It reads concepts and results into them that would stagger the men who drafted the text.

But this is true of *all* of constitutional law. The death-penalty cases pivoted on the words of the Eighth Amendment, which forbids "cruel and unusual punishment." It never occurred to the Founding Fathers that hanging was "cruel and unusual." The gallows was standard punishment for murder in the eighteenth century. Indeed, at the time the Constitution was adopted there were dozens of capital crimes, including burglary and rape in many states. The Bill of Rights itself presupposes capital punishment. This is clear from the very words of the Fifth Amendment. No one can be held to "answer for a capital . . . crime," without "presentment or indictment" by a grand jury. Every state in the Union used the gallows at the time the Constitution was adopted. Hangings were public events.

In this and other instances, the Court inflates the meaning of the text like an accordion. Yet some clauses have expanded only modestly or lie completely inert. In a few instances, the Court has dramatically narrowed the meaning of a provision, or retracted a previous expansion. This was true of the contracts clause. The Court made heavy use of the clause before the Civil War. After the war, the clause cropped up in cases on the debts of southern states, which the bankrupt governments were wriggling to get out of. Then the clause fell more or less asleep. And in the 1930s, during the Great Depression, the Court nearly destroyed its meaning altogether.

The case was *Home Building & Loan Ass'n v. Blaisdell.*[28] In the background was the agony of economic crisis and the catastrophic collapse of real-estate values. Hundreds of thousands of people could not make payments on their homes or their farms. Banks and creditors threatened to foreclose. Minnesota passed a law in 1933 which in effect postponed most foreclosures. This was exactly the kind of law the contracts clause was intended to prevent. But the Court refused to interfere. The Minnesota law was a "reasonable" attempt to "safeguard the economic structure upon which the good of all depends." History and precedent were swept away because of the Court's sense of crisis.

Civil Rights and Civil Liberties

We tend to think of the Supreme Court as a strong arm of defense for the downtrodden, as the very soul and armor of civil liberties. Yet this is a surprisingly recent role. Decisions about freedom of speech, freedom of the press, freedom of religion, and the like were extremely rare in the nineteenth century. As we have said, a good case can be made out that the Court's record, until the 1950s, was timid and patchy at best on issues of civil rights and civil liberties. There was little in this record to excite the admiration of partisans of such causes. This state of dormancy may be making something of a comeback in the 1990s—at least so some people think.

The Constitution is full of high words and noble sentiments. But words, after all, do not enforce themselves—even constitutional words. Repression of unpopular opinion has been far from unknown in our history. The Sedition Law[29] is a case in point. This law, passed during the presidency of John Adams, made it a crime to publish any "false, scandalous and malicious writing or writings" about the president, Congress, or the government, or any writings intended to defame them or bring them into "contempt or disrepute." The government used the law to harass opposition newspapers. The courts uttered hardly a peep of protest; the law died only because Adams lost the next election, and the incoming Congress repealed the law.

One can add other instances. The South was harsh on abolitionist opinion. Under the Virginia code of 1849, for example, it was a crime for a free person, "by speaking or writing," to "maintain that owners have not right of property in their slaves." Many southern states restricted "inflammatory" (antislavery) writings and newspapers.[30] The first civil-rights laws (passed after the Civil War) were emasculated by the courts.[31] In *Reynolds v. United States*[32] and other cases, the Supreme Court upheld strict laws directed against the Mormons in the period after the Civil War. The justices did next to nothing about the "red scare" during World War I and the 1920s. "Subversives" and "reds" went to jail; the Court affirmed their convictions. The Court was less than heroic in the 1950s, during the McCarthy era and throughout the Cold War period.[33] It accepted racial segregation in *Plessy v. Ferguson* (1896) and (as we saw) ratified the disgraceful treatment of the Japanese during World War II.[34] These were hardly proud chapters in Supreme Court history.

Nevertheless the United States was a free society in the nineteenth century. It was a very paradise of freedom compared to many countries, before and after. History is full of examples (Hitler and Stalin come to mind as extreme cases) of what murderous, evil governments can stoop to. Nothing in our domestic history sinks quite so low, although the treatment of Native Americans and, of course, slavery are egregious examples of what we have to be ashamed about. Still, it is not quite sugarcoating our history to stress the fact that many countries have been far, far worse.

The Bill of Rights was never a dead letter. Trials were usually fair, even when they did not meet today's more exacting standards. Concepts of rights change over time. We define liberty today to include rights our grandparents never thought of in that connection—rights of sexual freedom and expression, as we have noted.

In the nineteenth century, there was perhaps more consensus than there is today about the *limits* of rights. Of course, we do not have precise information about past public opinion on issues of freedom of speech or defendants' rights. There was no Gallup Poll, and our sources—newspapers, court cases—are almost certainly biased. What we can say is that we do not find much inclination to kick against the traces. In part, this is because the underdogs leave less behind in the way of historical records: it is easier to recover the words of slave owners than the words of slaves; "tramps" and deviants were mostly inarticulate and the most they hoped for was to stay out of trouble with the law— they did not dare to dream of legitimacy. Courts were not, on the whole, hospitable to rebels. Judicial activism, in the field of civil rights and civil liberties, took a long time to warm up.

At first, federal courts did not have the power (never mind the inclination) to enforce basic rights against the states. This was decided in the famous case of *Barron v. Baltimore*.[35] The Supreme Court held that the Bill of Rights bound the federal government only, not the states. Citizens could not bring actions in federal court claiming that the state had taken their property or infringed their basic rights. The states had their own constitutions, their own bills of rights, to be sure. But *Barron v. Baltimore* closed the door on hope for a single, national standard.

Barron v. Baltimore is still law, technically speaking. But later developments have taken away much of its bite. Today, citizens *can* enforce their basic rights against the states in federal court. Our old friend the Fourteenth Amendment, with its supple, expansive provisions, was the vehicle of change—specifically, its due-process clause. In a series of cases, the Supreme Court held that certain aspects of the Bill of Rights were so "fundamental" that the due-process clause scooped them up and swallowed them whole. In this way, the Fourteenth Amendment bypassed *Barron v. Baltimore.* Justice Benjamin Cardozo, in *Palko v. Connecticut,*[36] one of the key cases, said that freedom of speech was "the matrix, the indispensable condition, of nearly every other form of freedom." Hence, said the Court, any state that impairs freedom of speech steps over the line and violates "due process of law." Through cases like this, the First Amendment, which covers free speech, became a *national* standard, enforced by the Supreme Court, and as understood by the Supreme Court.

Over the years, the Court has slowly but steadily "incorporated" more and more provisions of the Bill of Rights into the Fourteenth Amendment, thus imposing them on all fifty states and vesting enforcement power in federal courts. Most of the provisions on criminal justice have been incorporated bag and baggage. There are a few exceptions. The Fifth Amendment requires indictment by grand jury in criminal cases. In 1884, in *Hurtado v. California,*[37] the Court refused to read this requirement into the Fourteenth Amendment. This decision still stands.

So much for the technical side of the story. But "incorporation" is more than a device. It means, first of all, greater sensitivity to rights; it also means that the federal courts have assumed broad *national* powers. The Supreme Court led the way. It built up a rampart of rules giving national scope to the Bill of Rights and lending its weight to one underclass after another: blacks, women, the poor, and, most particularly, those caught in the web of the criminal law. The most dramatic developments came after 1950. Many are associated with the Court under Earl Warren, appointed chief justice in 1953 by President Eisenhower.

Of course, one man—a chief justice—is never responsible for so strong a trend. Not even the whole panel of nine justices can claim the credit or take the blame. Courts are instruments of social change. They deal with issues that other people raise; they do not, on the whole, invent policies. They give policies a legal basis and help to carry them out. The 1950s was the decade of the burgeoning civil-rights movement. Black people had become more militant. This militance was one of the great social realities behind the *Brown* case. In the years since then, other minorities and underclasses have claimed their rights. On these social foundations the Court has built its house of doctrine.

The Supreme Court has no power to promote its own docket. It does have the right to pick and choose among the thousands of cases that beg for the ear of the Court. This right to choose, to be sure, is a source of great power. But a case that comes before the Court is at the end of the line, not the beginning. Each case is about a real problem, issue, or claim which began in the world outside the Court. To be sure, when courts show they are receptive to a certain type of claim, they encourage people to bring more such claims to court.

For example, the *Brown* case dealt, on the surface, only with Jim Crow schools. It outlawed segregation in public schools. In fact, for years the courts had only moderate success in forcing the reluctant South to inch slowly toward this goal—so that some have questioned whether *Brown* had any efficacy at all.[38] But the case also delivered a powerful message to the black community: the Court announced it was willing—even eager—to advance the cause of racial justice. Still, it was the black community and its allies that had to act. It takes nothing away from the Court to recognize that it had these partners—groups and individuals who demanded expansion or recognition of their rights. The "rights revolution" is a partnership, between an active court and an active society.

To explain where law comes from, what it does, and where it is going, one always has to look at social context. The law of obscenity is another example. The Court has been struggling with this issue for at least forty years. The First Amendment protects freedom of speech. In most states the sale of "pornography" or "obscene" books and pictures is a crime. Oklahoma, for example, prohibits selling "obscene, lewd, lascivious, filthy, or indecent" matter.[39] Where is the boundary line between obscenity, which can be forbidden, and free expression, which cannot? How far can people go, in words and pictures, before they lose the protection of the First Amendment?

The Court has never come up with a satisfying answer. The issue is on the whole surprisingly recent. The Supreme Court did not deal with it squarely until 1957, when it decided *Roth v. United States*.[40] Litigation on the point was rare in the nineteenth century. There were dirty books and dirty pictures, but they stayed in the closet, so to speak. Obscenity rarely showed its face in public.

State cases on the subject, apparently, were rare to nonexistent before the early nineteenth century. One case in Massachusetts (1821) dealt with *Memoirs of a Woman of Pleasure*, a book better known as

Fanny Hill. For more than a century after the Massachusetts case, this famous erotic novel, written by John Cleland, continued its underground life. It passed from clammy hand to clammy hand. In December 1923, two New York booksellers, Maurice Inman and Max Gottschalk, were arrested, convicted, and fined $250 for selling *Fanny Hill* (along with two other "classics," *A Night in a Moorish Harem* and *Only a Boy*).[41] During all this period, rarely if ever did anyone claim that the First Amendment's sweep was capacious enough to cover the adventures of the likes of Ms. Fanny Hill.

Then, in the 1960s, *Fanny Hill* went dramatically public, and this time with a difference. The publishers demanded (and got) constitutional protection. In the years after 1960, there was a great wave of obscenity cases. *Fanny* was the star of some of these cases. And generally speaking, the courts made an honest woman of her. The First Amendment, it turned out, was broad enough, and broad-minded enough, to protect this "woman of pleasure."[42]

By this time, *Fanny* was about 150 years old—about the same age, in fact, as the First Amendment. Yet their definitive meeting took place only in the 1960s. The words, of the book and of the First Amendment, were the same as they had been since the eighteenth century. But society had changed, and with it legal doctrine; the very meaning of freedom of speech had altered in the course of time.

Despite *Fanny's* triumph, the obscenity issue has never been finally resolved. Legal doctrine on the point is a hopeless muddle. The courts have been unable to find and announce workable rules and workable limits. It is clear, of course, that standards have dramatically shifted. Some forty years ago, a mild movie comedy, *The Moon Is Blue,* provoked an uproar simply because the word "virgin" was uttered on the screen. Today "adult" bookstores, peep shows, and pornographic movie houses exist in most towns of any size. Customers can see and buy hardcore pornographic magazines, and books for every brand and off-brand of sex—in living color, if you please, or in 3-D—and all without crackdowns or raids. This rank permissiveness shocks and disgusts millions of people; some feminists believe pornography is one key to male domination. Obviously, millions of others disagree, but quietly: they vote by watching and buying hard-core products. Those who prefer traditional morality tend to blame the courts for the flood of pornography, for stretching the First Amendment so that it protects this "filth." No doubt the courts have played a role. The courts have opposed censorship; they have vetoed restrictive laws; they have allowed very broad standards. But the major change has been, unquestionably, not legal but social.

There is a demand for these movies, books, and magazines, and, what is more, customers want to buy them cheaply, easily, legally, and openly. For the most part, these views have prevailed.

The issue is by no means a simple one. The Court faces, here as elsewhere, a difficult question: where to draw the line. There are, after all, bluenoses who want to censor Shakespeare, who find *Catcher in the Rye* too raw for high-school libraries, who want to ban any movie that even hints at sex. In one of the Supreme Court's obscenity cases,[43] the movie in question was *Carnal Knowledge*. A major studio produced it; it was a serious, important film on serious themes, starring Jack Nicholson, and obscene by no stretch of the imagination. Yet the defendant had been convicted of a crime for showing this movie in Albany, Georgia. The Supreme Court reversed the conviction. Another case, *Erznoznik v. City of Jacksonville*,[44] wrestled with the problem of (the now almost extinct) drive-in movies. Jacksonville, Florida, banned movies if they showed "the human male or female bare buttocks, human female bare breasts, or human bare pubic areas" whenever the screen was visible from a public street. The Supreme Court felt the rule went much too far: taken literally, it would ban a film containing a "picture of a baby's buttocks . . . the opening of an art exhibit . . . shots of bathers on a beach."

On the whole, the Court has tried to move cautiously in this delicate and controversial field. It does not wander too far ahead of elite public opinion. It does not give either side everything it wants. It certainly rejects the standards of prudery, but it has also never said that anything goes. It pays at least lip service to the idea of "community standards" of obscenity";[45] but it also held, in 1987, that works that claim literary, scientific, or artistic value were subject to a different standard (whether a "reasonable" person would see the good in them).[46] And in contemporary times, the problem of obscenity on the Internet looms large.

The Court, in other words, has waffled so far on the issue of obscenity. It has tried to strike a balance. This is often the posture of the Court in civil-liberty cases. The Court can lead public opinion, and it sometimes tries to. It wants to show the way at times, or act as a (self-appointed) teacher or vanguard. But it cannot march all by itself, way ahead of the rest of the crowd.

This is especially true because courts have only limited power. They make pronouncements, but somebody else must carry them out. Enforcement, however, is crucial. Real rights are more important than rights on paper. What happens to Supreme Court doctrines when they reach the street, the station house, the chambers of trial-court judges? Generally speaking, there is a lot of slippage between command and execution; whether the gap is scandalously large or tolerable depends on the time, the subject, the people, and the place.

One historical example might be useful. The case is *Bailey v. Alabama*,[47] decided in 1911. Lonzo Bailey was a poor black farm worker, working in Alabama for a white landowner. He quit his job in the middle of the growing season and was arrested for breaking his contract "fraudulently." This was a crime in Alabama, under a statute passed with people like Bailey in mind. The whole point was to tie black farm workers to the land, at least during the growing season—to make it impossible for them to quit, whatever their reasons.

The system smacked of serfdom, or even slavery. It had been going on for years. But a tiny band of progressive lawyers made a test case out of Lonzo Bailey's problem. They took the case all the way to the Supreme Court. Here Alabama lost. The court declared the law unconstitutional; the justices felt it was part of a system of peonage, forbidden by federal law, and by the Thirteenth Amendment, which banned slavery and "involuntary servitude." Black people in the South and their allies had won a great victory.

But in fact nothing much happened. The underlying problem did not go away. Bailey, of course, won his case. Alabama tinkered with its law, making small, cosmetic changes. Other southern states simply ignored the decision. The Southern labor system continued just as before. Southern peonage lived on.[48] *Bailey*, in short, was "ahead of its time." It gave liberals a warm glow, a sense of accomplishment. But there was no movement, no organization, no plan to follow through, no muscle and will to enforce the case. Thus, in a real sense, it was an empty victory, dead, as it were, on arrival.

More than forty years later, the Supreme Court decided *Brown v. Board of Education*.[49] The Court declared that racial segregation in public schools was unconstitutional and had to be ended. *Brown* was also the first of a series of cases that banned segregation everywhere, in all its forms. What happened after *Brown* was nothing short of a revolution—an incomplete revolution, to be sure, but a revolution nonetheless.

Brown, in other words, did not suffer the fate of the *Bailey* case. There is controversy over exactly how much *Brown* itself accomplished.[50] There is disillusionment with the results, among many African-Americans. But it is at least clear that *Brown* did not fade away. Why? Not because of anything in the opinion, in the doctrines announced, in the way it was written, in its style, or in its craftsmanship. The answer lies elsewhere, in changed social conditions and, especially, in the civil-rights movement. The great events that followed *Brown*, the sit-ins, marches, protests, the eloquence of Martin Luther King, the constant litigation, the struggle in the South and the North—all of this, and more, put power and passion behind the doctrines expressed in *Brown* and made them a working reality. The "revolution" happened because of the partnership between court and constituents, between legal force and social force.

The "revolution," like all revolutions, remains incomplete. Race is still, in the late 1990s, a major issue in the United States, and it is therefore, by an iron law of American society, a major *legal* issue as well. The Supreme Court now wrestles not with issues of segregation but with "reverse discrimination," "affirmative action," and similar issues. In 1995, the Supreme Court struck down a federal practice of giving "general contractors on government projects a financial incentive to hire subcontractors" who were controlled by "socially and economically disadvantaged individuals" (a code phrase for racial minorities).[51] "Affirmative action" in universities is also under attack.[52] Surely the last word has not been spoken on this issue.

Here and Abroad

A final word, this time about American constitutional law as an export commodity. Our system is old, as systems go, and since it began, it has served as a model for other nations. When the countries of Latin America broke away from Spain, many adopted written constitutions. The United States Constitution was an important source of ideas for these documents. Unfortunately, dictatorships in these countries often made a mockery of constitutional guarantees. The words speak of liberty, equality, and justice. But many countries have ignored or suspended those guarantees.

The Latin American countries come out of a different legal tradition—the tradition of Spain and the civil law. Judicial review, American-style, is alien to this tradition. Nonetheless, in some countries (for example, Colombia and Costa Rica) courts have played a strong constitutional role. From 1910 to 1953, the supreme court of Colombia invalidated more than fifty statutes, in whole or in part.[53] In some countries, there is a "diffuse" system of judicial review—the highest court simply adds this function to its workload (as is true of the United States Supreme Court). Other countries have a "concentrated" system, in which a special court exercises judicial review.[54]

After the Second World War, Germany, Italy, and Japan also wrote new constitutions. In each case, American ideas about constitutionalism and the rule of law made a deep impression. We had, after all, won the war; we had armies stationed in the losing nations. Bloody, repressive regimes had been overthrown. The United States was bound and determined to install something like its brand of government—which included constitutions, control of centralized power, and bills of rights.

The new constitutions included provisions for judicial review. Germany and Italy established special "constitutional courts" to exercise this power (the "concentrated" system). This was a startling break with national tradition. The German court, after a rather slow start, now shows strong signs of "activism"; it exercises power with a certain relish. For example, it jumped into the abortion issue as boldly as the United States Supreme Court. It came out, however, on the other side: in February 1975, it struck down liberal abortion laws, in the constitutional interests of the unborn child.[55] In 1995, the German constitutional court struck down a law in Bavaria, one of the most conservative (and Catholic) sections of Germany, which mandated crucifixes in public-school classrooms; the decision evoked a storm of protest.[56]

Other postwar courts have so far been quite cautious about their new powers. The Japanese court, for the first twenty years at least, was almost inert constitutionally; it almost never disapproved of legislation on constitutional grounds. But this reluctance, too, may be slowly eroding.[57] In general, newer constitutional courts (those in Cyprus, Austria, and Spain are examples) tend to grow stronger, more assertive, more self-confident over the years. When the Soviet Union disintegrated, in 1989, and the countries of Eastern Europe overthrew their old regimes, there was a new wave of constitution-building, and constitution-tinkering; here too, American models played a strong role—at least on paper.

We hear a lot about "American influence" in all of this constitutional ferment. Of course, American example has been significant, and in some cases so have American scholars (and American armies). But it would be wrong to put too much weight on this point. Context is crucial, as always. Societies in the contemporary world are all undergoing rapid social change. In many ways, we live now as part of a single world culture. In the major industrial countries of the West, and in Japan and the smaller "tigers" of the Far East, populations are much more mobile than before, and wealth is widely, though unequally, distributed. Old patterns of authority are decaying—very fast in some places, more slowly in others. Jet airplanes, computers, satellites, and the Internet have turned the world into a single village, at least in some respects.

Judicial review did not spring up in the United States by magic. By now it is a tradition, but it did not start that way. There was no such thing as judicial review in England, any more than there was in Spain or in Germany. Judicial review developed in this country almost from scratch. It grew because, in some mysterious way, it worked. Certain social conditions (and legal tools) made possible the American pattern. If these conditions reproduce themselves in, say, Germany or Japan, and if the tools are there, we would expect some sort of parallel development. Hollywood movies and Coca-Cola conquered the world because they appealed to people. No one forced them down foreign throats. People in other countries turned out to have much the same tastes, good or bad, as Americans. No one should have been surprised. Judicial review is an export of a similar type, in some ways—though on a higher plane, one hopes.

11

On Legal Behavior

*W*E HAVE SPENT a good deal of time so far on legal rules and on the structures that make and carry out those rules. But once again, it must be emphasized that a legal system is more than structures and rules. Rules, after all, are supposed to be followed—at least some of the time. The key element in any legal system is behavior—what people actually do. Otherwise rules are nothing but words, and the structures are a ghost town, not a living city. There is no way to understand a legal system, including ours, unless we pay attention to what we might call "legal behavior."

The term "legal behavior," as used in this book, means behavior influenced in some way by a rule, decision, order, or act which has been given out by somebody with legal authority. If I behave in a certain way, or change my behavior in a certain way, because of something the law commands—or because of some government action, or some message or order coming from government or from the legal system or from some functionary in it—then this is legal behavior. If I am driving along the road and see a speed-limit sign (or spot a policeman) and slow down, this then would be legal behavior.

It would also be legal behavior, though of a somewhat different sort, if I saw the policeman and started going a hundred miles an hour, to try to get away from him. After all, here, too, I am reacting to something going on in the legal system. It is also legal behavior, of course, to file income-tax returns, sue somebody, register to vote, and do countless other ordinary and extraordinary acts.

There are many things we might want to know about legal behavior. It is obvious that some laws are mostly obeyed and some are mostly disobeyed. How do we account for these differences? Why do people follow some rules and not others? This is an important question, because most of us have an interest, most of the time, in seeing that the rules are obeyed. (This is, of course, not universally true.)

Actually, we should try to steer clear of the words "obey" and "disobey." They can be somewhat misleading. Legal behavior is more than a matter of obeying and disobeying. One example will do to show this point. When married life has been too bumpy for a couple, they may consider divorce. In almost every state today, there is a "no-fault" system, which makes divorce fairly easy to get. It is a matter of filing papers in court, paying a small fee, going through certain formalities, and waiting awhile. If neither party makes a fuss, which is usually the case, and if they have come to an agreement, the court dissolves the marriage, splits up the property according to plan, issues custody orders if there are children, and so on. The man and woman are free now to marry again.

Clearly, all of this activity—going to court and getting a divorce—is legal behavior. Certainly the couple followed forms and rules. But we would hardly say they "obeyed" the law. The law does not order anybody to get a divorce. What it does is tell you how to get one if you want one. Thus it makes no sense to talk about obeying or disobeying the law in this instance. Rather, we should talk about using (or not using) the law of divorce. And, in general, except in criminal law and in certain provisions of regulatory law, legal behavior is more a matter of using or not using than of obeying or disobeying.

Not that obeying and disobeying are unimportant. It seems clear that the legal system would collapse if everybody disobeyed certain laws, such as laws against violent behavior, or if so many people disobeyed that the law lost its point completely. There is, in fact, a lot of crime, lawlessness, and deviance in our country. But we are still a long way from anarchy.

Some laws, of course, are more widely obeyed than others. There are many examples of laws that "nobody pays attention to." Prohibition is often cited as a good example of a major law which came to grief because of massive disobedience. Prohibition, the "noble experiment," was a total ban on selling or dealing in liquor. It went into effect in 1920. According to conventional accounts, it was a dismal failure. Millions of people kept right on drinking. Bootleggers and gangsters took over the liquor business. In 1928, to be sure, there were 55,729 prosecutions for violations of the National Prohibition Act in federal courts, and more than 48,000 convictions. But most of these were resolved by fines, and in any event, prosecutions were a drop in the bucket compared to the number of violations. Some scholars even feel that liquor consumption went up during Prohibition. This was probably not true, but the mere fact that one can make the argument suggests that violation was widespread indeed.[1]

Prohibition is, of course, not the only example of a law widely flouted. Marijuana laws were once called the "new Prohibition." John Kaplan's 1970 book had that phrase as part of its title. Kaplan reported on a survey in a California city (1967–68), where 49 percent of the males and 32 percent of the females between eighteen and twenty-four had tried marijuana. Yet marijuana was strictly illegal.[2] In 1993, a third of the population over twelve reported that they had used the drug—59 percent of those between twenty-five and thirty-four had done so, 11 percent within a month of the survey.[3] Obviously, if the laws were enforced, huge prison cities would be needed to hold all the violators. To take a more prosaic example, thousands—maybe millions—of drivers ignore the posted speed limit, every day. Yet these laws are not dead letters: they are enforced somewhat, even though imperfectly or sporadically or unfairly.

Many "dead" laws are not, after all, as dead as we may think. Even during Prohibition many people (perhaps most) obeyed the law. And the law had an important effect on legal behavior, including the behavior of people who regularly broke the law: it changed the time, manner, and mode of their drinking. After all, before Prohibition, it was legal to drink openly or in public. During Prohibition, drinking had to be kept more or less secret. Today, even where laws against "pot" are enforced very weakly, nobody dares light up in front of a policeman at high noon. Similarly, nobody drives a hundred miles an hour when the police are around, and where the speed limit is officially sixty-five.

Obedience and disobedience are not matters of black and white. There are all sorts of shades of gray. We have used the example of speed limits before. The speed limit is sixty-five on interstate highways, yet by custom, sixty-five means (more or less) seventy. Many people drive at seventy; some drive even faster. Technically, all these drivers are violating the law. But what if the speed limit were raised to seventy-five, or if there were no limit at all? In this case, no doubt some people would drive at eighty-five, or ninety or one hundred. Probably, then, the speed limit has *some* effect on the behavior of drivers, even though they "disobey" this law. It seems to dampen some of their passion for speeding. How much is an open question.

Similarly, how "ineffective" are the laws against marijuana? In some communities (not all), it is widely believed that these laws are not obeyed at all. But of course this is loose if not downright wrong. We have no idea how many people would smoke marijuana if it were completely legal to do so. There must be some (or many) timid souls who are deterred even by weak enforcement; there must be some people who refuse to smoke because it is against the law. And everywhere, as we said, illegality tends to affect time, manner, and quantity of "disobedience." The laws, then, have a real effect on behavior, including the behavior of violators. The law influences conduct, for better and for worse. Poor old Prohibition, on history's ash heap, probably made more of a dent on behavior than most people give it credit for.

Much the same can be said about use and nonuse of law. There are rules, doctrines, provisions that are used or not used, as a matter of individual choice. A person can either make out a will or not, as he or she sees fit. The law certainly does not insist on a will. A study of Cuyahoga County (Cleveland), Ohio, which took a sample of 659 estates closed in 1964–65, found that 31 percent of them were intestate—that is, the deceased never bothered to make out a will.[4] A study by the American Institute for Cancer Research, published in 1994, found that fewer than 30 percent of Americans had a valid will when they died. Those with large estates were more likely to have a will, but in a study conducted by an insurance company, slightly more than a third of respondents with fairly substantial estates—averaging $280,000— lacked a will.[5] When a marriage breaks up, the couple can simply live apart, or they can get a divorce. It is up to them.

The law of divorce is, in a way, a kind of commodity: the legal system offers it for sale to the public like a bar of soap or a car. The public can buy or not, as it chooses. A lot depends on the product and on the price. A divorce costs money. It also has a value: without a divorce, a person cannot legally remarry and start a legitimate new family. The laws of divorce, and rules about divorce procedures, have an impact on what divorce costs (in dollars and in psychic costs) and also on the benefit side: what people *get* from a divorce. These costs and benefits influence whether or not people choose to "buy" a divorce. Since the 1970s, when no-fault divorce came into being, divorce has become easier and cheaper. This influences the number of "sales." But of course a happily married couple does not rush out and get a divorce just because divorce is cheaper than before—or even free.

No law is 100 percent effective. We always have to tolerate a certain amount of slippage. The amount we can tolerate varies tremendously from one type of behavior to another. Let us take speeding as our example again. We tolerate a high level of violation. This does create problems—accidents, for one thing—but though literally millions of people break the law every day, this level of "disobedience" does not produce a crisis in society.

Contrast this with skyjacking. This is a very rare crime, committed by a tiny handful of disturbed people—terrorists, extremists. The potential pool of violators is and always will be small. But even a tiny violation rate (one out of a hundred thousand flights, or even a million) is simply intolerable; it could throw the whole transportation system into chaos. Society spends untold millions of dollars and devotes thousands of hours of effort to try to prevent all skyjacking. The toleration rate is very low. The same is true of political assassination.

Influencing Legal Behavior

What can we say about the factors that influence legal behavior? First of all, both *communication* of the law and *knowledge* of it are essential. It makes no sense to say that I obey or disobey a rule, use it, or evade it unless I know what the rule actually *is*. The rule, in other words, has to be communicated to me, and I must have some knowledge of its contents.

The size of the audience is a crucial point in any discussion about communication of legal rules. Some rules of law apply to only a few people; others apply to a whole class; some apply to everybody. If a rule applies only to a small group (manufacturers of cars, for example), it is easier to make the rule known to the audience. It is easy to pinpoint and locate *everybody* who falls into the category of "car manufacturer"; the numbers are small, and car manufacturers are not exactly inconspicuous. A rule which is supposed to reach all burglars is trickier, and a rule directed at everybody—the whole public—is hard to get across; and quite expensive .

The way the rule is communicated is also important. Some rules are, in fact, common knowledge; they are part of very general, very early learning. Most rules, and certainly all technical, detailed administrative rules, have to be specially delivered to their audience. There are all sorts of ways to do this: a sign that says "No smoking" is one way; a presidential speech is another. Some rules or orders are delivered to their audience in the flesh; a police officer, for example, stands at an intersection, in the midst of traffic, and tells drivers when and how they can turn left or continue.

The form of a rule also has a bearing on communication. A rule which is specific is better at conveying its message than a rule which is vague and general. The extreme case is a speed limit. It is posted in big letters at the side of the road, and its message is simple and direct: 40 MPH or 65 MPH or 70 MPH. We have little doubt that this rule reaches its audience. At the other extreme are subtle, difficult, vaguely worded doctrines of law. The Uniform Commercial Code, for example, provides that a court need not enforce an "unconscionable" clause in a contract.[6] Only lawyers, by and large, know that there is such a rule; even they have no way of knowing exactly what it means. There is no earthly way such a rule can reach a larger audience—businesspeople in general, or consumers.

Knowledge of the Law

How much do Americans know about their own legal system? One survey carried out in Michigan (1973) reported, to nobody's great surprise, that the general public knew less about law than law students did, and that better-educated people knew more about law than the less-educated. This was hardly news, but at least it confirmed people's guesses. The study also provided some bits of detail. People seemed to have a better grasp of criminal matters than of civil matters. Take, for example, this question: "If a person remains silent when questioned by the police, may his silence be used against him in court?" The right answer is no, and 82 percent of the subjects knew this. On the other hand, people were asked whether a car dealer could simply repossess a car parked on the street if the buyer missed a payment; 71 percent said yes, which is definitely the wrong answer.[7]

A Texas survey taken slightly earlier found important class differences in what people knew about law. It is disheartening to learn that poor people know very little about their rights. For example, nearly 40 percent of the low-income blacks who were surveyed thought police had a right to search their houses whenever they wanted to, which is certainly not the law.[8] These answers may reflect either pure ignorance or (sad to say) a degree of realism. That is, low-income people may experience law in a way that leads them to expect injustice. Their answers are technically wrong, but match their experience of living law.

Knowledge of law, like knowledge of anything else, is a matter of degree. We are not surprised to find that people are fairly ignorant about the legal system; people are fairly ignorant about most things. Lawyers know some law; yet their heads may be crammed full of misinformation about medicine, science, and world history. People in general do tend to have enough working knowledge of law to get by in their daily lives. On the whole, people can be expected to know more about rules that are relevant to themselves, their groups, and their jobs and situations. Taxi drivers are likely to know (more or less) the taxi regulations and the rules about taxi licenses. A police officer knows more about the laws of arrest than a plumber does. A plumber knows more about building codes than a police officer. A person in the export-import trade knows very little about taxi licenses, arrests, or plumbing rules, but a lot about export-import law. And so it goes.

What about rules that apply to everybody? Some are common knowledge. The aspects of law "everybody" knows are, in a way, the most primitive—the most closely connected to general customs and norms. Everybody above the age of five or so knows that the law forbids stealing—that it is a crime to rob a gas station. Details of the law, where to find the law, exactly what the law says—these are things most people may not know. They also probably do not know or understand technical distinctions, such as the difference between first-degree and second-degree murder or the nuances that separate robbers from burglars from larcenists. They know that a check has to be endorsed (signed on the back) before it can be transferred, but they may not understand the various refinements of the concept of "negotiability" which lie behind the practice of endorsement. Still, the guts of these rules are part of everyday life in society.

These very basic, very elementary rules are part of general and early learning. Even grade-school children have some idea about the rules and what they are. One study asked children of various ages, "What is a rule?" A boy in primary school gave this answer: "A rule is not to run around, not to hit anybody, not to break anything." Another question was "What would happen if there were no rules?" A second-grade girl said: "Then people would go around killing other people, and . . . stealing things, and . . . kidnapping people." These young children, then, have a clear sense that some behaviors (killing, stealing) are forbidden.[9] They learn these things from their parents, teachers and friends, and from TV.

Not all rules are learned this way, of course, and most are not learned at all. Otherwise there would be no need for lawyers and other experts. In fact, nobody can know all the rules, or even 1 percent of them. The federal government alone produces hundreds of new regulations every year, some of them tremendously complicated. The new rules and regulations are printed in the *Federal Register*, which runs to thousands of pages a year, as we have seen. It is also a very technical, very boring book, hardly something to keep on your bedside table. But lawyers will keep up with rules and regulations in the area of their specialties. Food-and-drug lawyers or corporate tax lawyers make sure they know the latest "regs" on their subjects; they might also subscribe to a loose-leaf service with up-to-date material, or learn what's new "on line." They probably read reports of the latest, most important cases.

These lawyers are important to the business world. They are mid-dlemen—brokers of information. They store up knowledge of legal rules and pass them on to clients when and as needed. In this regard, of course, they are like any other experts—doctors, auto mechanics, engineers. Lawyers are experts on rules and regulations. They are, of course, not the only such experts in society. Tax accountants are experts on tax rules; they compete with lawyers for business. There are many other examples. Every big company probably has many people working for it whose job is to keep up with rules and regulations of one kind or another: labor rules, business-law rules, regulations of all sorts. Some of these people will be lawyers; some will not.

In short, most people have working knowledge of truly essential rules; lawyers and knowledge brokers take care of much of the rest. Some people will learn about relevant rules from newsletters or other communications of this type, coming from an occupational group, for example. The California Supreme Court decided a case in 1976 which held that psychotherapists owed a duty of care to a person killed or injured by a patient. (In the case, a patient whose girlfriend had dumped him told his psychiatrist that he felt murderous urges toward her. The psychiatrist did not report this to anybody, and the boyfriend did murder the woman.)[10] Later studies showed that most psychothera-pists knew about the case; they learned about it mostly from the litera-ture of their profession..[11]

The psychotherapists "knew" about the case, but how accurate was their information? Not very, according to the study. Even large, sophisti-cated corporations do not necessarily get accurate knowledge of legal rules (and legal risks): they overestimate, for example, the legal dangers lurking in the doctrine of "wrongful discharge" of employees, according to a study published in 1992.[12] In general, there are large knowledge gaps about the law, and they can be socially destructive. More sophisti-cation about law and legal process would be useful, if only to educate voters and make them better judges of policy. Ignorance and misinfor-mation can be hazardous to society's health.

Occasionally, mistakes in legal knowledge can be shown to have terrible consequences. Joseph Wambaugh's book *The Onion Field* (1973) is the history of a crime, the brutal murder of a policeman in California. The killer, according to Wambaugh, misunderstood the state's "Little Lindbergh Law." This was a law about the punishment for kidnapping. The killer thought he could be sent to the gas chamber just for kidnapping a policeman. If this had been so, he would have had nothing to lose if he got rid of the policeman—besides, he would eliminate a dangerous witness. This was a mistake about the law, and it led to a pointless murder.

People in society probably have many wrong beliefs and ideas about law. There is, in a way, a kind of legal folklore in every society, including ours. The folklore consists of notions about law that are baseless or distorted, for one reason or another. Some people think it is illegal to sign a document in pencil. In fact, this is perfectly okay, though for obvious reasons it is also a bad idea. Or they may think they are not allowed to leave a hospital unless they pay the bills. In fact, they can. The hospital is not a prison and has no right to hold people prisoner. The folklore of American law is an intriguing subject which has not yet been systematically explored.

Much of what people know about law, or think they know, comes from the media. The O. J. Simpson trial, in 1994–95, was supposed to be a great educational experience; in fact, it was a highly misleading one, as we have seen. Coverage of important legal news is spotty at best. Court decisions are not routinely reported, except in sensational cases; and even important cases tend to be reduced to slogans and sound bites. A lot of what is reported in the press is propaganda or worse. The great panic over liability insurance in 1986 was fueled by reports of tort-law horror stories: for example, a psychic who had a CAT scan, lost her psychic powers, sued, and got $1 million from a Philadelphia jury. But almost none of these widely reported stories (including the story about the psychic) turned out to be factually accurate.[13] Of course, *misinformation* is an important social fact: people believe what they want to believe, and what fits in with their values and worldviews.

Sanctions

Suppose a norm or rule has been communicated to the necessary audience. People now know it, at least well enough to understand what is expected of them. At this point, the choice is theirs—to obey or not to obey, to use or not to use. Which will they choose? For simplicity, let us concentrate on obedience to rules of the criminal law.

First of all, there is probably no rule or law in the land which everybody follows all of the time. If such a rule existed, there would be no point making it a law in the first place; people would obey it on their own. At the same time, it is hard to think of a rule or law universally disobeyed. Almost everything falls in the middle. Of course, that middle is very broad. Every driver has broken traffic rules, and probably frequently. On the other hand, few people (fortunately) have tried their hand at murder.

What is it that moves people to make the choices they do? What pushes them in the direction of obeying this or that norm or disobeying it? Why are some laws observed more than others? The simplest and most general explanation is in terms of "sanctions," that is, rewards and punishments. People follow rules because they are afraid of what will happen if they don't. In other words, the law and its sanctions deter them.

The word "deterrence" conjures up certain images: we think of fines, jail, and other forms of punishment. The word "sanctions," however, covers more than punishment. It also includes rewards. The positive side of sanctions (rewards, incentives) is less obvious, because the literature tends to stress criminal law, and ordinary people, when they think of the law at all, tend to think in these terms as well. But incentives are an important part of the legal system. Government at every level hands out billions of dollars in subsidies. To encourage people to save energy, we might give them a tax break for insulating their homes, rather than putting them in jail if they do not cooperate. If farmers are growing too much cotton or peanuts, we might pay them to put land in the "soil bank." To get men and women for the army, we can force them with a "draft," or persuade them to volunteer with bonuses and other incentives.

Do rewards and punishment work? Of course they do, as a general proposition. There is plenty of proof, in case we needed it—first, in everyday experience, and second, in the scholarly literature. We know that many people hesitate to cheat on their income tax, not out of patriotic zeal, but because they are afraid of the IRS. We know that nobody speeds when the police car is watching.

We can take the following for granted: if there is a rule that includes some kind of punishment for breaking it, and if we increase the punishment, keeping all other factors the same, the new level of punishment will increase the deterrent effect. That is, some people (not everybody) will stop doing the deed, out of fear of punishment. Similarly, an increase in rewards will stimulate a desired behavior if all other factors are held constant. If a state offers $10 apiece for coyote skins, it will get a certain number of skins. If it raises the offer to $1,000 a skin, and nothing else changes, there will be a bigger harvest of skins. If we raise the fine for overtime parking from $5 to $20, at the same level of enforcement, some people will think twice about violating the rules. If we get serious and start towing cars away, there will be an even greater effect.

So much is obvious. The real issues are more difficult and complex. We know that threat of punishment deters people, but we do not know how much, in any given case. Nor do we understand who is deterred, and why. Yet these are crucial questions. Argument rages over whether capital punishment is an effective deterrent or not, or effective enough to be worthwhile. At one point, the Supreme Court, by a five-to-four vote, threw out all of the country's death-penalty laws. This was *Furman v. Georgia,* decided in 1972 (the death penalty, as we shall see, made a comeback a few years later).[14] Thurgood Marshall, one of the five in the majority in *Furman,* asserted that there was no justification for the death penalty, partly because it did not deter. This is, in fact, a hotly disputed question. There were scholars who agreed with Marshall, and others who disagreed. One economist, Isaac Ehrlich, went so far as to claim that every execution prevents between eight and twenty murders.[15] His methods and findings, however, have been vigorously—and plausibly—attacked.

The death penalty is an emotional issue; feelings run high on both sides. It is not easy to sort out facts from emotions. Probably capital punishment, as a general proposition, does, in principle, deter—that is, it does have an impact on behavior. If a dictator suddenly announced that anybody on the streets after dark would be shot, and if he meant business, people would scurry for cover as soon as the sun started sinking in the west. There would be an obvious impact on behavior—no question.

But this is not really the issue in the current debate. The issue is not whether the death penalty is effective compared to no punishment at all. Nobody suggests letting murderers go free or punishing them with a slap on the wrist. The question is whether capital punishment adds a measurable *extra* deterrent, compared to life imprisonment or a long "jolt" in prison. Or, if it adds something, does it add enough to make it worthwhile? Does using capital punishment cost too much? Does it have negative side effects? On these questions, we have relatively little information. The death penalty has not been used that much in this country over the last twenty years or so—its use is concentrated in a handful of states, mostly in the South—and we frankly do not know how much, if at all, it enters into the calculations of potential criminals. The vast majority of the public seem to favor the death penalty—at least they say they do. A minority, but a very committed one, object to killing prisoners, on moral grounds. Statistics and survey research, of course, cannot resolve ethical issues; neither can econometrics. This does not make these techniques unimportant.

We talk about the way punishment deters people; but what we really mean is the threat of punishment. After all, *most* people do not actually go to prison or suffer punishments. The literature on crime speaks about two kinds of deterrence, "general" and "special." General deterrence is deterrence in advance: people obey the law because they know there is such a thing as punishment. Special deterrence is after the fact: a criminal is caught and sent to jail. If he "learns a lesson" and goes straight, he has been specially deterred.[16]

General deterrence is more important than special deterrence. Sending a thief to jail may or may not get thievery out of his system. There are, in fact, lots of backsliders ("recidivists"). What the thief does, however, is far less important than the presumed effect of jails and punishment on millions of other people, who think twice before stealing, out of fear. The Internal Revenue Service, with a loud clang of publicity, often indicts a few prominent tax evaders right before April 15. The idea is general deterrence: putting the fear of the Lord, so to speak, into taxpayers. It probably works, at least on some people.

What is important, of course, is not the actual sanction, but what people know or think about sanctions—the knowledge and notions they carry around in their heads. A completely secret system of punishment, if such a thing were possible, would not change anybody's behavior. This points up a weakness in much of the literature on deterrence. Scholars have tried to prove that harsh punishments cut down the crime rate. They cannot run experiments, so they try to find "natural" experiments. They compare, for example, the situation in two or more states. They look at the average prison term in state A, and compare it with the term in state B; then they look at the crime rates in these states. Does the tough state have less crime?[17]

But this is tricky business. In the first place, it is not easy to measure crime rates with precision. Comparing the rates of two or more states compounds the problem. Secondly, all sorts of other factors besides punishment influence crime rates. Thirdly, unless the differences in prison terms from state to state are extremely great, criminals are unlikely to know the differences. Suppose state A gives out, on average, prison sentences 12 percent more severe than those in state B. If burglars and thieves are not aware of the different levels of severity, then we should not expect any difference in the behavior of potential criminals in the two states. And if it takes a team of social scientists to discover the precise levels of severity, would a pickpocket or shoplifter know the same facts simply by intuition?

The reverse of this point is a kind of scarecrow or bogeyman effect. People are deterred by sanctions that are not really there—people only think they are. A study of subway crime in New York City found this "phantom effect." When the city put more policemen in subway cars, the crime rate went down, even during hours when the police were not actually there.[18] Of course, a phantom effect is not likely to last; it will wear off as soon as people learn the true picture. This is, alas, the fate of many of the campaigns against drunk driving. The zeal dribbles away, and then so too does the deterrent effect.[19]

When people talk loosely about the punishment for some particular crime, they often mean the official level of punishment—that is, the simple, blunt words on the law books ("five years in prison"). But punishment is both more and less than these five years. It is a complex process—a whole package of events—that an arrest sets in motion. A woman is picked up for shoplifting; she is taken to a strange, scary place; she is held in a cold, filthy cell; her name gets into the newspapers; she misses work and may lose her job; the neighbors gossip about her case; her husband files for divorce. All this can happen even if the police or the prosecutors or a jury let her go in the end without any "punishment." As Malcolm Feeley put it, in a study of a New Haven court, in the "lower criminal courts the process itself is the primary punishment."[20]

Process is punishment, no question. This makes it even harder to compare deterrent effects across state lines. It is easy to compare the *words* of the statutes of, say, Connecticut and Mississippi; harder, but still possible, to compare average sentences in the two states; much harder, and almost impossible, to compare real punishments. Shoplifting may carry more shame in a small town than in a big city, where life is more anonymous. Even "one year in prison" is not the same thing everywhere. Some prisons are harsher than others. There are maximum-security prisons where life is as tough and brutal as outside on the streets. Some prisons are filthy and corrupt; their guards are vicious; prisoners are victimized and raped. Then there are "model" prisons, well run, with more freedom and humanity. In theory at least, the kind of punishment experienced in prison should make a difference, both to general and special deterrence.

Deterrence is a psychological concept, at bottom. It is a guess about the way people will react to certain expectations. It obviously varies with the individual. People do not all react alike. Punishment, for example, is stigmatic: it imposes shame. But the impact of stigma is quite variable. An arrest might ruin a respectable businessman for life. It might humiliate him to the point of suicide. On the other hand, a young, street-wise thief might accept arrest as a cost of doing business. These assumptions are at least plausible.

People today are frightened, worried, and obsessed with the problem of crime. There is no question that the problem is extremely serious; there is little doubt that the rates of serious and violent crime have exploded in the period since the Second World War—rates of robbery, burglary, even murder. This may, in fact, be more or less a worldwide trend; the crime rates in London, Stockholm, and Sydney, though much lower than ours, have also risen dramatically in this period, according to a careful study.[21] In the early 1990s, in the United States, the rates seemed to moderate, or even decline, but the figures remain very, very high. The causes of the jump in crime in the last half of the twentieth century are, frankly, rather obscure.

What is to be done? For many people the solution is obvious: tighten the screws. Punishment deters; we need more punishment. Put more people in prison. Put more people to death. Lengthen the sentences. Make prison harsher, more austere. These ideas are simple and seem very attractive. The question is, can such tactics really work?

For better or for worse, tightening the screws is more easily said than done. The legislature can try to toughen the system, by passing harsh laws, but it cannot make punishments stick. The legislature does not catch or prosecute criminals, or carry out trials, or run the jails. The individual parts of the system can all frustrate each other. The system, to repeat the analogy we used in Chapter 9, is like a leaky hose.

Evidence of this fact keeps mounting up. Malcolm Feeley, in his studies of reforms in criminal justice, found a record of repeated failure. Laurence Ross, who analyzed studies of traffic crackdowns on speeders and drunk drivers, found that most of the crackdowns ultimately failed, as we noted before. When there is a move to control discretion at one point in the system, discretion simply shifts to another point: "The serpent held by one coil of his body may wriggle more energetically elsewhere."[22]

We can call this the problem of the "cadres." We talk as if a law or rule is a simple order which goes directly from some commander (the legislature, say) immediately to a subject—someone supposed to listen and obey. But in fact the process is rarely that simple, at least in our legal system. The process is more like chains of complex molecules. When the legislature orders longer jail sentences for drug pushers, it sends a message down the chain of command. The people in charge at each stage (the cadres) have the power to misunderstand, to pervert, to divert, to drag their feet, to frustrate the order. They may do this either consciously or unconsciously. It is a general problem of bureaucracy, and is especially severe in criminal justice because the system is so loose, so gangly, so uncoordinated.

There is another problem with "tightening the screws." The layman forgets that punishment can be self-defeating; it may have toxic side effects. In theory, a vicious, brutal prison should do a better job of deterring than a country-club prison, but it may also make inmates more criminal, more brutal—more likely to commit crime when they get out. We frequently hear that juvenile halls and jails are schools for crime; if this is so, it is another side effect of harshness. Probation, after all, whatever its failings, is not in itself a school for crime.

I do not mean to suggest that programs of toughness *always* fail. There is, for better or for worse, ample evidence that the toughness campaign of the late 1980s and early 1990s did have a notable impact— prison populations have skyrocketed, after all. The laws did succeed in locking up tens of thousands of men and women. What is less certain is what, if anything, has been accomplished by way of deterrence and "incapacitation."[23]

The stigma and shame of a criminal record are also punishments, in theory, and should deliver extra deterrence. In practice this, too, does not quite work out. The stigma can close so many doors that the ex-con is forced back to crime. This is the problem of the side effects. It is hard to measure, to be sure. But if we are convinced that these side effects are real, we might try, instead of more punishment, programs of jobs or rehabilitation. Alas, these seem out of step with the public mood in the 1990s.

The Deterrence Curve

Another point about rewards and punishments is worth making. We assume that if we jack up the threat of punishment, or punishment itself, we get some additional deterrent. That is, if we make a parking ticket $20 instead of $5, fewer people will park overtime. Can we tell in advance how much more compliance we will get?

The simple answer is no. Everything depends on the social setting, the circumstances, who the people are. But even if we know all this, we have no way to predict the amount of deterrence that more punishment buys. One thing is clear: the relationship is not simple and linear. Doubling the fine does not double the effect. It may produce much more than double, or very much less. There is no known way to predict.

Can we say anything about typical patterns? It seems that often they are more or less curvilinear. Suppose there is a $5 fine for parking over-time on Main Street; suppose the police catch one out of every three violators. Suppose, too, that half the drivers disobey the rules. They have two chances out of three of succeeding, and if they are caught, the fine is low. (Assume, to keep things simple, that the drivers know these facts.) What happens if enforcement stays the same, but we raise the fine to $50? Do we get ten times more compliance?

Almost certainly not. Half the drivers are already obeying, despite the pitiful fine. They are already deterred, or are law-abiding people for other reasons. We are concerned, in other words, with only half the drivers. They may be a tougher and more daring and less law-abiding group.

Still, $50 is real money. We cannot expect ten times more results, but we can expect some improvement in the situation. Suppose now we find that only one out of four drivers is willing to take the risk and park overtime. Raising the fine to $100 would flush out a few more—but probably not many, since only hard-core cases are left. To get at *this* group, we might start towing cars away. This is a big leap forward. Overtime parkers now have to pay a big fine and run around the city to reclaim their cars—a colossal nuisance. Nonetheless, a towaway system brings about little change, because there are not many drivers left to deter. The curve has flattened out. If we try punishments that are even more severe—taking away driver's licenses, or putting the drivers in jail—we would get only piddling results. There are too few violators left to deter. At some point, the curve becomes almost perfectly flat.

Let us transfer this reasoning to a more serious crime, for example, arson. The punishment for arson, assuming we catch most arsonists, is, let us say, five to ten years in prison. This is already pretty severe. Most people do not burn down buildings. The people who do are sick, violent, or unconscionable people. There are only a few of them, compared to the general population. Morality and fear of heavy punishment already prevent most acts of arson. Only a few people are left for new deterrence to work on. Some of these are hard-core cases—perhaps people who have trouble controlling their urge to burn things down. If we double the punishment and make this new punishment stick, we might get some fresh deterrent effect, but probably not very much. The curve has already flattened out. In theory, the effect of greater punishment will never be zero, but in practice, for some crimes, the effect comes very close to zero. Whether we have reached that point, or almost reached it, with certain *very* serious crimes—rape, for example, or murder—is a difficult question.

Capital Punishment

The debate about capital punishment is so loud and so passionate that it is worth spending a little more time on the subject. For some people, as we noted, the basic issue is moral. They do not want the state to kill, regardless of the deterrent effect. Similarly, some people favor capital punishment whether it deters or not; they feel that cruel, savage killers have forfeited the right to live and that executing such scum is a simple matter of justice. But there is also a group in between, who might be for or against, depending on whether the penalty worked.

Does fear of the gallows, the gas chamber, the electric chair, the firing squad, or lethal injection keep people from killing? (Murder is, practically speaking, the only capital crime left in this country.)[24] Our homicide rate is scandalously high. We kill each other in shocking numbers compared to (say) the Japanese or the Belgians. Moreover, the killing spree seems to be on a scale much higher than in the nineteenth and early twentieth centuries. Violence may be as American as apple pie, but this kind of pie seems unusually popular today. In Philadelphia, for example, in the years 1839–1901, on average only 3 persons per 100,000 were accused of criminal homicide each year. In the period 1969–71, however, 1,499 people were accused of this crime—a yearly rate of 25.7 per 100,000; in 1994, in Washington, D.C., the murder rate was about 70 per 100,000.[25] Government statistics estimate there were about 8,000 homicide victims nationally in 1950; then came the murder boom, and in 1978 there were more than 20,000 victims. The murder rate has remained at this high plateau; in 1994 there were over 23,000 victims of murder, about 9 per 100,000, nationwide.[26] There are some problems with all of these figures, and some indications that in the late 1990s the numbers are now leveling off or even declining. Still, the differences between time periods are so vast that there is no doubt about the general trend. We live in a golden age of murder.

Crime is a national scandal; yet the actual number of murderers, considering the size of our population, is nonetheless quite small. It is not hard to think of reasons why. Moral scruples, fear of revenge, and the likelihood of severe punishment, short of the death penalty, are more than enough to keep most of us away from violent crime. The curve, in other words, has flattened out enormously. This means that the added bang which the death penalty might provide is not likely to produce much *fresh* deterrence. In other words, a person can argue against the death penalty on many grounds—moral or social scruples or assumed side effects—but also because it may not work very well. It is not necessary to argue that the death penalty flatly does not deter. This would be questionable in principle, and it skates on very thin empirical ice.

Most discussions of the death penalty are, in a way, unnecessarily abstract. They ignore the facts of this particular society. The death penalty may work efficiently in some societies—societies that use it quickly, mercilessly, and frequently. It cannot work well in the United States, where it is relatively rare, slow, and controversial. This point gets lost in the shouting and the arguments.

To deter, a threat must be real. If we ticket an illegal parking spot once every thirty years, we cannot expect anybody to be afraid to park there. Except in a few states (Texas, very notably), the death penalty is not often carried out in the United States. In California, with over 10 percent of the nation's population (and a big contingent on death row), there had been, as of the beginning of 1997, fewer actual executions since 1976 than the fingers on one hand. This means that in California, the death penalty must be fairly feeble as an extra deterrent. In order to pack more muscle, we would have to put the death penalty into effect reasonably often, though how often is not easy to say. But because this form of punishment has some intense and dedicated enemies, and because it is hedged about with so many procedural safeguards, the number of executions is likely to stay quite limited, at least in the foreseeable future.

In fact, the death penalty was never as common in this country as it was in England in early modern times. American did, however, make more use of it in the past than they do now. At the time of the American Revolution, people could be hung for dozens of crimes; there were 113 separate offenses that carried the death penalty in South Carolina in 1813. By 1850, the list was down to twenty-two.[27] The northern states were stingier with capital offenses. In practice, murder and rape were the only important crimes that carried the death penalty. As far back as the early nineteenth century, there was a movement to get rid of the death penalty. Some states—Wisconsin is one—have never had it at all.

A law on the books is one thing; actual hangings are another. Here, too, the South was more lavish with death penalties than the North. The chief victims were slaves. In Virginia, between 1706 and 1865, 628 slaves were hanged.[28] South Carolina put 296 slaves to death between 1800 and 1855—sixty-four for murder, forty-six for insurrection, thirty-one for burglary, twenty-eight for assault, seventeen for arson, twenty-one for poisoning, seventeen for rape. (In seventy-two cases, the exact crime was unknown.) By contrast, Massachusetts, with a white population twice as large as the black population of South Carolina, executed only twenty-eight people between 1801 and 1845.[29] This is less than one a year.

Public opinion, especially in the past, is a slippery and elusive topic. There were, of course, no opinion polls in the nineteenth century. But we do know something about how the system actually behaved, and we know the rhetoric of public debate. Behavior and rhetoric both suggest that support for the death penalty suffered a long-term decline in America. The number of people actually put to death went down steadily. In the decade of the 1930s, 1,667 prisoners were executed. As late as 1951, there were 105 deaths from capital punishment. In 1966, there was only one. After that time, capital punishment almost, though not quite, ground to a halt.

The main reason was the success of the legal campaign against the death penalty. In 1972, in the famous case of *Furman v. Georgia*,[30] the Supreme Court, as we mentioned before, dropped a bombshell. The Court struck down as unconstitutional every death-penalty law in the country and made a clean sweep of death row. It was a startling decision and a close call: the majority was a bare five out of nine justices, and the decision was so fragmented that it was hard to tell exactly what was decided and why. In fact, every justice wrote a separate opinion.

A few justices felt that the death penalty was "cruel and unusual," or had somehow become cruel and unusual in the course of social evolution. This made capital punishment unconstitutional under the Eighth Amendment, in all circumstances. Most justices did not support this view. In fact, the majority—the five justices on the winning side—said all sorts of things, some contradicting the others. One basic theme was that there was too much discretion in the system. The death penalty was imposed in arbitrary, unpredictable, almost irrational ways. It also fell too heavily on black people, on underdogs, on the unpopular. Some justices argued that it was a poor deterrent, or that it was immoral, or that enlightened public opinion had turned against it, and so on.

Some of these arguments rested on empirical assertions—statements of fact—at least in part. For example, was it really true that the death penalty offends "enlightened" public opinion? Of course, there is no standard for judging what is and what is not "enlightened." What is "enlightened" to one person is foolish or bigoted to another. At any rate, only one thing was clear after *Furman:* for the time being, capital punishment was dead.

It did not stay dead. The soaring crime rate breathed new life into it. Public opinion (enlightened or otherwise) apparently turned. Capital punishment began to do better in public-opinion polls. Most state legislatures showed their disagreement with *Furman* in the most direct possible way: they passed new death laws. They had to take into account what the Court said in *Furman,* as best they could; hence they tried to write less offensive statutes. In this sense, at least, the decision was a powerful force for change. But it failed to put the issue to rest.

In 1976, the Supreme Court decided a new batch of cases on the death penalty. The lead case was *Gregg v. Georgia.*[31] In many ways, the results were just as chaotic as in *Furman.* The Court split badly, and the justices wrote many separate opinions, ranging all over the lot. The Court ruled on several new kinds of statute. It accepted some and struck down others. Most of the justices were not willing to go the last step and destroy the death penalty absolutely and finally and under all circumstances. Beyond this, the law was left rather murky. Later decisions have not quite cleared up the murk.

Meanwhile, legislatures have not been idle either. The issue is still alive and very active politically. The popularity of the death penalty has grown tremendously. The population on death row numbers over three thousand, as of 1997. Mostly these prisoners wait, and wait, and wait. There are endless court hearings, appeals, and reappeals. Relatively few are actually put to death; blizzards of suits, claims, writs, and petitions pile up delay after delay. Since 1976 and up to the time of this writing (1997), something over three hundred people have been put to death, starting with Gary Gilmore in Utah, who (at the end) had given up the struggle.

The death penalty is indeed a rallying cry for "law-and-order" people. Few politicians dare to utter a word against it. President Clinton's crime bill in 1994 trumpeted loudly the creation of new capital crimes at the federal level[32] Determined enemies of capital punishment fight these developments, at every step of the way. They are losing ground, and yet the result does seem to be a kind of stalemate. The death penalty is the law in most states, but even in Texas, the state with the biggest appetite for executions, it is not a quick and easy form of punishment— no matter how vicious the criminal and how heinous his crime. In the 1950s, it was already possible to hold the executioner off for years; legal moves seemed almost endless. A famous instance was the case of Caryl Chessman. Chessman was sentenced to die in California on May 21, 1948. Not until twelve years later, in May 1960, did he lose his final hope and die in the gas chamber.

Today, there are dozens and dozens of Chessmans—men (and a few women) who have spent years and years on death row, fighting their fate. Jerry Joe Bird, executed in Texas in 1991, had been on death row for seventeen years.[33] The end of the torture, one way or another, is still in doubt for most of the death-row denizens. Their number continues to grow. They sit tight and struggle on from court to court. The pace of executions quickened in the late 1980s and 1990s, and the Supreme Court indicated real impatience with the endless delays. The Court, and the public, seemed to be saying: get on with it. Some observers do expect the harvest of executions to increase in the near future.

But it would be too simple, still, to say flatly that the United States "uses the death penalty." Capital punishment, in most states, either does not exist—some twelve states lack it entirely—or is half dead, as in California. Only in some of the southern states is it much of a working reality. It is tied up in knots that have proved very difficult to unravel. A death penalty of the American sort cannot act as much of a deterrent, compared to the toughest form of life sentence—life without possibility of parole. A real death penalty—one that worked, one that had a strong effect on criminal behavior—would have to be more certain and more swift.

Is there much of a chance of a death penalty of this sort, in the United States? I doubt it. The opposition will never give up. Many people (including judges and juries) find the death penalty awesome, frightening, extreme. No doubt many people who tell pollsters they favor the death penalty would shrink from it on an actual jury. Our tradition of due process, whatever its deficiencies, stands in the way of any "quick and dirty" solutions. Is there anybody who thinks a person sentenced to death should *not* have a careful review, and at least one appeal to a higher court? Yet all this takes time—lots of time—and a shortage of lawyers to handle such cases is one of the prime causes of delay.

The situation, then, is confused, uncertain, endlessly complex—and as a result, frustrating to both sides of the argument. The pros and the cons both grumble and complain, and no wonder: neither side can, for the moment, win a meaningful and decisive victory. Yet this situation reflects current social reality. Society is of two minds on the subject. The law faithfully mirrors public hesitation, disagreement, and doubt, just as it reflects its deeper convictions.

The death penalty is an extreme example of a more general issue in deterrence theory, and it also points up problems in the plan, so popular today, to make the legal system more effective by giving it more muscle and more bite. Many scholars have worked on deterrence theory in recent years. They tend to agree that deterrence is no humbug: if we jack up real penalties, we will definitely scare away some customers for crime, just as a stiff rise in the price of lettuce or toys would scare off some buyers. In the real world, this is a mighty big if. "Severity" is easier said than done. The system is too complex to move easily and quickly. Severe laws can be controversial (like the death penalty); they may produce nasty, unwanted side effects. All of this makes deterrence hard to measure and hard to predict, and also hard to harness and control.

12

Legal Culture: Legitimacy and Morality

*N*OT ALL LEGAL behavior can be explained in terms of reward and punishment. To some extent, we are indeed animals that respond to the carrot and the stick. But we are also moral and social beings. We react to messages we get from other people—to what other people think and say—and we also listen to the voice of conscience, to messages from inside. These messages are extremely important in explaining how we respond to legal acts. They may be, in fact, more important than rewards and punishments.

The "social" factor, reduced to its simplest form, simply means that people care what other people think. No man or woman is an island. We are all powerfully influenced by family, friends, neighbors, coworkers, fellow students, members of our church. All of us feel the silent and not-so-silent pressure of these people who co-inhabit our lives. This pressure may push us to obey the law or to disobey, or to use the law in particular, patterned ways.

There has been much talk, for example, about the influence of peer groups—a phrase that refers, basically, to the people around us, the people we consider to be our group ("peers" means equals). We know from everyday experience that the group has a tremendous influence. Such a term as "delinquent subculture," for example, is merely an elegant way to express a simple idea. The point is this: it is a kind of punishment if your friends taunt you, laugh at you, treat you as inferior; it is a real and strong reward when they admire you and praise you. Suppose you belong to some big-city gang whose code gives high marks to macho behavior—breaking the law, acting tough, defying the police—but gives low marks if you tattle or are "yellow" or refuse to go along with some illegal caper. You are certainly more likely to break the law than if you were not a member of the gang. This is because breaking the law in your case represents conformity to group norms, and if you conform to *official* norms—that is, if you act "good"—you are breaking the law of your group. In "Clarendon Heights," a housing project in a Northeastern city, a member of the "Hallway Hangers" reports, "You hafta make a name for yourself, to be bad, tough, whatever. . . . If you're to be bad, you hafta be arrested." Thus "good grades in school can lead to ostracism, whereas time spent in prison earns respect."[1]

Even outside the gang context, we can use similar ideas to help account for delinquency: the adolescent chooses rebellion because it "allows conformity to the standards of an alternate social system," which (for a number of reasons) suit his psychological and other needs more than the mainstream system.[2] And the delinquency label, when it is pinned on an adolescent, only serves to isolate him from respectable society and makes it more likely that his real rewards will come from the members of his group, and only from them.

There is nothing startling, then, in all this, either as theory or as practice. Everybody likes to be rewarded and practically everybody wants to avoid punishment; a whipping is a whipping whether it comes from the state or from the people next door. The groups we belong to are, in a way, miniature societies, with tiny "governments" and "laws" of their own. If we follow gang norms instead of the norms of the "real" government, we are in a way simply acting as the subjects of competing rulers. Very often, the scarier and more threatening "government" is the one that sits on our doorstep. After all, for most people, it may be easier to avoid or evade the police than to get out from under disapproval (or worse) that comes from friends, neighbors, or parents. In many prisons, gang leaders are more effective and powerful rulers of prison society than the warden or guards.

This much seems fairly obvious, though there is not much research directly relevant. It is sometimes possible to show how other people influence legal behavior. Johannes Feest, for example, did a little study of traffic behavior in Berkeley, California. His study showed that people drive one way when they are alone, quite another when other people sit next to them. Among drivers who were alone, only one out of ten came to a full stop at a stop sign; when someone shared the car with the driver, full stops rose to 21 percent.[3]

In other words, people do not obey traffic rules only because they are afraid of the police. They also respond to the person sitting next to them—to what that person thinks and feels, what that person says about the driver's behavior. Some of us will go through a red light late at night, with nobody around and nobody with us, although we would never do the same by day, police or no police.

Feest gathered his data by sitting in a parked car and watching how drivers behaved. He did not talk to the drivers, and we do not know who the other people were who influenced the driver. No doubt they were relatives or friends. A study by Lionel Dannick, however, suggests that even a stranger can affect behavior, simply by being nearby. Dannick did research on pedestrians in New York City. Pedestrians often crossed the street illegally, that is, when the sign said "Don't walk." But if the experimenters planted somebody to stand on the corner and cross only when the sign said "Walk," the rate of violation dropped dramatically. Contrariwise, when the "plant" clearly broke the rule, the rate of violation went up.[4] Violators, in other words, "reinforce" other violators, and compliers do the same.[5]

We have to draw a distinction, of course, between the effect of other people on our own behavior and the effect of our own ideas about right and wrong. Of course, what we see when we stand on the corner or peek out from a parked car is people's behavior; their motives are invisible. Why is it that somebody stops himself from jaywalking when he sees other people who obey the rule? Perhaps he wants to avoid embarrassment, and of course it is embarrassing if people see you breaking rules. But the "good" people are also teachers, of a sort: they show us that the rule is alive, that it means something to them, that they choose (for whatever reason) not to break it. That may influence the way we feel about the rule.

The point, in other words, is that peer pressure (or other messages from the crowd) may in the long run change our thoughts as well as our behavior. The civil-rights laws have forced hotels and restaurants to open their doors to people of all races; there was a time when many of them—and not only in the South—refused to let black people in. The fact that these hotels and restaurants *must* not discriminate does not in itself change bigots to nonbigots; the owners may still feel the same way about race. But coercion creates a new situation—it changes public behavior—and when this happens, real or imagined peer pressure may start to work on people's minds. A segregated restaurant first becomes illegal, then impossible, and finally unthinkable. Somewhat similarly, corporations, mindful of antidiscrimination laws, set up offices and departments to deal with "equal opportunity" within the company, and these bring in committed people and set up waves of dynamics that affect the behavior of companies, employees, and everybody they come in contact with.[6]

Legitimacy and Morality

As we have suggested, ideas about right and wrong, about morality, about legitimacy, are very important in explaining how people behave. This is plain common sense. Most of us (one hopes) would not steal, cheat, murder, or set fire to buildings, whether or not there was any chance the police would catch us and whether or not there was any chance that peers would find out and disapprove. We would do the right thing because we want to, because of the voice inside, because we have been taught to avoid evil deeds, and the lessons of our childhood took hold.

The penal code, in other words, is not the only source—or even the main source—of our ideas about right and wrong. We learn the moral code from our parents and teachers, and we drink in ideas simply by living in society. Every community has its own definitions of right and wrong, and every community has its own way of imparting them to members. Ideas of right and wrong are constantly in flux; it is interesting to watch them shift, bend, and change colors. Some norms (about killing and stealing) are very stable, of course; others (about sexual behavior, for example) seem much more changeable, and have changed most radically over time.

In any event, our consciences are powerful motors. Most of us want to do what is right, and if this means obeying the law, then we will obey. Conversely, there may be times when people feel strongly that the law is wrong or immoral. Conscience can lead to disobedience as well as obedience. There are many examples in our history. People have often gone to jail as a matter of conscience. In protest against the war in Vietnam, for example, many men refused to register for the draft. It was a way to oppose what they felt was an immoral war; they were willing to suffer punishment rather than obey. Some people are so appalled by abortion that they are willing to disrupt family planning clinics, even if it means going to jail. A few fanatics have even been willing to kill.

We obey—and want to obey—what we think is *right;* and also what we consider *legitimate.* These two words do not mean the same thing. Social scientists and legal scholars—at least since the days of Max Weber, the great German sociologist—talk a great deal about legitimate rules and about legitimacy in general. But the words are not always used very precisely, and there are many definitions floating about in the literature. The imprecision is so great that at least one scholar, Alan Hyde, feels that the whole concept should be junked as useless and confusing.[7] Of course, no single definition of legitimacy is right or wrong, but the concept does have a core of value. Basically, when people say that laws are "legitimate," they mean that there is something rightful about the way in which the laws came about. Legitimacy is mostly used as a procedural concept, in other words—or, if you will, a legal one.

An example will make this clear. What makes a law passed by Congress "legitimate"? Not what is in the law—that might be foolish, short-sighted, or deficient in all sorts of ways. No, the law is legitimate because Congress passed it; for most of us that is enough in itself. In other words, we do not question the legitimacy of a law so long as it was regularly passed by Congress or a state legislature or a city council.

We can push this idea further and ask *why* the fact that Congress passed the law makes the law "legitimate." If we put this question to people, they might answer with something like this: Congress has the right to do this because the people elected its members, or because the law reflects what the majority of people want. Very few members of the public have thought deeply about political theory, but they do have vague, commonsense ideas floating around in their heads. In any case, the legitimacy of law rests on the way it comes to be: if that is legitimate, then so are the results, at least most of the time. And what is true for legislative bodies is also true for actions of the president, rules of the Seattle school board, and decisions of the Supreme Court of Arkansas: all are legitimate insofar as the public accepts them as part of the normal, rightful way of doing public business.

The binding force of these legal acts comes, then, from the procedure or from the institution, not from what the acts do or say. Obeying a rule because it is legitimate is not at all the same as obeying it because it is moral or ethical, or even because it is fair. In fact, we should probably distinguish carefully between various ways in which a rule or act can be "right." People in their legal behavior do follow the voice of conscience. But conscience is a complicated organ; its voice is made up of many tones.

Legitimacy is only one of these factors of conscience. Another we can call "civic-mindedness." This is the notion that we ought to obey some rules for social or patriotic reasons. Civic-minded people are willing to take fewer showers and let their lawns die if there is a water shortage; they enlist in the army during wartime; they resist the impulse to throw beer cans on the trail in Yellowstone; they pay taxes on time and in full. For some people, this is a powerful impulse, even in situations where there is no chance violators will get caught and no peers are around to wag their fingers. For others, of course, such a motive is weak or absent.

"Morality," strictly speaking, is a somewhat different motive. This may perhaps be the most powerful and important factor of all: obedience to rules for moral or religious reasons. It is our moral training that explains why most of us do not cheat, steal, murder, or lie. It is why devout Mormons refuse to drink, why Orthodox Jews refrain from eating pork, why observant Catholics do not divorce. The normative structure of society is as important as its political structure, and just as essential.

"Fairness" is still another concept. Sometimes I might feel that a rule deserves support because of some purely formal characteristic—for example, because it affects everybody in the country, and why should I be different? If the government imposed a $5 tax on every man, woman, and child, some people might decide to pay because they felt it was only fair to do so, whether or not they thought the tax made sense, was morally sound, or was good for the country. Still another conscience factor is what we might call "trust." This is the feeling that we should go along with some rule or order because of faith in the authorities. They know so much and we know so little. If they tell us to do something, they must have a good reason, and we should go along, whether we understand the reasons or not.

These factors are all different from legitimacy, and they are all motives for obeying or disobeying law. Motives are invisible, but motives or attitudes are social facts as much as behavior is. What people think is as real as what they eat and how they vote or swim, only harder to observe or to measure. Like all attitudes, attitudes toward laws and rules are not poured in concrete. They change over time. Different ages and types of people have them in different degrees, and they also rise and fall with the social tides.

Many people feel, for example, that trust is in short supply today. Studies have suggested that people have gotten more cynical over the years. They are less likely than before to say that they trust or believe in the authorities. One study asked people, "How much of the time do you think that you can trust the government in Washington to do what is right?" In 1964, 14 percent said "always"; 62 percent said "most of the time"; only 22 percent said "only some of the time." Six years later, in 1970, only 6 percent trusted the government "always"; 47 percent said "most of the time"; the doubters who said "only some of the time" had risen to 44 percent.[8]

Trust declined even further after 1970. Survey research picked up a definite loss of confidence in government, and probably in experts and authorities of all sorts. In 1981 the governor of California (after much controversy) gave an order for aerial spraying of pesticides on parts of northern California. The problem was the insidious medfly, whose larvae threatened to chew the fruit industry to death. The public was told that the spray was harmless, that there was nothing to fear. A generation earlier, almost everybody would have accepted this as gospel; it was the governor's word and the word of the scientists employed by the state. In 1981, many people simply refused to believe; some people left the area in panic; blind faith was in short supply. A survey published in 1996 found a "precipitous decline in ordinary Americans' confidence in . . . government." Only 32 percent of the people surveyed had a "great deal" or "quite a lot" of confidence in the federal government. More than two-thirds felt that the federal tax system was "basically unfair."[9]

What follows from a loss of trust? If people are distrustful of government, and dissatisfied, do they tend to break the law? Not necessarily. People can comply even if they are more or less fed up with the system.[10] There is some reason to be skeptical about the so-called spillover effect. This is the hypothesis that people who think one part of the legal system is unfair or illegitimate, or who do not trust it in one regard, will disobey or lose faith in the rest of it.

In a way, this seems plausible. People frequently make this point about laws that are badly or unfairly enforced; they claim that this leads to disrespect for law in general. Supposedly, this was a side effect of Prohibition. We hear the same argument about criminalizing marijuana. In fact, there is little or no evidence for the spillover effect. If you think the marijuana laws are unfair or ridiculous, are you more likely to cheat on your income tax, park overtime, or shoot your brother-in-law? It seems unlikely. There may be spillover into "neighboring" areas of legal behavior: a person with contempt for marijuana laws may be more likely than others to use cocaine or break the liquor laws. Somehow, we feel sure a dope pusher will not shy away from breaking vice laws. But we are not sure how far these "neighborhoods" extend or what constitutes a neighborhood.

It is logical to assume some connection between the way we behave and what we think about legitimacy and the moral status of law. In one classic study, Harry V. Ball studied landlords in Honolulu. The city was under rent control at the time. Ball found that landlords who thought rent control was unfair tended to act accordingly: these were the landlords who overcharged their tenants.[11]

This shows some relationship between attitude and behavior. But exactly what relationship? We have a chicken-and-egg puzzle here. Which comes first, the moral attitude or the lawbreaking? The sense of unfairness may be one way a landlord soothes his conscience. Ball assumes the sense of unfairness led landlords down the path to law-breaking; but the causation might go the other way around: landlords who violated the law came to excuse themselves by blaming bad law. The Honolulu data do not show which way the causal arrows point.

In an important study published in 1990, Tom R. Tyler studied residents of Chicago, to try to find out (among other things) whether legitimacy and other such factors influenced actual obedience to law. He found that most people—over 80 percent—agreed that people "should obey the law even if it goes against what they think is right." He also found that there was a relationship between *belief* in compliance and *actual* compliance—at least with the handful of rules he actually studied (for example, rules against drunk driving and overtime parking).[12] The subject is intriguing, important, and difficult, and deserves a lot of further careful study.

The Inverse Factors

We have discussed a variety of inner motives for legal behavior—morality, fairness, trust, civic-mindedness, legitimacy. Each of them, as the discussion implies, also has its opposite: mistrust, illegitimacy, a sense of unfairness, and so on. We assume that the more we make people think of a law as moral, trustworthy, and legitimate, the more likely it is that they will comply, and there are bits of evidence that support this proposition. Similarly, an increase in a sense of a law's unfairness or illegitimacy should weaken the feeling of duty, leading to less obedience (or none) or—if the moral feelings are strong enough—to actual defiance or revolt.

This is plain common sense. It is confirmed by experience as well. If Tyler's findings are true, people in general do think they ought to obey the law, whether they like the law or not. But there seem to be limits—at least for some people. As we said, there are men and women so ardently opposed to legal abortion that they are willing to terrorize family planning clinics. There are also people so fanatically opposed to government that they are willing to bomb federal installations, as the Oklahoma City tragedy of 1995 suggests. Dissent can, of course, take milder forms: refusal to pay income tax, court cases attacking the constitutionality of statutes, and so on; some of these methods (the court cases) are plainly legitimate and operate wholly within the system.

For most people, loss of faith is not necessarily across-the-board.

When people become disgusted with or mistrustful of one law or one part of government, they do not necessarily turn outlaw. A few do; most do not. Most simply grumble and accept things as they are. Some turn to other channels for expressing dissatisfaction. We have mentioned the courts. There is, in other words, what one might call a *transfer* of legitimacy. People who lose faith in Congress, city hall, or the bureaucracies might turn to the judges in hopes of salvation. That is, they "judicialize" their problems.

In the medfly crisis in California, which we mentioned a few pages back, the state government announced it would spray a pesticide (malathion) over the counties near San Francisco Bay. They assured the public that malathion was safe. Many people did not believe them. They suspected the government was lying, to protect big fruit growers.

As it happens, the spraying went off as planned. Those who opposed it did not take it lying down. They went to court. This strategy for the disgruntled is becoming more common. It is the way the battle against capital punishment is carried on. It was the keystone of the civil-rights movement. As the malathion case shows, the strategy does not always work (the case was lost), but it can at least achieve delay. And delay is often valuable—if the goal is to stop some government action dead in its tracks. The battle against nuclear power plants goes on and on; court tactics make nuclear power more costly through delay and through obstructive measures that are all perfectly legal, though sometimes extremely legalistic. The enemies of the death penalty, too, count on delay. They try measure after measure to keep the convicts on death row alive.

Much of this litigation reflects a loss of faith and trust in government. Yet, in one crucial sense, it implies *more*, not less, trust: trust in the courts. Environmental groups, prisoners'-rights groups, civil-liberties groups—such bands of activists would not waste time and money on litigation if they were cynical about court systems, or if they trusted the courts as little as they trusted certain other agencies of government. In many societies, there would be no such faith in the courts—not in their will nor in their power. The trend toward judicialization is, to some extent, an indicator of loss of legitimacy and trust with regard to government in general. It is thus a sign of what we called a transfer or shift of legitimacy to courts.

Legitimacy and Conscience: How Strong?

How strong are our feelings of legitimacy or trust, or conscience in general? Common sense tells us that we have more attachment to some norms than to others. Most of us would not kill except in dire emergency, if then, but we are nonchalant about breaking the speed limits. These differences make it hard to say much, in general, about how people resolve conflicts *among* the various motives for legal behavior. Everything depends on the circumstances, the situation, and the particular rule. People who feel that speeding is dangerous and antisocial, and who are afraid of the police, are still willing to go at lightning speed if the situation is serious enough.

If sanctions, the people around us, and our inner feelings all pull in the same direction, then the norm will be tough and durable indeed. This is basically the case with norms against killing. The law takes murder very seriously and punishes it severely. Conscience is against it, too, and neighbors and friends share the general revulsion against killing. Hence this norm is one of the strongest known.

It is not easy to go much beyond this simple point. Suppose conscience pulls one way and the law, with its sanctions, pulls another: who wins? Is the threat of punishment more powerful than appeal to conscience? There is no general answer. An occasional researcher has tried to study the question experimentally. In one such project, two researchers used college students in Florida as their guinea pigs. The students were allowed to grade their own quizzes in a course. Without the students' knowledge, the teachers were able to check the real scores against self-graded ones and find out how much cheating was going on. Quite a bit, it turned out. Some students were then threatened with spot checks and punishment; this cut down cheating considerably. Others were given a moral pep talk. This hardly worked at all. Threat of punishment was much more powerful than appeals to conscience.[13] In another study, the researchers probed to see whether students (always handy subjects) were likely to violate certain norms—drunk driving, petty theft; they were then asked questions about whether shame (inner guilt), embarrassment (peer pressure), or legal sanctions were likely to present a "problem." In this study, "shame" seemed to make a difference; "embarrassment" did not count for very much at all.[14]

But these studies hardly prove the general case—or *any* general case. In fact, the general case is unprovable, because the terms "punishment," "conscience," and "peer group" do not refer to single or constant factors. There are many types of conscience, and many ways to try to stir it into action. They cannot be summed up in a single formula. Sometimes, in the midst of a war, appeals to the public for sacrifice have been tremendously successful: many people have been willing, after all, to die for their country or for a cause. At other times and under other circumstances, moral appeals and sermons simply fall on deaf ears.

Wage-price guidelines, for example, have often been dismal failures; they need strong sanctions to back them up.

Also, sanctions themselves come in all shapes and sizes, from money rewards to fines, jail, whipping, and even the threat of death. Some sanctions terrify us; some have very little bite. Some incentives are strong and some are weak. Again, much depends on the circumstances.

These studies of student behavior, then, cannot provide us with general answers to the questions we are asking. At best, they pit one sort of moral appeal against one sort of sanction, or one form of peer-group pressure against one form of moral appeal, and in only one or two types of situation. We do not know what happens when there is conflict between state sanctions and private conscience, between conscience and the pull and tug of group loyalty, between peer pressure and the government, in a *different* situation. Conflicts of this kind are everyday occurrences. Nothing is more common than to find ourselves in the middle, torn between a feeling that we ought to obey (or disobey) the law, and contradictory messages coming from the people around us or from our own inner feelings. There are no rules on how to resolve these conflicts, and there are no general research findings that tell us how people do resolve them.

Civil disobedience is an important social fact in our history. Civil disobedience is an open challenge to law, but one based on principle. People who civilly disobey do not deny that the laws they attack are formally valid. But they feels that the laws are so repulsive morally, or so harmful to society, that the citizen has a higher duty to disobey. The higher duty may be grounded in religion. The Mormons in Utah in the nineteenth century believed that God permitted and encouraged men to have several wives. The idea was enormously offensive to the rest of the country, but the Mormons stuck to their guns and defied the authorities for many years, and in the face of tremendous persecution. The Boston Tea Party, the abolitionist movement, the civil-rights movement, draft protests, the right-to-life movement—the historical record is full of examples of civil disobedience. Some of it has been extremely effective in changing the law or in teaching the larger society a moral lesson. It is enough to mention Martin Luther King and the black protest movements of the 1950s and 1960s.

Civil disobedience is not always nonviolent. The Boston Tea Party destroyed private property. John Brown was willing to kill innocent people in his crusade against slavery. In this society, nonviolence may tend to add moral strength to civil disobedience. This was the lesson taught by Mahatma Gandhi in India, and applied since then in many countries. One reason is that nonviolence expresses, in a particularly dramatic way, the morality of civil disobedience. It expressly denies any spillover effect. It is a way of saying, "We object to *this* law, but not to law in general." The protesters, in fact, are deeply committed to order, justice, and organized society. Indeed, they may often appeal—as did Martin Luther King—to a higher but secular law (the Constitution, for example). This legitimates their disobedience to local laws which, they claim, are themselves illegitimate. In any event, they assert, with their words and their body language, that some laws, though formally or superficially valid, are simply too morally corrupt to survive.

Law and Morality

We often hear talk about the conflict between law and morals. Many writers stress how different law is from morality, and how much the legal code differs from the moral code. Others insist that law cannot be separated from morality, or even that unjust rules or an unjust regime cannot be law. There are complex and fascinating issues here, which are at the core of the philosophy of law.[15]

The relationship between legal codes and the moral norms and customs of society—and specifically of United States society—is a simpler, less normative issue. It is obvious that the law embodies a moral code, and does so explicitly. The law books of any state and of the federal government (and of other countries, too) make this point in the most elementary way. Murder, theft, rape, and income-tax fraud are immoral acts, and they are certainly illegal as well.

But every complicated society (and ours is certainly complicated) has more than a single moral code: it has many different ones. People disagree, sometimes quite bitterly, about issues of right and wrong, morality and immorality, and how to deal with situations in which the various versions clash. Some disagreements over norms can be compromised, or the norms can be treated as deserving of equal treatment. The law, for example, is neutral on the subject of religion, by and large. It does not require anyone to practice any faith, and there is no official church or statement of faith. In many societies there were, or are, state religions, and those who hold unorthodox beliefs and follow unorthodox practices are persecuted, sometimes to the point of death. There is certainly no "separation of church and state" in Iran, or in Saudi Arabia.

But there are situations, in the United States, where neutrality is impossible. The law cannot be both for or against something at the same time. This means that conflicts arise continually between law and morals, or rather between law and the morals of *some* part of the population. The polygamy dispute in territorial Utah can serve as a good historical example. Before the Civil War, abolitionists clashed with those who defended slavery. There have been innumerable other instances, up to the present day.

One of the most poignant instances today is the abortion controversy. The Supreme Court, in *Roe v. Wade*,[16] held that the Constitution, our highest law, protects a woman's right to have an abortion, at least in the early months of pregnancy. The Court struck down state laws that interfered with this right. Many people feel *Roe v. Wade* was a wise, just, and even moral decision. But many people were, and continue to be, outraged. To them, abortion is nothing more or less than murder, and any law that permits it permits the worst possible crime, the slaughter of innocent beings. Obviously, these believers in the "right to life" cannot accept the present law, which goes against their own moral code. "Pro-choice" people, on the other hand, may believe just as strongly in the justice of their cause—in the sanctity of a woman's right to control her own body.

There is a sense, however, in which law and morality seem to clash, even without sharp differences of opinion of this sort. Most of us would probably agree that it is wrong to tell lies or to cheat at cards. Neither of these is a crime; neither is found in the penal code. Some lies are so gross or harmful that they may amount to slander, and card-cheating may, under some circumstances, amount to fraud, but these are exceptional situations. Why does the law leave lying and cheating alone? Why not at least a small fine? Is overtime parking really worse than cheating at poker or bridge?

Perhaps these examples prove that law and morality are different spheres and have different aims. But there is another way to describe the situation. If we made card-cheating a crime, we might set off some nasty consequences. People might start informing on other people. We would give great discretion and power to police if we let them arrest people for lying. We might open the door to blackmail and corruption. We might punish people beyond what they deserve.

Notice that all these statements about adverse side effects are also statements about morality—about what is right and what is wrong, just and unjust. In other words, when "immoral" acts are left out of the penal code it is not because of some inherent difference between law and morality, but because there are many competing moral principles and we have to make choices among them. Society has to make these choices all the time; and it does not always choose correctly, by any means. The Mann Act, passed in the early part of the twentieth century,[17] made it a federal crime to "transport" a woman across state lines "for the purpose of prostitution or debauchery, or for any other immoral purpose." This law was supposed to help stamp out "white slavery" (note the racist overtones of this popular phrase): the practice of forcing women into the degrading status of prostitution. The act probably had no impact on prostitution. It probably did open the door to blackmail, which is another evil, and a serious one. The law also permitted the harassment of some defendants who offended public opinion—Jack Johnson, for example, the boxer, and Chuck Berry, the rock-and-roll star; these were black men involved with white women. In 1986, in the face of changing ideas about sexual morality, and in the light of the act's checkered history, it was substantially revised and defanged.[18]

The legal system is based on social norms; it has to be. It reflects principles and ideas which fit ideas about morality held somewhere in society. But not necessarily by everybody. Morality is an abstraction. Debates and conflicts are hard, specific, concrete; they are about abortion, the death penalty, polygamy; about drug laws, gambling, pornography on the Internet, gays in the military, prostitution, air pollution, endangered species. The list is long and the struggle is hard. But the issue is not whether or not the law should enforce morality. Of course it should; it must. The issue is, whose morality, and how?

To put it another way: in a complex, pluralistic society—a society made of up all sorts, shapes, and tastes of people, with many ways of life—how far should the legal system go in upholding a single, official moral code? Many people would answer rather quickly, "Not far at all." We should live and let live. An open, democratic society can and should tolerate different ways of life.

Not everybody, of course, would agree with this philosophy. In fact, nobody agrees with it entirely. After all, there are people whose personal moral code allows or even requires them to rob banks, burn buildings, and skyjack planes "for the cause." Even the Ku Klux Klan or the American Nazi Party has "principles," which the rest of us find repulsive. There are people who actually *believe* in sex with children. We can argue that people who hold these views have the right of free speech— they can say what they want. But beyond that, there is no reason why we should actually accommodate or legitimate the behaviors and principles in question. Nor do we.

On the other hand, a live-and-let-live philosophy *will* accommodate a range of viewpoints—a variety of beliefs, opinions, and styles of life. It is not a case of one code of norms, or else infinity. The issue is not that general. So-called victimless crime, for example, is at least in part an issue of minority rights. Our legal system is supposed to be based on the idea of limits: the majority has moral and physical power, but the wishes and needs of minorities must be protected, too. Where are the limits? No one can say exactly. There have been times when tolerance, despite our lip service to minority rights, has been in very short supply. Today, many of the most strident conflicts turn on issues of the "social revolution," which is considered in Chapter 14.

13

The American Legal Profession

*T*HE AMERICAN LEGAL profession is the largest in the world, in absolute numbers. It may also be the largest in the world in proportion to population. There were over 800,000 lawyers in the United States in 1991; the 1995 estimate was nearly 900,000. The numbers are growing rapidly. By the time you read this, there may be close to a million lawyers in America: almost certainly, that figure will be reached by the end of the twentieth century.[1]

Technically, of course, there is no such thing as an "American lawyer"; every state admits its own, and a lawyer licensed to practice in Florida is strictly speaking a layperson as far as Alabama or Alaska is concerned. Nonetheless, in the aggregate, this is a vast army of law-trained men and women. The growth of this profession, what lawyers do (and don't do), and the professional ethics and practices of the bar cannot be ignored, then, in any discussion of the nature of American law.

The American Bar: A Thumbnail Historical Sketch

There was a time, long ago—a golden age, if you will—when there were very few lawyers in what is now the United States. In some colonies, especially those dominated by the clergy, there was a good deal of hostility to lawyers. It may or may not be significant that Plymouth Colony, in the seventeenth century, expelled its first lawyer, Thomas Morton, for various "misdemeanors," including trading with the Indians, drinking to excess, and other "beastly practices."[2]

Yet the lawyers found a niche for themselves, despite their unpopularity, as they would do time and time again. By the eighteenth century, they had become quite indispensable in a country whose lifeline was the sea and which depended heavily on trade with the West Indies and the mother country. Wherever there is business, trade, or dealings with government, the American lawyer plays a role. After independence, the legal profession took a quantum leap in size. There were only fifteen lawyers in Massachusetts in 1740, serving a population of about 150,000. In 1840, a century later, there were 640 lawyers, ten times as many in ratio to the population. The big push came after the Revolution.[3]

What was true in this one state was no doubt true in other states as well. In the nineteenth century, lawyers increased far faster than population. Sometime before 1900, their numbers crossed the 100,000 mark. In the twentieth century, and especially in recent years, growth has been even more explosive. Between 1960 and 1970, the number of lawyers increased by about a third; new admissions to the bar grew by an astonishing 91 percent between 1970 and 1975.[4] The total number of lawyers may have doubled in the last twenty years or so. In 1950, there was about one lawyer for every 700 people in the country; in 1980, one for every 400 or so; in 1995, about one for every 290 people.[5] About 30,000 new lawyers a year are added to the swarm. If this trend continues, the whole country might in the end consist of nothing but lawyers. Fortunately, that day is a long way off.

Where are these lawyers, what are they up to, and what kinds of work do they do? They are mostly in big cities, mostly in private practice, mostly handling the affairs of business firms. Some private practitioners are "solos," who work by themselves. Others work in law firms as partners or as "associates"—lawyers who work for the partners, on a salary basis. Most of these "associates" are young, and hope to "make partner" someday. A smaller number of lawyers work as "house counsel." That is, they are lawyers on the payroll of one particular company. They are lawyers with a single client, their company. The number of these lawyers also seems to be growing fast. In 1951, there were 11,000 house counsel; in 1979, 50,000. AT&T had 895 lawyers on its payroll in 1981; Exxon had 454; General Electric had 340.[6] By 1991, there were over 70,000 lawyers who worked as house counsel in private industry.[7] Governments—state, federal, and local—also hire thousands of lawyers. Other members of the bar have jobs related to law, but not quite of it; these include insurance-claims adjusters and FBI agents. A few lawyers teach or write about law. A few lawyers serve as judges of high and low courts. And, of course, some lawyers never quite make it, or choose not to; they dribble out of the profession into business, real estate, or insurance; they make pottery, or sell shoes, or teach school.

The work habits, lifestyle, and collective behavior of lawyers has, naturally, changed a good deal over the years. Nowadays, many lawyers never see the inside of a courtroom. They give advice and, if possible, keep clients out of litigation. In the early nineteenth century, lawyers' work centered much more on the courtroom than today. Judges in many parts of the country "rode circuit." That is, they went from county seat to county seat, hearing cases. Lawyers traveled along with them. Abraham Lincoln rode circuit in Illinois, before he went into politics.

In such a system, bench and bar formed a cozy little unit. The lawyer had no clients "on retainer." He picked up clients as he went along—if he was lucky. When he came to the county seat, and if he was well known, two or three clients who needed his services would approach him, almost before he had a chance to get down from his horse. A good lawyer, with a quick mind and aggressive tactics, could earn a reputation on circuit and get clients and business this way.[8]

The traveling lawyer, of course, had no time or place to do research; he had few books, or none, and no staff of clerks to help him. His brains and his mouth were his assets. Speeches to the jury were important; a silver tongue was a definite advantage. The most famous lawyers in the first half of the nineteenth century were those known as great orators. Daniel Webster was one of these talker-lawyers. In the higher courts, speeches might go on for hours, even days. Alexander Hamilton argued for six hours before a New York court in Albany, in a criminal libel case (1804). In the *Dartmouth College* case (1818), Daniel Webster spoke on behalf of the college for three to five hours; his speech, especially its ending, has gone into legend. According to one account (probably exaggerated), the audience "dissolved in tears"; when Webster finished, the whole courtroom was so overcome with emotion that for a while no one could speak.[9]

Some such courtroom speeches have come down to us; by modern standards, they seem flowery and overblown, full of purple passages. But in the days before radio and television, speeches were a form of entertainment; they were also the key to a lawyer's reputation. With his oratory, he could catch the eye and ear of potential clients.

Lawyers, of course, were more than orators. Law was a job for quick, clever people—young men (and, at the time, only men) with good heads on their shoulders, who knew their way around. Law was an easy profession to get into. Lawyers scrambled for any kind of work they could get. They investigated real estate titles; they defended petty criminal cases; they collected debts. They oozed into any crack or cranny of the business world they could find. They bought land and sold land, on their own or for investors. George Gale, a Vermont lawyer who settled in Trempealeau County, Wisconsin, in 1851, "acted as a kind of real estate broker . . . as a one man mortgage company . . . as a collection or serving agent on the lands."[10] Lawyers also went into politics, and took political jobs when they could. They swarmed all over Congress, the statehouses, the county seats, the city halls, the territorial governments.

Even before the Civil War, of course, not all lawyers were cast in the mold of Abraham Lincoln—country lawyers who rode from town to town on horseback. There were rich, established lawyers in big cities, harvesting the commercial practice of the seaports. Alexander Hamilton, in the years around 1800, was one of these lawyers. He dealt, for example, with problems of marine insurance—policies written on ships and cargo. This lucrative work, with its tang of salt water and money, was worlds apart from the petty land deals and debt-collecting that were staple work for the prairie lawyers.[11]

A few lawyers, as early as the first half of the nineteenth century, avoided the courtroom altogether. They specialized in book work, office work, business planning. After the Civil War, the rise of big business created new legal demands, and hungry lawyers rushed to fill them. In this period, from roughly 1870 on, the "Wall Street lawyer" came into prominence. This new breed of lawyer had a new style of work. Practice and professional life revolved around clients, mostly businesses and businessmen, not around judges and fellow lawyers.

It was a natural process. Businesses needed skilled hands to solve the thousand and one legal problems that confronted them. A big company like Standard Oil or Sears Roebuck or United States Steel, as it traveled the road from shop or store to interstate giant, had the greatest needs of all. Lawyers had skills that were useful to these big businesses. The legal problems of a large enterprise are many, and they are continuous. Lawyers for big business were not hired for this case or that; rather, they were kept on retainer.

The great enterprises were willing to pay well, and they wanted to stay out of court. They wanted their counsel to know their business inside and out; they wanted to steer a clear course among the reefs and shoals of the law and the hazards of competition. Lawyers were valuable to big business not because of any gift of gab but because they were shrewd at business deals, creative in drawing up papers, nimble at finance and the securities market, sophisticated about government and rules. Railroad receiverships, deeds of trust, municipal-bond issues—none of these had the glamour of a murder trial or the homely interest of a suit to replevy a horse. But Wall Street was built on these drab, essential pillars of paper, sweat, and guile.

Daniel Webster and Alexander Hamilton worked by and for themselves. The Wall Street lawyer worked, more and more, in partnership. Before the Civil War, there were a few two-man firms. Once in a while, the partners tended to specialize: one acted as the courtroom man, the other as the office or inside man. After the Civil War, there was a slow expansion of firms. By 1900 or so, all major cities had firms of some size. New York, of course, led the way. The firm of Carter, Hughes, and Dwight listed fourteen lawyers in *Hubbell's Legal Directory* for 1903—eight partners and six associates. Sullivan and Cromwell had ten lawyers on its payroll. The biggest firm in Denver, Colorado, was Dines and Whitted—two lawyers and three associates. In Chicago, two firms had seven lawyers each.

Size carried definite advantages. One man could have only so much knowledge and skill. A large bank or steel mill needed more than one man could provide: a firm could better cover the relevant aspects of law. And only a firm was likely to have manpower and brainpower enough to cope with a major bond issue, or to merge two giant businesses, or to reorganize a sprawling network of railroads.

It was almost as if a hormone were at work on the legal profession, pushing the growth of firms. The process continues. In the 1960s, according to one survey, there were forty-three American law firms with fifty or more lawyers each. Twenty of these were in New York City. The largest law firm, Shearman and Sterling, was made up of 125 lawyers—thirty-five partners and ninety associates on salary.[12] This seemed immense at the time, a "law factory" of massive proportions. But the biggest firms today utterly dwarf it in size. In 1980, Baker & McKenzie, with headquarters in Chicago, had 512 lawyers and branches in eleven cities.[13] In 1995, Baker & McKenzie was still the largest firm, but now it had 1,754 lawyers and branches or affiliates in over fifty cities worldwide; there were 158 lawyers in Chicago, 146 in Hong Kong, all the way down to one in Hanoi and one in Ho Chi Minh City, Vietnam. Two other law firms had more than a thousand lawyers, and there were twenty firms that could boast more than five hundred lawyers.[14]

The very large firms, with their exotic branches, are unusually cosmopolitan. Most law firms stick to a single office. At most they have a branch or two. But the habit of branching is definitely on the march. In 1982, Sullivan and Cromwell, besides its mother office on Wall Street, had branches in Washington, D.C., London, and Paris. By 1995, it had added Los Angeles, Hong Kong, Melbourne, Tokyo, and Frankfurt. The San Francisco firm of Morrison & Foerster (with 533 lawyers) had branches as close as Palo Alto and as far away as Tokyo and Brussels.[15] This is at the upper end of the scale. At the popular end, there are now a number of "law clinics," with offices in many neighborhoods. There was even, at one time, talk about putting mini-offices in department stores so that a person could buy underwear, get glasses, eat a sandwich, and consult a lawyer, all under a single roof. The Wall Street lawyer of 1900 would surely whirl in his grave at the very thought.

What Lawyers Do

The big firms grow bigger, but thousands of lawyers still work on their own, as "solos." There are also tiny firms and middle-sized firms. Some of the small firms are general firms—they will take on any kind of work. Others are "boutique" firms—highly specialized in some small corner of the practice. There are lawyers in big cities and lawyers in sleepy towns. Thousands of young people pour out of law schools every year and take the bar examination. In California alone, 6,702 men and women passed this test in 1995. These new recruits take up all sorts of jobs and fill many slots. Not all of them, of course, will stay in law.

The profession is, and always has been, quite diverse. There are many legal worlds. To begin with, there is the world of the big firm, the "Wall Street lawyer." There are, of course, "Wall Streets" all over the country—La Salle Street in Chicago, Montgomery Street in San Francisco. There are "Wall Street" firms in Houston, Atlanta, Boston, Los Angeles, Denver, and so on.

These big firms recruit their lawyers, by and large, from the "national" law schools—schools with big reputations and long traditions, like Harvard and Yale, and brash newcomers like Chicago and Stanford. A few state schools have elbowed their way into the ranks of the elite (Michigan, Berkeley). We know in general who the clients are: big corporations and wealthy families. We know in general what the work is: it includes securities law, antitrust law, bond issues, mergers, tax work, international trade. But we have little systematic knowledge about the details. Researchers find it hard to pierce the curtain of privacy that surrounds these firms. Their taste for publicity is muted, but growing. There is also the reason—or excuse—that much of the information is confidential. Sociological literature on the big law firm is not as large as one would like, but the volume is increasing.[16]

In both big and little firms, there will probably be some litigation. How much is uncertain. Business lawyers used to pride themselves on staying out of court. But there has been a litigation boom since at least the 1970s at some of the larger firms. In 1978, at the Cravath firm in

New York, a very large firm, 10 percent of the lawyers were working on litigation, double the manpower effort of the past.[17] Cravath was up to its neck at the time in a monster lawsuit (the government's attempt to hack IBM's "monopoly" to pieces, an attempt which ultimately failed) and the workload in litigation was probably somewhat out of the ordinary, but other firms also reported increases in their trial and courtroom work. This is a response, among other things, to increased regulation and to new causes of action. Sears Roebuck, after all, had no sex-discrimination suits in 1930. By the 1990s, in some big firms, up to half the work could be described as "litigation."

Another staple of law practice is real estate: buying and selling houses or (on a more sophisticated level) concocting elaborate deals for shopping centers, suburban developments, and office buildings, or converting luxury apartments into condominiums. Estate work is also common to big firms and little firms alike—writing wills and trusts, guiding the dead through the dark rivers of probate. Big firms handle these affairs for captains of industry and for great old families. Middle-sized firms do the same for the medium-rich—manufacturers of plastic novelties, owners of restaurants, car-wash companies, apartment buildings. Small-town lawyers handle farm estates. And so on.

Big firms and solo practitioners are alike, curiously enough, in one key regard: they tend to be generalists. In medicine, the specialists have more prestige and make more money than "GPs," or doctors who practice "family medicine." The legal profession is somewhat different. Big firms make the most money and enjoy the highest status, yet they are general firms, or at least general-business firms. Their senior partners earn as much as half a million a year, or even more. Specialization is not the way to the top, for firms. On the other hand, big law firms are *internally* specialized. They are rather like clinics, hospitals, or HMOs. This is one reason why the firms grew large in the first place.

Some branches of practice, to be sure, do tend toward specialization. There are lawyers who carve out niches in almost any and every conceivable area of law. Lawyers have specialized in patents, will contests, tax appeals, divorce, civil rights. There are lawyers who work on export-import trade, on chartering ships, on show business ("entertainment law"), on trademarks and copyrights. Some boutique firms, especially in Washington, specialize in administrative law. There are "PI" (personal-injury) lawyers, who confine themselves to tort cases growing out of accidents or bring products-liability and malpractice suits. There are lawyers who do nothing but sue airlines.

On the other hand, few lawyers are totally specialized. This is one finding from a massive study of the Chicago bar. Criminal prosecutors are exceptional in that they stick to criminal work and do not stray into other fields. But even patent lawyers have more than one string to their bow; only 40 percent of those in the survey restricted themselves totally to patents. Only 22 percent of the corporate tax specialists did nothing else.[18]

Big-firm lawyers cover many fields and many problems. But there are areas they definitely do not touch. One is divorce. Wall Street does very little family law, except perhaps to mop up financial fallout when multimillionaire couples split apart. It is the lawyers in smallish firms and in law clinics, and the solos, who handle "one-shot" clients—couples who want a divorce, victims of car crashes, people arrested for drunk driving.

Some lawyers with one-shot clients struggle to make ends meet; others earn heaps of money. The better-known personal-injury lawyers do very well indeed. They take cases on a "contingent-fee" basis. That is, the lawyer gets nothing if the client loses, but if the client wins, the lawyer takes a hefty chunk of the winnings, often one-third. This is true whether the case is settled or goes to trial. If the recovery is big—if it is one of the rare multimillion-dollar recoveries, in a medical-malpractice case, or a products-liability case—so is the fee. It does not take many cases of this type to put a lawyer in clover.

Money, of course, is not everything, and "PI" work never carries the prestige of a Wall Street practice. Partly this is because Wall Street has a richer, more elegant clientele. Tort lawyers serve all classes, top to bottom. Criminal lawyers, in particular, dirty their hands with the problems of our less savory citizens. And all "one-shot" lawyers constantly face the problem of finding new business. Their clients come and go; the lawyers need continuous infusions of fresh blood. After all, no one gets run over by trains, divorced, or arrested for murder consistently. Many Wall Street firms keep their clients "on retainer"; their business is steady, year in and year out. Of course, they scramble for new business and fight to keep old business. But the struggle has been, on the whole, genteel. What is more, they tend not to hustle in public. In fact, they hate publicity. A flamboyant style hurts them more than it helps. The opposite is true for tort lawyers, criminal lawyers, and divorce lawyers.

In recent years, however, the nature of the practice, even for the very big firms—or especially for them—has been changing. More and more, some of these firms are dependent on large, one-time transactions—a giant merger, for example. Hence these huge firms are becoming more like "one-shot" firms writ large. Their business has become more volatile and precarious. They may not advertise, but they hire public-relations firms, and they welcome publicity. The quiet, lucrative practice of the 1950s looks more and more like the "good old days," forever gone.

Who Are the Lawyers?

Since the early nineteenth century, law has been a prominent way to get ahead in this society, a means of upward mobility. Young men on the make have shimmied up this greasy pole, which has been a bit easier and less slippery than other alternatives. Who were these men? In the first place, the word "men" is to be taken literally. For much of our history, lawyer meant "white male." Not a single woman was admitted to the bar before the 1870s, and precious few blacks.

Indeed, when women tried to break into this all-male club, they met resistance and reluctance, to say the least. One pioneer was Myra Bradwell, wife of an Illinois lawyer and mother of four children, who applied for admission to the bar in 1869. She passed the exam, but the Supreme Court of Illinois turned her down. Women, especially married women, were not suitable lawyers. Like lunatics and children, they were under "disability"; they lacked full legal rights themselves. Besides, the very idea of a woman lawyer was repulsive to most male lawyers. Law practice would endanger the "deference and delicacy with which it is the pride of [the] . . . ruder sex to treat her." Mrs. Bradwell appealed to the United States Supreme Court, but did no better there. The traditional family, according to Justice Bradley, was "founded in the divine ordinance, as well as in the nature of things." This meant that women belonged inherently to "the domestic sphere" (the kitchen, in other words), not to the world of public affairs, and certainly not to the world of the law.[19]

Opinion changed, but slowly and grudgingly. In the same year that Myra Bradwell was shut out in Illinois, Iowa admitted Arabella Mansfield to practice. The first woman lawyer in Illinois was Alta M. Hulett (who was unmarried); she broke the barrier in 1873. The first woman lawyer in California was Clara Shortridge Foltz. The University of Michigan decided to admit women to its law school in 1870; Yale's law school followed in 1886, Cornell's in 1887.

Despite this, the bar stayed largely a man's world. As recently as 1960, less than 3 percent of the country's lawyers were women. Change did not take place until the 1970s. In 1965, 4 percent of the country's law students were women; in 1973, 16 percent; in 1979, 32 percent, in 1995, 42 percent. About a quarter of the lawyers practicing law in the late 1990s were women, and as the older men die off or retire, the percentage is bound to grow. Meanwhile, from the 1960s on, a trickle of women began to show up on law faculties, in big firms, and on the bench. In 1981, President Reagan appointed Sandra Day O'Connor of Arizona, a graduate of Stanford University's law school, to the United States Supreme Court. She was the first woman ever to sit there. Ruth Bader Ginsberg, appointed by President Clinton in 1993, was the second. The chief justice of California during the late 1970s and early 1980s was a woman, Rose Bird. In 1967, no American law school had more than two women on its faculty. Most had none at all. By 1996, the situation had changed quite dramatically; there were, for example, eleven women on the faculty at Harvard, ten at Stanford. Women are, to be sure, nowhere close to parity, but women deans are no longer a novelty, and the trend lines are pretty clear and dramatic.

Black lawyers were rare birds, too, in American history. John Mercer Langston was one of the first. Langston was the son of a white plantation owner and a slave woman. He became a lawyer in Ohio in 1854; later, he served as the first head of the law department of Howard University, which opened its doors after the Civil War and trained a small but crucial corps of black lawyers.[20]

Progress here too was painfully slow. In 1965, blacks made up 11 percent of the population, but less than 2 percent of the legal profession and only 1.3 percent of the law students, nearly half of these in all-black law schools. At this point, the doors began to open a bit wider, both in law schools and at the bar. Some law schools devised special programs to get and train black students and help correct the extreme imbalance at the bar. In 1977, about 5 percent of the law students in the country were black; many of these—perhaps most—would have been shut out of places in law schools if the schools admitted students purely "by the numbers."[21] Chicanos would have fared just as badly. There is, of course, controversy over programs of "affirmative action" and a federal court, in 1996, declared these programs unconstitutional in Texas.[22]

Law firms, in the past, were as discriminatory as law schools, and even more so. Through the 1950s, most were solidly WASP. Jews were taboo, Catholics suspect and rare. Jews tended to have their own firms, some quite large. Barriers against Jews in the big firms have by now totally crumbled. Barriers against blacks are more stubborn, but are definitely receding. At any rate, they are no longer blatant and overt. True, many firms settle for a "token" black. But even a token is important; it proves to the firm of Chicken and Little that the sky will not fall in if the firm is no longer lily-white. Discrimination against women has also become much less pronounced—partly because of the sheer number of women pouring out of the law schools. Women now hold the majority of associate-level positions at larger San Francisco law firms. Women seem to be slow to make partner—one hears a lot about the "glass ceiling"—and it is still more difficult for women compared to men to "have it all" (career *and* family). But the times are definitely, and dramatically, changing.

Still, equality of opportunity is not an easy goal to achieve, especially with regard to barriers of class. There are structural hurdles. The cost of legal education is one of these barriers. Tuition alone at top private schools was over $20,000 a year in 1995–96. The Chicago survey reported some disquieting facts. Lawyers tend to come from the families of businessmen, teachers, professionals; they are not sons of grocery clerks or coal miners' daughters. Over 73 percent of the practicing lawyers in Chicago came from "solidly middle-class or upper-middle-class homes," far more than if lawyers were selected from Chicago families at random. Many came from lawyerly or professional backgrounds. And the percentage of lawyers from working-class backgrounds was probably going down, not up, at least at the time of the Chicago survey.[23]

Becoming a Lawyer

The English legal system historically made a sharp distinction between two kinds of lawyer: barristers and solicitors. Barristers, in their wigs and robes, acted as cuortroom lawyers; solicitors did everything else, but could not appear before the higher courts. Solicitors, on the whole, were less tony and prestigious than barristers, but only solicitors dealt with clients face-to-face on a regular basis. A few American states once made distinctions between ranks or classes or lawyers (New York, New Jersey, Massachusetts, Virginia), but by the middle of the nineteenth century these had all died out and we were left with a single category: lawyer.

It was not a hard label to earn. In the nineteenth century, the law was fairly wide open, as professions went (and bearing in mind that women were excluded). To some extent, it flatters the nineteenth-century lawyer to call him a professional. Nowadays, the road to the bar is a long hard grind—first college, then three years of law school (if you can get in), then a cram course, then the bar examination itself. In many states, the bar exam is itself quite a hurdle; 40.6 percent of those who took the California bar exam in July 1995 failed to pass.

Admission to the bar was a different beast entirely in the nineteenth century. Legal education as we know it did not exist in 1800. The way to the bar was through apprenticeship. The young man who wanted to be a lawyer "read law" in a lawyer's office. He sat in the office for a period, and plowed through a number of law books. Often the apprentice made himself useful doing the lawyer's drudge work: copying documents, writing out pleadings, running errands. In the days before typewriters, telephones, stenographers, Xerox machines, and word processors, a lawyer *needed* clerks. If the clerk was lucky, he got some actual training out of the deal. Not all clerks or apprentices were lucky.[24]

In most states, the bar examination did not do much filtering; it was hardly a significant hurdle. A few states (Indiana, for one) got rid of it altogether for a while. Elsewhere, it was short and not very tough. Young Salmon P. Chase, later chief justice of the United States, was admitted to the bar in Washington, D.C., around 1829. Seldom, he wrote, "has any candidate for admission to the bar presented himself for examination with a slenderer stock of learning." Chase had spent time in the office of William Wirt, then attorney general, as a "student-at-law." He read Blackstone and a few other books. Wirt "never examined me. Only once did he put a question to me about my studies." The "bar examination" itself was just as perfunctory. Justice Cranch asked him a few questions; Chase answered them, though "not very well." The judge said, "You must study another year." But Chase begged for mercy: "I have made all my arrangements to go to the Western country and practice law." The judge "yielded," and Chase was sworn in.[25] Those were the good old days.

Legal education in a school setting developed only slowly, though in a sense it can be traced to the end of the eighteenth century. Two streams of education ultimately flowed together. The first was a kind of glorified clerkship. It came about this way: A few lawyers discovered that they really liked teaching clerks, and were good at it. They spent less and less time with clients, more and more time with their clerks. They took on extra clerks, for pay, in order to teach them law. Finally, the law practice withered away, and the office turned into a school.

This is more or less the story of the famous Litchfield School, the first law school in the country. It was founded by Judge Tapping Reeve in Litchfield, Connecticut, in 1784. It lasted until 1833, and was quite successful in its day. The Litchfield School had little in common with modern law schools. In looks, it was modest: a simple frame building, much like a country schoolhouse. There were no entrance requirements, no prerequisites, no final examinations. Litchfield used the lecture method. The full course took a bit more than a year. There were lectures every day. Students copied down as much of the lectures as they could. On Saturdays, there were quizzes covering the work of the week. Instruction was, needless to say, intensely practical.

There were a number of other schools on the Litchfield plan, in all parts of the country. Eventually, they died out. Their influence merged with the other stream—instruction in a university setting. Here William Blackstone was an early model. He gave lectures on law, at Oxford, in the middle of the eighteenth century. To be sure, these lectures were not meant to train lawyers. They were supposed to be part of the education of young laymen. Still, his example gave a strong push to the notion of learning law at a university. Blackstone's lectures were the source of his *Commentaries,* a book that was fantastically successful, on both sides of the Atlantic. American colleges and universities began to copy the Blackstone idea. The first American chair of law was at William and Mary College. A holder of this chair, St. George Tucker, published an American edition of Blackstone in 1803, up-to-date and with American notes and additions.

Harvard, however, was the first university with a separate department of law. In its early years, from about 1816 on, legal education at Harvard was a kind of mixture of Litchfield and Blackstone. Its intellectual pretensions, of course, went beyond those of Litchfield, especially under Joseph Story. Story was the first professor to occupy a new chair endowed by Nathan Dane (1829). Story was a justice of the Supreme Court of the United States, and he wrote many learned (though somewhat ponderous) legal treatises. Despite Story and his successors, Harvard Law School in the middle of the nineteenth century was not the tough, rigorous Harvard of *The Paper Chase.* When Joseph Hodges Choate entered Harvard Law School in 1852, he found the standards "very low." "There were absolutely no examinations to get in, or to proceed, or to get out. All that was required was the lapse of time, two years, and the payment of the fees."[26]

All this changed radically in 1870. In that year, legal education as we know it was born. It sprang from the brain of Christopher Columbus Langdell, who became dean of Harvard Law School in that year. Langdell worked a revolution in legal education. He invented the case method, practically speaking—instead of listening to lectures, students read and discussed published reports of cases decided by appellate courts. These cases were collected in casebooks, and Langdell put the first one of these together. He also insisted on the so-called Socratic method of teaching—teaching through questions and answers. Lectures were out.

He also, in a way, invented the law professor. Before Langdell, judges and practicing lawyers taught law. Usually they kept their "real" jobs; teaching was a sideline. Joseph Story was a sitting justice of the Supreme Court during the years he taught at Harvard. Other professors taught after successful careers in practice or on the bench. Chief Justice

Joel Parker of New Hampshire was appointed to a Harvard chair in 1847, at the age of fifty-two.[27] Langdell put an end to this practice at Harvard. He hired James Barr Ames, who was almost fresh out of law school, to join Harvard's faculty. Ames had no practical experience at all. Langdell believed in him—not as a lawyer but as a teacher. Law, to Langdell, was a science; it had to be taught by people adept in the science. Whether they had dirtied their hands in practice was irrelevant.

Langdell's methods were novel and disturbing; they evoked bitter opposition, even at Harvard. Gradually, the opposition died down, and the Langdell method won out over all of its rivals. By the second decade of the twentieth century, the Harvard case method was almost universal in American law schools. It remains dominant to this day. To be sure, there have been many changes in curriculum. Some schools have experimented with a more "clinical" approach, teaching a few courses through real or simulated work on actual cases. The casebooks contain a lot of material that would have shocked and horrified Langdell: besides the cases themselves, we find much more in the way of notes, questions, and explanatory material along with excerpts from articles, mostly "legal" but occasionally economic, historical, or sociological. The curriculum has changed greatly, too: nobody taught environmental law in Langdell's days, or feminist jurisprudence. Still, the core of the Langdell method has been remarkably resistant to change, and the names of the first-year courses would, on the whole, be perfectly familiar to him if he came back to life.

Law schools also tightened their standards after the Langdell revolution. A definite curriculum was established; each class was topped off with a final exam. The Langdell method was austere, abstract. Langdell's conception of law as a science divorced the study of law from the grubby world of practice—and also from politics, history, economics, and anything that smacked of social context. His schools taught only legal principles; everything else was banished from the law school, exiled to the rest of the university—for example, departments of politics or government. Yet in other ways the new-model law schools were tied more closely to their universities. Nineteenth-century university law schools were independent kingdoms, on the whole. They ran themselves; they collected their own fees; they had almost nothing to do with their universities, except to share a famous university name.

Meanwhile, law school pushed out clerkship as the high road to the bar. In 1850 there were fifteen law schools in the country; in 1870, thirty-one; in 1900, 102. In 1996, the American Bar Association accredited 178 schools. Apprenticeship is theoretically possible as a path to the bar in a few states, but in practice it is virtually extinct. In a few states, notably California, there are a number of schools that are unaccredited (the total number of these schools, in 1996, was something on the order of thirty-seven). Some of these schools are "proprietary"— that is, they make money, or try to. Their entrance requirements are low, but so are their success rates in training students who can pass the bar. For example, in July 1995, almost two-thirds of the students from unaccredited law schools who took the California bar for the first time flunked the exam; 80.7 percent of those from ABA-approved law schools, on the other hand, passed.

There are law schools in every major city and in almost every state; Alaska is one of the few that lacks this modern amenity. These law schools are both different from each other and much the same. They are remarkably similar in curriculum and method. They also tend to impose the same general requirements: a college degree, and the Law School Admission Test (LSAT). This test began its reign of terror around 1950; a good score is a must for entry into all but the weakest law schools. Law schools are, on the other hand, quite different in prestige, money, and power—and in quality of faculty and students, at least on paper. A tremendous surge of applicants in the 1960s and 1970s battered at the doors of law schools. The stronger, older schools were able to "skim off the cream." In 1992, for example, LSAT administered over 140,000 exams, and about 86,000 students applied to accredited law schools—more than two for every available slot for that year. The flood of applicants now seems to have crested, but the demand is still very strong.

Law schools, as we said, all rest on a kind of base of similarity, but it would be naive to deny that money and prestige do not make a difference. Harvard, Yale, Berkeley, and Chicago can afford huge research libraries; small schools cannot. For a long time, the rich (private) schools were mostly schools for the rich, but public legal education has a distinguished history, especially in the Middle West (Michigan, Wisconsin, Minnesota) and the West (California). In the late nineteenth century, many schools were founded to teach law at night. There were twenty of these schools by 1900. (Many of them survive to this day, though they usually offer day courses, too.) Their students were mostly drawn from the working class. Out of these schools came the immigrant lawyers, Polish, Italian, Jewish, Irish, and Greek, who often went back to their neighborhoods and served their ethnic constituents. Graduates of these schools rarely made it to Wall Street or La Salle Street. The big firms were and are staffed with graduates of national schools, not these "local" schools.[28] But the night schools and other local law schools have been breeding grounds for local judges and politicians; thus, in their own way, they wield great influence and power. Their alumni run the statehouses, or at least city hall.

The Organized Bar

Lawyers, like Americans in general, are joiners. Yet the bar did not have a strong, permanent organization until the 1870s. The first modern bar association was the Association of the Bar of the City of New York. It was founded in 1870 by what one lawyer called "the decent part of the profession." This "decent part" had boiled over in indignation because of the plague of corrupt lawyers, judges, and politicians in Boss Tweed's New York. A few years later, in 1878, "seventy-five gentlemen" of the bar, meeting in Saratoga, New York, founded a national group, the American Bar Association.

Bar associations in their early days made no attempt to recruit the mass of American lawyers. They were basically clubs of like-minded, high-class lawyers. Indeed, that was their point: they kept the riffraff out and admitted only the "best elements" of the profession. The purpose was reform—drafting better laws, fighting against corruption, raising the prestige of the profession.

They had other, less defensible, ideas. The ABA had at one time a rather shameful history of snobbery and bias. In 1912, through carelessness, the ABA let in three black lawyers; when the leadership realized what had happened, they tried to undo this dreadful mistake, since the "settled practice" was to "elect only white men." The three blacks were allowed to remain, but future applicants had to reveal their race, to prevent any more such "mistakes." The ABA also took reactionary stands on matters of free speech and political dissent. Its record during the Cold War was unenviable. Instead of standing up for the Bill of Rights, the ABA resolved, in 1950, "that all lawyers attest to their loyalty with an anti-Communist oath."[29]

The ABA, in short, represented the conservative upper crust of the profession for most of its history. It stood for elite values and goals. Early on, the ABA promoted codes of ethics for the bar and tried to upgrade the lawyer's reputation by defining, and upholding, ethical conduct. This had its good side and its bad side. The good side was the struggle for honesty and higher standards. The bad side was elitism, a kind of dogged conservatism on professional issues, and a failure to consider the rights of consumers of legal services. Even the ethics were class-biased. Under the old ABA canons of ethics, advertising was forbidden. Wall Street, after all, did not need to advertise. The small lawyer did, but the ABA was not concerned with his wishes. Ordinary laypeople, too, were disadvantaged: it was hard for them to find out what lawyers had to offer. The rule, in other words, made sure that "knowledge would remain unevenly, and unfairly, distributed."[30] The bar did not like price competition, either. In many states there were tables of minimum fees. Price cutting was unwelcome.

The ABA today has come a long way since the 1950s. But it is still not an association of all American lawyers. No one has to join. In 1996, it had a huge membership—over 340,000—but this made up less than half the practicing bar. Under pressure from inside and out, the ABA has has tried to become more representative. It is no longer a club for white males; it is definitely open to any American lawyer. It was a sign of the times that in 1995 a woman, Roberta Cooper Ramo, was elected president of the ABA.

The bar has also done some reexamination of its ethical codes. The so-called Kutak Commission proposed a major revision; the bar in 1983 refused to accept it, but the debate opened up discussion on matters the bar once accepted without question. The outside world, too, has intervened. In 1976, the Supreme Court struck down minimum fee schedules.[31]

The next year, the Court killed the ban on advertising, too. This was the case of *Bates v. State Bar of Arizona.*[32] John R. Bates, with his partner Van O'Steen, ran a "legal clinic" in Phoenix, Arizona. His ads in the paper ("Do You Need a Lawyer?") touched off the case. Bates won, and since then more and more lawyers advertise. Today, there are even ads on TV. Obviously, these ads are not aimed at rich Americans, let alone General Motors or IBM; they appeal, for example, to people arrested for drunk driving, or people with work injuries, or immigration problems—people who never, perhaps, dealt with a lawyer before, and had only the vaguest idea how to get one. Advertising makes the old-time lawyer squirm, and its virtues are certainly debatable. What it will mean to the profession in the long run remains to be seen.

The ABA is a national organization of lawyers; there are also state, county, and city bar associations. They too have been expanding and trying to shed their image of elitism.[33] In more than half the states, starting with North Dakota in the early 1920s, the bar has been "integrated." This has nothing to do with race; it means that lawyers cannot practice unless they join their state bar and pay dues. The integrated bar uses these forced contributions for a number of purposes; disciplinary processes eat up a lot of the money. In theory, a state bar is better able to control its members and keep them on the straight and narrow path if the bar is integrated. Some lawyers are skeptical. Some states have rejected the idea, and the plan has been attacked as a kind of "closed shop" for lawyers—an infringement of individual rights and autonomy. The debate continues.

Lawyers have always insisted, to a skeptical world, that they are mostly honest, skilled, high-toned. There are, of course, rotten apples in every barrel, but the bar insists on the right to pick them out itself. The bar's record in doing so is spotty, at best. State bar associations and state judiciaries are the ultimate enforcers; the ultimate sanction is disbarment, that is, losing the right to practice law. In 1961–62, the fifty states disbarred seventy-four lawyers and suspended nine.[34] In 1978, according to Deborah L. Rhode, agencies received 30,836 complaints serious enough to warrant opening a file, but only 124 lawyers in the whole country were disbarred.[35] The pace of complaints has increased—there were 54,600 complaints in 1986—but the penalties continue to be infrequent and light.[36] Some of the states, however, are fairly active. In 1995, there were 6,505 complaints received by the Attorney Registration and Disciplinary Commission in Illinois. In that year, the Supreme Court of Illinois disbarred fifty-four lawyers, suspended fifty-seven, censured or reprimanded twenty-two, and put fifteen on probation. The most common offenses were "improper handling of funds" and "neglect."[37]

It is hard to be sure, but it does seem that relatively few lawyers pay for their sins. Most complaints go nowhere. Disciplinary proceedings are a drop in the bucket. Unless lawyers are impossibly honest and the clients impossibly demanding and neurotic, something is amiss. The disciplinary agencies are, in Rhode's view, "grossly unresponsive" to clients and their complaints. Lawyers punish other lawyers for very flagrant violations—stealing a client's money, for example. For most other offenses, and for plain incompetence, lawyers are (understandably) rather gentle with themselves. And many rules are simply not enforced.

For example, under professional codes of ethics, it is wrong for a lawyer to farm out a case to another lawyer and split the fees. That is, if a client brings a case to Lawyer X, Lawyer X is supposed to handle it himself. But if he does bring in another lawyer for some reason, they must divide the fees in a way that reflects the actual work done by each of them. In New York, according to a study of personal-injury lawyers published in the 1970s, the rule was "systematically broken." Moreover, there was a "tacit understanding" not to treat this violation "as a serious matter"; the organized bar would discipline only truly outrageous cases.[38]

Lawyers, however, can be sued for malpractice by their clients, and such lawsuits do happen. In 1992, an event occurred which shook the Wall Street bar to its foundations. A government agency, the Office of Thrift Supervision, brought an administrative action against Kaye, Scholer—a major Wall Street firm. The firm had represented a failed savings-and-loan association, and the OTS claimed that its actions on behalf of its client crossed the line between advocacy and fraud or malpractice. Faced with possible disaster, the firm settled with OTS for $41 million.[39] Whatever the facts of the case, it was a signal to the upper bar that its ethical practices were not beyond question or dispute.

The Social Role of Lawyers: Do Lawyers Run the Country?

From the very beginning of the republic, lawyers have swarmed all over government, at federal, state, and local levels. In Indiana, for example, seven out of the first eight governors were lawyers, eleven out of the first thirteen lieutenant governors, eight of the first nine senators, and forty-five out of sixty-one congressmen, up to the 1850s.[40] Many presidents, from John Adams to Richard Nixon, Gerald Ford, and Bill Clinton, have been lawyers; no other profession has contributed so many presidents. Abraham Lincoln and Franklin D. Roosevelt were lawyers. Lawyers have served in droves as secretaries of state and cabinet members. President Clinton, on his election in 1992, promised to give America a cabinet that looked like them. He meant women and minorities; what his cabinet mostly looked like was a meeting of lawyers. Over 75 percent of the cabinet members were lawyers. More than 35 percent of key subcabinet posts went to lawyers.[41] In general, lawyers have occupied political offices, down to the lowliest township level, in numbers far, far outstripping their "proper" share.

This is no accident. For one thing, the business of lawyers is intimately connected to the business of government. Government makes and administers law; law is what lawyers know. For many lawyers, too, a political career goes hand in glove with a private career. If a Chicago woman who is a doctor or dentist goes down to Springfield to serve in the Illinois assembly, she hurts her career quite badly. If she is a lawyer, it may have the opposite effect; politics may be good for an assemblywoman's law business, especially if she has partners back home. She gets a reputation as somebody who knows the right people and who knows the ropes—a lawyer who can get things done.

This works for federal service also. Lawyers appointed to a high position in the State Department or the Department of Transportation or the Department of Housing and Urban Development are not interrupting their careers. The job may in fact be a step up the ladder. The lawyer learns what to do, whom to know. When these lawyers leave government service, they often get fat partnerships in major law firms.

Experience in a regulatory agency like the SEC or the Internal Revenue Service or the antitrust division of the Justice Department makes a lawyer more valuable to private clients. Lawyers often end up working for companies they used to regulate. It is no surprise when an attorney general becomes chief counsel for IBM, or when a manpower specialist at the Pentagon becomes a partner in a firm whose clients build missiles and tanks.

In recent years, lawyers have lost a little of their dominance in Congress and state legislatures. In 1966, 26 percent of state legislators were lawyers; in 1979, 20 percent; in 1986, it was down to 16 percent.[42] By 1980 or so, lawyers made up less than half the members of Congress for the first time in years.[43] In 1996, 43 percent of the members of Congress were lawyers. One reason for the decline may be that these jobs (Congress, the state legislatures) have gotten tougher. They are definitely full-time now—certainly Congress is. And for the first time in our history, state political positions *may* interfere with a lawyer's career.

The decline in lawyer-legislators, apparently, leveled off in the 1990s. It is also highly variable at the state level. In 1992, lawyers made up 48 percent of the Massachusetts senate, but only 18 percent of the lower house in Colorado, and in the lower house of Delaware, with forty-one members, there was only one lonely lawyer.[44] Nonetheless, it is still fair to say that lawyers are as common as sparrows in government; wherever one turns, one stumbles over lawyers, either inside the bureaucracy or outside of it, acting as lobbyists or attorneys for companies with government business. Many people think lawyers have too much influence in America. Lawyers, on the whole, have a terrible image. The poet Carl Sandburg asked rhetorically why the hearse horse "snickers" when he carries the lawyer's bones. Even worse things are said about lawyers. "Superlawyers," the powerful Washington firms, are suspected of running the country, and on behalf of their big, nasty clients. Lower down, we hear about shysters, ambulance chasers, ticket fixers. The criminal bar has its own special, odious image. Lawyer-politicians combine two bad reputations in one. The Watergate scandal made matters worse: the connivers who surrounded Richard Nixon—and President Nixon himself—were mostly members of the bar, their morals dulled by "blind ambition." Lawyer jokes (none of them complimentary) are so common that whole books of them are published; there is nothing comparable for architects, accountants, and even doctors.[45]

Still, the ethical practices of lawyers may not be any worse than those of other professions. Lawyers bring some of the trouble on themselves by claiming too much—by claiming, in a sanctimonious way, that they are interested only in justice, not power or wealth. They also suffer guilt by association. Their clients are often people in trouble. Saints do not need lawyers; gangsters do. Companies that wheel and deal—or pollute rivers—need lawyers more than stable, law-abiding firms. Happy couples do not consult lawyers; divorcing couples do. And so it goes.

Despite the joke books and the endless complaints, most people who use lawyers seem to be satisfied with them, according to surveys. Yet, on the other hand, in 1993, 73 percent of the population thought there were too many lawyers; and a 1992 survey of business executives found that 62 percent thought the American legal system hampered them in their competition with foreigners.[46] Apparently, most people think *their* lawyers are helpful, but that lawyers in the aggregate do more harm than good.

Is this the case? Are lawyers making things better, or worse? What difference do lawyers make, anyway? Would it be an improvement if we had fewer lawyers? It is not easy to answer these questions. A few studies give a clue or two. Some scholars have tried to measure the behavior of lawyers in state legislatures and compare this to the behavior of nonlawyers. Do lawyers in the Tennessee assembly, say, vote and act in ways systematically different from the other assemblymen? If they do, we might decide that legal training shapes a certain personality, a certain cluster of opinions; if you fill up a legislature or agency with people of this type, you bend it in some particular way.

On the whole, the studies turn up negative results. There are few, if any, differences between the way lawyers and nonlawyers vote and behave in state assemblies.[47] The job of being a legislator and the social situation—pressure from voters, for example—bend the lawyer, not the other way around. A few studies *have* come up with differences: lawyers are more independent politically, more reform-minded, more effective, more active in sponsoring legislation, than nonlawyers.[48] But even these results do not show that lawyers share some special ideology or that they influence how the country runs.

Most of the criticism these days focuses on lawyers *outside* the government: on those lawyers who are supposedly ruining the country by formenting wild and harmful lawsuits, bankrupting respectable businesses, and driving municipalities to the wall. There have been attempts to show that lawyers and their machinations cost the country countless billions of dollars a year, and that the lawyers really *are* ruining the economy. These demonstrations are, however, based on tenuous and dubious statistics.[49] Nor do these arguments take the *benefit* side of lawyering into account. It is easy to add up the costs, if lawsuits force a company to retool the designs of its autos, or take breast implants off the market, but isn't society better off? Discrimination lawsuits add to the cost of doing business, but what about the increase in social justice? Unfortunately, these benefits are not easy to measure.

It is interesting to compare the American profession with the bar in other countries. Japan is an amazing contrast. In 1960, Japan had a population of over ninety million and only 9,114 lawyers, concentrated in a few large cities.[50] In 1986, despite the tremendous increase in the Japanese economy, there were still only something on the order of 13,000 lawyers.[51] There are more than twenty times as many lawyers in the United States per 1,000 population. And the Japanese elites seem content to keep down the number of lawyers. In 1986, almost 24,000 students took the Japanese National Legal Examination; only 2 percent of them passed.[52]

Yet Japan is no primitive country. It is an industrial giant. Its huge industrial firms sell cars, radios, cameras and computer chips all over the world. Sony and Toyota, if they were American companies, would have hundreds of lawyers on their payroll or at their beck and call on Wall Street. (Perhaps their American subsidiaries do.) Obviously, lawyers in the United States do things that are not done—or not done by lawyers—in Japan.

It is not clear what these things are. Supposedly the Japanese do not like to litigate, but neither do American businesses, and actual litigation does not begin to account for the vast number of American lawyers. Obviously, the two countries define lawyers' work very differently. The Japanese have plenty of laws, rules, and regulations, but they seem to do quite nicely without an American-type legal profession. We can conclude that there is no inevitable, necessary connection between a legal profession of the American type and modern society, or capitalism, or the welfare state, or industrial society. Rather, our profession is at least in part unique or peculiar, shaped to the characteristics of American society. But exactly how, or what these features are, is not at all clear.

This is not to say that lawyers make no difference to the United States. Clearly they do. Nine hundred thousand lawyers do not sit around twiddling their thumbs. They work; they accomplish; they do. A culture has grown up in this country which somehow depends on this crowd of lawyers. *Our* business system, unlike Japan's, cannot get along without lawyers, and the social system, too, is curiously dependent on the bar. Would we be better off, then, with fewer lawyers? There is no way to answer this question. Without the lawyers, this would be a different society, in a different sort of world.

Lawyers and Social Justice

The business of lawyers is justice. That, at least, is what they claim. A man or woman accused of crime or of tax fraud, or hounded by government in some way, or sued by a nasty neighbor, wants fairness, justice, a crack at vindication. Only a good lawyer can get these for him. Of course, a smart lawyer can pervert justice, too, in some cases. This certainly happens.

In fact, the business of lawyers is both justice and injustice. They are on all sides of every issue, on both sides of every case. Some lawyers are attracted to lost causes, like moths to a flame—men like Clarence Darrow, "attorney for the damned," who defended anarchists and murderers.[53] There have been left-wing lawyers, like the late William Kunstler, who took up the causes of clients despised by most of the rest of society. There are ACLU lawyers, who defend free speech for left wing and right wing alike; some of their clients—American Nazis, for example—spit on everything the ACLU stands for.

Thousands of lawyers, however, work for the status quo. They represent American business, especially big business, and the people who own great wealth. They work for oil interests, computer companies, real estate syndicates. We sometimes hear it said that lawyers are by nature conservative. It is more accurate to say that lawyers, like most people, are anxious to make a living. They go where the money is, and the money is concentrated at top levels of business and society. Lawyers gravitate to whatever regime is in power; in this sense they are conservative, but only if the regime is conservative. In Communist countries, the lawyers tended to be faithful party members. And of course there are exceptions to every generalization. There are, as we said, left-wing lawyers, dissident lawyers. Some lawyers have even been prominent revolutionaries—like Fidel Castro or India's Nehru.

Law and lawyers are expensive. Many people who want or need a lawyer have trouble paying the price. Justice is for sale, but most people would agree that in a just society it should not be *totally* for sale. Hence the state provides a lawyer, free of charge, to anyone accused of a serious crime who cannot afford to pay on his own. Many states had long recognized such a constitutional right; in 1963, as we have seen, the Supreme Court, in the famous case of *Gideon v. Wainwright*,[54] imposed it on all the states. Today, "public defenders," who are on the state payroll, defend most people charged with serious crime.[55]

For civil cases, the situation is more complicated. A few lawyers have always made it a practice to do some work free for poor clients. Since the late nineteenth century, some cities have had programs of legal aid. The Legal Aid Society of New York began as an organization called Deutscher Rechts-Schutz Verein, in 1876, to help out German immigrants. It broadened its scope over the years and changed its name officially in 1896. By 1913, there were forty active societies, all over the country, and growth continued afterward.[56] But though these societies did good work, they merely scratched the surface. The poor were basically shut out of civil courts. Even the small-claims movement was not much of a help.

A major change came during the "War on Poverty," in the 1960s, under President Lyndon Johnson. The Office of Economic Opportunity established neighborhood law offices to serve poor clients. Bright young lawyers staffed these offices. In 1974, the work was transferred to a new body, the Legal Services Corporation, chartered and paid for by Congress. In the early 1980s, the corporation funded 320 legal-aid programs and 1,200 neighborhood offices all around the country. It paid for 5,000 lawyers and 2,500 paralegals. The price tag was $300 million a year.

From the start, there was controversy over the program. Landlords were annoyed when poverty lawyers helped tenants fight evictions. Conservatives thought it was absurd to pay one agency of government to bring lawsuits against the rest of the government. They considered poverty lawyers radicals, whose main aim was to drum up "activist" lawsuits, not to help the poor with ordinary legal problems. Many political leaders agreed. OEO lawyers had the annoying habit of fighting city hall. Some governors, too, tried to get rid of the program in their states. One of these was the governor of California, Ronald Reagan. Later he became president, and as president he proposed cutting off all federal money, leaving the states in charge of legal aid if they chose to support this kind of program. Congress balked, and the program continued. But the opposition made its mark. The program, in the 1990s, is a muted version of what began so boldly in a prior generation. Its vital fuel—money—has been reduced, and recent law has reined in some of its more visible—and effective—tactics. Since 1995, staff lawyers, for example, can no longer bring class actions.

The public-interest lawyer is another departure from past practice. There are now a number of law firms organized for the "public interest." They do not represent private clients. Rather, they represent "the public" (as they define it): people who want to preserve wilderness lands in Alaska or who oppose nuclear power plants. They speak up for the snail darter and the black-footed ferret; they tilt lances against government red tape in housing and welfare administration. They fight for convicted murderers and for victims of discrimination.

Who pays for these lawyers? The government itself contributes something; foundations contribute something; members of organizations (the Sierra Club, for example) contribute their share. There are only a handful of these firms. One study found about "forty charity-supported public-interest law firms" in 1973. They averaged ten lawyers each.[57] The number has grown a little since then, but public-interest lawyers make up no more than a tenth of 1 percent of the practicing bar. These are truly little Davids, up against the Goliaths of government and big business. Their opponents have thousands of lawyers and tremendous resources. Financially speaking, too, the public-interest bar leads a hand-to-mouth existence.

Yet these firms have accomplished miracles; they have done heroic work (some think too heroic). They have brought giant enterprises to a halt. They delayed the Alaska pipeline and have helped kill nuclear power plants and projects to develop wilderness areas. They have forced the government to shift direction or change programs in many different ways. They have helped revolutionize the law of landlord and tenant. They have monitored the work of dozens of agencies.

One sign of their success is the bitterness of the opposition. Another is the rise of conservative counterparts. "Public-interest" firms on the right sprang up to counterbalance the liberal firms. The Mountain States Legal Foundation in Denver, Colorado, was one of these counterbalances. James G. Watt, President Reagan's first secretary of the interior, served as its president before he entered the cabinet. The foundation was formed to defend "free enterprise." It believed in "privatization" of the public domain; in assigning more of the public lands to "mineral development" or leaving the land in the hands of ranchers.[58] It was, in other words, as if the Environmental Defense Fund or the Natural Resources Defense Council had been turned on its head. The Center for Individual Rights, founded in 1989, brought a lawsuit which successfully attacked the affirmative-action program of the University of Texas Law School.[59] This and other groups are conservative versions of the NAACP Legal Defense Fund or the American Civil Liberties Union. Imitation is the sincerest form of flattery.

14

Law and Social Change

*I*T IS OBVIOUS to the naked eye that we live in a period of very rapid social change. There is change in every aspect of life—social life, the family, sex, technology, politics, the economy. Why the world is changing so fast, compared to older times, is a complicated question. But whatever the reason, mankind and womankind are speeding along on a fast-moving train, and there are no signs that the train is slowing down. Nor is there any way to stop it and get off. Since law is a mirror of society, rapid social change means rapid legal change as well. This chapter will explore a few facets of the way in which social change and legal change are related.

First, a theoretical question about the relationship. Does law lead in the process of social change, or does it simply follow along? In other words, can we point the finger of praise, or of blame, at law and the legal system for what is happening in the world? Is law a motor—or one of the motors—generating social change? Or does social change always originate in the larger society, later spilling over into the legal system? Is the legal system a system which merely adjusts or accommodates itself to big changes taking place outside it?

Nobody can give full, final answers to these questions. As a matter of general theory, this book takes the point of view that major social change begins outside the legal system, that is, in society. The legal system is not wholly autonomous. It is not a world in itself. It is not insulated from outside influence.

To be sure, many people argue that the law is tough, conservative, and resistant to change. They sense a good deal of autonomy in the system. Experience suggests a rather different story, at least over the long haul. The legal systems of Western countries have been completely transformed since the Middle Ages, most notably in the years since the Industrial Revolution began. When we look at the changes, it is clear that over the centuries the legal system has been carried along by great waves of social force. Social movements sweep across it with the strength of a mighty sea. The legal system may seem like a powerful warship to those on deck, but its power shrinks to nothing compared with the might of the ocean it sails on and the wind and weather all about.

Of course, we can carry this point of view too far. We need not downgrade the power and importance of law—in this culture, at least. We must keep in mind the tremendous size of the legal profession; the vast bulk of the substantive law; the striking way in which political, social, and economic issues somehow end up as lawsuits; the massive activity of administrative agencies; the ceaseless creation of new norms by Congress, states, and cities. All of this must have some independent impact on society.

What *is* the place of law in society? A purely social theory of law, taken to an extreme, would look at the legal system as if it were some kind of puppet, dancing on its master's strings. The puppet master is the larger society. The picture may be somewhat overdrawn. A parable may provide a better image. Imagine a town on the banks of a swift, wide river. The people who live in the town want some way to cross the river. They want to reach people on the other side, to buy and sell goods, to travel to other places, and so on. The only way across is by ferry, which is slow and inefficient. The townspeople get together and demand a bridge. Taxes are levied; contracts are let; the bridge is built. Now both sides of the river are linked.

Clearly, the bridge did not get built by itself. It owes its existence to the political process; ultimately, a social demand—a social force—called the bridge into being. But once the bridge is in place, spanning the river, it begins inevitably to have its own, independent effect on community life. People construct their lives around the bridge. They move back and forth across the river. Some people live on one side and shop on the other. Some people commute to jobs on the opposite side. The towns on both sides grow larger and become more interdependent.

The bridge is now a familiar presence; it is part of consciousness and tradition. Poets write poems about it. Young people cannot remember a time when the bridge was not there. They expect a bridge; they find it natural. They take for granted the flow of people, goods, and cars from bank to bank—the freedom to cross the river at will. The bridge determines once and for all exactly where and how people cross. It excludes all other crossing points. The ferry is long since gone. The bridge has drilled itself into people's minds and taken root there. In other words, it affects more than their way of life; it affects the way they look at the world—what they expect, how they live, how they think.

The bridge is a metaphor for law and the legal system. Social forces in the larger society create it, shape it, twist it and turn it, pull it and push it. But these forces produce a system that itself becomes a part of social life; once in place, the system works its own influence on society, on how we live, how we think, how we feel. This independent effect of the legal system does not mean that there is something wrong with theory that shifts the burden of causation from "law" to "society." The legal system is not autonomous, not independent of society. It is not a system all to itself, insulated from the life of society. The legal system does not march to a separate drummer. It is a part of the social order, a soldier in the army of society. But its sheer size and presence, its importance, its scale, its interactions with the rest of the social organism give it an impact and a *meaning* beyond that of some limp marionette. Law is society's servant, to be sure. But it is not a quiet, invisible servant in an old-fashioned household; it is the noisy, bumptious workforce of a modern factory.

The legal system has clearly been an important player in the dramatic development of American society and economy over the years. J. Willard Hurst's classic study of the lumber industry in Wisconsin is full of lessons on this point.[1] Many aspects of law were relevant to this industry. But these aspects of law did not create the lumber industry; it would be more accurate to turn this sentence around—that is, the law was bent to suit the needs of the industry. This was because the politically and economically active citizens, the people who counted, wanted it that way. But like the bridge in the story, once the legal system was in place, it channeled development along set lines. There were old, familiar notions of contract and property, and although the law was sometimes changed and restructured to meet what the actors in the business wanted, these changes nonetheless took place within a specific and definite tradition of law and legal action. Thus, the legislature had the power to grant franchises; it made use of this old power to give lumber enterprises exclusive rights to improve streams and use these streams for the transport of logs.[2] Law also "offered ordered procedures for exploring facts, mustering evidence, defining values and the range of value choices, and setting decent bounds and terms for controversy."[3] In other words, the legal order defined the rules of the game, and in the short run at least, the players all accepted these rules, just as one accepts—and must accept—the bridge, and where it is, in the game of crossing the river.

In some respects, of course, the metaphor of the bridge is misleading. Generally speaking, law is far more flexible than an ordinary bridge. It is perhaps more like a pontoon bridge—a bridge which is not totally fixed; we can move it somewhat, upriver or downriver, if the need is great.

In short, then, the general thesis of this book is that law follows social change and adapts to it. Yet the legal system also crystallizes and channels social change, and plays an important role in community life. After all, it is through law, legal institutions, and legal processes that customs and ideas take on a more permanent, rigid form, like the bridge—or the pontoons—in our story. The legal system is a structure. It has shape and form. It lasts. It is visible. It sets up fields of force. It affects ways of thinking. When practices, habits, and custom turn into law, they tend to become stronger, more fixed, more explicit. They can be imposed on people who do not share these customs and habits or are downright hostile to them. Law has its hidden persuaders—its moral basis, its legitimacy, its ideology—but in the last analysis it has force, too, to back it up. Custom can also be powerful, but in complex societies custom is far too flabby to do all the work—to run the machinery of order. Law carries a powerful stick: the threat of force. This is the fist inside its velvet glove.

Revolution and Evolution in Legal Change

Thus far, the term "social change" has been used without explanation. Of course, there is no single process of social change. There are many kinds of change. Some social change is total, cataclysmic—revolutionary, in a word—breaking sharply with the past. Other forms of social change are incremental, evolutionary, step-by-step. There are also many grades and levels in between. Social change in the modern world, unless appearances deceive us, is racing along faster than in older, traditional societies. We live in an age of constant revolution.

There are legal revolutions as well as social revolutions. The Russian Revolution (1918) destroyed czarist society, and the czarist laws came tumbling down as well. The Soviets wiped out all the old codes and—temporarily, at least—established a new, radical form of justice. When the Soviet Union disintegrated, around 1990, there were almost equally radical changes in Russia and the surrounding new countries. The whole socialist order was dismantled, and the successor states embarked on a feverish course of writing new constitutions and new laws.

No sudden changes on this scale ever took place in this country. Our own revolution was not as sharp a break with the past, legally speaking. Independence brought about a change in government, of course, and some dramatic innovations (the Constitution, for example), but the ordinary legal system kept going with business (almost) as usual. Rules, court procedures, daily routines were hardly disturbed, except where there was actual fighting. The common law was like a clock that kept on ticking all through a raging storm.

A real revolution, with guns and mobs, can bring about drastic, sudden change. But we often talk, somewhat dramatically, about "revolutions" that are legal, social, economic—bloodless "revolutions" like the civil-rights revolution, the Industrial Revolution, even the so-called sexual revolution. These expressions are a bit overheated, but they make an important point. Social change does not move at a uniform pace. It accelerates and decelerates. There are fairly static periods and periods of rapid change. In American history, the Civil War and the two world wars, the Great Depression, and the New Deal of the 1930s were probably periods of unusually active and dramatic change. Major changes in social relations and in the economy almost inevitably produce major *legal* change. Between 1954 and 1970, the law of race relations altered completely. The sexual revolution came at about the same time; it, too, has had major legal fallout. Neither of these "revolutions" has been completely successful, and both are still engaged in skirmishes if not outright struggle of one sort or another. For the race revolution and the sexual revolution, there are plenty of counterrevolutionaries about, fighting their rearguard actions.

Today, we seem to live in an age of constant acceleration—a restless, even frantic era of perpetual change. And, after all, even small differences year by year add up to big ones over time. If we compare American law today with the law as it was in 1800, we are necessarily struck by the fact of change—enormous, fundamental, revolutionary change. But no single step was of revolutionary size; there was nothing to compare with what happened in Russia in 1918 or 1989, or China in the late 1940s, when the whole order crumbled at once.

Race Relations

Exactly how does law respond to social change? What is the mechanism? There are no general answers. One can trace some aspects of the relationship by following the course of race relations in the United States. We will, for the sake of relative simplicity, confine ourselves to black-white relations. This is only part of the story (the treatment of Hispanics, of Native Americans, of Asians, is left out), but this part, of course, is long and complex enough for our purposes. In many ways, it is an ugly and depressing tale. Most black Americans are descendants of slaves. They were brought to this country from the seventeenth century on. They were Africans, kidnapped, turned over to slave traders, and transported here or to the West Indies in the dirty, crowded holds of slave ships.

The law of slavery was discussed in Chapter 3. As was pointed out there, slavery was unknown to England or to the common law. Many whites, however, came to the colonies as indentured servants. Servitude was a kind of temporary slavery: a servant was bound to a master or mistress for a specific term of years. At the end of this time the servant went free. Some blacks probably had this status in the beginning, that is, in the seventeenth century.

But from the beginning, too, there were signs of a different status for blacks, and from the very first, the line between servant and slave was in part a color line.[4] By the middle of the seventeenth century, it was clear that some blacks were slaves, not servants. A slave is a servant for life, a servant who can never work off his status. In Virginia, at least some African blacks were treated as slaves before there is any evidence that the law officially recognized slave status. There are some hints of a custom of slavery perhaps as early as the 1620s; court records from about 1640 on show this custom clearly.[5] In 1644, there is mention of a mulatto boy named Manuel, sold "as a slave for-Ever."[6] In 1662, a Virginia statute made one aspect of the relationship official: slave status was to be inherited; children of a black slave mother would be slaves themselves from birth. The same statute recognized the color line in another way. Anyone who committed "fornication with a Negro" was to be fined twice the usual fine for fornication.[7]

Another law, in 1667, dealt with Christian slaves. Suppose a black slave became a Christian. Was he then free "by vertue of baptisme"? The answer was no: baptism did not "alter the condition of the person as to his bondage."[8] The slave might be free in heaven, but not here on earth. Later laws hammered home the legal reality of slavery. Slaves could not vote, hold office, own property. They were chattels, pieces of property; they could be bought and sold, given away, mortgaged, or rented out. They could be left to an heir by will or transferred by deed. The colonies spelled out these rules in elaborate codes of laws.

Meanwhile, slaves arrived by the boatload and the local population multiplied. On Southern plantations, slaves made up the basic workforce. They provided the muscles for planting and harvesting; they were the servants in the master's great house or in town. In fact, there were slaves in every colony—in New York, Massachusetts, and Rhode Island as well as in the South. But only in the South—in Maryland, Virginia, the Carolinas, Georgia—did slaves make up the bulk of the labor force. In the middle of the eighteenth century, 40 percent of the population of Virginia were blacks; some 96 percent of these blacks were held as slaves.

The differences between North and South became sharper after the Revolution. All of the northern states abolished slavery. There was some reaction in the South, too, against slavery. Some slaveholders took seriously the rhetoric of the Revolution, with its talk about inherent, inborn rights. A few Southern slave owners set their slaves free or wrote their slaves' freedom into their wills. George Washington was one of these; his will provided that at the death of his wife all the slaves he owned "shall receive their freedom."

But these were exceptions. Slavery kept a powerful hold on the Southern mind, and the economy needed black bodies. King Cotton demanded slaves. Slave codes became stricter and stricter in the nineteenth century. Fear of slave rebellion and of Northern abolitionists made the South more stubborn and defiant in the years before the Civil War. Slave states by law discouraged manumission (setting slaves free), and even moved to abolish the practice. There were free blacks in every southern state—descendants of other free blacks, or slaves freed by their masters. But these free blacks were barely tolerated, and were at best semifree. Like slaves, they could not vote or hold office. They could not testify in court against a white man. In many southern states, a freed slave was required by law to leave the state and never return. The actual practice was somewhat more lenient, but the message was clear: slavery was the natural condition of the black. Finally, Arkansas, just before the Civil War, passed a law to expel its few free blacks.[9]

The South imposed many restrictions on antislavery activity. It resisted attempts to reform or limit slavery. The slavery question, in general, poisoned relations with the North. Two issues, perhaps, stand out: the problem of the fugitive slave, and the spread of slavery to the territories. Northern abolitionists were dead set against returning runaway slaves; slaveowners insisted on their rights; Northern courts were caught in the middle. The territorial question raged on for at least forty years, from the Missouri Compromise (1820) to the Civil War, in 1860. The South, of course, lost this long and bloody war. Slavery was finally abolished; emancipation was rammed down white Southern throats.

But the white South did not give up its privileges so easily. When the war ended, the old oligarchy held fast to power—at least for a while.

The defeated states (starting with Mississippi) passed new race laws in 1865 and 1866, the so-called Black Codes. In these laws the white legislatures somewhat grudgingly conceded that slavery was dead; they allowed blacks to marry, and to own certain kinds of property. But they tried to keep the old social system alive, as far as they could. Blacks would be slaves without slavery—landless peasants, forced to work for white masters. In Mississippi, any "freedmen, free Negroes and mulattoes" who were over eighteen but had no "lawful employment or business" were declared "vagrants." A vagrant was liable to be fined, up to $50. A vagrant who could not pay—and few blacks had any cash—would be hired out to anybody who was willing to pay off the fine. The employer (often the vagrant's old master) would recoup the fine from the black man's or woman's wages. Through this and other legal arrangements, the South planned to force blacks to go back to work under conditions of virtual serfdom.

But war emotions were too fresh in the North for these laws to prevail. The North insisted on repeal of the Black Codes. The South was forced to accept three new amendments to the federal Constitution, which ended slavery and guaranteed civil liberties to the blacks (the Thirteenth, Fourteenth, and Fifteenth). Blacks were to be full citizens; they were given the legal right to vote and to share in political life. Federal troops patrolled the South.

Blacks were indeed legally free, as never before. They could go to school, start businesses, come and go as they pleased. At least this was true on paper. But Southern blacks were still at the bottom of the heap, still poor and illiterate, still treated as inferior by whites. During Reconstruction, blacks voted in some numbers. Blacks sat in Southern legislatures and even on Southern courts; a black man, J. J. Wright, was a justice of the Supreme Court of South Carolina. These were important developments. In the long run, black political power might have led to better, more equal relationships with whites. But this was not to be.

Racial equality, North or South, was in fact a house of cards. It fell apart at the touch. White people, whether high or low in the social scale and regardless of where they lived, were overwhelmingly opposed to full racial equality. Blacks had never been really welcome in the North, and Northern blacks were not treated as equals. School segregation, for example, was an invention of the North, not the South—though in fairness, the North was also the first to repudiate it. The South made little attempt to educate black children, segregated or not.

The legal structure of equality was also a house of cards. When the federal troops marched home, in the late 1870s, white supremacy came back to the South with a vengeance. Black workers were tied to the soil, as before. They were tenants or sharecroppers; they lived from hand to mouth, desperately poor, completely dependent on white landowners. A network of law and legal techniques helped keep blacks in their place; the crushing weight of the law-enforcement system added to poverty, illiteracy, and social prejudice, reinforcing the structure of discrimination.

Laws against "vagrancy," for example, were still on the books. Other laws made it a crime for black workers to "defraud" employers by quitting their work on white farms. It was also illegal for outsiders to "entice" workers away from their jobs—by offering them better jobs, for example. In practice, then, black farmhands were chained to white masters.[10]

The formal legal system was hardly any help. In the Reconstruction period, Congress passed a number of civil-rights laws. The Civil Rights Act of 1875 was a far-reaching law which banned discrimination in "inns, public conveyances on land or water, theatres, and other places of public amusement." But in the *Civil Rights Cases* (1883),[11] the Supreme Court declared the law unconstitutional. Congress, said the Court, had overstepped the bounds of the Fourteenth Amendment. The amendment applied only to "state action," that is, to acts of public authorities; it banned "discriminative and unjust laws" but not "individual offenses." People were still free to "discriminate," if they wished, in their homes, their social lives, their businesses; the Fourteenth Amendment had no power to reach into these spheres.

By this time, Reconstruction was in full retreat. The resurgent South swept off the table whatever crumbs of political influence blacks had picked up. There would be no more black faces in Southern legislatures, no more black judges in courtrooms. Some black officeholders were voted out; a few were impeached. Toward the end of the nineteenth century, the South began to weave a tight new fabric of legal segregation—the Jim Crow laws. These crystallized and formalized the attitudes and customs of the dominant whites. They made a rigid set of rules out of fluid social practice.[12] Any dissenters, white or black, had to face the fact that law as well as custom was against them. Blacks sank further into a swamp of oppression and injustice.

A few black voices were raised in protest in the courts, but the courts turned a deaf ear. In 1890, Louisiana passed a Jim Crow railroad law, an "Act to promote the comfort of passengers." Its message had nothing to do with comfort, however, and everything to do with segregation. Blacks were no longer free to sit in the same railroad cars as whites; the only exception was for "nurses attending children." All other blacks had to be rigidly separated from the whites. A light-skinned black named Homer Plessy ran afoul of the law. He tried to sit in the white section of a train, but was thrown off, and for his impudence landed in the parish jail of New Orleans. His protests ultimately reached the United States Supreme Court, whose famous (or infamous) decision, *Plessy v. Ferguson*,[13] was handed down in 1896.

By a vote of eight to one, the Supreme Court gave a green light to segregation. Nothing in the Constitution made Jim Crow laws illegal, said the Court. So long as facilities were "equal," it did not matter that they were "separate." The law could take into account the "established usages, customs and traditions of the people," especially when "the preservation of the public peace and good order" were at stake. What these words meant was clear: the Southern (white) way of life would prevail. The struggle for racial equality suffered a deadly blow; the highest court in the country accepted, and even praised, the American brand of apartheid.

John Marshall Harlan wrote a passionate, vigorous dissent. He insisted that the Constitution was "color-blind." It neither "knows nor tolerates classes among citizens. In respect of civil rights, all citizens are equal before the law." The Louisiana statute, "under the guise of . . . equal accommodation," was an act of oppression—a device to compel blacks "to keep to themselves while travelling." This, Harlan thought, violated the spirit and letter of the Civil War amendments to the Constitution. It was an evil act, and it would encourage race hatred and violence for years to come.

Harlan's predictions were accurate, but he was swimming against the tide. *Plessy v. Ferguson* encouraged the South to continue with its program of segregation. Soon every southern state had an arsenal of Jim Crow laws. Even jails were segregated: Arkansas law called for separate "apartments" for white and black convicts, "separate bunks, beds, bedding, separate dining tables and all other furnishings."[14]

At the same time, the southern states moved to strip blacks of political influence. They destroyed the right of black citizens to vote. This was, in theory, illegal, but the South found ways to do it: poll taxes, literacy tests, sometimes sheer terror. Whites were generally excused from literacy and other tests, sometimes by virtue of "grandfather clauses." The Oklahoma version, struck down later by the Supreme Court, required voters to be able to read and write any section of the Oklahoma constitution. But it exempted anybody who was entitled to vote on January 1, 1866, in any country, and anybody descended from such a voter. Of course, this meant that almost all whites were excused and hardly any blacks. The tactics worked. The number of black voters in most southern states dropped off to almost nothing. The rest of the country stood silent.

Stripped of political rights, the Southern black was now helpless. A black who dared cross the color line or who outraged local opinion ran the risk of sudden death. The bloody law of lynch mob and rope enforced the grim Southern code. Lynching was at its height around the turn of the century. Hundreds of prisoners, most of them black, were dragged from prison and hanged or burned; local authorities looked the other way. The North was uncomfortable with lynching; many voices, black and white, cried out against the practice; but the Southern system was deeply, firmly entrenched, and the national will to oppose it was weak and diffuse.

White supremacy was the cornerstone of Southern culture—and the Southern economy. Segregation survived legally because strong social forces held it in place. A counterattack began early in the twentieth century. It was slow and tortuous at first, but it, too, was persistent. Like segregation itself, it had an important legal aspect and embodied an important legal strategy. The fight for racial justice was a fight for power in society, but part of its strength came from its appeal to morality and its firm commitment to law.

The National Association for the Advancement of Colored People (NAACP) was founded in the years before the First World War. From the start, it had a strong legal arm. The NAACP defended black rights in court and brought lawsuits to expand those rights. Not all these lawsuits were successful, but some were, and spectacularly so. In *Guinn v. United States* (1915),[15] the NAACP took part in the fight against Oklahoma's grandfather clause, and won. But even victories in the courts did not produce real change in race relations. Southern states, despite cases like *Guinn,* had plenty of ways to keep blacks out of the voting booth. The United States Civil Rights Commission, in a report issued in 1961, found sixteen counties in the Deep South in which not a single black was registered to vote, even though blacks were a majority in these counties.[16]

Time, however, was ultimately on the side of the NAACP and the black population. The world outside the courtroom was rapidly changing. By 1950, the plantation system was dying in the South. In the twentieth century, blacks migrated north in great numbers, looking for work. The Second World War drew more blacks to the North, with the promise of factory jobs. The black community developed more militance, more cohesion, in the course of time. Internationally, colonialism was in decline. The Second World War was in part a war against racist ideology. It was jarring and discordant to fight the war with segregated troops, but the system of segregation hung on. President Harry Truman ordered the army, navy, and air force desegregated, though he did so only after the end of the Second World War. By then, broad change was in the air.

A climax was reached in 1954, when the Supreme Court, on one of its most historic Mondays, announced the stupendous, unanimous decision in *Brown v. Board of Education.*[17] There was only one opinion. By Supreme Court standards, it was short and direct. The chief justice, Earl Warren, recently appointed by President Eisenhower, wrote the opinion of the Court, but he spoke for a unanimous body.

The *Brown* case dealt with segregated schools. In the Deep South and in some border states, black and white children, by law, had to go to separate schools. Oliver Brown, the black plaintiff, lived in Topeka, Kansas; his daughter, Linda, went to a segregated school.

The Court in *Brown* gave the plaintiffs, and their attorneys, a smashing victory and boosted, immeasurably, the cause of racial equality. Segregation in the schools, the court said, was illegal—unconstitutional. That was startling enough—a massive shock to the South. But *Brown* was only the beginning. A chain of decisions struck down race discrimination and segregation in every aspect of public life—in parks, swimming pools, beaches, municipal services. Despite howls of protest from the South, the Court never backed down, never looked back. The cases sent an important signal to the black community and its allies: federal courts would not waver in defense of minority rights. Their doors would be open to blacks, for the enforcement of racial equality. The promise of the Fourteenth Amendment would at last be fulfilled. More: courts would redefine and expand the classic rights.

Enforcement of *Brown* was never easy. The South resisted, dragged its heels, dug in. "Massive resistance" was the slogan in the former Confederacy. In 1962, eight years after *Brown,* not a single black child went to school with whites in Mississippi, Alabama, or South Carolina. Even colleges and universities in these states were still rigidly segregated.[18]

Civil rights had become, quite literally, a struggle. At times blood was shed. Civil-rights workers were harassed, beaten, ostracized. Martyrs died for the cause, most of them black. A church was bombed and black children died. There were sit-ins, marches, petitions, riots; nonviolent protest spread throughout the South. Meanwhile, legal struggles went on in the law courts. Both modes of battle were vital. Neither was sufficient in itself: the marchers and battlers needed lawyers, and the work of the lawyers meant nothing without action on the streets. Perhaps a third element should be added: the civil-rights struggle was carried on in the age of TV. When civil-rights workers were beaten, and when howling mobs screamed at little black children marching to school under the protection of federal marshals, the whole country watched what was going on.

More than forty years have passed by since *Brown* was decided. School desegregation is still controversial, still an issue in the country. There are still hundreds of all-black (and all-white) schools. Most now are in the North, products of the neighborhood school system, segregated housing patterns, and "white flight"—that is, the migration of the white middle class to the suburbs. The school bus is one possible technique for mixing the races, but it has been bitterly resisted—and not always only by whites. The Supreme Court approved of busing in 1971,[19] but this did not end the debate or the constant stream of lawsuits. The Court itself has become, in recent years, more hesitant about this remedy.

In many big cities, public-school children are, in numbers, overwhelmingly black. Integration in the *Brown* sense is no longer even possible, at least not inside city limits. Yet this does not mean that *Brown* has failed. All-black schools are not segregated schools, in the older sense. They have integrated staffs, and the school boards tend to treat them fairly. Indeed, in some cities, blacks control the boards of education. Black schools face immense problems, but they are not Jim Crow schools in the same sense that they were in the South.

Race relations are in constant evolution. The Civil Rights Act of 1964 was a great leap forward. Title II outlawed race discrimination in "any place of public accommodation." This included inns, hotels, motels, restaurants, cafeterias, lunch counters, soda fountains, "any motion picture house, theater, concert hall, sports arena, stadium or other place of exhibition or entertainment," and "any gasoline station." The law was, of course, soon challenged in court. But this time the Supreme Court upheld the statute, and in sweeping terms.[20] The challenger in the second of these cases was a "family-owned restaurant in Birmingham, Alabama," Ollie's Barbecue by name, which specialized in "barbecued meats and homemade pies." This kind of small, local eatery stood at the very limit of the law, but the Supreme Court was willing, even eager, to validate the law to the maximum extent and smash segregation forever. The Court rested its decision on its power to regulate interstate commerce. Even a greasy-spoon restaurant used food products that had crossed state borders, and any motel was, after all, open to interstate travelers.

This time, the barriers in public places really did collapse. The Civil Rights Act took hold. A black man for the first time could drive a car across the country and eat at almost any restaurant, stay at almost any motel. A strong Voting Rights Act (1965) put another nail in the coffin of the old order. The federal government now promised to stand behind the right of blacks to vote. Black political power increased enormously. Blacks began to appear once more in legislatures and city halls, where they had been absent since Reconstruction. A black man, Douglas Wilder, served a term as governor of Virginia. The political power of African-Americans also increased in the North, especially where there were concentrations of black voters. Black mayors were elected in Detroit, Atlanta, Los Angeles, Newark, Cleveland, Chicago, New York, Philadelphia, and Washington, D.C. Many of the cities that elected black mayors had black majorities, or close to it. In a few instances—San Francisco in 1995, for example—a city in which blacks were a rather small minority nonetheless put a black in City Hall.

Race is still a burning issue in American life. Social and legal change have undoubtedly moved in the direction of racial equality. But the movement has not been smooth, especially in recent years. There have been many zigs and zags. Segregation is officially dead. There is no chance it will come back to life—officially. But there is still a huge black underclass in every major city and in the rural South; there is still a wide gap between the incomes of blacks and of whites. There are too few black doctors, lawyers, business executives, scientists, architects. More black babies die than white babies. Twice the percentage of blacks are unemployed. The prisons are jammed with black men.

Are new measures called for? Many blacks (and white liberals) say yes. What is needed is an extra helping hand—something that goes beyond desegregation. It is not enough to dismantle legal barriers. Affirmative steps are now needed, positive programs of help. But this touches a raw nerve. Many whites fear and resent these "favors" to blacks. They feel threatened in their jobs or their homes. "Affirmative action" generates strong backlash.

The issue came to a head in the famous *Bakke* case.[21] Alan Bakke, who was white, applied to the medical school of the University of California at Davis. Davis had a special admissions program for minorities; it had, in fact, a quota. A certain number of places in each entering class were set aside for blacks and other minorities. Davis rejected Alan Bakke's application, but at the same time (he claimed) the school admitted blacks with lower grades and scores than his. This, he felt, violated his constitutional rights.

The Supreme Court obviously found the case troubling. Its decision was fragmented and confused. The Court struck down the Davis system of quotas and (by a bare majority) ordered the school to let Bakke in.

But the justices wrote several separate opinions, and there was no true majority on any major point. A bare majority of the justices felt that some forms of "benign" discrimination were legal, but exactly which ones, and how far a school could go in its affirmative-action programs, remained unanswered.

In a sense, then, the *Bakke* case settled nothing, except for Alan Bakke himself, who forced open the door to a medical career. Affirmative action and benign discrimination remained living issues, very much unresolved. (The issue was posed as well with regard to women, and to other racial minorities.) Most blacks feel a strong claim of right to affirmative action. They feel these measures are necessary to undo centuries of injustice and to counteract the racism that still poisons American life. Blacks tend to think that equality, economic and political, is still a far-off goal. They are afraid that progress has ground to a halt. In the 1990s, a more conservative Supreme Court seemed to be turning back the clock. The Court disapproved of "minority set-asides" in public contracts, in 1995;[22] the Court also voiced disapproval of Congressional districts in the South, with crazy boundaries, that had been gerrymandered to make sure they had a majority of black voters.[23] A lower federal court, in 1996, ordered Texas universities to stop their affirmative action programs; the Supreme Court refused to intervene.[24]

Yet despite shifts in this or that direction, it is undeniable that immense changes in race relations—in law and fact—have taken place since *Brown.* Unlike many legal "victories" before *Brown,* the earth did move; the landscape shifted in a permanent way. How much of this was because of *Brown?* How much credit goes to courts, to law and legal process? The question has been vigorously debated, and there are those who feel that the role of the Court has been vastly exaggerated.[25]

It is impossible, of course, to separate cause and effect. The *Brown* case did not start the civil-rights movement; that much is obvious. The movement came first, and it "caused" *Brown,* if the word "cause" is appropriate at all. But once in place, *Brown* and later cases did play a role in the developing drama. They played a role something like the bridge in our parable. Congress added to the structural framework by passing strong new laws on civil rights. This tough, bony structure of law helped channel and concentrate power and influence in society. As more black people voted, it became more difficult for candidates to run for office on a white-racist basis. Segregationists virtually disappeared from public life. Senator Strom Thurmond of South Carolina ran for president in 1948, as a "Dixiecrat," in support of white supremacy and states' rights. Yet in the 1990s the same Senator Thurmond vigorously championed a conservative black man, Clarence Thomas—indeed, a black man who was married to a white woman—for a position on the Supreme Court of the United States. Race prejudice did not disappear, by any means; rather, on the whole, it went underground.

But this was not an unimportant development. The law was not merely an expression of power; it also expressed ideals, and when power and ideals became united, white supremacy was reduced to a fringe movement, almost an outlaw movement. Outlaws sometimes wield their own form of sinister strength. But in this case, they lost their legitimacy, and that loss can be crucial at times. The chain of events since *Brown* helped transform people's thoughts and ideas, their concepts of legal right; it modified their view of law and what they expected the law to perform. Social processes lay behind these changes in legal culture, but legal culture, like the bridge, reinforced these processes, and in time and in turn it led to further social change.

Law and the Social Revolution

Tremendous changes have also taken place in recent years in culture, lifestyle, and social behavior. These changes have gone far beyond race relations, though the civil-rights revolution may have played some role in these other domains of social change. There has been a revolution in customs and habits of life, and notoriously, a so-called sexual revolution. This "revolution" took, and takes, a number of forms. There is a huge increase in the number of young couples and not-so-young couples who live together without bothering to get married. There is the gay-rights movement, demanding legitimacy for the "sexual minorities." Pornography is sold more or less out in the open, and protected by law to a large extent. There are relaxed attitudes toward "dirty" speech both in public and in private, a decline in the double standard of sexual morality, and so on. The dreaded specter of AIDS may have altered behavior somewhat, in a "conservative" direction; but it has hardly affected, at all, the *ideology* of the sexual revolution. Promiscuous, unsafe sex may be hazardous to one's health, but the effect on the soul is another matter.

Our concern is with law—more specifically, with the role legal institutions play either in helping to bring these changes about, in resisting them, in adapting to them, or in altering their form. Of course, we must be more precise in describing our subject. Exactly what is this "revolution" in social norms and behaviors? Everyone probably has his or her own notion. At the core is the idea that certain standards of conduct, once widely accepted in the United States, or at least not often challenged, are now "in play," in dispute, or have simply broken down.

Specifically, what has changed is, first, the idea that a single official code of personal behavior governs (or should govern) the country; second, that the code more or less coincides with the moral commands of traditional Christianity, overlaid with a dose of Victorian morality; and third, and most relevant for our purposes, that government has the right—indeed, the duty—to turn these precepts into legal rules and to enforce them as best it can.

All three of these notions are under sustained attack, and their hold on the law has been drastically weakened. Many examples that come to mind have to do with sex and sexual morality, but by no means all. Consider, for example, gambling, once almost totally illegal, now a major industry—state lotteries, Las Vegas and Atlantic City, riverboat casinos, casinos on Indian reservations. Consider, too, the legal and social position of minority religions. There was never, of course, any official religion in the United States, and in theory everyone enjoys total freedom of religion. The First Amendment makes a bold, positive statement: "Congress shall make no law respecting an establishment of religion, or prohibiting the free exercise thereof." Some state constitutions are even more emphatic. The Wisconsin constitution states that "the right of every man to worship Almighty God according to the dictates of conscience shall never be infringed." The state cannot give "preference" to any religion or spend any public money on any "religious" society.[26] In fact, however, there has always been a semiofficial range of religions in the country, and Americans have found it hard to tolerate "free exercise" for religions that seemed too strange—that wandered too far from the familiar course.

The troubled history of the Church of Jesus Christ of Latter-Day Saints, usually called the Mormons, is a case in point. Joseph Smith founded this religion around 1830. From the beginning, his followers were persecuted; Smith himself was murdered by a mob. The Mormons traveled west, hoping to find a sanctuary. They founded a community in the basin of the Great Salt Lake, in what is now Utah. They wanted to make their own way in the world, but the world did not let them. The Mormons practiced polygamy, which was, they believed, God's will. This practice was too much for the rest of the country to stomach. "Mormonism," one Protestant minister proclaimed, is a "great surge of licentiousness . . . it is the concentrated Corruption of this land, it is the brothel of the nation, it is hell enthroned."[27] The "free exercise" of polygamy went against the grain of American opinion. There was no way the majority could tolerate polygamy, and therefore it could not tolerate the Mormons themselves.

In 1862, Congress passed the Morrill Act, aimed explicitly at the

Mormons, which made polygamy a federal crime in the territories, including Utah.[28] A man named George Reynolds was indicted under the act, convicted, and sentenced to prison. He appealed to the United States Supreme Court. His defense was freedom of religion—his rights under the First Amendment.

In *Reynolds v. United States*,[29] the Supreme Court affirmed Reynolds's conviction. Polygamy was "odious"; Congress was right to declare it a crime. Merely because polygamy was a tenet of someone's religion did not excuse the practice: if a person believed that "human sacrifices were a necessary part of religious worship," was that an excuse? Or if a wife "religiously believed it was her duty to burn herself upon the funeral pile of her dead husband," would the state allow this to happen?

The Mormons argued, with a good deal of justice, that they were not licentious people at all; they were religious people who had the highest moral standards. They put enormous stress on wholesome, traditional family life. But the rest of the country refused to believe them. Polygamy, to the ordinary American, was a barbaric custom, and socially dangerous besides. In the *Reynolds* case, the Court noted that polygamy was "exclusively a feature of the life of Asiatic and of African people"; it also "led to the patriarchal principle . . . which . . . fetters the people in stationary despotism."

Here, as is usually the case, the Court no doubt reflected what the country as a whole felt. The *Reynolds* case demonstrated the limits of national tolerance, which stopped far short of allowing multiple wives. Tolerance meant the right—for white people, at least—to blend into the dominant culture without barriers of caste or class. It did not imply the right to "do your own thing," that is, to live as a free, unconventional spirit. It never occurred to the justices that "Asiatic and African people" might claim the same level of civilization (and legality) as white Christians from northern Europe.

Wisconsin v. Yoder[30] is a more modern case (1975), and it, too, deals with offbeat religion. The contrast with *Reynolds* is striking. Jonas Yoder was a member of a minority religious group, the Old Order Amish. Another defendant, Adin Yutzy, belonged to the Conservative Amish Mennonite Church. The defendants lived in Wisconsin. Under state law, children had to go to school until sixteen. The defendants refused to keep their children in school past the eighth grade. They were fined $5, and appealed. The case (clearly a test case) went all the way to the United States Supreme Court.

The defense, once again, was freedom of religion. Public high school, or any advanced schooling, was "contrary to the Amish religion and way of life." If defendants obeyed the Wisconsin law, the Amish argued, it would "endanger their own salvation and that of their children." The Amish insisted on living in their own church community, "separate and apart from the world and worldly influence."

This time, the Supreme Court was willing to accept the claim. The First Amendment guaranteed the right to live outside the "conventional 'mainstream.' " The state had no power to impose its will on a religion and a way of life "that is odd or even erratic but interferes with no rights or interests of others." The Wisconsin school law was a valid use of state power in general, but the Amish also had rights, and they were entitled to be exempted from the law.

The opinions in the *Yoder* case, as some have pointed out, can be reconciled with some quite conservative features of American culture. The Amish are intensely religious, rural, old-fashioned people. Their values do not offend the majority; in some ways they are merely extreme forms of values which the dominant culture much admires. But the same could have been said about the Mormons. Polygamy itself was a Biblical practice, after all. Even though we can find big differences between *Reynolds* and *Yoder,* big enough to reconcile them, it seems fair to say that the 1970s Court was less wedded to the idea of cultural assimilation, more open-minded, more willing to tolerate groups different in lifestyle from the rest of the country, than it was in the nineteenth century.

Of course, even today there are limits to freedom of religion. It is of course still true that no court would accept human sacrifice or the burning of widows, in the name of religion, any more than in 1878. There is a deep suspicion of "cults." At Jonestown, Guyana, in November 1978, hundreds of Americans, followers of a fanatical leader, committed suicide at his orders, by drinking poisoned Kool-Aid. Nonstandard religions still make most Americans fearful, suspicious. The Unification Church (the "Moonies") has provoked intense legal action as well. The church is under the wing of the First Amendment, to be sure, but to what extent? Are the tactics of this church—its aggressive recruiting, its dictatorial demands on its members—protected by law? Desperate parents have snatched their children out of the clutches of this church and had them "deprogrammed." Since the "Moonies," and members of other "cults," are over eighteen, how can the parents legally do this? Young people certainly have the right to choose their way of life; if so, how can parents insist that their children submit to deprogrammers? Somewhat reluctantly, the courts have, on the whole, refused to take the side of parents and deprogrammers. Adults cannot be forced to leave their religion.[31]

Changes in laws about obscenity and sexual deviance also bring the legal system face to face with the social revolution. Chapter 9 discussed the rise and fall of laws against victimless crime and the upsurge of interest in enforcing the traditional moral code from the late nineteenth century on. Sex and obscenity laws were tightened in this period; abortion was criminalized; states also enacted stronger laws against gambling and Sabbath-breaking. This movement, which began around 1870, may have been the last gasp of a dying social order. Or, perhaps, it was the last stand of a beleaguered concept—the notion that there was, and ought to be, basically a single moral code for the country, essentially the code of Protestant America.

Millions of immigrants, many from Southern and Eastern Europe, swarmed into the United States in the late nineteenth century. These immigrants brought their own cultures with them; these cultures differed from the culture of the older Americans in certain crucial respects. Joseph Gusfield argued that this culture clash explains why the temperance movement became so strong in this period. He saw the movement as a kind of Protestant backlash, which snowballed until it reached its peak in the passage of the Prohibition Amendment.[32]

The Harrison Narcotics Act (1914) was another "triumph" of morality; it made criminals out of drug addicts, and was perhaps an even greater disaster than Prohibition in the long run. Culture clash was a factor in the war on "dope" and "dope fiends." The earliest drug laws—for example, the laws in California[33]—were directed against "opium dens." The Chinese ran these dens, and to white Californians, opium was just one more aspect of the "Chinese problem." The drive against marijuana was also aimed primarily at a single ethnic group, the Chicanos; marijuana was supposedly "a direct by-product of unrestricted Mexican immigration." In "areas with concentrations of Mexican immigrants, the fear of marihuana was intense."[34]

The old moral code, however vigorous it was in the pulpits, had begun to decay in the outside world. Behavior, as usual, precedes new law, and is decisive in creating new law. But ideas, attitudes, shift along with behavior. At one time, there was a standard notion of what respectable behavior meant. Respectable people had moderate sex lives, within the boundaries of Christian marriage. They did not get drunk and disorderly. They did not gamble or take drugs. They worked hard and obeyed the law. Of course, society had plenty of dirty secrets. There were millions of heavy drinkers. Prostitutes sold their bodies on the streets. Gambling and vice were available in every city. There were tramps and hoboes who drifted from place to place. But nobody *defended* vice and drink. People either behaved according to the code or, what is almost as important, they accepted it as right and authoritative; they pledged allegiance to it even if and as they broke every single commandment.

What happened from the late nineteenth century on was perhaps a subtle change in the legitimacy of the traditional code. More people began to question it, and not just through their conduct; they questioned the code as the norm, the ideal, as well—they attacked its official status. Italian Catholics, for example, saw nothing wrong in a glass of wine. Others attacked "Puritanism" and "prudery" more broadly. Most of the habits and norms of the new immigrants were not at all offensive, nothing to compare with Mormon polygamy or the alleged Chinese opium culture. Nonetheless, the old elites may have felt that the sun was setting on their empire of values; that the fine old house of American culture was rotting away.

They did not accept their fate lying down. If rot was attacking the house, then the timbers needed reconstruction. The majority turned to law to enforce their code and to shore up their monopoly of moral legitimacy. Law acts as a substitute for informal norms, in a complex society. It is used to keep a diverse population glued together in some reasonable working order, despite all the differences between groups in values and habits. It replaces informal methods—those methods which worked well enough on the tiny island of Tristan de Cunha, or among little clans and groups of hunters and gatherers, or in clubs, families, and groups of friends.

Society turns to law for help in shoring up the house—in preventing further dilapidation. But the law does not necessarily work as expected. Cultural diversity, the very fact that stimulates the use of formal law, dooms the legal process to imperfect performance. If the law chooses sides, if it outlaws the codes and customs of a minority, it may meet with severe resistance. Most people think Prohibition was a dismal failure, and in many ways it was. The Harrison Act and the severe modern drug laws have had an even more depressing history. Most fair-minded experts concede this point. The "war on drugs" has created a black market in drugs. It has driven addicts into lives of crime; it has contributed to urban decay. The policy has not only failed, it has also done incalculable harm. The effect on African-Americans is particularly harsh; in 1992, blacks made up 40 percent of the men and women arrested for drug abuse—out of all proportion to their share of the population, and out of all proportion to their actual use of drugs.[35] There may not be an easy solution to the drug problem,[36] but that does not alter the fact that drug laws have a lot to answer for.

On issues of sexual morality, law necessarily reflects what is happening in the larger society. The sexual revolution, it turns out, is not a flash in the pan. The old morality decayed and went right on decaying; in the last two generations, there has been tremendous pressure to change the law, to take the stigma of criminality (and stigma in general) out of behavior that does not fit the old models. That famous lustful couple, "consenting adults," no longer risks arrest and prosecution, in most states, no matter what they do with or to each other. The last word, of course, has not been spoken. "Moral" forces have counterattacked, and vigorously. Pornography is still intensely controversial. So are gay rights. The Supreme Court upheld, as constitutional, laws against "sodomy," in a Georgia case decided in 1986.[37] But the Court was deeply divided on the issue, and as of 1996, the status of the case is in some doubt, after the Court struck down a Colorado initiative that outlawed local gay-rights ordinances. Abortion remains a deeply controversial issue, too. Abortion rights were created by the Supreme Court in the 1970s, but the "pro-life" movement has never given up, and the issue remains deeply divisive in the 1990s. Many legal battles still lie ahead in Congress, in the courts, and in the public mind.

The Decay of Authority

What lies behind the social revolution? Some see it as part of a long-term trend, the general weakening of authority in the United States. This trend began, perhaps, early in our history. The Puritan colonies were dominated by the clergy, but the clergy did not keep its authority for very long. When the country became independent, it was a nation without an established church, a nobility, or an aristocracy of birth or merit. Such nineteenth-century visitors as Alexis de Tocqueville were amazed at how "democratic" this country was, which meant, among other things, that the population showed little respect for traditional authority, compared to countries like France. It was a nation of social and political equals, or at least it looked that way to a European, despite the slaves in the South. (The subordinate position of women was a feature most men never noticed.)

Every society has an authority structure. Every society has high and low. No society even comes close to pure equality. There were and are many kinds of authority, many forms of hierarchy, in this country. Millions of Americans are deeply religious, and are faithful to the word of their churches. Learning, skill, and money all command respect. So does political power. There is also the authority of custom, and the authority of traditional morality. These form a kind of inner monarchy, whose commands are passed along by parents, teachers, and preachers.

For many people, the old ways, or what they understand as the old ways, are a powerful source of control. Shifts in patterns of authority are relative, not absolute.

Authority is hard to measure. Undoubtedly, some traditional institutions have been slowly loosing or losing their grip, over time. There is considerable discussion, for example, of the fate of family authority. Clearly, family authority is very much alive. Father's word may not be "law" anymore, or mother's, but most children do obey their parents, and they care what their parents think and say. They do their homework and they listen to teacher in school, even if they do not show old-fashioned respect or obey like little Prussians. There are millions of single-parent families and unorthodox families, but they are families nonetheless. The family changes in form, but it is still a great power. Most people, too, follow a definite code of behavior, and it is a fairly traditional one. The decline of authority is, as we said, a matter of degree. Studies suggest a decline in respect for governmental authority, a decline in trust, a crisis of legitimacy; but the loss of faith may be, perhaps, rather selective.

Legal process, in a sense, rushes in to fill the vacuum. "Law" has in many ways replaced other forms of authority. In the colonial period, officials swore to be loyal to their king; they had a personal bond to the crown. The president of the United States takes an oath to support the Constitution. His "king" is a legal document, a symbol of law, rather than any human authority. In this country, ultimate power is supposed to rest with the people; more concretely, it lies in the legal structure of society, and in the laws themselves. We pledge allegiance to the flag, but true allegiance runs not to a piece of cloth, or even to the president, or to some sacred text in the National Archives. Rather, our commitment is to a way of governing, a process, a set of procedures, a way of making decisions—in other words, to *law*. There is a shared understanding that we obey and respect the rules of the game.

These rules hold society together. They are essential nuts and bolts that keep the structure from falling apart. As other forms of authorities weaken, the role of some aspects of law becomes stronger—becomes recognized as an impartial, impersonal arbiter of disputes. Law is a way out of the dilemmas of politics and controversy. The idea is that law stands above and beyond all politics—and even if this idea is, to a large extent, nothing but a myth, it is nonetheless powerful. It is a way to appeal to people's inner voices, to motives higher than their crude self-interest. All this may explain a striking American trend: all sorts of social and economic issues end up in court. And, in court, these questions get *answers;* moreover, both sides usually respect what the courts decide.

Other countries do not have quite the same system. De Tocqueville noticed the American habit in embryo in the nineteenth century. There is no political or social question in America, he said, that does not turn into a judicial one. Today De Tocqueville's insight seems even more obviously right. Of course, not everybody celebrates the American reliance on courts; we have noted before the cries of alarm and shouts of panic.

In any event, law and (rather surprisingly) the courts stand in the center, the core of crucial decisions, in the United States, in instance after instance. The courts are intimately concerned with such sticky issues as obscenity, abortion, sexual deviancy, personal morality, and drug laws—in short, with the whole social revolution. They are just as closely connected with the economy. They are players in the game of politics as well—they even decide whether states have drawn the right lines around Congressional districts, or whether Congress can regulate campaign finance.

A Twentieth Century Instance: The Palimony Case

Social forces constantly make and remake law. We often see this happening before our very eyes, so to speak. An example from 1976 was the notorious "palimony" case of *Marvin v. Marvin*.[38] A well-known movie actor, Lee Marvin, and Michele Triola, a singer, lived together in a single household for seven years. They never actually married. But Michele Triola called herself Michele Marvin, and they behaved in all respects like man and wife. Then the relationship ended. In 1970, Michele Marvin sued Lee Marvin, demanding half of his earnings—more than $1 million—for the years they lived together. She claimed he had promised her this share in return for *her* promise to come and live with him, a promise which she of course kept.

The trial court, in Los Angeles, dismissed the case. The judge relied on a long line of prior decisions refusing to enforce such agreements. To live together outside of marriage was immoral in the eyes of the law, and any supposed contract to behave this way could not be legally enforced. Michele Marvin appealed, and the California Supreme Court, by a six to one vote, reversed the lower court's decision. The trial court, it said, had acted too hastily; Michele might well have a good cause of action. She should be allowed to prove her case. They sent *Marvin v. Marvin* back to the lower court, to begin all over again.

The opinion of the California Supreme Court is at certain points blunt and direct, at other points technical and full of legal nuances. All the subtleties were lost, of course, on the millions of people who read about the case in the newspapers or heard about it on the evening news. Only a handful of lawyers read or have read the actual text. The public did understand one thing, however: Michele's case had opened the door to a new kind of lawsuit. Cohabitation was no longer an outlaw status, on the fringe of respectability and legality. It was or could be a definite legal relationship; rights and duties might flow out of it, and a court could enforce any reasonable arrangements the partners made with each other.

The Supreme Court of California had pushed legal doctrine in a new direction—but why? One point seems obvious to layman and lawyer alike: times had changed, morals had changed. The Census Bureau estimated that 2.2 million unmarried couples were living together as of 1978, two years after the *Marvin* case was decided.[39] Cohabitation, once shunned in respectable society, had become exceedingly popular. It has continued to be so.

The California Supreme Court lives in society along with the rest of us. The justices have eyes and ears; they read newspapers and watch TV. The justices who decided the *Marvin* case surely knew people—their own children, perhaps—who lived together without bothering to get married. Cohabitation had become a way of life, like it or not, and it had spread among all classes of society. When social arrangements change, it is no surprise that legal rights and duties rearrange themselves. The California court argued at various points in its opinion that *Marvin v. Marvin* was not really a break with past law. Courts like to stress the continuity of law, even when they create new doctrines. But at other points in the opinion the court frankly referred to the altered social context, to the "radical" changes taking place in "the mores of society."

Michele Marvin's victory in the California Supreme Court did not settle her claim. It now had to be assessed on the facts. The new trial was long and bitter. It made headlines, and was rich in gossip and scandal. Legally speaking, the outcome was something of an anticlimax. Michele Marvin won a modest victory, so modest it was almost defeat. She was awarded something on the order of $100,000. This was small potatoes, compared to the size of her claim (and considering her lawyers' fees). Probably she failed to win big money because her evidence was weak. She insisted she and Lee Marvin had come to an "agreement," but she had no convincing proof. In the end, both sides claimed victory. One thing was clear, though it was cold comfort for Michele Marvin: the law had changed. No moral or legal barrier stood in the way of claims like hers, at least in California.

The social revolution had touched one field of law, at one point in space and time. Duties and rights were realigned. The exact realignment was not, as far as we can tell, foreordained with iron logic. The spread of cohabitation meant that the issue was sure to bob to the surface somewhere in the legal system. Legal change was bound to happen, but the California solution was by no means inevitable or predetermined. No one can say the new legal pattern had to take exactly this form, at this time, or that this was the best way to handle the situation. We can say only that arrangements were bound to change—bound to take some new form, better suited to the new facts than the arrangements discarded.

What effect, in turn, did *Marvin v. Marvin* have on society? The case was famous—notorious, in fact. The *New York Times* ran seventeen articles on the case between 1976 and 1979. *Time* magazine featured it in a story; so did *Playboy;* comedians told jokes about it on TV; cartoons appeared in magazines. The word (or at least some word) got around. Millions of people learned that the law had changed. They learned this vaguely and inaccurately, but they did smell something happening.

What took place next is hardly surprising. Other disappointed lovers took their cue from *Marvin v. Marvin.* In the two years after the California case, about a hundred lawsuits of the *Marvin* type were filed in various courts.[40] Others were probably settled before getting that far. In many states, cases went up to higher courts on appeal. There the outcomes were mixed. Some states stuck to their guns, at least for the time being. Others climbed on the new bandwagon and followed the line laid down in *Marvin v. Marvin.* Trends of case law were established, though they pointed in different directions. Some legislatures were hostile; Minnesota, in 1980, made these contracts enforceable only if they were "written and signed by the parties" and ordered the courts to dismiss any lawsuits based on claims that did not comply.[41] In 1987, Texas, too, closed the door on such contracts unless they were in writing. But even in these states, what probably unsettled the legislators was fear of blackmail and fraud—not the morality of couples who lived together without getting married.

Did people change their behavior after *Marvin?* Some probably did. Some wealthy people with "live-ins" no doubt became more cautious about what they said and did. The case stimulated a few people to consult their lawyers; a few cohabitors probably drew up contracts with each other spelling out rights and duties and making explicit what claims they had, if any, to what the other partner earned. Once again, we can invoke the metaphor of the bridge. Social forces bent the law in one direction, but once the law changed, new forces and new alignments emerged; law itself became an influence on conduct. The California Supreme Court had come to a decision which was itself a response to social change; the court formalized and restated the problem, redefined the issue, and (in a blaze of publicity) gave rise to new expectations. The case also probably helped in a minor way to legitimize a way of life that in the past would have scandalized respectable people. It was definitely a sign of the times that when the American Bar Association published, in 1993, a "guide" to drafting and enforcing premarital agreements and the like, it included a chapter that discussed *Marvin*-like contracts for same-sex couples.[42] To be sure, there are many people who still think cohabitation is immoral. No doubt they would disapprove of the *Marvin* case and what followed it. But the California court, of course, did not invent, or spread, cohabitation.

Changes in morals, morality, ways of life—changes in culture and expectation—create new demands that press in on legal institutions, including the courts. These institutions then change their behavior, as they are pushed and pulled by rival social forces. Legal rules, processes, and behaviors shift; they move right or left, up or down. The new legal situation freezes customs into more solid forms, reinforces certain expectations, sends out new messages, subtly alters culture. It changes ways of thinking and looking at life the way a prism alters beams of light. This is a constant process in society.

Another case in point is surrogate motherhood. A New Jersey case of 1988, involving "Baby M," made as many headlines as the *Marvin* case. In *Baby M*, a married couple paid a woman to bear a child, using the husband's sperm. When a little girl was born, the womb mother refused to give her up. The highest court of New Jersey held that the contract could not be enforced, but it treated the case as an ordinary custody dispute (and awarded custody to the father).[43] By 1995, nineteen states had passed statutes to ban or regulate surrogacy contracts; the debate goes on.[44] The whole issue would have been unthinkable as late as, say, 1950.

To take still one more example, environmental law is a whole new field that has sprung up in the past generation. It cannot be understood without reference to the environmental *movement*. This movement did not begin inside the legal system. It began outside, in society. It burst into consciousness and spilled over into law. Today this field of law is a big, important, tangible reality. Lawyers and the public talk about "impact statements," "endangered-species lists," "clean-air amendments," the "superfund," and so on. A vice president of the United States, Al Gore, has written a book on the environment and has based much of his political career on defense of the environment. Environmental *law*—a complex, technical body of rules and procedures—in turn provides hooks or handles, which environmental groups use to put pressure on society, pressure to move still further in a particular direction.

The course of sociolegal change is not smooth and painless. It is at best a bumpy road. The environmental movement, for example, is continually embroiled in controversy. Many people think "things have gone too far." They believe that "extremists" have hurt the economy, all for the sake of a few trees or fish. An important countermovement became prominent in the 1970s. Some of its leaders gained political power during the Reagan administration. James Watt, who was President Reagan's secretary of the interior until late 1983, came out of this background. Arguments have raged over oil leases in California waters, over coal mines and timber cutting on public land, over nuclear wastes, over the dredging of canals, over policy in regard to national parks, and so on. The Republican Congress elected in 1994 was determined to bring back what some considered a better balance—favoring jobs and economic growth over spotted owls and endangered species. But the environmental movement proved to be a tough opponent. Both sides push and pull—in the courts, in legislatures, in the election booth. As they do, they push and pull at the doctrines and rules, the raw material of law. Environmental law is in constant flux.

Every major change in social behavior has an impact on law. And every major change in law has its roots in changes outside of it, in social behavior. The "medical-malpractice crisis" is on the surface a purely legal crisis. In the late twentieth century, there was a rash of lawsuits against doctors and hospitals; these stimulated, or panicked, insurance companies; insurance premiums for many doctors went sky-high; the doctors fought back, demanding legislative curbs on tort suits—with considerable success. But the whole dance of action and reaction would be inconceivable without deep changes in the organization of medicine. The changing structure of medical practice, the growth of specialization, the development of modern surgery and pharmacology, and the rise of health insurance have all altered the way doctors and patients relate to each other, and the legal rules of the horse-and-buggy days were bound to be swept away.

The struggles over the death penalty and over abortion rights also demonstrate how courts and law are exposed to outside pressure. In these battles, the courts are often in the spotlight. But in an important sense, they are not really the major actors in the drama. The crime rate, its effect on public opinion, vast shifts of political force; the sexual revolution, modern birth control, the women's movement—all of these are backstage, so to speak, pulling the strings.

Still, the sheer mass, the volume, of law seems to keep growing, one way or another. Where is it leading us? And can we say anything about future trends?

15

Epilogue: The Future of Law in the United States

*M*ANY PEOPLE FEEL that law is too much with us, that Americans are too involved with law, litigation, and legal process for their own good. This is a complaint we have noted several times in this book. To be sure, to the naked eye American society seems trapped in a net of law—more than is true of other countries or was true in the United States in older times. Some people think we are sinking deeper and deeper into legal quicksand. One national magazine bewailed the "suing society," in which "trust is undermined and creativity discouraged" because of endless litigation.[1] President Bush, in 1992, denounced "bizarre or frivolous lawsuits" and referred to "dead weights" that had "begun to slow the engine of growth."[2] Of course, some people take the growth of the American legal system as rather a matter of pride, a sign of commitment to justice for all.

The first fourteen chapters of this book emphasized the dependence of law on social forces, but despite this—or because of it—these chapters also stood for the proposition, among other things, that law, legal process, and legal institutions are crucially important in making American life what it is. Even the simple acts of everyday life—a trip to the grocery store—presuppose a vast superstructure of law. Law touches on both the ordinary and the extraordinary in this society. Much of the news on an average day is news about law, to an astonishing degree. Most of what makes news is what is public; nowadays what is public is almost sure to be legal or governmental, or to have some legal or governmental angle. This is true, too, of natural disasters (so-called acts of God, floods, hurricanes, earthquakes) and of major accidents (plane crashes, fires, collapsing walls). Somehow law gets involved. We cannot avoid the role of the Civil Aeronautics Board, air controllers, fire ordinances, disaster relief, government inspection of dams and levees, and so on. A plane crash or any other tragedy is bound to produce a flurry of investigations. It will also surely bring about a flock of lawsuits. These are now almost as certain as death and taxes.

Everybody talks about the "litigious society" and about "too much law." Is this just talk? Is there something more systematic we can say about the volume of law? Can it be measured rigorously? There is no real way to take a yardstick to the legal system and measure it. It has no definite beginning, middle, and end. But there are some crude ways to show the fact of growth. There are now nearly 900,000 practicing lawyers. They must be doing *something*. Statutes, state and federal, turn into printed books—a physical bulk that can be seen and its dimensions taken. The collected statutes of New Jersey of 1847 fit into one snug volume of about a thousand pages. Today, the statutes of New Jersey fill an entire shelf.

The population of New Jersey has also grown since 1847. The 1850 census recorded a population of 489,555 in New Jersey; it is nearly eight million today. But growth in the laws is more than a question of keeping up with population. The statutes left untouched in 1847 many aspects of life which are densely regulated today. If a state passes a law regulating dry cleaners, the law will apply whether there are thirty dry cleaners in the state or thirty thousand. Of course, regulation is unlikely if there are, in fact, only thirty dry cleaners. The growth of law is not unrelated to population size, but the relationship is not a simple one.

There were no dry cleaners at all in 1847. There were also no telephones, computers, automobiles, atomic wastes, oral contraceptives, television sets, and so on. There were no surrogate mothers, no gene-splicing, no Internet. The astonishing changes in science and industry since 1847 have blown apart the old limits of law. There was a little bit of traffic law before the automobile, but machines that swarm the streets by the millions and can speed at a hundred miles an hour create problems much greater than the problems of the horse and buggy days.

The automobile also expands the zone of personal freedom, in ways we take for granted. For centuries, most people in the world were tied to the soil almost literally. There was no easy way to see the world beyond the crest of some small hill near the family hut or shack. In 1847, even New Jersey farmers and textile workers in Lowell, Massachusetts, were essentially tied to home base. Travel was difficult and slow.

Technology vastly expanded the mobility of the average person. The railroad was already a great advance, but it was the automobile that worked the most fantastic change in American lives. Today, most families own or have access to a car. They can move from city to country, country to city, state to state, almost at will. The car means freedom to explore parks and museums, to visit relatives who moved to Colorado, to go camping, to live in the suburbs and commute to work.

At the same time, the auto generates need for an immense body of rules—rules about auto accidents, rules about auto safety, rules of the road, traffic regulations, parking restrictions, rules about driver's licenses and drunk driving, and so on. All this is part of the price for the vast extension of freedom the automobile has brought with it. It is not so obvious, then, that more laws, more rules, as such, cut down on personal freedom. This may or may not be true. Some level of regulation is a natural product of new technology—a cost or side effect of machines that expand our freedom and our possibilities. The computer opens the door to communication with vast numbers of other people at almost instantaneous speed and at enormous distances. It also raises the issue of "cyberporn," which the bluenoses of the nineteenth century did not have to contend with. Law is essentially about rules of the game in a complex society. The questions of freedom and its limits are impossible to resolve. This book has touched on these questions here and there, but certainly has not given definitive answers.

Crude as they are, then, all indicators strongly suggest great growth in the outer aspects of law: the rules themselves, the personnel, the institutions. The legal system has swollen in size over the years, growing faster than the population, and the rate of growth itself seems to be growing. Administrative law came up almost out of nothing and is now a major force in society. Particularly striking is the explosion in federal law in the last two generations, roughly since the New Deal. The Reagan administration took office in 1981 with a firm resolve to cut and slash. It is a popular idea, and later administrations (Republican or Democratic) have not dared to disagree. But cutting government has not gotten very far. And no one even dreams of rolling the federal government back to the days of Harding and Coolidge. No such reversal is possible. Conservative governments can only hope to privatize a bit, deregulate a bit, sent some tasks back to the state; for the rest, they can only hope to keep the state from swelling until it bursts like a giant balloon.

The Litigation Explosion: Fact and Fiction

One special area of growth may be litigation. The clamor over litigation and litigation rates is especially great. Litigation, people say, is rising rapidly, faster than courts can cope, faster than is good for us. For some time, there has been talk about an "explosion" of lawsuits, about "hyperlexis," a dreadful disease that has "overloaded" the legal circuits.[3] According to the magazine article quoted earlier, "employees sue employers, students sue teachers, taxpayers sue bureaucrats and friends sue friends."[4] Former President Bush's judgment was equally severe, as we just saw.

What is wrong with a "litigation explosion," if we have one? First of all, lawsuits might overwhelm the courts and interfere with the orderly administration of justice. Second, the flood of cases might disrupt and destroy the ordinary processes of government. Courts take over roles that do not belong to them: they meddle in affairs of state. They move into areas which should be left alone or handled by others. Third, lawsuits can disrupt and destroy normal social relations. Suing your physician, for example, does not make for good relations between doctor and patient. Fourth, excessive litigation is bad for the economy—this was President Bush's point; it distorts the allocation of resources; it drives good products off the market, stifles innovation, and acts as a kind of tax on business.

The people who complain come up with many horrible examples to show what they mean. Some point to the busing of schoolchildren, some cite the way courts stop or delay big projects, some refer to the death-penalty cases or the abortion cases, some point to the "crisis" in malpractice and in products liability, to frivolous suits for damages, to endless litigation by "jailhouse lawyers," and so on. Judges themselves have complained of a crisis in the courts. They talk of a crushing burden of lawsuits.

Actually, we know surprisingly little about litigation rates in the United States and even less about the way these rates change over time. There is really no solid proof of a "litigation explosion." The gross amount of litigation has certainly been rising over the years. But when we talk about a litigation rate, we must mean some sort of relationship between cases and population. Here the talk about "explosions" has nothing much to back it up. Judicial statistics are poor. Historical statistics (where we have any) are almost worthless. It is hard to say anything about long-term trends.

Litigation rates are definitely rising in one court system, the federal courts. These courts on the whole keep good records. In 1900, the United States District Courts disposed of 29,094 cases. The volume rose to 152,585 in 1932 (swelled artificially by Prohibition cases), dropped to 69,466 in 1942, and then began rising again. In 1971 it reached 126,145; in 1980, 189,778.[5] In 1992–93, 228,162 civil cases were filed in federal court, along with 47,850 criminal cases. In addition, the federal system handled 939,935 bankruptcy matters.[6]

This boom in federal cases helps give the impression of a litigation explosion. But there is only one federal system, and there are fifty states. The states account for over 90 percent of the lawsuits in the country. Studies of state courts are sparse and somewhat inconclusive. In St. Louis, for example, Wayne McIntosh found a high litigation rate in the early nineteenth century, until 1850. The rate then declined, and bottomed out in the 1890s. After 1900, there was an upward trend, but an extremely modest one. Essentially, he concludes, the litigation rate remained "fairly stable" in the period of the twentieth century his study covered, roughly to the late 1970s.[7] No explosion here. Nor was any explosion found in a study of two California counties, Alameda County and San Benito County, for the period 1870–1970.[8]

In fact, the litigation rate is a rather elusive figure. One reason is that it is hard to say exactly what litigation is. For example, there is a high divorce rate in the United States. The courts churn out hundreds of thousands of divorces. Almost all of them are uncontested. Each is a "case," in the sense that somebody files a piece of paper in court, the clerk opens a file, and *Smith v. Smith* gets a case number. But most of the time, nothing will actually happen in court that deserves to be called litigation. The case is completely cut-and-dried. The Smiths and their lawyers have worked out everything far in advance. There is legal behavior here, but hardly litigation.

The same is true of cases of other kinds: adoption proceedings, petitions to change one's name, and so on. Most tort cases, as we noted, are settled out of court. Even most of those that are filed in court drop out before trial. As with divorce cases, the clerk gives them a file number and they are tallied in court statistics. Yet when people talk about litigation, they probably have in mind real disputes which actually get resolved in the courtroom by a judge, or a judge and jury. Are *these* cases increasing in number? Nobody really seems to know.

Of course, some kinds of litigation *are* increasing. Judicial review is more common than in the past, as we have seen. In an important way it feeds on itself. If courts are willing to monitor, revise, and oversee what Congress, legislatures, and administrative agencies do, then they encourage social groups to bring their demands into court. People band together to challenge a law they do not like—to stop a highway or a jetport, to force the state of Arkansas to clean up its prisons, to get Alabama to reform its mental hospitals, to prevent the execution of a murderer, and so on. This is a strong trend, and a growing one. It is part of an international trend, but it is perhaps strongest in the United States.

Whenever and wherever a new "field" of law emerges, or a new cause of action, a bulge in cases at the trial level may result. These cases may make a social splash even when they are not statistically significant. Chapter 14 discussed *Marvin v. Marvin*. This case opened a door that had once been shut; it has probably led to some new litigation—several hundred cases, perhaps. This is in many ways an important development. But a few hundred cases would not show up at all in judicial statistics. Filings in the United States are in the millions; a few hundred cases are a spit in the ocean.

What is important, then, is not the numbers, but the *types* of cases filed—especially the new areas of litigation that have opened up in the last decades. Malpractice and products liability have blossomed. The Civil Rights Act of 1964 and associated laws inspired a flock of novel cases. Before the 1960s, there was the merest handful of cases about race discrimination, and there were basically none at all on sex and age discrimination, or discrimination against the handicapped—the most recent development. Congress and the courts have created new rights. Discrimination in the job market was outlawed—first for race and sex and religion, then for other categories. Today, employment discrimination is a major field of law. It gives work to hundreds of lawyers and has hatched a whole battery of lawsuits. Compared to the number of divorces, the numbers are insignificant. But many of these cases are huge, class-action cases against great corporations, involving millions of dollars and the structure of whole job markets. Numbers do not do justice to the situation. There are more mice in the world than there are elephants, but each elephant makes a good deal more of a splash.

In general, "megacases" are increasing: monster lawsuits, massive and incredibly expensive. Private antitrust suits are one prominent example. The Sherman Act (1890)[9] made monopoly and restraint of trade a crime. The government, of course, had primary powers of enforcement. But Section 7 of the law gave private citizens or companies the right to sue for damages against any person or company who had "injured" them by violating the act. Indeed, the plaintiff could collect three times the actual damages. This was meant to provide an incentive to sue, and also to be a sort of punishment for wrongdoers. Yet private suits were not common for many years. They averaged one hundred a year in the 1940s. At one time—1979—there were as many as thirteen hundred or more; in 1995, the number had dropped to 781, but it was still substantially greater than during the first half century of the Sherman Act.[10]

Private antitrust suits tend to be elephant cases. Some may drag on for months, even years. The biggest of them can cost each side tens of millions of dollars. The amounts at stake can be staggering—in the millions or billions. Tons of documents may be filed in court. Whole platoons of lawyers might be thrown into the fray. Some public antitrust cases are also supercases. One prime example was the great IBM case. It began in 1969, and became a champion lawsuit in size. The documents might have filled a dozen warehouses. Costs on both sides were staggering. At one time it looked as if the case would never end—that it would literally go on forever. But in 1981, the Reagan administration threw in the towel and the mighty lawsuit fizzled out, after millions of dollars, millions of documents, and millions of hours. This case too made no dent on judicial statistics. It was essentially one case. Obviously, it does not take many megacases of this sort to give off the smell of an "explosion." The same can be said of some of the massive, class-action tort suits. In the "Agent Orange" case, veterans sued chemical manufacturers. They were exposed in Vietnam to a pesticide called Agent Orange, and they claimed it harmed them physically. The case was "actually a consolidation into one class action of more than 600 separate actions originally filed by more than 15,000 named individuals," plus 400 additional individual cases. The plaintiffs were represented by a network of about 1,500 law firms; the defendants spent, it is estimated, about $100 million on their defense. After six years of litigation, a settlement was reached in 1984, creating a fund of $180 million with interest.[11]

On the other hand, lawsuits of some sorts may be traveling in the opposite direction, that is, decreasing. Some scholars claim the courts are handling fewer cases of types that were once quite common—ordinary contract cases, disputes between landlord and tenant, quarrels between two people who claim the same piece of land, arguments over Uncle Harry's will. The evidence is imperfect here, too, but it is clear that many staples of nineteenth-century litigation have all but disappeared from the dockets. Debt collection, for example, has been "routinized," and "contested litigation" on this subject has declined dramatically since the nineteenth century.[12]

Not everybody, by any means, is convinced that there is too much suing going on. There are those who think there is too little—that the courts are falling down on their job. The ordinary person cannot get justice. Courts are too slow and expensive. Businessmen would, on the whole, not disagree with this last point; they tend, if at all possible, to avoid the courts, and to use arbitration or other alternatives.

The courts, then, may be neglecting "issues that affect the quality of everyday life." The phrase is from Laura Nader, in the preface to a book which explores "alternatives"—ways of handling disputes and grievances outside of the court system, everything from the Better Business Bureau to the activities of a congressman's office.[13] Chapter 2 of this book also looked briefly at "informal justice." From time to time, there are plans to improve or revivify the courts or to provide more effectively for popular justice. In 1977, the Department of Justice set up, on an experimental basis, three Neighborhood Justice Centers. They were located in Atlanta, Kansas City, and Los Angeles and were supposed to be alternatives to courts for resolving minor disputes.[14] Only the Atlanta center was still around as such in 1997, but meanwhile, local mediation and dispute-resolving bodies had multiplied like weeds. A directory of the American Bar Association listed four hundred "dispute resolution programs" in 1993.[15]

Perhaps the courts are not doing a good job in small cases, but they certainly play a role in society at large. They are muscling their way into more and more of the business of government—or being asked to do so. They provide some sort of check or control over the work of those who do govern. Of course, their power to do this work, and particularly their power to follow through, leaves a lot to be desired. Still, the boundaries between what is traditionally thought of as fit stuff for courts and what is not seems to be eroding. Areas of life that were off limits to courts in the past are no longer immune to intervention.

We see constant signs of this evolution. Newspapers report the extremes. One man threatened to sue a young woman because she stood him up on a date. Another man tried to sue his own mother and father for "malpractice." They botched the job of bringing him up, he said, and turned him into a psychological wreck. A Yale graduate, disgruntled at something or other, wanted a federal court to wipe his degree off Yale's records.[16] According to the magazine story we quoted earlier, the parents of a nine-year-old girl in Indiana filed a lawsuit because the girl found no prize in a box of Cracker Jack.[17] (This may be apocryphal.)

The courts usually throw such cases out (though not always). These cases are oddities, freaks; after all, that is why they appear in the newspapers. Some of the worst reported "freaks" never actually happened—they are urban legends. Still, these cases, and these reports, do illustrate one general point: almost anything can end up as a court case today. No area of life is sacrosanct. Courts routinely make decisions about the inner workings of factories, hospitals, schools, and prisons. Decision on these subjects would have been unthinkable a century ago. These subjects were "private" and beyond the reach of courts—or, in some cases, were within the unrestrained discretion of public officials.

Courts even intervene in what were once very private family affairs. In a 1972 case, a fourteen-year-old girl in Minnesota sued her parents in juvenile court. The parents had built themselves a boat and were about to go off with their daughters on a cruise around the world. The girl, Lee Anne, wanted to stay at home with her friends. She went to court and won a partial victory. The juvenile judge allowed her to stay behind, in custody of an aunt.[18] In 1992, a twelve-year-old boy, Gregory Kingsley, went to court in Florida to "divorce" his mother and father and get himself adopted by his foster parents; the Florida courts indeed agreed to terminate his parents' rights.[19]

These cases are striking, perhaps alarming and deplorable. We can see why many people would wonder if it is right for courts to meddle in private, family affairs. In other areas, it seems easier to defend an active, even intrusive judiciary. After all, despite all the talk of "downsizing" government and shrinking the federal monster, it is still the case that hardly any area of life is beyond the scope of government at *some* level. The more the government does, the more we need to control it. In most countries, courts do not exercise this power, or do it only feebly. In most modern countries, governments are powerful, gargantuan in size, and quite pervasive. The ordinary citizen has few ways to get somebody in government to listen, let alone persuade government to see things the citizen's way. There is no meaningful judicial review in much of the world, even though the habit does seem to be spreading. In the many one-party systems—in China, for example, home to more than a billion people—courts of justice are essentially powerless to thwart the will of the regime.

Courts in the United States, for all their faults, give people at least some realistic way to right wrongs done by the government and by private centers of power. There are, to be sure, countries that are just as democratic, but whose courts are relatively supine or inactive. Some of these countries have evolved other means, perhaps, to keep Leviathan under control. But courts are part of *our* system of control, geared to our needs and traditions.

Regular courts may be too expensive and formal for ordinary cases and for day-by-day disputes. But they are well suited for big cases, group claims, class actions. As for the little cases, we do need fresh ideas and new institutions; we need debate and research about dispute settlement, grievance procedures, access to law. Ideas are in the air; some are getting a hearing. We have seen some examples. "Alternative dispute resolution" is not just a buzzword; it is a growing institution. Perhaps more will happen along these lines.

The Society of Strangers

A society like ours is one of great interdependence. All of us are in the same boat, in many ways. Imagine, at one extreme, a pioneer family in the nineteenth century—a family, let us say, living miles away from its nearest neighbor, building its own house, growing its own food, weaving its own clothing. The parents themselves taught the children to read and to do figures, they provided their own entertainment, acted as their own doctors, dentists, barbers, nurses—they did everything, took every role.

This is an extreme case, and was rare even in the past. But it points up how different our way of life really is. The world of the 1990s is a far cry from the world of these pioneers. It is a far cry, too, from the way of life of tribal society, where custom rules, where life is bound to a tiny village and a few miles of woods all about it. Village life is life lived wholly in the so-called primary group—in a face-to-face culture. Each man, woman, and child is related by blood or marriage or clan to everybody who matters to that person. Similarly, on the island of Tristan da Cunha, the primary group was the only group. In our society, to be sure, we are as profoundly dependent on each other as the people in any tribal culture. But most of the links in our chain of dependence are links to strangers, not kinfolk or friends.

We are, in short, a "nation of strangers, a country where the greatest number of potential abuses occurs between people who are strangers to each other."[20] Most of us work for big companies. We buy ready-made food and clothing. Strangers protect us, as police, or threaten us, as criminals, when we walk the streets. Strangers put out our fires. Strangers teach our children, build our houses, invest our money. Strangers on radio and TV or in the newspapers give us our news of the world. When we travel by bus or train or plane, our lives are in the hands of strangers. If we fall sick and go to the hospital, strangers cut open our bodies, wash us, nurse us, kill us or cure us. When we die, strangers lower us into the earth.

We accept all this. We are used to it. The environment of strangers is part of our lives. The line between intimate life and impersonal public life is growing a shade indistinct. Strangers even intrude on the most private, inward corners of our lives. Love, sex, and marriage are not immune. Social workers, psychiatrists, marriage counselors—there are thousands of "experts" in these matters, and millions of people, at one point or another in their lives, go to these experts with their personal problems. (Sometimes, in extreme cases, we may even be forced to go.) More and more, a technical, professional, bureaucratic world elbows its way into the outskirts of the last of the private sanctuaries.

This does not mean that there is less space for us to grow as individuals, less scope for us to experiment with ways of life, or less personal privacy in American society in the 1990s. Quite the contrary. There is probably far greater room for personal autonomy than ever before in history. Certainly there is far more than in tribal societies, or even among the pioneers, whose lives were rigidly constrained, and whose energies were absorbed by sheer survival—growing food, keeping warm, and staying alive. There is far more leisure today, and more options for the average person. But the boundaries between what is supposed to be private and personal and what is not no longer carry the same meaning as before.

And law moves along, following society, responding to these social facts. It is no surprise, then, that in the 1990s no zone is so intimate, personal, or private that it is immune from the staring eye of law. And why not? "Custom" is what we call the norms that regulate face-to-face relationships; "law" is the word for norms that regulate relations among strangers. When customary norms break down, society turns to law. This is the central thesis of this book. A small society, a tribe, a tiny island, can go on from year to year on the basis of shared norms, unspoken premises, rules of behavior made sacred through tradition. Our society cannot do this. Americans hold many things in common—there *are* shared norms—but not enough so that the country runs itself automatically. The country is just too big. There are too many of us, and we are too different from each other. We need (or feel we need) formal, structured ways to govern ourselves. And this means law.

No doubt a lot is gained and a lot is lost in a social order built up in this way. This is not the place to explore the gains and the losses in detail. Some economists argue that a regulated economy is less efficient in every regard than a free economy, run entirely by the "invisible hand." But even the "invisible hand" needs some help: law and order, a court system, enforcement of contracts, a framework of rules. And almost everyone would have to concede that if we want to craft a fairer and more equitable—or safer and healthier—society, we need some kind of structure, some methods of control. Some kinds of collective control are virtually beyond controversy. We simply must have police. A few zealots of the right would stop just about there; a small, diminishing band on the left wants massive collective control. The rest of us want a good deal of government, though exactly how much and where to draw the line is a subject of constant political debate; it is one of the major cleavages in democratic society.

In a complex world, freedom does not necessarily mean no government control. Paradoxically, law may be needed to maximize freedom. When the air people breathed was fresh and clean, nothing much had to be done to keep it that way. Streams ran pure and clear; there seemed to be no end to wildlife, trees, and space, or to oil, gas, and coal. Those times have passed. The automobile has generated not only new freedom but also new rules. The courts and the legislatures have created or expanded many rights and doctrines, in an attempt to counterbalance the strength of big government, big business, and other large collectivities. There is, and will be, constant tension between freedom and control. But there is no escape from interdependence. The people of this country are tied together in organic knots, and forever. Nobody expects "the law" to wither away.

The specific role of courts in our society is hard to predict. The future is, as always, cloudy. The particular jobs courts do now may change. Nothing is engraved in stone. Some of the present trends—the heavy use of judicial review, for example—will probably continue into coming years, as far ahead as we can see. The courts are responding to certain felt needs, and these needs are not going to become obsolete. If not the courts, then some other agency will take over the social functions which the courts now perform.

Law is a creature of society. Society is rapidly changing, but it shows no signs of going back to the simple habits of the old days. Nor does anybody really expect a Utopia in which government would disappear. Law, legal process, and the legal system are facts of life in the United States. They have a central place, and that is likely to continue. Perhaps the role of law will grow, perhaps not, but it is not about to shrivel or go away. And the legal system will continue to bend and turn in response to social change. Institutions may change a bit (or a lot) in what they do; taxes may go up, or down; government may expand into this area, retract its horns from that. But short of some mammoth reworking of our way of life, law will be with us for as far ahead as we can see—a massive presence in our lives.

Documents

In this book, we have discussed many different kinds of law and many sources of law. This short collection of documents illustrates some of the most prominent of these sources: constitutions, legislation, administrative regulations, and case law.

In our legal system, the federal Constitution is the supreme law of the land. It outranks all other sources. No state or federal law, no city ordinance, no administrative rule, is valid if it violates the federal Constitution. Of course, there are also state constitutions, and they have the final word on local, state matters.

The documents in Part I begin with excerpts from the federal Constitution which have a particular bearing on the material in this book. A small portion of the constitution of Oregon is also presented. It illustrates state constitutional law: the section chosen discusses lawmaking through the initiative and referendum—sources of law which are unknown to the federal Constitution. The Oregon material also includes a few typical features of state constitutions which, again, have no parallel in the federal Constitution, for example, the prohibition against "local" and "special" laws.

"Legislation" is a term that covers a vast range of activity; the documents in Part II give some idea of that range. The Sherman Act, a federal statute of great historical and economic significance, is in form quite general and brief: it sets out a few broad principles and leaves entirely open all questions of interpretation and administration. The short excerpt from the federal Food, Drug, and Cosmetic Act, with its mixture of broad principle and meticulous detail, shows what modern regulatory law is often like. Title VII of the Civil Rights Act of 1964, with the 1991 amendments, is similar in style and shows how deeply federal law has penetrated into areas of life that were immune from federal regulation in earlier generations.

Part II also includes two examples of state legislation. The Idaho statute is a typical workmen's compensation law. Workmen's compensation replaced the old system of dealing with work accidents through private lawsuits. The new system, in Idaho and elsewhere, is an elaborate, detailed, highly "administered" body of law. The brief excerpt from the California Structural Pest Control Board Law is an example of a common and important form of state legislation: occupational licensing.

Part III deals with the administrative process. The main theme is the way in which administrative agencies fill in the blanks in bodies of statutory law, by writing rules and regulations. The three examples given are drawn from the rules laid down by the federal Food and Drug Administration, the Equal Employment Opportunity Commission, and the California Structural Pest Control Board. These examples are keyed to statutes reprinted in Part II.

In our legal system, of course, courts play a major role in interpreting law, which in practice often means making law. Part IV contains six cases; each of them, in its own way, illustrates this theme. In *Brown v. Board of Education*, the celebrated school-desegregation case, the Supreme Court of the United States boldly made policy, in a decision which is perhaps the most important that institution ever handed down. *Brown* is also an example of judicial review: the Supreme Court swept aside dozens of state laws and city ordinances which required segregated schools, on the grounds that the federal Constitution outlawed such segregation.

In *Dothard v. Rawlinson*, the Supreme Court made policy in a somewhat different context. The case presented a tricky issue of sex discrimination; formally, the task was to interpret the policy set out in Title VII of the Civil Rights Act of 1964. The *Hopgood* case raises the question of "affirmative action," a much-debated policy issue. In *Louie v. Bamboo Gardens*, the Idaho Supreme Court had the job of resolving a dispute in the light of what it saw as the principles embodied in the Idaho workmen's compensation statute. The facts of the case made the situation difficult—it was a situation at the very edge of the statutory policy. The decision can be read as a kind of reaching out, an extension of principles of liability beyond the text of the statute. In *Marvin v. Marvin*, the famous California "palimony" case which was discussed in Chapter 14, we see how courts respond to changing customs and changing times in areas where there is no statute or constitutional mandate to bind them or guide them. In the *Baby M* case, the New Jersey court was also confronted with a new-minted problem; its decision, however, was not pure judge-made law—in the opinion we see the court citing and working within a framework of enacted law.

PART I

The Constitutional Experience

A. Constitution of the United States

B. Constitution of Oregon

A. Constitution of the United States

We the People of the United States, in Order to form a more perfect Union, establish Justice, insure domestic Tranquility, provide for the common defence, promote the general Welfare, and secure the Blessings of Liberty to ourselves and our Posterity, do ordain and establish this Constitution for the United States of America.

. . .

ARTICLE III

Section 1. The judicial Power of the United States, shall be vested in one supreme Court, and in such inferior Courts as the Congress may from time to time ordain and establish. The Judges, both of the supreme and inferior Courts, shall hold their Offices during good Behaviour, and shall, at stated Times, receive for their Services, a Compensation, which shall not be diminished during their Continuance in Office.

Section 2. [1] The judicial Power shall extend to all Cases, in Law and Equity, arising under this Constitution, the Laws of the United States, and Treaties made, or which shall be made, under their Authority:—to all Cases affecting Ambassadors, other public Ministers and Consuls:—to all Cases of admiralty and maritime Jurisdiction:—to Controversies to which the United States shall be a Party:—to Controversies between two or more States:—between a State and Citizens of another State:—between Citizens of different States:—between Citizens of the same State claiming Lands under Grants of different States, and between a State, or the Citizens thereof, and foreign States, Citizens or Subjects.

[2] In all Cases affecting Ambassadors, other public Ministers and Consuls, and those in which a State shall be a Party, the supreme Court shall have original Jurisdiction. In all the other Cases before mentioned, the supreme Court shall have appellate Jurisdiction, both as to Law and Fact, with such Exceptions, and under such Regulations as the Congress shall make.

[3] The trial of all Crimes, except in Cases of Impeachment, shall be by Jury: and such Trial shall be held in the State where the said Crimes shall have been committed; but when not commit-

ted within any State, the Trial shall be at such Place or Places as the Congress may by Law have directed.

Section 3. [1] Treason against the United States, shall consist only in levying War against them, or in adhering to their Enemies, giving them Aid and Comfort. No Person shall be convicted of Treason unless on the Testimony of two Witnesses to the same overt Act, or on Confession in open Court.

[2] The Congress shall have Power to declare the Punishment of Treason, but no Attainder of Treason shall work Corruption of Blood, or Forfeiture except during the Life of the Person attainted.

ARTICLE IV

Section 1. Full Faith and Credit shall be given in each State to the public Acts, Records, and judicial Proceedings of every other State. And the Congress may by general Laws prescribe the Manner in which such Acts, Records and Proceedings shall be proved, and the Effect thereof.

Section 2. [1] The Citizens of each State shall be entitled to all Privileges and Immunities of Citizens in the several States.

[2] A Person charged in any State with Treason, Felony, or other Crime, who shall flee from Justice, and be found in another State, shall on demand of the executive Authority of the State from which he fled, be delivered up, to be removed to the State having Jurisdiction of the Crime.

[3] No Person held to Service or Labour in one State, under the Laws thereof, escaping into another, shall, in Consequence of any Law or Regulation therein, be discharged from such Service or Labour, but shall be delivered up on Claim of the Party to whom such Service or Labour may be due.

Section 3. [1] New States may be admitted by the Congress into this Union; but no new State shall be formed or erected within the Jurisdiction of any other State; nor any State be formed by the Junction of two or more States, or Parts of States, without the Consent of the Legislatures of the States concerned as well as of the Congress.

[2] The Congress shall have Power to dispose of and make all needful Rules and Regulations respecting the Territory or other Property belonging to the United States; and nothing in this Constitution shall be so construed as to Prejudice any Claims of the United States, or of any particular State.

Section 4. The United States shall guarantee to every State in this Union a Republican Form of Government, and shall protect each of them against Invasion; and on Application of the Legislature, or of the Executive (when the Legislature cannot be convened) against domestic Violence.

ARTICLE V

The Congress, whenever two thirds of both Houses shall deem it necessary, shall propose Amendments, to this Constitution, or, on the Application of the Legislatures of two thirds of the several States, shall call a Convention for proposing Amendments, which, in either Case, shall be valid to all Intents and Purposes, as part of this Constitution, when ratified by the Legislatures of three fourths of the several States, or by Conventions in three fourths thereof, as the one or the other Mode of Ratification may be proposed by the Congress; Provided that no Amendment which may be made prior to the Year One thousand eight hundred and eight shall in any Manner affect the first and fourth Clauses in the Ninth Section of the first Article; and that no State, without its Consent, shall be deprived of its equal Suffrage in the Senate.

ARTICLE VI

[1] All Debts contracted and Engagements entered into, before the Adoption of this Constitution, shall be as valid against the United States under this Constitution, as under the Confederation.

[2] This Constitution, and the Laws of the United States which shall be made in Pursuance thereof; and all Treaties made, or which shall be made, under the Authority of the United States,

shall be the supreme Law of the Land; and the Judges in every State shall be bound thereby, any Thing in the Constitution or Laws of any State to the Contrary notwithstanding.

[3] The Senators and Representatives before mentioned, and the Members of the several State Legislatures, and all executive and judicial Officers, both of the United States and of the several States, shall be bound by Oath or Affirmation, to support this Constitution; but no religious Test shall ever be required as a Qualification to any Office or public Trust under the United States.

ARTICLE VII

The Ratification of the Conventions of nine States shall be sufficient for the Establishment of this Constitution between the States so ratifying the Same.

Done in Convention by the Unanimous Consent of the States present the Seventeenth Day of September in the Year of our Lord one thousand seven hundred and Eighty seven and of the Independence of the United States of America the Twelfth.

ARTICLES IN ADDITION TO, AND AMENDMENT OF, THE CONSTITUTION OF THE UNITED STATES OF AMERICA, PROPOSED BY CONGRESS, AND RATIFIED BY THE LEGISLATURES OF THE SEVERAL STATES, PURSUANT TO THE FIFTH ARTICLE OF THE ORIGINAL CONSTITUTION.

AMENDMENT I [1791]

Congress shall make no law respecting an establishment of religion, or prohibiting the free exercise thereof; or abridging the freedom of speech, or of the press; or the right of the people peaceably to assemble, and to petition the Government for a redress of grievances.

AMENDMENT II [1791]

A well regulated Militia, being necessary to the security of a free State, the right of the people to keep and bear Arms, shall not be infringed.

AMENDMENT III [1791]

No Soldier shall, in time of peace be quartered in any house, without the consent of the Owner, nor in time of war, but in a manner to be prescribed by law.

AMENDMENT IV [1791]

The right of the people to be secure in their persons, houses, papers, and effects, against unreasonable searches and seizures, shall not be violated, and no Warrants shall issue, but upon probable cause, supported by Oath or affirmation, and particularly describing the place to be searched, and the persons or things to be seized.

AMENDMENT V [1791]

No person shall be held to answer for a capital, or otherwise infamous crime, unless on a presentment or indictment of a Grand Jury, except in cases arising in the land or naval forces, or in the Militia, when in actual service in time of War or public danger; nor shall any person be subject for the same offence to be twice put in jeopardy of life or limb; nor shall be compelled in any criminal case to be a witness against himself, nor be deprived of life, liberty, or property, without due process of law; nor shall private property be taken for public use, without just compensation.

AMENDMENT VI [1791]

In all criminal prosecutions, the accused shall enjoy the right to a speedy and public trial, by an impartial jury of the State and district wherein the crime shall have been committed, which district shall have been previously ascertained by law, and to be informed of the nature and cause of the accusation; to be confronted with the witnesses against him; to have compulsory process for obtaining witnesses in his favor, and to have the Assistance of Counsel for his defence.

AMENDMENT VII [1791]

In Suits at common law, where the value in controversy shall exceed twenty dollars, the right of trial by jury shall be preserved, and no fact tried by a jury, shall be otherwise re-examined in any Court of the United States, than according to the rules of the common law.

AMENDMENT VIII [1791]

Excessive bail shall not be required, nor excessive fines imposed, nor cruel and unusual punishments inflicted.

AMENDMENT IX [1791]

The enumeration in the Constitution, of certain rights, shall not be construed to deny or disparage others retained by the people.

AMENDMENT X [1791]

The powers not delegated to the United States by the Constitution, nor prohibited by it to the States, are reserved to the States respectively, or to the people.

AMENDMENT XI [1798]

The Judicial power of the United States shall not be construed to extend to any suit in law or equity, commenced or prosecuted against one of the United States by Citizens of another State, or by Citizens or Subjects of any Foreign State.

. . .

AMENDMENT XIII [1865]

Section 1. Neither slavery nor involuntary servitude, except as a punishment for crime whereof the party shall have been duly convicted, shall exist within the United States, or any place subject to their jurisdiction.

Section 2. Congress shall have power to enforce this article by appropriate legislation.

AMENDMENT XIV [1868]

Section 1. All persons born or naturalized in the United States, and subject to the jurisdiction thereof, are citizens of the United States and of the State wherein they reside. No State shall make or enforce any law which shall abridge the privileges or immunities of citizens of the United States; nor shall any State deprive any person of life, liberty, or property, without due process of law; nor deny to any person within its jurisdiction the equal protection of the laws.

Section 5. The Congress shall have power to enforce, by appropriate legislation, the provisions of this article.

AMENDMENT XV [1870]

Section 1. The right of citizens of the United States to vote shall not be denied or abridged by the United States or by any State on account of race, color, or previous condition of servitude.

Section 2. The Congress shall have power to enforce this article by appropriate legislation.

. . .

AMENDMENT XVIII [1919]

Section 1. After one year from the ratification of this article the manufacture, sale, or transportation of intoxicating liquors within, the importation thereof into, or the exportation thereof from the United States and all territory subject to the jurisdiction thereof for beverage purposes is hereby prohibited.

Section 2. The Congress and the several States shall have concurrent power to enforce this article by appropriate legislation.

Section 3. This article shall be inoperative unless it shall have been ratified as an amendment to the Constitution by the legislatures of the several States, as provided in the Constitution, within seven years from the date of the submission hereof to the States by the Congress.

AMENDMENT XIX [1920]

[1] The right of citizens of the United States to vote shall not be denied or abridged by the United States or by any State on account of sex.

[2] Congress shall have power to enforce this article by appropriate legislation.

. . .

AMENDMENT XXI [1933]

Section 1. The eighteenth article of amendment to the Constitution of the United States is hereby repealed.

Section 2. The transportation or importation into any State, Territory, or possession of the United States for delivery or use therein of intoxicating liquors, in violation of the laws thereof, is hereby prohibited.

Section 3. This article shall be inoperative unless it shall have been ratified as an amendment to the Constitution by conventions in the several States, as provided in the Constitution, within seven years from the date of the submission hereof to the States by the Congress.

. . .

AMENDMENT XXIV [1964]

Section 1. The right of citizens of the United States to vote in any primary or other election for President or Vice President, for electors for President or Vice President, or for Senator or Representative in Congress, shall not be denied or abridged by the United States or any State by reason of failure to pay any poll tax or other tax.

Section 2. The Congress shall have power to enforce this article by appropriate legislation.

. . .

AMENDMENT XXVI [1971]

Section 1. The right of citizens of the United States, who are eighteen years of age or older, to vote shall not be denied or abridged by the United States or by any State on account of age.

Section 2. The Congress shall have power to enforce this article by appropriate legislation.

B. Constitution of the State of Oregon

ARTICLE IV: LEGISLATIVE DEPARTMENT

Section 1. Legislative power; initiative and referendum. (1) The legislative power of the state, except for the initiative and referendum powers reserved to the people, is vested in a Legislative Assembly, consisting of a Senate and a House of Representatives.

(2) (a) The people reserve to themselves the initiative power, which is to propose laws and amendments to the Constitution and enact or reject them at an election independently of the Legislative Assembly.

(b) An initiative law may be proposed only by a petition signed by a number of qualified voters equal to six percent of the total number of votes cast for all candidates for Governor at the election at which a Governor was elected for a term of four years next preceding the filing of the petition.

(c) An initiative amendment to the Constitution may be proposed only by a petition signed by a number of qualified voters equal to eight percent of the total number of votes cast for all candidates for Governor at the election at which a Governor was elected for a term of four years next preceding the filing of the petition.

(d) An initiative petition shall include the full text of the proposed law or amendment to the Constitution. A proposed law or amendment to the Constitution shall embrace one subject only and matters properly connected therewith.

(e) An initiative petition shall be filed not less than four months before the election at which the proposed law or amendment to the Constitution is to be voted upon.

(3) (a) The people reserve to themselves the referendum power, which is to approve or reject at an election any Act, or part thereof, of the Legislative Assembly that does not come effective earlier than 90 days after the end of the session at which the Act is passed.

(b) A referendum on an Act or part thereof may be ordered by a petition signed by a number of qualified voters equal to four percent of the total number of votes cast for all candidates for Governor at the election at which a Governor was elected for a term of four years next preceding the filing of the petition. A referendum petition shall be filed not more than 90 days after the end of the session at which the Act is passed.

(c) A referendum on an Act may be ordered by the Legislative Assembly by law. Notwithstanding section 15b, Article V of this Constitution, bills ordering a referendum and bills on which a referendum is ordered are not subject to veto by the Governor.

(5) The initiative and referendum powers reserved to the people by subsections (2) and (3) of this section are further reserved to the qualified voters of each municipality and district as to all local, special and municipal legislation of every character in or for their municipality or district. The manner of exercising those powers shall be provided by general laws, but cities may provide the manner of exercising those powers as to their municipal legislation. In a city, not more than 15 percent of the qualified voters may be required to propose legislation by the initiative, and not more than 10 percent of the qualified voters may be required to order a referendum on legislation.

Section 18. Where bills to originate. Bills may originate in either house, but may be amended, or rejected in the other; except that bills for raising revenue shall originate in the House of Representatives.—

. . .

Section 20. Subject and title of Act. Every Act shall embrace but one subject, and matters properly connected therewith, which subject shall be expressed in the title. But if any subject shall be embraced in an Act which shall not be expressed in the title, such Act shall be void only as to so much thereof as shall not be expressed in the title.

· · ·

Section 21. Acts to be plainly worded. Every act, and joint resolution shall be plainly worded, avoiding as far as practicable the use of technical terms.—

· · ·

Section 23. Certain local and special laws prohibited. The Legislative Assembly, shall not pass special or local laws, in any of the following enumerated cases, that is to say:—

Regulating the jurisdiction, and duties of justices of the peace, and of constables;

For the punishment of Crimes, and Misdemeanors;

Regulating the practice in Courts of Justice;

Providing for changing the venue in civil, and Criminal cases;

Granting divorces;

Changing the names of persons;

For laying, opening, and working on highways, and for the election, or appointment of supervisors;

Vacating roads, Town plats, Streets, Alleys, and Public squares;

Summoning and empanneling (sic) grand, and petit jurors;

For the assessment and collection of Taxes, for State, County, Township, or road purposes;

Providing for supporting Common schools, and for the preservation of school funds;

In relation to interest on money;

Providing for opening, and conducting the elections of State, County, and Township officers, and designating the places of voting;

Providing for the sale of real estate, belonging to minors, or other persons laboring under legal disabilities, by executors, administrators, guardians, or trustees.—

PART II.

Federal and State Legislation

A. Sherman Antitrust Act (1890)

B. Food, Drug, and Cosmetic Act

C. Civil Rights Act of 1964, Title VII

D. Workmen's Compensation Law (Idaho)

E. Structural Pest Control Board Law (California)

A. Sherman Antitrust Act (1890)

U.S. Statutes at Large, Volume 26, p. 209.

CHAP. 647.—An act to protect trade and commerce against unlawful restraints and monopolies.

Be it enacted by the Senate and House of Representatives of the United States of America in Congress assembled.

SEC. 1. Every contract, combination in the form of trust or otherwise, or conspiracy, in restraint of trade or commerce among the several States, or with foreign nations, is hereby declared to be illegal. Every person who shall make any such contract or engage in any such combination or conspiracy, shall be deemed guilty of a misdemeanor, and, on conviction thereof, shall be punished by fine not exceeding five thousand dollars, or by imprisonment not exceeding one year, or by both said punishments, in the discretion of the court.

SEC. 2. Every person who shall monopolize, or attempt to monopolize, or combine or conspire with any other person or persons, to monopolize any part of the trade or commerce among the several States, or with foreign nations, shall be deemed guilty of a misdemeanor, and, on conviction thereof, shall be punished by fine not exceeding five thousand dollars, or by imprisonment not exceeding one year, or by both said punishments, in the discretion of the court.

SEC. 3. Every contract, combination in form of trust or otherwise, or conspiracy, in restraint of trade or commerce in any Territory of the United States or of the District of Columbia, or in restraint of trade or commerce between any such Territory and another, or between any such Territory or Territories and any State or States or the District of Columbia, or with foreign nations, or between the District of Columbia and any State or States or foreign nations, is hereby declared illegal. Every person who shall make any such contract or engage in any such combination or conspiracy, shall be deemed guilty of a misdemeanor, and, on conviction thereof, shall be punished by fine not exceeding five thousand dollars, or by imprisonment not exceeding one year, or by both said punishments, in the discretion of the court.

Sec. 4. The several circuit courts of the United States are hereby invested with jurisdiction to prevent and restrain violations of this act; and it shall be the duty of the several district attorneys of the United States, in their respective districts, under the direction of the Attorney-General, to institute proceedings in equity to prevent and restrain such violations. Such proceedings may be by way of petition setting forth the case and praying that such violation shall be enjoined or otherwise prohibited. When the parties complained of shall have been duly notified of such petition the court shall proceed, as soon as may be, to the hearing and determination of the case; and pending such petition and before final decree, the court may at any time make such temporary restraining order or prohibition as shall be deemed just in the premises.

Sec. 5. Whenever it shall appear to the court before which any proceeding under section four of this act may be pending, that the ends of justice require that other parties should be brought before the court, the court may cause them to be summoned, whether they reside in the district in which the court is held or not; and subpoenas to that end may be served in any district by the marshal thereof.

Sec. 6. Any property owned under any contract or by any combination, or pursuant to any conspiracy (and being the subject thereof) mentioned in section one of this act, and being in the course of transportation from one State to another, or to a foreign country, shall be forfeited to the United States, and may be seized and condemned by like proceedings as those provided by law for the forefeiture, seizure, and condemnation of property imported into the United States contrary to law.

Sec. 7. Any person who shall be injured in his business or property by any other person or corporation by reason of anything forbidden or declared to be unlawful by this act, may sue therefor in any circuit court of the United States in the district in which the defendant resides or is found, without respect to the amount in controversy, and shall recover three fold the damages by him sustained, and the costs of suit, including a reasonable attorney's fee.

Sec. 8. That the word "person," or "persons," wherever used in this act shall be deemed to include corporations and associations existing under or authorized by the laws of either the United States, the laws of any of the Territories, the laws of any State, or the laws of any foreign country.

Approved, July 2, 1890.

B. Food, Drug, and Cosmetic Act

(21 U.S.C.A., Section 352)

Misbranded drugs and devices

A drug or device shall be deemed to be misbranded—

(a) If its labeling is false or misleading in any particular.

(b) If in package form unless it bears a label containing (1) the name and place of business of the manufacturer, packer, or distributor; and (2) an accurate statement of the quantity of the contents in terms of weight, measure, or numerical count: *Provided,* That under clause (2) of this paragraph reasonable variations shall be permitted, and exemptions as to small packages shall be established, by regulations prescribed by the Secretary [of Health and Human Services].

(c) If any word, statement, or other information required by or under authority of this chapter to appear on the label or labeling is not prominently placed thereon with such conspicuousness (as compared with other words, statements, designs, or devices, in the labeling) and in such terms as to render it likely to be read and understood by the ordinary individual under customary conditions of purchase and use.

(d) If it is for use by man and contains any quantity of the narcotic or hypnotic substance alpha eucaine, barbituric acid, betaeucaine, bromal, cannabis, carbromal, chloral, coca, cocaine, codeine, heroin, marihuana, morphine, opium, paraldehyde, peyote, or sulphonmethane; or any chemical derivative of such substance, which derivative has been by the Secretary, after investigation, found to be, and by regulations designated as, habit forming; unless its label bears the name and quantity or proportion of such substance or derivative and in juxtaposition therewith the statement "Warning—may be habit forming."

· · ·

(f) Unless its labeling bears (1) adequate directions for use; and (2) such adequate warnings against use in those pathological conditions or by children where its use may be dangerous to health, or against unsafe dosage or methods or duration of administration or application, in such manner and form, as are necessary for the protection of users: *Provided,* That where any requirement of clause (1) of this subsection, as applied to any drug or device, is not necessary for the protection of the public health, the Secretary shall promulgate regulations exempting such drug or device from such requirement.

· · ·

(i) (1) If it is a drug and its container is so made, formed, or filled as to be misleading; or (2) if it is an imitation of another drug; or (3) if it is offered for sale under the name of another drug.

(j) If it is dangerous to health when used in the dosage or manner, or with the frequency or duration prescribed, recommended, or suggested in the labeling thereof.

C. Civil Rights Act of 1964, Title VII (as amended)

42 U.S.C. Section 2000e-2

(a) It shall be an unlawful employment practice for an employer—

(1) to fail or refuse to hire or to discharge any individual, or otherwise to discriminate against any individual with respect to his compensation, terms, conditions, or privileges of employment, because of such individual's race, color, religion, sex, or national origin; or

(2) to limit, segregate, or classify his employees or applicants for employment in any way which would deprive or tend to deprive any individual of employment opportunities or otherwise adversely affect his status as an employee, because of such individual's race, color, religion, sex, or national origin.

(b) It shall be an unlawful employment practice for an employment agency to fail or refuse to refer for employment, or otherwise to discriminate against, any individual because of his race, color, religion, sex, or national origin, or to classify or refer for employment any individual on the basis of his race, color, religion, sex, or national origin.

(c) It shall be an unlawful employment practice for a labor organization—

(1) to exclude or to expel from its membership, or otherwise to discriminate against, any individual because of his race, color, religion, sex, or national origin.

(2) to limit, segregate, or classify its membership or applicants for membership, or to classify or fail or refuse to refer for employment any individual, in any way which would deprive or tend to deprive any individual of employment opportunities, or would limit such employment opportunities or otherwise adversely affect his status as an employee or as an applicant for employment, because of such individual's race, color, religion, sex, or national origin; or

(3) to cause or attempt to cause an employer to discriminate against an individual in violation of this section.

(d) It shall be an unlawful employment practice for any employer, labor organization, or joint labor-management committee controlling apprenticeship or other training or retraining, including on-the-job training programs to discriminate against any individual because of his race, color, religion, sex, or national origin in admission to, or employment in, any program established to provide apprenticeship or other training.

(e) Notwithstanding any other provision of this subchapter, (1) it shall not be an unlawful employment practice for an employer to hire and employ employees, for an employment agency to classify, or refer for employment any individual, for a labor organization to classify its membership or to classify or refer for employment any individual, or for an employer, labor organization, or joint labor-management committee controlling apprenticeship or other training or retraining programs to admit or employ any individual in any such program, on the basis of his religion, sex, or national origin in those certain instances where religion, sex, or national origin is a bona fide occupational qualification reasonably necessary to the normal operation of that particular business or enterprise, and (2) it shall not be an unlawful employment practice for a school, college, university, or other educational institution or institution of learning to hire and employ employees of a particular religion if such school, college, university, or other educational institution or institution of learning is, in whole or in substantial part, owned, supported, controlled, or managed by a particular religion or by a particular religious corporation, association, or society, or if the curriculum of such school, college, university, or other educational institution or institution of learning is directed toward the propagation of a particular religion.

. . .

(h) Notwithstanding any other provision of this subchapter, it shall not be an unlawful employment practice for an employer to apply different standards of compensation, or different terms, conditions, or privileges of employment pursuant to a bona fide seniority or merit system, or a system which measures earnings by quantity or quality of production or to employees who work in different locations, provided that such differences are not the result of an intention to discriminate because of race, color, religion, sex, or national origin, nor shall it be an unlawful employment practice for an employer to give and to act upon the results of any professionally developed ability test provided that such test, its administration or action upon the results is not designed, intended or used to discriminate because of race, color, religion, sex or national origin. . . .

(i) Nothing contained in this subchapter shall apply to any business or enterprise on or near an Indian reservation with respect to any publicly announced employment practice of such business or enterprise under which a preferential treatment is given to any individual because he is an Indian living on or near a reservation.

(j) Nothing contained in this subchapter shall be interpreted to require any employer, employment agency, labor organization, or joint labor-management committee subject to this subchapter to grant preferential treatment to any individual or to any group because of the race, color, religion, sex, or national origin of such individual or group on account of an imbalance which may exist with respect to the total number or percentage of persons of any race, color, religion, sex, or national origin employed by any employer, referred or classified for employment by any employment agency or labor organization, admitted to membership or classified by any labor organization, or admitted to, or employed in, any apprenticeship or other training program, in comparison with the total number or percentage of persons of such race, color, religion, sex, or national origin in any community, State, section, or other area, or in the available work force in any community, State, section, or other area.

D. Workmen's Compensation Law (Idaho)

Idaho Code, Title 72

72-102. Definitions.—Words and terms used in the workmen's compensation law, unless the context otherwise requires, are defined in the subsections which follow.

. . .

(14) "Injury" and "accident."

(a) "Injury" means a personal injury caused by an accident arising out of and in the course of any employment covered by the workmen's compensation law.

(b) "Accident" means an unexpected, undesigned, and unlooked for mishap, or untoward event, connected with the industry in which it occurs, and which can be reasonably located as to time when and place where it occurred, causing an injury.

(c) "Injury" and "personal injury" shall be construed to include only an injury caused by an accident, which results in violence to the physical structure of the body. The terms shall in no case be construed to include an occupational disease and only such nonoccupational diseases as result directly from an injury.

(15) "Medical and related benefits" means payments provided for or made for medical, hospital, burial and other services as provided in this law other than income benefits.

(16) "Medical services" means medical, surgical, dental or other attendance or treatment, nurse and hospital service, medicines, apparatus, appliances, prostheses, and related services, facilities and supplies.

(17) "Occupational diseases."

(a) "Occupational disease" means a disease due to the nature of an employment in which the hazards of such disease actually exist, are characteristic of, and peculiar to the trade, occupation, process, or employment, but shall not include psychological injuries, disorders or conditions unless the conditions . . . [of] 72-451 are met.

72-208. Injuries not covered—Wilful intention—Intoxication. (1) No compensation shall be allowed to an employee for injury proximately caused by the employee's wilful intention to injure himself or to injure another.

(2) If an injury is the proximate result of an employee's intoxication, all income benefits shall be reduced by fifty per cent (50%), provided that such reduction shall not apply where the intoxicants causing the employee's intoxication were furnished by the employer or where the employer permits the employee to remain at work with knowledge by the employer or his supervising agent that the employee is intoxicated.

72-209. Exclusiveness of liability of employer.—(1) . . . [T]he liability of the employer under this law shall be exclusive and in place of all other liability of the employer to the employee, his spouse, dependents, heirs, legal representatives or assigns.

. . .

(3) The exemption from liability given an employer by this section shall also extend to the employer's surety and to all officers, agents, servants and employees of the employer or surety, provided that such exemptions from liability shall not apply in any case where the injury or death is proximately caused by the wilful or unprovoked physical aggression of the employer, its officers, agents, servants or employees, the loss of such exemption applying only to the aggressor and shall not be imputable to the employer unless provoked or authorized by the employer, or the employer was a party thereto.

72-211. Exclusiveness of employee's remedy.— . . . [T]he rights and remedies herein granted to an employee on account of an injury or occupational disease for which he is entitled to compensation under this law shall exclude all other rights and remedies of the employee, his personal representatives, dependents or next of kin, at common law or otherwise, on account of such injury or disease.

72-212. Exemptions from coverage.—None of the provisions of this law shall apply to the following employments unless coverage thereof is elected [by the employer in writing.] . . .

(1) Household domestic service.

(2) Casual employment.

(3) Employment of outworkers.

(4) Employment of members of an employer's family dwelling in his household.

(5) Employment which is not carried on by the employer for the sake of pecuniary gain.

(6) Employment as the owner of a sole proprietorship; employment of a working member of a partnership . . . employment of an officer of a corporation who at all times during the period involved owns not less than ten per cent (10%) of all of the issued and outstanding voting stock of the corporation and, if the corporation has directors, is also a director thereof.

. . .

(8) Agricultural pursuits. Agricultural pursuits, as used herein, shall include the raising or harvesting of any agricultural or horticultural commodity including the raising, pelting, shearing, feeding, caring for, training and management of livestock, bees, poultry and fur-bearing animals and wildlife raised in captivity, on inclosed lands and public ranges. Agricultural pursuits shall include the loading and transporting, by motor vehicle, of any agricultural or horticultural commodity to any storage, processing, distribution or manufacturing destination and the unloading of the commodity at such destination; provided, that the exemption for the transportation, loading or unloading of agricultural or horticultural commodities shall apply only to individuals, corporations, partnerships or other legal entities who are transporting, loading or unloading only those agricultural or horticultural commodities which the individual, corporation, partnership or other legal entity produced, raised or harvested. The return trip from a manufacturing, processing, storage or distribution destination is exempted if: the return trip to the original point of debarkation is by the safest and most direct route reasonably possible, the cargo transported on the return trip, if any, is to be used exclusively by the individual, corporation, partnership, or other legal entity which is transporting the cargo, and the cargo transported is to be used only in direct connection with the agricultural pursuit.

(9) Pilots of agricultural spraying or dusting planes. Employment as a pilot of an aircraft, used to apply fertilizers and pesticides to agricultural crops, when actually operating an aircraft, shall be exempt from the provisions of the workmen's compensation law, if: the employer files with, and has written approval by, the industrial commission, prior to employing a pilot for the purpose of engaging in the application of pesticides to agricultural crops by aircraft, proof of coverage of an insurance policy that will provide to the employed pilot of such aircraft while actually operating an aircraft, benefits in an amount of not less than: twenty-five thousand dollars ($25,000) accidental death and dismemberment, ten thousand dollars ($10,000) medical expense payments, and five hundred dollars ($500) per month disability income for a minimum of forty-eight (48) months.

(10) Associate real estate brokers and real estate salesmen. Service performed by an individual for a real estate broker as an associate real estate broker or as a real estate salesman, if all such service performed by such individual for such person is performed for remuneration solely by way of commission.

(11) Volunteer ski patrollers.

(12) Officials of athletic contests involving secondary schools . . .

. . .

72-428. Scheduled income benefits for loss or losses of use of bodily members.—An employee who suffers a permanent disability less than total and permanent shall, in addition to the income benefits payable during the period of recovery, be paid income benefits for such permanent disability in an amount equal to fifty-five percent (55%) of the average weekly state wage stated against the following scheduled permanent impairments respectively:

	Weeks
(1) Amputations of Upper Extremities	
Forequarter amputation	350
Disarticulation at shoulder joint	300
Amputation of arm above deltoid insertion	300
Amputation of arm between deltoid insertion and elbow joint	285
Disarticulation at elbow joint	285
Amputation of forearm below elbow joint proximal to insertion of biceps tendon	285
Amputation of forearm below elbow joint distal to insertion of biceps tendon	270
Disarticulation at wrist joint	270
Midcarpal or mid-metacarpal amputation of hand	270
Midcarpal or mid-metacarpal amputation of hand	270
Amputation of all fingers except thumb at metacarpophalangeal joints	160
Amputation of thumb	
At metacarpophalangeal joint or with resection of carpometacarpal bone	110
At interphalangeal joint	80
Amputation of index finger	
At metacarpophalangeal joint or with resection of metacarpal bone	70
At proximal interphalangeal joint	55
At distal interphalangeal joint	30
Amputation of middle finger	
At metacarpophalangeal joint or with resection of metacarpal bone	55
At proximal interphalangeal joint	45
At distal interphalangeal joint	25
Amputation of ring finger	
At metacarpophalangeal joint or with resection of metacarpal bone	25
At proximal interphalangeal joint	20
At distal interphalangeal joint	12
Amputation of little finger	
At metacarpophalangeal joint or with resection of metacarpal bone	15
At proximal interphalangeal joint	10
At distal interphalangeal joint	5
(2) Amputations of Lower Extremities	
Hemipelvectomy	250
Disarticulation at hip joint	200
Amputation above knee joint with short thigh stump (3″ or less below tuberosity of ischium)	200
Amputation above knee joint with functional stump	180
Disarticulation at knee joint	180
Gritt-Stokes amputation	180
Amputation below knee joint with short stump (3″ or less below intercondylar notch)	180
Amputation below knee joint with functional stump	140
Amputation at ankle (Syme)	140
Partial amputation of foot (Chopart's)	105
Mid-metatarsal amputation	70
Amputation of all toes	
At metatarsophalangeal joints	42
Amputation of great toe	
With resection of metatarsal bone	42
At metatarsophalangeal joint	25

At interphalangeal joint	25
Amputation of lesser toe (2nd–5th)	
With resection of metatarsal bone	7
At metatarsophalangeal joint	4
At proximal interphalangeal joint	3
At distal interphalangeal joint	1
(3) Loss of Vision and Hearing	
Total loss of vision of one eye	150
Loss of one eye by enucleation	175
Total loss of binaural hearing	175

. . .

72-432. Medical services, appliances and supplies—Reports.—(1) The employer shall provide for an injured employee such reasonable medical, surgical or other attendance or treatment, nurse and hospital service, medicines, crutches and apparatus, as may be required by the employee's physician or needed immediately after an injury or disability from an occupational disease, and for a reasonable time thereafter. If the employer fails to provide the same, the injured employee may do so at the expense of the employer.

(2) The employer shall also furnish necessary replacements or repairs of appliances and prostheses, unless the need therefor is due to lack of proper care by the employee. If the appliance or prosthesis is damaged or destroyed in an industrial accident, the employer, for whom the employee was working at the time of accident, will be liable for replacement or repair, but not for any subsequent replacement or repair not directly resulting from the accident.

(3) In addition to the income benefits otherwise payable, the employee who is entitled to income benefits shall be paid an additional sum in an amount as may be determined by the commission as by it deemed necessary, as a medical service, when the constant service of an attendant is necessary by reason of total blindness of the employee or the loss of both hands or both feet or the loss of use thereof, or by reason of being paralyzed and unable to walk, or by reason of other disability resulting from the injury or disease actually rendering him so helpless as to require constant attendance. The commission shall have authority to determine the necessity, character and sufficiency of any medical services furnished or to be furnished and shall have authority to order a change of physician, hospital or rehabilitation facility when in its judgment such change is desirable or necessary.

(6) Nothing in this chapter shall be construed to require a workman who in good faith relies on Christian Science treatment by a duly accredited Christian Science practitioner to undergo any medical or surgical treatment, providing that neither he nor his dependents shall be entitled to income benefits of any kind beyond those reasonably expected to have been paid had he undergone medical or surgical treatment, and the employer or insurance carrier may pay for such spiritual treatment.

. . .

72-437. Occupational diseases—Right to compensation.—When an employee of an employer suffers an occupational disease and is thereby disabled from performing his work in the last occupation in which he was injuriously exposed to the hazards of such disease, or dies as a result of such disease, and the disease was due to the nature of an occupation or process in which he was employed within the period previous to his disablement as hereinafter limited, the employee, or, in case of his death, his dependents shall be entitled to compensation.

72-438. Occupational Diseases.—Compensation shall be payable for disability or death of an employee resulting from the following occupational diseases:

(1) Poisoning by lead, mercury, arsenic, zinc, or manganese, their preparations or compounds in any occupation involving direct contact therewith, handling thereof, or exposure thereto.

(2) Carbon monoxide poisoning or chlorine poisoning in any process or occupation involving direct exposure to carbon monoxide or chlorine in buildings, sheds, or inclosed places.

(3) Poisoning by methanol, carbon bisulphide, hydrocarbon distillates (naphthas and others) or halogenated hydrocarbons, or any preparations containing these chemicals or any of them, in any occupation involving direct contact therewith, handling thereof, or exposure thereto.

(4) Poisoning by benzol or by nitro, amido, or amino-derivatives of benzol (dinitro-benzol, anilin and others) or their preparations or compounds in any occupation involving direct contact therewith, handling thereof, or exposure thereto.

(5) Glanders in the care or handling of any equine animal or the carcass of any such animal.

(6) Radium poisoning by or disability due to radioactive properties of substances or to Roentgenray (X-ray) in any occupation involving direct contact therewith, handling thereof, or exposure thereto.

(7) Poisoning by or ulceration from chromic acid or bichromate of ammonium, potassium, or sodium or their preparations, or phosphorus preparations or compounds, in any occupation involving direct contact therewith, handling thereof, or exposure thereto.

(8) Ulceration due to tar, pitch, bitumen, mineral oil, or paraffin, or any compound product, or residue of any of these substances, in any occupation involving direct contact therewith, handling thereof, or exposure thereto.

(9) Dermatitis venenata, that is, infection or inflammation of the skin, furunculosis excepted, due to oils, cutting compounds, lubricants, liquids, fumes, gases, or exposure thereto.

(10) Anthrax occurring in any occupation involving the handling of or exposure to wool, hair, bristles, hides, skins, or bodies of animals either alive or dead.

(11) Silicosis in any occupation involving direct contact with, handling of, or exposure to dust of silicon dioxide (SiO_2).

(12) Cardiovascular or pulmonary or respiratory diseases of a paid fireman, employed by a municipality, village or fire district as a regular member of a lawfully established fire department, caused by overexertion in times of stress or danger or by proximate exposure or by cumulative exposure over a period of four (4) years or more to heat, smoke, chemical fumes or other toxic gases arising directly out of, and in the course of, his employment. Recognizing that additional toxic or harmful substances or matter are continually being discovered and used or misused, the above enumerated occupational diseases are not intended to be exclusive, but such additional diseases shall not include hazards which are common to the public in general. . . .

72-451. Psychological accidents and injuries.—Psychological injuries, disorders or conditions shall not be compensated under this title, unless the following conditions are met:

(1) Such injuries of any kind or nature emanating from the workplace shall be compensated only if caused by accident and physical injury as defined in section 72-102(15)(a) through (15)(c), Idaho Code, or only if accompanying an occupational disease with resultant physical injury, except that a psychological mishap or event may constitute an accident where: (i) it results in resultant physical injury so long as the psychological mishap or event meets the other criteria of this section, and (ii) it is readily recognized and identifiable as having occurred in the workplace, and (iii) it must be the product of a sudden and extraordinary event; and

(2) No compensation shall be paid for such injuries arising from conditions generally inherent in every working situation or from a personnel related action including, but not limited to, disciplinary action, changes in duty, job evaluation or employment termination; and

(3) Such accident and injury must be the predominant cause as compared to all other causes combined of any consequence for which benefits are claimed under this section; and

(4) Where psychological causes or injuries are recognized by this section, such causes or injuries must exist in a real and objective sense; and

(5) Any permanent impairment or permanent disability for psychological injury recognizable under the Idaho worker's compensation law must be based on a condition sufficient to constitute a diagnosis using the terminology and criteria of the American psychiatric association's diagnostic and statistics manual of mental disorders, third edition revised, or any successor manual promulgated by the American psychiatric association, and must be made by a psychologist, or psychiatrist duly licensed to practice in the jurisdiction in which treatment is rendered; and

(6) Clear and convincing evidence that the psychological injuries arose out of and in the course

of the employment from an accident or occupational disease as contemplated in this section is required.

Nothing herein shall be construed as allowing compensation for psychological injuries from psychological causes without accompanying physical injury.

This section shall apply to accidents and injuries occurring on or after July 1, 1994, and to causes of action for benefits accruing on or after July 1, 1994, notwithstanding that the original worker's compensation claim may have occurred prior to July 1, 1994.

E. Structural Pest Control Board Law (California)

(California Business and Professional Code)

§ 8505.2 Performance of fumigation under direction and supervision of licensee. Fumigation shall be performed only under the direct and personal supervision of an individual who is licensed by the board as an operator or field representative in a branch of pest control which includes fumigation or who is the qualified partner or responsible natural person of a partnership which is so licensed or the qualified officer or responsible natural person of a corporation or association which is so licensed.

§ 8520. Structural pest control board; existence; membership; powers There is in the Department of Consumer Affairs a Structural Pest Control Board, which consists of seven members. . . .

The board is vested with the power to and shall administer the provisions of this chapter.

§ 8521. Qualifications of members The board is composed of seven members, three of whom shall be, and shall have been for a period of not less than five years preceding the date of their appointment, operators licensed under this chapter actively engaged in the business of pest control and who are residents of this state, and four public members who shall not be licentiates of the board.

§ 8525. Rules and regulations. The board . . . may . . . adopt, amend, repeal, and enforce reasonably necessary rules and regulations relating to the practice of pest control and its various branches. . . .

The board shall give notice of adoption of such rules and regulations to all persons licensed under this chapter at least 30 days prior to the effective date of the regulations.

§ 8550. Necessity of license or registration. (a) It is unlawful for any individual to engage or offer to engage in the business of, act in the capacity of, or advertise himself or herself as, or assume to act as, an operator or a field representative, or to engage or offer to engage in the practice of structural pest control, unless he or she is licensed under this chapter. For purposes of this subdivision, "engage in the practice of structural pest control" shall not include price quotations given by unlicensed employees of a registered company in response to a request for that information.

§ 8551. Fumigation in public structure. It is unlawful for any unlicensed person to perform fumigation with dangerous or lethal fumigating chemicals in any public structure, including rooming houses, or households when used as public structures, hotels, apartment houses, or any part thereof.

§ 8553. Violation as misdemeanor Any person who violates any provision of this chapter, or who conspires with another person to violate any provision of this chapter, is guilty of a misdemeanor, and is punishable by a fine of not less than one hundred dollars ($100) nor more than one thousand dollars ($1,000), or by imprisonment in the county jail for not more than six months, or by both such fine and imprisonment.

§ 8565. Examination; operators The board shall ascertain by written examination that an applicant for a license as operator is qualified in the use and understanding of all of the following:

(a) The English language, including reading, writing, and spelling.

(b) The building and safety laws of the state and any of its political subdivisions, if the branch or branches of pest control, or wood roof cleaning and treatment for which he or she is applying, require that knowledge.

(c) The labor laws of the state.

(d) The provisions of this chapter.

(e) Poisonous and other dangerous chemicals used in pest control, if the branch license or licenses for which he or she is applying, require that knowledge.

(f) The theory and practice of the branch or branches of pest control or wood roof cleaning and treatment in which the applicant desires to be licensed.

(g) Other state laws, safety or health measures, or practices that are reasonably within the scope of structural pest control in the various branches or in wood roof cleaning and treatment, including an applicant's knowledge of the requirements regarding health effects and restrictions on applications. . . .

§ 8568. Grounds for denial; powers and proceedings After a hearing the board may deny a license or a company registration unless the applicant makes a showing satisfactory to the board that the applicant, if an individual, has not, or if the applicant is a company applying for a company registration, that its manager and each of its officers, directors, employees, members and partners have not:

(a) Committed any act or crime constituting grounds for denial of licensure. . . .

(b) While unlicensed or not registered, knowingly committed or aided and abetted the commission of any act for which a license or company registration is required under this chapter.

(c) While acting as a partner, officer, managing employee, or qualifying manager of a firm, partnership, or corporation, had knowledge of and participated in the commission of any act resulting in the suspension or revocation of a license or company registration.

PART III.

Administrative Regulations

A. Food and Drug Administration Regulations

B. Equal Employment Opportunity Commission Regulations

C. Structural Pest Control Board Regulations (California)

A. Food and Drug Administration Regulations.

Code of Federal Regulations, Title 21

Subpart F—Labeling Claims for Drugs in Drug Efficacy Study

§ 201.200 Disclosure of drug efficacy study evaluations in labeling and advertising.

(a)(1) The National Academy of Sciences—National Research Council, Drug Efficacy Study Group, has completed an exhaustive review of labeling claims made for drugs marketed under new-drug and antibiotic drug procedures between 1938 and 1962. The results are compiled in "Drug Efficacy Study, A Report to the Commissioner of Food and Drugs from the National Academy of Sciences (1969)." As the report notes, this review has made "an audit of the state of the art of drug usage that has been uniquely extensive in scope and uniquely intensive in time" and is applicable to more than 80 percent of the currently marketed drugs. The report further notes that the quality of the evidence of efficacy, as well as the quality of the labeling claims, is poor. Labeling and other promotional claims have been evaluated as "effective," "probably effective," "possibly effective," "ineffective," "ineffective as a fixed combination," and "effective but," and a report for each drug in the study has been submitted to the Commissioner.

(2) The Food and Drug Administration is processing the reports, seeking voluntary action on the part of the drug manufacturers and distributors in the elimination or modification of unsupported promotional claims, and initiating administrative actions as necessary to require product and labeling changes.

(3) Delays have been encountered in bringing to the attention of the prescribers of prescription items the conclusions of the expert panels that reviewed the promotional claims.

(b) The Commissioner of Food and Drugs concludes that:

(1) The failure to disclose in the labeling of a drug and in other promotional material the conclusions of the Academy experts that a claim is "ineffective," "possibly effective," "probably effective," or "ineffective as a fixed combination," while labeling and promotional material bearing any such claim are being used, is a failure to disclose facts that are material in light of the representations made and causes the drug to be misbranded.

(2) The Academy classification of a drug as other than "effective" for a claim for which such

drug is recommended establishes that there is a material weight of opinion among qualified experts contrary to the representation made or suggested in the labeling, and failure to reveal this fact causes such labeling to be misleading.

(c) Therefore, after publication in the FEDERAL REGISTER of a Drug Efficacy Study Implementation notice on a prescription drug, unless exempted or otherwise provided for in the notice, all package labeling. . . promotional labeling, and advertisements shall include, as part of the information for practitioners under which the drug can be safely and effectively used, an appropriate qualification of all claims evaluated as other than "effective" by a panel of the National Academy of Sciences–National Research Council, Drug Efficacy Study Group, if such claims continue to be included in either the labeling or advertisements. . . .

(e) Qualifying information required in drug labeling by paragraph (c) of this section in order to advise prescribers of a drug of the findings made by a panel of the Academy in evaluating a claim as other than "effective" shall be at least of the same size and color and degree of prominence as other printing in the labeling and shall be presented in a prominent box using one of the following formats and procedures:

(1) In drug labeling the box statement may entirely replace the indications section and be in the following format:

INDICATIONS

Based on a review of this drug by the National Academy of Sciences—National Research Council and / or other information, FDA has classified the indication(s) as follows:

Effective: (list or state in paragraph form).

"Probably" effective: (list or state in paragraph form).

"Possibly" effective: (list or state in paragraph form).

Final classification of the less-than-effective indications requires further investigation.

---

(2) Or the indication(s) for which the drug has been found effective may appear outside the boxed statement and be followed immediately by the following boxed statement:

Based on a review of this drug by the National Academy of Sciences–National Research Council and / or other information, FDA has classified the other indication(s) as follows:

"Probably" effective: (list or state in paragraph form).

"Possibly" effective: (list or state in paragraph form).

Final classification of the less-than-effective indications requires further investigation.

· · ·

(g) The Commissioner may find circumstances are such that, while the elimination of claims evaluated as other than effective will generally eliminate the need for disclosure about such claims, there will be instances in which the change in the prescribing or promotional profile of the drug is so substantial as to require a disclosure of the reason for the change so that the purchaser or prescriber is not misled by being left unaware through the sponsor's silence that a basic change has taken place. The Food and Drug Administration will identify these situations in direct correspondence with the drug promoters, after which the failure to make the disclosure will be regarded as misleading and appropriate action will be taken.

B. *Equal Employment Opportunity Commission Regulations*

Code of Federal Regulations, Title 29

§ 1604.2 Sex as a bona fide occupational qualification.

(a) The commission believes that the bona fide occupational qualification exception as to sex should be interpreted narrowly. Label—"Men's jobs" and "Women's jobs"—tend to deny employment opportunities unnecessarily to one sex or the other.

(1) The Commission will find that the following situations do not warrant the application of the bona fide occupational qualification exception;

(i) The refusal to hire a woman because of her sex based on assumptions of the comparative employment characteristics of women in general. For example, the assumption that the turnover rate among women is higher than among men.

(ii) The refusal to hire an individual based on stereotyped characterizations of the sexes. Such stereotypes include, for example, that men are less capable of assembling intricate equipment: that women are less capable of aggressive salesmanship. The principle of nondiscrimination requires that individuals be considered on the basis of individual capacities and not on the basis of any characteristics generally attributed to the group.

(iii) The refusal to hire an individual because of the preferences of coworkers, the employer, clients or customers except as covered specifically in paragraph (a)(2) of this section.

(2) Where it is necessary for the purpose of authenticity or genuineness, the Commission will consider sex to be a bona fide occupational qualification, e.g., an actor or actress.

(b) Effect of sex-oriented State employment legislation.

(1) Many States have enacted laws or promulgated administrative regulations with respect to the employment of females. Among these laws are those which prohibit or limit the employment of females, e.g., the employment of females in certain occupations, in jobs requiring the lifting or carrying of weights exceeding certain prescribed limits, during certain hours of the night, for more than a specified number of hours per day or per week, and for certain periods of time before and after childbirth. The Commission has found that such laws and regulations do not take into account the capacities, preferences, and abilities of individual females and, therefore, discriminate on the basis of sex. The Commission has concluded that such laws and regulations conflict with and are superseded by title VII of the Civil Rights Act of 1964. Accordingly, such laws will not be considered a defense to an otherwise established unlawful employment practice or as a basis for the application of the bona fide occupational qualification exception.

(2) The Commission has concluded that State laws and regulations which discriminate on the basis of sex with regard to the employment of minors are in conflict with and are superseded by title VII to the extent that such laws are more restrictive for one sex. Accordingly, restrictions on the employment of minors of one sex over and above those imposed on minors of the other sex will not be considered a defense to an otherwise established unlawful employment practice or as a basis for the application of the bona fide occupational qualification exception.

(3) A number of States require that minimum wage and premium pay for overtime be provided for female employees. An employer will be deemed to have engaged in an unlawful employment practice if:

(i) It refuses to hire or otherwise adversely affects the employment opportunities of female applicants or employees in order to avoid the payment of minimum wages or overtime pay required by State law; or

(ii) It does not provide the same benefits for male employees.

(4) As to other kinds of sex-oriented State employment laws, such as those requiring special rest and meal periods or physical facilities for women, provision of these benefits to one sex only will be a violation of title VII. An employer will be deemed to have engaged in an unlawful employment practice if:

(i) It refuses to hire or otherwise adversely affects the employment opportunities of female applicants or employees in order to avoid the provision of such benefits; or

(ii) It does not provide the same benefits for male employees. If the employer can prove that business necessity precludes providing these benefits to both men and women, then the State law is in conflict with and superseded by title VII as to this employer. In this situation, the employer shall not provide such benefits to members of either sex.

(5) Some States require that separate restrooms be provided for employees of each sex. An employer will be deemed to have engaged in an unlawful employment practice if it refuses to hire or otherwise adversely affects the employment opportunities of applicants or employees in order to avoid the provision of such restrooms for persons of that sex.

§ 1604.3 Separate lines of progression and seniority systems.

(a) It is an unlawful employment practice to classify a job as "male" or "female" or to maintain separate lines of progression or separate seniority lists based on sex where this would adversely affect any employee unless sex is a bona fide occupational qualification for that job. Accordingly, employment practices are unlawful which arbitrarily classify jobs so that:

(1) A female is prohibited from applying for a job labeled "male," or for a job in a "male" line of progression; and vice versa.

(2) A male scheduled for layoff is prohibited from displacing a less senior female on a "female" seniority list; and vice versa.

(b) A Seniority system or line of progression which distinguishes between "light" and "heavy" jobs constitutes an unlawful employment practice if it operates as a disguised form of classification by sex, or creates unreasonable obstacles to the advancement by members of either sex into jobs which members of that sex would reasonably be expected to perform.

§ 1604.4 Discrimination against married women.

(a) The Commission has determined that an employer's rule which forbids or restricts the employment of married women and which is not applicable to married men is a discrimination based on sex prohibited by title VII of the Civil Rights Act. It does not seem to us relevant that the rule is not directed against all females, but only against married females, for so long as sex is a factor in the application of the rule, such application involves a discrimination based on sex.

(b) It may be that under certain circumstances, such a rule could be justified within the meaning of section 703(e)(1) of title VII. We express no opinion on this question at this time except to point out that sex as a bona fide occupational qualification must be justified in terms of the peculiar requirements of the particular job and not on the basis of a general principle such as the desirability of spreading work.

§ 1604.5 Job opportunities advertising.

It is a violation of title VII for a help-wanted advertisement to indicate a preference, limitation, specification, or discrimination based on sex unless sex is a bona fide occupational qualification for the particular job involved. The placement of an advertisement in columns classified by publishers on the basis of sex, such as columns headed "Male" or "Female," will be considered an expression of a preference, limitation, specification, or discrimination based on sex.

· · ·

§ 1604.7 Pre-employment inquiries as to sex.

A pre-employment inquiry may ask "Male........., Female........."; or "Mr. Mrs. Miss," provided that the inquiry is made in good faith for a nondiscriminatory purpose. Any pre-employment inquiry in connection with prospective employment which expresses directly or indirectly any limitation, specification, or discrimination as to sex shall be unlawful unless based upon a bona fide occupational qualification.

§ 1604.10 Employment policies relating to pregnancy and childbirth.

(a) A written or unwritten employment policy or practice which excludes from employment applicants or employees because of pregnancy, childbirth or related medical conditions is in prima facie violation of title VII.

(b) Disabilities caused or contributed to by pregnancy, childbirth, or related medical conditions, for all job-related purposes, shall be treated the same as disabilities caused or contributed to by other medical conditions, under any health or disability insurance or sick leave plan available in connection with employment. Written or unwritten employment policies and practices involving matters such as the commencement and duration of leave, the availability of extensions, the accrual of seniority and other benefits and privileges, reinstatement, and payment under any health or disability insurance or sick leave plan, formal or informal, shall be applied to disability due to pregnancy, childbirth or related medical conditions on the same terms and conditions as they are applied to other disabilities. Health insurance benefits for abortion, except where the life of the mother would be endangered if the fetus were carried to term or where medical complications have arisen from an abortion, are not required to be paid by an employer; nothing herein, however, precludes an employer from providing abortion benefits or otherwise affects bargaining agreements in regard to abortion.

(c) Where the termination of an employee who is temporarily disabled is caused by an employment policy under which insufficient or no leave is available, such a termination violates the Act if it has a disparate impact on employees of one sex and is not justified by business necessity. . . .

§ 1604.11 Sexual harassment.

(a) Harassment on the basis of sex is a violation of section 703 of title VII. Unwelcome sexual advances, requests for sexual favors, and other verbal or physical conduct of a sexual nature constitute sexual harassment when (1) submission to such conduct is made either explicitly or implicitly a term or condition of an individual's employment, (2) submission to or rejection of such conduct by an individual is used as the basis for employment decisions affecting such individual, or (3) such conduct has the purpose or effect of unreasonably interfering with an individual's work performance or creating an intimidating, hostile, or offensive working environment.

(b) In determining whether alleged conduct constitutes sexual harassment, the Commission will look at the record as a whole and at the totality of the circumstances, such as the nature of the sexual advances and the context in which the alleged incidents occurred. The determination of the legality of a particular action will be made from the facts, on a case by case basis.

(c) Applying general title VII principles, an employer, employment agency, joint apprenticeship committee or labor organization (hereinafter collectively referred to as "employer") is responsible for its acts and those of its agents and supervisory employees with respect to sexual harassment regardless of whether the specific acts complained of were authorized or even forbidden by the employer and regardless of whether the employer knew or should have known of their occurrence. The Commission will examine the circumstances of the particular employment relationship and the job junctions performed by the individual in determining whether an individual acts in either a supervisory or agency capacity.

(d) With respect to conduct between fellow employees, an employer is responsible for acts of sexual harassment in the workplace where the employer (or its agents or supervisory employees) knows or should have known of the conduct, unless it can show that it took immediate and appropriate corrective action.

(e) An employer may also be responsible for the acts of non-employees, with respect to sexual harassment of employees in the workplace, where the employer (or its agents or supervisory employees) knows or should have known of the conduct and fails to take immediate and appropriate corrective action. In reviewing these cases the Commission will consider the extent of the employer's control and any other legal responsibility which the employer may have with respect to the conduct of such non-employees.

(f) Prevention is the best tool for the elimination of sexual harassment. An employer should take all steps necessary to prevent sexual harassment from occurring, such as affirmatively raising the subject, expressing strong disapproval, developing appropriate sanctions, informing employees of their right to raise and how to raise the issue of harassment under title VII, and developing methods to sensitize all concerned.

(g) Other related practices: Where employment opportunities or benefits are granted because of an individual's submission to the employer's sexual advances or requests for sexual favors, the

employer may be held liable for unlawful sex discrimination against other persons who were qualified for but denied that employment opportunity or benefit.

C. Structural Pest Control Board Regulations (California)

California Code of Regulations
Title 16: Professional and Vocational Regulations
Division 19,
Article 4. Fumigation and Pesticide Use

§ 1970. Standards and Record Requirements.

For the purpose of maintaining proper standards of safety and the establishment of responsibility in handling the dangerous gases used in fumigation and the pesticides used in other pest control
operations, a registered company shall compile and retain for a period of at least two years, a log
or report for each fumigation job and for each pesticide control operation in which a pesticide is
used by the registered company or the registered company's employee.

(a) The report or log for each fumigation job shall contain the following information:
Name and address of prime contractor.
Name and address of subcontractor, if any.
Address of property.
Name of owner or his or her agent.
Type of structure as to details of roofing and walls.
Cubic feet fumigated.
Target pest or pests controlled.
Kind of fumigant or fumigants used and amount.
Name of warning agent and amount used. Type of sealing method used.
Weather conditions as to temperature and wind.
Time gas introduced (date and hour).
Name of licensee testing for leaks.
List of any extraordinary safety precautions taken.
Time gas released (date and hour).
Name of licensee making final test.
Names of crew at fumigation.
Names of crew at opening.
Time fire department was notified, where required by local ordinance.
Time police department notified, where required by local ordinance.
Time ready for occupancy.
Signature of licensed operator or field representative in charge.

(b) The report for each pest control operation, other than fumigation, in which a pesticide is
used shall contain the following information:
Date of treatment.
Name of owner or his or her agent.
Address of property.
Total area treated. Target pest or pests controlled.
Pesticide and amount used.
Identity of person or persons who applied the pesticide.

§ 1983. Handling, Use, and Storage of Pesticides.

(a) Each container in which any pesticide is stored, carried or transported shall be adequately labeled in accordance with the provisions of Articles 1 and 5, Chapter 2, Division 7 of the Food and Agriculture Code (relating to economic poisons) and regulations adopted by the Department of Pesticide Regulation thereunder.

(b) Service kits which contain any pesticide or preparation thereof shall be handled with extreme caution and in no case shall such a kit be left where children or other unauthorized persons might remove the contents.

(c) When any pesticide or preparation thereof is carried on a truck or other vehicle, a suitable storage space shall be provided thereon. Under no circumstances shall such storage be left either unlocked or unattended when containing any pesticide or preparation thereof.

(d) Where there is danger of food or drug contamination, all food or drug commodities and all utensils or equipment used in the preparation of food or drugs shall be adequately covered to insure against contamination by pesticidal materials, unless the contamination will be dissipated or otherwise removed prior to the time the food or drugs are consumed or the utensils or equipment used.

(e) No rodenticide or avicide shall be used in such manner as to be readily accessible to children or pets.

(f) All rodenticides and avicides shall be removed from readily accessible places upon termination of the particular service.

(g) Under no circumstances shall oil base insecticidal materials be used in or near open flames or active heaters.

(h) Tracking powders shall be used only at floor level or in such places as warrant their safe use.

(i) When a covered or uncovered bait station is used for any pesticide the bait station shall be adequately marked with the signal word or symbols required on the original pesticide label, the generic name of the pesticide, and the name, address and telephone number of the structural pest control company. A building which is vacated, posted, locked and in the care, custody and control of the registered company shall be considered the bait station.

PART IV.

American Case Law

A. *Brown v. Board of Education of Topeka et al.* (1954)

B. *Dothard v. Rawlinson* (1977)

C. *Hopwood v. State of Texas* (1996)

D. *Louie v. Bamboo Gardens et al.* (1947)

E. *Marvin v. Marvin* (1976)

F. *In the Matter of Baby M* (1988)

Brown et al. v. Board of Education of Topeka et al.

347 U.S. 483, 74 S.Ct. 686, 98 L.Ed. 873 (1954)

MR. CHIEF JUSTICE WARREN delivered the opinion of the Court.

These cases come to us from the States of Kansas, South Carolina, Virginia, and Delaware. They are premised on different facts and different local conditions, but a common legal question justifies their consideration together in this consolidated opinion.

In each of the cases, minors of the Negro race, through their legal representatives, seek the aid of the courts in obtaining admission to the public schools of their community on a nonsegregated basis. In each instance, they had been denied admission to schools attended by white children under laws requiring or permitting segregation according to race. This segregation was alleged to deprive the plaintiffs of the equal protection of the laws under the Fourteenth Amendment. In each of the cases other than the Delaware case, a three-judge federal district court denied relief to the plaintiffs on the so-called "separate but equal" doctrine announced by this Court in *Plessy v. Ferguson,* 163 U.S. 537. Under that doctrine, equality of treatment is accorded when the races are provided substantially equal facilities, even though these facilities be separate. In the Delaware case, the Supreme Court of Delaware adhered to that doctrine, but ordered that the plaintiffs be admitted to the white schools because of their superiority to the Negro schools.

The plaintiffs contend that segregated public schools are not "equal" and cannot be made "equal," and that hence they are deprived of the equal protection of the laws. Because of the obvious importance of the question presented, the Court took jurisdiction. Argument was heard in the 1952 Term, and reargument was heard this Term on certain questions propounded by the Court.

Reargument was largely devoted to the circumstances surrounding the adoption of the Fourteenth Amendment in 1868. It covered exhaustively consideration of the Amendment in Congress, ratification by the states, then existing practices in racial segregation, and the views of proponents and opponents of the Amendment. This discussion and our own investigation convince us that, although these sources cast some light, it is not enough to resolve the problem with which we are faced. At best, they are inconclusive. The most avid proponents of the post-War Amendments undoubtedly intended them to remove all legal distinctions among "all persons born or naturalized in the United States." Their opponents, just as certainly, were antagonistic to both the letter and the spirit of the Amendments and wished them to have the most limited effect. What others in Congress and the state legislatures had in mind cannot be determined with any degree of certainty.

An additional reason for the inconclusive nature of the Amendment's history, with respect to segregated schools, is the status of public education at that time. In the South, the movement toward free common schools, supported by general taxation, had not yet taken hold. Education of white children was largely in the hands of private groups. Education of Negroes was almost nonexistent, and practically all of the race were illiterate. In fact, any education of Negroes was forbidden by law in some states. Today, in contrast, many Negroes have achieved outstanding success in the arts and sciences as well as in the business and professional world. It is true that public school education at the time of the Amendment had advanced further in the North, but the effect of the Amendment on Northern States was generally ignored in the congressional debates. Even in the North, the conditions of public education did not approximate those existing today. The curriculum was usually rudimentary; ungraded schools were common in rural areas; the school term was but three months a year in many states; and compulsory school attendance was virtually unknown. As a consequence, it is not surprising that there should be so little in the history of the Fourteenth Amendment relating to its intended effect on public education.

In the first cases in this Court construing the Fourteenth Amendment, decided shortly after its adoption, the Court interpreted it as proscribing all state-imposed discriminations against the Negro race. The doctrine of "separate but equal" did not make its appearance in this Court until 1896 in the case of *Plessy* v. *Ferguson, supra,* involving not education but transportation. American courts have since labored with the doctrine for over half a century. In this Court, there have been six cases involving the "separate but equal" doctrine in the field of public education. In *Cumming* v. *County Board of Education,* 175 U.S. 528, and *Gong Lum* v. *Rice,* 275 U.S. 78, the validity of the doctrine itself was not challenged. In more recent cases, all on the graduate school level, inequality was found in that specific benefits enjoyed by white students were denied to Negro students of the same educational qualifications. *Missouri ex rel. Gaines* v. *Canada,* 305 U.S. 337; *Sipuel* v. *Oklahoma,* 332 U.S. 631; *Sweatt* v. *Painter,* 339 U.S. 629; *McLaurin* v. *Oklahoma State Regents,* 339 U.S. 637. In none of these cases was it necessary to re-examine the doctrine to grant relief to the Negro plaintiff. And in *Sweatt* v. *Painter, supra,* the Court expressly reserved decision on the question whether *Plessy* v. *Ferguson* should be held inapplicable to public education.

In the instant cases, that question is directly presented. Here, unlike *Sweatt* v. *Painter,* there are findings below that the Negro and white schools involved have been equalized, or are being equalized, with respect to buildings, curricula, qualifications and salaries of teachers, and other "tangible" factors. Our decision, therefore, cannot turn on merely a comparison of these tangible factors in the Negro and white schools involved in each of the cases. We must look instead to the effect of segregation itself on public education.

In approaching this problem, we cannot turn the clock back to 1868 when the Amendment was adopted, or even to 1896 when *Plessy* v. *Ferguson* was written. We must consider public education in the light of its full development and its present place in American life throughout the Nation. Only in this way can it be determined if segregation in public schools deprives these plaintiffs of the equal protection of the laws.

Today, education is perhaps the most important function of state and local governments. Compulsory school attendance laws and the great expenditures for education both demonstrate our recognition of the importance of education to our democratic society. It is required in the performance of our most basic public responsibilities, even service in the armed forces. It is the very foundation of good citizenship. Today it is a principal instrument in awakening the child to cultural values, in preparing him for later professional training, and in helping him to adjust normally to his environment. In these days, it is doubtful that any child may reasonably be expected to succeed in life if he is denied the opportunity of an education. Such an opportunity, where the state has undertaken to provide it, is a right which must be made available to all on equal terms.

We come then to the question presented: Does segregation of children in public schools solely on the basis of race, even though the physical facilities and other "tangible" factors may be equal, deprive the children of the minority group of equal educational opportunities? We believe that it does.

In *Sweatt* v. *Painter, supra,* in finding that a segregated law school for Negroes could not provide them equal educational opportunities, this Court relied in large part on "those qualities which are incapable of objective measurement but which make for greatness in a law school." In *McLaurin* v. *Oklahoma State Regents, supra,* the Court, in requiring that a Negro admitted to a white graduate school be treated like all other students, again resorted to intangible considerations: ". . . his ability to study, to engage in discussions and exchange views with other students, and, in general, to learn his profession." Such considerations apply with added force to children in grade and high schools. To separate them from others of similar age and qualifications solely because of their race generates a feeling of inferiority as to their status in the community that may affect their hearts and minds in a way unlikely ever to be undone. The effect of this separation on their educational opportunities was well stated by a finding in the Kansas case by a court which nevertheless felt compelled to rule against the Negro plaintiffs:

> "Segregation of white and colored children in public schools has a detrimental effect upon the colored children. The impact is greater when it has the sanction of the law; for the policy of separating the races is usually interpreted as denoting the inferiority of the negro group. A sense of inferiority affects the motivation of a child to learn. Segregation with the sanction of law, therefore, has a tendency to [retard] the educational and mental development of negro children and to deprive them of some of the benefits they would receive in a racial[ly] integrated school system."

Whatever may have been the extent of psychological knowledge at the time of *Plessy* v. *Ferguson,* this finding is amply supported by modern authority.[*] Any language in *Plessy* v. *Ferguson* contrary to this finding is rejected.

We conclude that in the field of public education the doctrine of "separate but equal" has no place. Separate educational facilities are inherently unequal. Therefore, we hold that the plaintiffs and others similarly situated for whom the actions have been brought are, by reason of the segregation complained of, deprived of the equal protection of the laws guaranteed by the Fourteenth Amendment. This disposition makes unnecessary any discussion whether such segregation also violates the Due Process Clause of the Fourteenth Amendment.

Because these are class actions, because of the wide applicability of this decision, and because of the great variety of local conditions, the formulation of decrees in these cases presents problems of considerable complexity. On reargument, the consideration of appropriate relief was necessarily subordinated to the primary question—the constitutionality of segregation in public education. We have now announced that such segregation is a denial of the equal protection of the laws. In order that we may have the full assistance of the parties in formulating decrees, the cases will be restored to the docket, and the parties are requested to present further argument on Questions 4 and 5

---

[*] K. B. Clark, Effect of Prejudice and Discrimination on Personality Development (Midcentury White House Conference on Children and Youth, 1950); Witmer and Kotinsky, Personality in the Making (1952), c. VI; Deutscher and Chein, The Psychological Effects of Enforced Segregation: A Survey of Social Science Opinion, 26 J. Psychol. 259 (1948); Chein, What are the Psychological Effects of Segregation Under Conditions of Equal Facilities?, 3 Int. J. Opinion and Attitude Res. 229 (1949); Brameld, Educational Costs, in Discrimination and National Welfare (MacIver, ed., 1949), 44–48; Frazier, The Negro in the United States (1949), 674–681. And see generally Myrdal, An American Dilemma (1944). [This original footnote, itself controversial, lists psychological studies which, it was claimed, support the Court's conclusion.—AUTHOR'S NOTE.]

previously propounded by the Court for the reargument this Term.† The Attorney General of the United States is again invited to participate. The Attorneys General of the states requiring or permitting segregation in public education will also be permitted to appear as *amici curiae* upon request to do so by September 15, 1954, and submission of briefs by October 1, 1954.

It is so ordered.

Dothard v. Rawlinson

433 U.S. 321, 97 S.Ct. 2720, 53 L.Ed. 2d 786 (1977)

MR. JUSTICE STEWART delivered the opinion of the Court.

Appellee Dianne Rawlinson sought employment with the Alabama Board of Corrections as a prison guard, called in Alabama a "correctional counselor." After her application was rejected, she brought this class suit under Title VII of the Civil Rights Act of 1964, 78 Stat. 253, as amended, 42 U. S. C. § 2000e *et seq.* (1970 ed. and Supp. V), and under 42 U. S. C. § 1983, alleging that she had been denied employment because of her sex in violation of federal law. A three-judge Federal District Court for the Middle District of Alabama decided in her favor. *Mieth* v. *Dothard,* 418 F. Supp. 1169. . . .

I

At the time she applied for a position as correctional counselor trainee, Rawlinson was a 22-year-old college graduate whose major course of study had been correctional psychology. She was refused employment because she failed to meet the minimum 120-pound weight requirement established by an Alabama statute. The statute also establishes a height minimum of 5 feet 2 inches.

After her application was rejected because of her weight, Rawlinson filed a charge with the Equal Employment Opportunity Commission, and ultimately received a right-to-sue letter. She then filed a complaint in the District Court on behalf of herself and other similarly situated women,

---

† "4. Assuming it is decided that segregation in public schools violates the Fourteenth Amendment.

"(*a*) would a decree necessarily follow providing that, within the limits set by normal geographic school districting, Negro children should forthwith be admitted to schools of their choice, or

"(*b*) may this Court, in the exercise of its equity powers, permit an effective gradual adjustment to be brought about from existing segregated systems to a system not based on color distinctions?

"5. On the assumption on whcih questions 4 (*a*) and (*b*) are based, and assuming further that this Court will exercise its equity powers to the end described in question 4 (*b*),

"(*a*) should this Court formulate detailed decrees in these cases;

"(*b*) if so, what specific issues should the decrees reach;

"(*c*) should this Court appoint a special master to hear evidence with a view to recommending specific terms for such decrees;

"(*d*) should this Court remand to the courts of first instance with directions to frame decrees in these cases, and if so what general directions should the decrees of this Court include and what procedures should the courts of first instance follow in arriving at the specific terms of more detailed decrees?"

challenging the statutory height and weight minima as violative of Title VII and the Equal Protection Clause of the Fourteenth Amendment. A three-judge court was convened. While the suit was pending, the Alabama Board of Corrections adopted Administrative Regulation 204, establishing gender criteria for assigning correctional counselors to maximum-security institutions for "contact positions," that is, positions requiring continual close physical proximity to inmates of the institution. Rawlinson amended her class-action complaint by adding a challenge to Regulation 204 as also violative of Title VII and the Fourteenth Amendment.

Like most correctional facilities in the United States, Alabama's prisons are segregated on the basis of sex. Currently the Alabama Board of Corrections operates four major all-male penitentiaries—Holman Prison, Kilby Corrections Facility, G. K. Fountain Correction Center, and Draper Correctional Center. The Board also operates the Julia Tutwiler Prison for Women, the Frank Lee Youth Center, the Number Four Honor Camp, the State Cattle Ranch, and nine Work Release Centers, one of which is for women. The Julia Tutwiler Prison for Women and the four male penitentiaries are maximum-security institutions. Their inmate living quarters are for the most part large dormitories, with communal showers and toilets that are open to the dormitories and hallways. The Draper and Fountain penitentiaries carry on extensive farming operations, making necessary a large number of strip searches for contraband when prisoners re-enter the prison buildings.

A correctional counselor's primary duty within these institutions is to maintain security and control of the inmates by continually supervising and observing their activities. To be eligible for consideration as a correctional counselor, an applicant must possess a valid Alabama driver's license, have a high school education or its equivalent, be free from physical defects, be between the ages of 20½ years and 45 years at the time of appointment, and fall between the minimum height and weight requirements of 5 feet 2 inches, and 120 pounds, and the maximum of 6 feet 10 inches, and 300 pounds. Appointment is by merit, with a grade assigned each applicant based on experience and education. No written examination is given.

At the time this litigation was in the District Court, the Board of Corrections employed a total of 435 people in various correctional counselor positions, 56 of whom were women. Of those 56 women, 21 were employed at the Julia Tutwiler Prison for Women, 13 were employed in noncontact positions at the four male maximum-security institutions, and the remaining 22 were employed at the other institutions operated by the Alabama Board of Corrections. Because most of Alabama's prisoners are held at the four maximum-security male penitentiaries, 336 of the 435 correctional counselor jobs were in those institutions, a majority of them concededly in the "contact" classification. Thus, even though meeting the statutory height and weight requirements, women applicants could under Regulation 204 compete equally with men for only about 25% of the correctional counselor jobs available in the Alabama prison system.

II

A

The gist of the claim that the statutory height and weight requirements discriminate against women does not involve an assertion of purposeful discriminatory motive. It is asserted, rather, that these facially neutral qualification standards work in fact disproportionately to exclude women from eligibility for employment by the Alabama Board of Corrections. We dealt in *Griggs* v. *Duke Power Co., supra,* and *Albemarle Paper Co.* v. *Moody,* 422 U.S. 405, with similar allegations that facially neutral employment standards disproportionately excluded Negroes from employment, and those cases guide our approach here.

Those cases make clear that to establish a prima facie case of discrimination, a plaintiff need only show that the facially neutral standards in question select applicants for hire in a significantly discriminatory pattern. Once it is thus shown that the employment standards are discriminatory in effect, the employer must meet "the burden of showing that any given requirement [has] . . . a manifest relationship to the employment in question." *Griggs* v. *Duke Power Co., supra,* at 432. If the employer proves that the challenged requirements are job related, the plaintiff may then show that other selection devices without a similar discriminatory effect would also "serve the employer's legitimate interest in 'efficient and trustworthy workmanship.'" *Albemarle Paper Co.* v. *Moody, supra,* at 425, quoting *McDonnell Douglas Corp.* v. *Green,* 411 U.S. 792, 801.

Although women 14 years of age or older compose 52.75% of the Alabama population and 36.89% of its total labor force, they hold only 12.9% of its correctional counselor positions. In considering the effect of the minimum height and weight standards on this disparity in rate of hiring between the sexes, the District Court found that the 5'2" requirement would operate to exclude 33.29% of the women in the United States between the ages of 18–79, while excluding only 1.28% of men between the same ages. The 120-pound weight restriction would exclude 22.29% of the women and 2.35% of the men in this age group. When the height and weight restrictions are combined, Alabama's statutory standards would exclude 41.13% of the female population while excluding less than 1% of the male population. Accordingly, the District Court found that Rawlinson had made out a prima facie case of unlawful sex discrimination. . . .

B

[Appellants argue] that they have rebutted the prima facie case of discrimination by showing that the height and weight requirements are job related. These requirements, they say, have a relationship to strength, a sufficient but unspecified amount of which is essential to effective job performance as a correctional counselor. In the District Court, however, the appellants produced no evidence correlating the height and weight requirements with the requisite amount of strength thought essential to good job performance. Indeed, they failed to offer evidence of any kind in specific justification of the statutory standards.

If the job-related quality that the appellants identify is bona fide, their purpose could be achieved by adopting and validating a test for applicants that measures strength directly. Such a test, fairly administered, would fully satisfy the standards of Title VII because it would be one that "measure[s] the person for the job and not the person in the abstract." *Griggs* v. *Duke Power Co.,* 401 U.S., at 436. But nothing in the present record even approaches such a measurement.

For the reasons we have discussed, the District Court was not in error in holding that Title VII of the Civil Rights Act of 1964, as amended, prohibits application of the statutory height and weight requirements to Rawlinson and the class she represents.

III

Unlike the statutory height and weight requirements, Regulation 204 explicitly discriminates against women on the basis of their sex. In defense of this overt discrimination, the appellants rely on § 703(e) of Title VII, 42 U.S.C. § 2000e-2(e), which permits sex-based discrimination "in those certain instances where . . . sex . . . is a bona fide occupational qualification reasonably necessary to the normal operation of that particular business or enterprise." . . .

We are persuaded—by the restrictive language of § 703(e), the relevant legislative history, and the consistent interpretation of the Equal Employment Opportunity Commission—that the bfoq exception was in fact meant to be an extremely narrow exception to the general prohibition of discrimination on the basis of sex. In the particular factual circumstances of this case, however, we conclude that the District Court erred in rejecting the State's contention that Regulation 204 falls within the narrow ambit of the bfoq exception.

The environment in Alabama's penitentiaries is a peculiarly inhospitable one for human beings of whatever sex. Indeed, a Federal District Court has held that the conditions of confinement in the prisons of the State, characterized by "rampant violence" and a "jungle atmosphere," are constitutionally intolerable. *Pugh* v. *Locke,* 406 F. Supp. 318, 325 (MD Ala.). The record in the present case shows that because of inadequate staff and facilities, no attempt is made in the four maximum-security male penitentiaries to classify or segregate inmates according to their offense or level of dangerousness—a procedure that, according to expert testimony, is essential to effective penological administration. Consequently, the estimated 20% of the male prisoners who are sex offenders are scattered throughout the penitentiaries' dormitory facilities.

In this environment of violence and disorganization, it would be an oversimplification to characterize Regulation 204 as an exercise in "romantic paternalism." Cf. *Frontiero* v. *Richardson,* 411 U.S. 677, 684. In the usual case, the argument that a particular job is too dangerous for women may appropriately be met by the rejoinder that it is the purpose of Title VII to allow the individual woman to make that choice for herself. More is at stake in this case, however, than an individual woman's decision to weigh and accept the risks of employment in a "contact" position in a maximum-security male prison.

The essence of a correctional counselor's job is to maintain prison security. A woman's relative ability to maintain order in a male, maximum-security, unclassified penitentiary of the type Alabama now runs could be directly reduced by her womanhood. There is a basis in fact for expecting that sex offenders who have criminally assaulted women in the past would be moved to do so again if access to women were established within the prison. There would also be a real risk that other inmates, deprived of a normal heterosexual environment, would assault women guards because they were women. In a prison system where violence is the order of the day, where inmate access to guards is facilitated by dormitory living arrangements, where every institution is understaffed, and where a substantial portion of the inmate population is composed of sex offenders mixed at random with other prisoners, there are few visible deterrents to inmate assaults on women custodians. . . .

There was substantial testimony from experts on both sides of this litigation that the use of women as guards in "contact" positions under the existing conditions in Alabama maximum-security male penitentiaries would pose a substantial security problem, directly linked to the sex of the prison guard. On the basis of that evidence, we conclude that the District Court was in error in ruling that being male is not a bona fide occupational qualification for the job of correctional counselor in a "contact" position in an Alabama male maximum-security penitentiary.

The judgment is accordingly affirmed in part and reversed in part, and the case is remanded to the District Court for further proceedings consistent with this opinion.

It is so ordered.

MR. JUSTICE MARSHALL, with whom MR. JUSTICE BRENNAN joins, concurring in part and dissenting in part.

I agree entirely with the Court's analysis of Alabama's height and weight requirements for prison guards, and with its finding that these restrictions discriminate on the basis of sex in violation of Title VII. . . . I must, however, respectfully disagree with the Court's application of the bfoq exception in this case.

. . .

It appears that the real disqualifying factor in the Court's view is "[t]he employee's very womanhood." *Ante,* at 336. The Court refers to the large number of sex offenders in Alabama prisons, and to "[t]he likelihood that inmates would assault a woman because she was a woman." *Ibid.* In short, the fundamental justification for the decision is that women as guards will generate sexual assaults. With all respect, this rationale regrettably perpetuates one of the most insidious of the old myths about women—that women, wittingly or not, are seductive sexual objects. The effect of the decision, made I am sure with the best of intentions, is to punish women because their very presence might provoke sexual assaults. It is women who are made to pay the price in lost job opportunities for the threat of depraved conduct by prison inmates. Once again, "[t]he pedestal upon which women have been placed has . . . , upon closer inspection, been revealed as a cage." *Sail'er Inn, Inc. v. Kirby,* 5 Cal.3d 1, 20, 485 P.2d 529, 541 (1971). It is particularly ironic that the cage is erected here in response to feared misbehavior by imprisoned criminals.

. . .

The proper response to inevitable attacks on both female and male guards is not to limit the employment opportunities of law-abiding women who wish to contribute to their community, but to take swift and sure punitive action against the inmate offenders. Presumably, one of the goals of the Alabama prison system is the eradication of inmates' antisocial behavior patterns so that prisoners will be able to live one day in free society. Sex offenders can begin this process by learning to relate to women guards in a socially acceptable manner. To deprive women of job opportunities because of the threatened behavior of convicted criminals is to turn our social priorities upside down.

Hopwood v. State of Texas

78 F.3rd 932 (C.A. 5, 1996)

JERRY E. SMITH, Circuit Judge:

With the best of intentions, in order to increase the enrollment of certain favored classes of minority students, the University of Texas School of Law ("the law school") discriminates in favor of those applicants by giving substantial racial preferences in its admissions program. The beneficiaries of this system are blacks and Mexican Americans, to the detriment of whites and non-preferred minorities. The question we decide today . . . is whether the Fourteenth Amendment permits the school to discriminate in this way.

We hold that it does not. The law school has presented no compelling justification, under the Fourteenth Amendment or Supreme Court precedent, that allows it to continue to elevate some races over others, even for the wholesome purpose of correcting perceived racial imbalance in the student body. . . .

As a result of its diligent efforts in this case, the district court concluded that the law school may continue to impose racial preferences. *See Hopwood v. Texas,* 861 F.Supp. 551 (W.D.Tex.1994). . . . [W]e reverse and remand, concluding that the law school may not use race as a factor in law school admissions. Further, we instruct the court to reconsider the issue of damages in accordance with the legal standards we now explain. . . .

I.

A.

The University of Texas School of Law is one of the nation's leading law schools, consistently ranking in the top twenty. . . . Accordingly, admission to the law school is fiercely competitive, with over 4,000 applicants a year competing to be among the approximately 900 offered admission to achieve an entering class of about 500 students. Many of these applicants have some of the highest grades and test scores in the country.

Numbers are therefore paramount for admission. In the early 1990's, the law school largely based its initial admissions decisions upon an applicant's so-called Texas Index ("TI") number, a composite of undergraduate grade point average ("GPA") and Law School Aptitude Test ("LSAT") score. The law school used this number as a matter of administrative convenience in order to rank candidates and to predict, roughly, one's probability of success in law school. Moreover, the law school relied heavily upon such numbers to estimate the number of offers of admission it needed to make in order to fill its first-year class.

Of course, the law school did not rely upon numbers alone. The admissions office necessarily exercised judgment in interpreting the individual scores of applicants, taking into consideration factors such as the strength of a student's undergraduate education, the difficulty of his major, and significant trends in his own grades and the undergraduate grades at his respective college (such as grade inflation). Admissions personnel also considered what qualities each applicant might bring to his law school class. Thus, the law school could consider an applicant's background, life experiences, and outlook. Not surprisingly, these hard-to-quantify factors were especially significant for marginal candidates.

Because of the large number of applicants and potential admissions factors, the TI's administrative usefulness was its ability to sort candidates. For the class entering in 1992—the admissions group at issue in this case—the law school placed the typical applicant in one of three categories according to his TI scores: "presumptive admit," "presumptive deny," or a middle "discretionary zone." An applicant's TI category determined how extensive a review his application would receive. . . .

Most, but not all, applicants in the presumptive admit category received offers of . . . admission with little review. . . .

Applications in the middle range were subjected to the most extensive scrutiny. For all applicants other than blacks and Mexican Americans, the files were bundled into stacks of thirty, which were given to admissions subcommittees consisting of three members of the full admissions committee. Each subcommittee member, in reviewing the thirty files, could cast a number of votes—typically from nine to eleven—among the thirty files. Subject to the chairman's veto, if a candidate received two or three votes, he received an offer; if he garnered one vote, he was put on the waiting list; those with no votes were denied admission.

Blacks and Mexican Americans were treated differently from other candidates, however. First, compared to whites and non-preferred minorities, the TI ranges that were used to place them into the three admissions categories were lowered to allow the law school to consider and admit more of them. In March 1992, for example, the presumptive TI admission score for resident whites and non-preferred minorities was 199. Mexican Americans and blacks needed a TI of only 189 to be presumptively admitted. The difference in the presumptive-deny ranges is even more striking. The presumptive denial score for "nonminorities" was 192; the same score for blacks and Mexican Americans was 179.

While these cold numbers may speak little to those unfamiliar with the pool of applicants, the results demonstrate that the difference in the two ranges was dramatic. According to the law school, 1992 resident white applicants had a *mean* GPA of 3.53 and an LSAT of 164. Mexican Americans scored 3.27 and 158; blacks scored 3.25 and 157. The category of "other minority" achieved a 3.56 and 160. . . .

The stated purpose of this lowering of standards was to meet an "aspiration" of admitting a class consisting of 10% Mexican Americans and 5% blacks, proportions roughly comparable to the percentages of those races graduating from Texas colleges. The law school found meeting these "goals" difficult, however, because of uncertain acceptance rates and the variable quality of the applicant pool. In 1992, for example, the entering class contained 41 blacks and 55 Mexican Americans, respectively 8% and 10.7% of the class.

In addition to maintaining separate presumptive TI levels for minorities and whites, the law school ran a segregated application evaluation process. Upon receiving an application form, the school color-coded it according to race. If a candidate failed to designate his race, he was presumed to be in a nonpreferential category. Thus, race was always an overt part of the review of any applicant's file.

The law school reviewed minority candidates within the applicable discretionary range differently from whites. Instead of being evaluated and compared by one of the various discretionary zone subcommittees, black and Mexican American applicants' files were reviewed by a minority subcommittee of three, which would meet and discuss every minority candidate. Thus, each of these candidates' files could get extensive review and discussion. And while the minority subcommittee reported summaries of files to the admissions committee as a whole, the minority subcommittee's decisions were "virtually final."

Finally, the law school maintained segregated waiting lists, dividing applicants by race and residence. Thus, even many of those minority applicants who were not admitted could be set aside in "minority-only" waiting lists. Such separate lists apparently helped the law school maintain a pool of potentially acceptable, but marginal, minority candidates.

B.

Cheryl Hopwood, Douglas Carvell, Kenneth Elliott, and David Rogers (the "plaintiffs") applied for admission to the 1992 entering law school class. All four were white residents of Texas and were rejected.

The plaintiffs were considered as discretionary zone candidates. Hopwood, with a GPA of 3.8

and an LSAT of 39 (equivalent to a three-digit LSAT of 160), had a TI of 199, a score barely within the presumptive-admit category for resident whites, which was 199 and up. She was dropped into the discretionary zone for resident whites (193 to 198), however, because Johanson decided her educational background overstated the strength of her GPA. Carvell, Elliott, and Rogers had TI's of 197, at the top end of that discretionary zone. Their applications were reviewed by admissions subcommittees, and each received one or no vote.

II

The plaintiffs sued primarily under the Equal Protection Clause of the Fourteenth Amendment; they also claimed derivative statutory violations of 42 U.S.C. §§ 1981 and 1983 and of title VI of the Civil Rights Act of 1964, 42 U.S.C. § 2000d ("title VI"). The plaintiffs' central claim is that they were subjected to unconstitutional racial discrimination by the law school's evaluation of their admissions applications. They sought injunctive and declaratory relief and compensatory and punitive damages. . . .

III

[1] The central purpose of the Equal Protection Clause "is to prevent the States from purposefully discriminating between individuals on the basis of race." . . .

In order to preserve these principles, the Supreme Court recently has required that any governmental action that expressly distinguishes between persons on the basis of race be held to the most exacting scrutiny. . . .

Strict scrutiny is necessary because the mere labeling of a classification by the government as "benign" or "remedial" is meaningless. . . .

Under the strict scrutiny analysis, we ask two questions: (1) Does the racial classification serve a compelling government interest, and (2) is it narrowly tailored to the achievement of that goal? . . .

Finally, when evaluating the proffered governmental interest for the specific racial classification, to decide whether the program in question narrowly achieves that interest, we must recognize that "the rights created by . . . the Fourteenth Amendment are, by its terms, guaranteed to the individual. The rights established are personal rights." *Shelley v. Kraemer,* 334 U.S. 1, 22, 68 S.Ct. 836, 846, 92 L.Ed. 1161 (1948). Thus, the Court consistently has rejected arguments conferring benefits on a person based solely upon his membership in a specific class of persons.

With these general principles of equal protection in mind, we turn to the specific issue of whether the law school's consideration of race as a factor in admissions violates the Equal Protection Clause. . . .

[6] We agree with the plaintiffs that any consideration of race or ethnicity by the law school for the purpose of achieving a diverse student body is not a compelling interest under the Fourteenth Amendment. . . .

Indeed, recent Supreme Court precedent shows that the diversity interest will not satisfy strict scrutiny. Foremost, the Court appears to have decided that there is essentially only one compelling state interest to justify racial classifications: remedying past wrongs. . . .

Within the general principles of the Fourteenth Amendment, the use of race in admissions for diversity in higher education contradicts, rather than furthers, the aims of equal protection. Diversity fosters, rather than minimizes, the use of race. It treats minorities as a group, rather than as individuals. It may further remedial purposes but, just as likely, may promote improper racial stereotypes, thus fueling racial hostility.

The use of race, in and of itself, to choose students simply achieves a student body that looks different. Such a criterion is no more rational on its own terms than would be choices based upon the physical size or blood type of applicants. Thus, the Supreme Court has long held that governmental actors cannot justify their decisions solely because of race. . . .

Accordingly, we see the caselaw as sufficiently established that the use of ethnic diversity simply to achieve racial heterogeneity, even as part of the consideration of a number of factors, is unconstitutional. Were we to decide otherwise, we would contravene precedent that we are not authorized to challenge.

While the use of race *per se* is proscribed, state-supported schools may reasonably consider a host of factors—some of which may have some correlation with race—in making admissions decisions. The federal courts have no warrant to intrude on those executive and legislative judgments unless the distinctions intrude on specific provisions of federal law or the Constitution.

A university may properly favor one applicant over another because of his ability to play the cello, make a downfield tackle, or understand chaos theory. An admissions process may also consider an applicant's home state or relationship to school alumni. Law schools specifically may look at things such as unusual or substantial extracurricular activities in college, which may be atypical factors affecting undergraduate grades. Schools may even consider factors such as whether an applicant's parents attended college or the applicant's economic and social background.

For this reason, race often is said to be justified in the diversity context, not on its own terms, but as a proxy for other characteristics that institutions of higher education value but that do not raise similar constitutional concerns. Unfortunately, this approach simply replicates the very harm that the Fourteenth Amendment was designed to eliminate.

The assumption is that a certain individual possesses characteristics by virtue of being a member of a certain racial group. This assumption, however, does not withstand scrutiny. . . .

To believe that a person's race controls his point of view is to stereotype him. . . .

Instead, individuals, with their own conceptions of life, further diversity of viewpoint. Plaintiff Hopwood is a fair example of an applicant with a unique background. She is the now-thirty-two-year-old wife of a member of the Armed Forces stationed in San Antonio and, more significantly, is raising a severely handicapped child. Her circumstance would bring a different perspective to the law school. The school might consider this an advantage to her in the application process, or it could decide that her family situation would be too much of a burden on her academic performance.

We do not opine on which way the law school should weigh Hopwood's qualifications; we only observe that "diversity" can take many forms. To foster such diversity, state universities and law schools and other governmental entities must scrutinize applicants individually, rather than resorting to the dangerous proxy of race.

The Court also has recognized that government's use of racial classifications serves to stigmatize. . . . While one might argue that the stigmatization resulting from so-called "benign" racial classifications is not as harmful as that arising from invidious ones, the current Court has now retreated from the idea that so-called benign and invidious classifications may be distinguished. . . .

Finally, the use of race to achieve diversity undercuts the ultimate goal of the Fourteenth Amendment: the end of racially-motivated state action. . . .

In sum, the use of race to achieve a diverse student body, whether as a proxy for permissible characteristics, simply cannot be a state interest compelling enough to meet the steep standard of strict scrutiny. These latter factors may, in fact, turn out to be substantially correlated with race, but the key is that race itself not be taken into account. Thus, that portion of the district court's opinion upholding the diversity rationale is reversibly flawed.

B

We now turn to the district court's determination that "the remedial purpose of the law school's affirmative action program is a compelling government objective." 861 F.Supp. at 573. The plaintiffs argue that the court erred by finding that the law school could employ racial criteria to remedy the present effects of past discrimination in Texas's primary and secondary schools. The plaintiffs contend that the proper unit for analysis is the law school, and the state has shown no recognizable present effects of the law school's past discrimination. The law school, in response, notes Texas's well-documented history of discrimination in education and argues that its effects continue today at the law school, both in the level of educational attainment of the average minority applicant and in the school's reputation.

[7] In contrast to its approach to the diversity rationale, a majority of the Supreme Court has held that a state actor may racially classify where it has a "strong basis in the evidence for its conclusion that remedial action was necessary." . . .

1

The Supreme Court has "insisted upon some showing of prior discrimination by the governmental unit involved before allowing limited use of racial classifications in order to remedy such discrimination." . . .

Strict scrutiny is meant to ensure that the purpose of a racial preference is remedial. Yet when one state actor begins to justify racial preferences based upon the actions of other state agencies, the remedial actor's competence to determine the existence and scope of the harm—and the appropriate reach of the remedy—is called into question. The school desegregation cases, for example, concentrate on school districts—singular government units—and the use of interdistrict remedies is strictly limited. . . .

Here, however, the law school has no comparative advantage in measuring the present effects of discrimination in primary and secondary schools in Texas. Such a task becomes even more improbable where, as here, benefits are conferred on students who attended out-of-state or private schools for such education. Such boundless "remedies" raise a constitutional concern beyond mere competence. In this situation, an inference is raised that the program was the result of racial social engineering rather a desire to implement a remedy.

No one disputes that in the past, Texas state actors have discriminated against some minorities in public schools. In this sense, some lingering effects of such discrimination is not "societal," if that term is meant to exclude all state action. But the very program at issue here shows how remedying such past wrongs may be expanded beyond any reasonable limits.

Even if, *arguendo,* the state is the proper government unit to scrutinize, the law school's admissions program would not withstand our review. For the admissions scheme to pass constitutional muster, the State of Texas, through its legislature, would have to find that past segregation has present effects; it would have to determine the magnitude of those present effects; and it would need to limit carefully the "plus" given to applicants to remedy that harm. A broad program that sweeps in all minorities with a remedy that is in no way related to past harms cannot survive constitutional scrutiny. Obviously, none of those predicates has been satisfied here.

We further reject the proposition that the University of Texas System, rather than the law school, is the appropriate governmental unit for measuring a constitutional remedy. The law school operates as a functionally separate unit within the system. As with all law schools, it maintains its own separate admissions program. The law school hires faculty members that meet the unique requirements of a law school and has its own deans for administrative purposes. Thus, for much the same reason that we rejected the educational system as the proper measure—generally ensuring that the legally-imposed racially discriminatory program is remedial—we conclude that the University of Texas System is itself too expansive an entity to scrutinize for past discrimination.

In sum, for purposes of determining whether the law school's admissions system properly can act as a remedy for the present effects of past discrimination, we must identify the law school as the relevant alleged past discriminator. The fact that the law school ultimately may be subject to the directives of others, such as the board of regents, the university president, or the legislature, does not change the fact that the relevant putative discriminator in this case is still the law school. In order for any of these entities to direct a racial preference program at the law school, it must be because of past wrongs at that school. . . .

In such a case, one cannot conclude that a hostile environment is the present effect of past discrimination. Any racial tension at the law school is most certainly the result of present societal discrimination and, if anything, is contributed to, rather than alleviated by, the overt and prevalent consideration of race in admissions.

Even if the law school's alleged current lingering reputation in the minority community—and the perception that the school is a hostile environment for minorities—were considered to be the present effects of past discrimination, rather than the result of societal discrimination, they could not constitute compelling state interests justifying the use of racial classifications in admissions. A bad reputation within the minority community is alleviated not by the consideration of race in admissions, but by school action designed directly to enhance its reputation in that community.

Minority students who are aided by the law school's racial preferences have already made the decision to apply, despite the reputation. And, while prior knowledge that they will get a "plus" might make potential minorities more likely to apply, such an inducement does nothing, *per se*, to change any hostile environment. As we have noted, racial preferences, if anything, can compound the problem of a hostile environment. . . .

VI

In summary, we hold that the University of Texas School of Law may not use race as a factor in deciding which applicants to admit in order to achieve a diverse student body, to combat the perceived effects of a hostile environment at the law school, to alleviate the law school's poor reputation in the minority community, or to eliminate any present effects of past discrimination by actors other than the law school. Because the law school has proffered these justifications for its use of race in admissions, the plaintiffs have satisfied their burden of showing that they were scrutinized under an unconstitutional admissions system. The plaintiffs are entitled to reapply under an admissions system that invokes none of these serious constitutional infirmities. We also direct the district court to reconsider the question of damages, and we conclude that the proposed intervenors properly were denied intervention.

Louie v. *Bamboo Gardens et al.*

67 Ida. 469, 185 P.2d 712 (1947)

MILLER, Justice.

This case was submitted to the Industrial Accident Board on a stipulation of the facts as agreed to between the parties, and from which, among other things, it is made to appear:

That Tom Louie, claimant and appellant, about 45 years of age, on the 18th day of October, 1946, and for more than three months prior thereto, was in the employ of the Bamboo Gardens, a restaurant in Boise, Idaho, as a dishwasher therein; that he was casually acquainted with one Fook Lee Hong, another Chinaman, but that said Hong was not a patron of the Bamboo Gardens, nor a customer thereof in that he had never taken his meals thereat and was in nowise interested therein. September 21, 1946, Fook Lee Hong and three other Chinese were arrested on a narcotic charge by officials of the United States; that during the latter part of September 1946, Hong was fined $50 by the U. S. District Judge, at Boise, Idaho, on account of his plea to said charge and thereupon discharged from further custody. Hong was a discharged veteran of World War II. After his discharge for the violation of the Narcotic Act, 26 U.S.C.A. Int. Rev. Code, §§ 2550 et seq., 3220 et seq., he seems to have labored under the delusion that it was thought that he had turned "State's evidence," and that someone was going to kill him. After his said discharge and prior to October 18, 1946, he stated to an Assistant United States District Attorney that members of a tong society to which Tom Louie belonged, and to which Hong did not belong were going to import "hatchet men" from Walla Walla, Washington to Boise, Idaho to kill him because members of such tong thought he had turned State's evidence against his former companions on the narcotic charge; that for several days before October 18, 1946, he was more or less in hiding at the American Legion Building in Boise, Idaho, asserting that someone was going to kill him. The Prosecuting Attorney of Ada County, Idaho, made an investigation and found there were no reasonable grounds for his suspicions that someone was going to kill him, but in his own mind he suffered the delusion that an attempt would be made upon his life.

October 18, 1946, at about 5:45 P.M., Tom Louie, claimant and appellant, received an injury, during his regular hours, and in the course of his employment, and while he was on duty performing the tasks for which he was employed at his employer's place of business, at 107 South 7th Street, Boise, Idaho, in that while taking water glasses from the kitchen to the serving table in the dining room, Fook Lee Hong entered the restaurant by the front door on 7th Street, carrying a loaded 38 caliber revolver, which he brandished in a threatening manner, and then shot the same within the restaurant three times, one of which shots struck Tom Louie, claimant and appellant, in the upper back region, piercing his chest cavity and his lungs. The employer was notified of such accident and injury sustained by said claimant and appellant, during the evening of October 18, 1946, and that a claim in writing, stating the name and address of the employer, the time, place, nature and cause of the injury, signed by claimant and appellant, was filed with the Industrial Accident Board on October 30, 1946; that as the result of the injury sustained, claimant and appellant was hospitalized at St. Luke's Hospital at Boise, Idaho, for a period commencing the evening of October 18, 1946, and until and including November 9, 1946, and that the hospital and medical charges in the sum of $475.55 were paid by claimant and appellant; that claimant and appellant was under medical care at the time of filing the stipulation of facts with the Industrial Accident Board and that at the time he was totally disabled for work and would continue to be so totally disabled for a period of time subsequently to be determined; that he was not then surgically healed and whether or not he will sustain a permanent injury is yet to be determined as well as the degree thereof, if permanent injury results therefrom.

On or about October 21, 1946, a criminal complaint was filed against Fook Lee Hong by the Prosecuting Attorney of Boise, Idaho, and on October 31, 1946, Hong was held by the Committing Magistrate to answer to the District Court for the crime of assaulting Tom Louie with a deadly weapon with intent to commit murder. An information was filed in said District Court, November 1, 1946, charging Hong with an assault to commit murder. A plea was interposed under I.C.A. Sec. 19-3202, that Fook Lee Hong was insane. The issue was tried to a jury, which returned a verdict of insanity and which was duly filed and entered in said District Court on November 18, 1946. November 20, 1946, the said District Court made and entered its commitment, committing Hong to the State Hospital South at Blackfoot, Idaho, by virtue of his having been found insane as aforesaid.

The Industrial Accident Board considered the stipulated facts and on January 6, 1947, made and entered its findings of fact, rules of law and order dismissing appellant's claim. The findings of fact follow very closely the stipulation. Finding No. 7, among other things, recites as follows: "The sole issue presented is one of law. It is conceded that the accidental injury to claimant Tom Louie arose in the course of his employment by the Bamboo Gardens. The precise issue is whether said accidental injury arose out of such employment." There is no dispute as to the facts.

. . .

We fail to find any evidence that would indicate that Fook Lee Hong, at the time he entered the restaurant at which Tom Louie was employed, or at the time he fired the shot resulting in the accidental injury of said Tom Louie, was looking for the appellant and had a real or imaginary grievance against him. There is no evidence to the effect that at the time Hong entered the restaurant that he knew that Tom Louie was employed there or that he would find him therein. In the conversation he had with various officials, no mention was ever made of Tom Louie and the only manner in which Tom Louie seems to have been connected with his delusion, is that Louie was a member of a tong that Hong asserted was going to bring in hatchet men from Walla Walla to kill him.

It may, however, be of no significance as to whether or not said Hong was looking for Tom Louie at the time he shot him and had either a real or imaginary grievance against him. The fact remains that it was an accidental injury and under the Workmen's Compensation Law, claimant and appellant is entitled to receive compensation as a result of said injury.

. . .

. . . The modern tendency of the decisions, in keeping with the spirit of the law, is to award compensation in all cases where a liberal construction of the statute would justify it. Even in view of this liberal construction, it is not enough for the applicant to say that the accident would not have happened if he had not been engaged in the particular employment or if he had not been at the particular place. He must go further and say that the accident arose because of something he was doing in the course of his employment and because he was exposed by the nature of his employment to some particular danger.

. . .

It would seem that the evidence in this case is such as justifies the conclusion that the injury was the result of a risk to which appellant was subjected in the course of his employment, and to which he would not have been subjected had he not been so employed. Appellant was injured not merely because he was a dishwasher in the Bamboo Gardens' restaurant, but because he was an employee within the Bamboo Gardens restaurant, and engaged in the performance of duties which his employment imposed upon him. It was his employment that placed him in the position and environment wherein he was assaulted and sustained the accidental injury. Appellant did not in any manner provoke the assault and attending accidental injury. At the precise time of the injury he was placed and engaged in the business of his employer. There is nothing to show that the brandishing of the pistol and the firing thereof was a deliberate intention to injure appellant. The intention of the assailant from the record may have been limited to "shooting up the place," and that it was a random shot that struck appellant.

. . .

The order of the board denying compensation constitutes a clear error of law. The order is, therefore, vacated and set aside, with directions to conduct such proceedings as may be necessary in a further consideration of appellant's claim and to make such findings and award as the evidence and law require consistent with the views herein expressed. Costs to appellant.

Marvin v. *Marvin*

18 Cal.3d 660, 557 P.2d 106, 134 Cal.R. 815 (1976)

TOBRINER, Justice.

. . .

Plaintiff avers that in October of 1964 she and defendant "entered into an oral agreement" that while "the parties lived together they would combine their efforts and earnings and would share equally any and all property accumulated as a result of their efforts whether individual or combined." Furthermore, they agreed to "hold themselves out to the general public as husband and wife" and that "plaintiff would further render her services as a companion, homemaker, housekeeper and cook to . . . defendant."

Shortly thereafter plaintiff agreed to "give up her lucrative career as an entertainer [and] singer" in order to "devote her full time to defendant . . . as a companion, homemaker, housekeeper and cook;" in return defendant agreed to "provide for all of plaintiff's financial support and needs for the rest of her life."

Plaintiff alleges that she lived with defendant from October of 1964 through May of 1970 and fulfilled her obligations under the agreement. During this period the parties as a result of their efforts and earnings acquired in defendant's name substantial real and personal property, including motion picture rights worth over $1 million. In May of 1970, however, defendant compelled plaintiff to leave his household. He continued to support plaintiff until November of 1971, but thereafter refused to provide further support.

On the basis of these allegations plaintiff asserts two causes of action. The first, for declaratory relief, asks the court to determine her contract and property rights; the second seeks to impose a constructive trust upon one half of the property acquired during the course of the relationship.

Defendant demurred unsuccessfully, and then answered the complaint. Following extensive discovery and pretrial proceedings, the case came to trial. Defendant renewed his attack on the complaint by a motion to dismiss. . . .

After hearing argument the court granted defendant's motion and entered judgment for defendant. . . . [Plaintiff] appealed from the judgment.

Defendant first and principally relies on the contention that the alleged contract is so closely related to the supposed "immoral" character of the relationship between plaintiff and himself that the enforcement of the contract would violate public policy. He points to cases asserting that a contract between nonmarital partners is unenforceable if it is "involved in" an illicit relationship . . . or made in "contemplation" of such a relationship. . . . A review of the numerous California decisions concerning contracts between nonmarital partners, however, reveals that the courts have not employed such broad and uncertain standards to strike down contracts. The decisions instead disclose a narrower and more precise standard: a contract between nonmarital partners is unenforceable only *to the extent* that it *explicitly* rests upon the immoral and illicit consideration of meretricious sexual services.

. . .

Although the past decisions hover over the issue in the somewhat wispy form of the figures of a Chagall painting, we can abstract from those decisions a clear and simple rule. The fact that a man and woman live together without marriage, and engage in a sexual relationship, does not in itself invalidate agreements between them relating to their earnings, property, or expenses. Neither is such an agreement invalid merely because the parties may have contemplated the creation or continuation of a nonmarital relationship when they entered into it. Agreements between nonmarital partners fail only to the extent that they rest upon a consideration of meretricious sexual services. Thus the rule asserted by defendant, that a contract fails if it is "involved in" or made "in contemplation" of a nonmarital relationship, cannot be reconciled with the decisions.

. . .

In summary, we base our opinion on the principle that adults who voluntarily live together and engage in sexual relations are nonetheless as competent as any other persons to contract respecting their earnings and property rights. Of course, they cannot lawfully contract to pay for the performance of sexual services, for such a contract is, in essence, an agreement for prostitution and unlawful for that reason. But they may agree to pool their earnings and to hold all property acquired during the relationship in accord with the law governing community property; conversely they may agree that each partner's earnings and the property acquired from those earnings remains the separate property of the earning partner. So long as the agreement does not rest upon illicit meretricious consideration, the parties may order their economic affairs as they choose, and no policy precludes the courts from enforcing such agreements.

In the present instance, plaintiff alleges that the parties agreed to pool their earnings, that they contracted to share equally in all property acquired, and that defendant agreed to support plaintiff. The terms of the contract as alleged do not rest upon any unlawful consideration. We therefore conclude that the complaint furnishes a suitable basis upon which the trial court can render declaratory relief. . . . The trial court consequently erred in granting defendant's motion for judgment on the pleadings.

. . .

. . . [We] believe that the prevalence of nonmarital relationships in modern society and the social acceptance of them, marks this as a time when our courts should by no means apply the doctrine of the unlawfulness of the so-called meretricious relationship to the instant case. As we have explained, the nonenforceability of agreements expressly providing for meretricious conduct rested upon the fact that such conduct, as the word suggests, pertained to and encompassed prostitution. To equate the nonmarital relationship of today to such a subject matter is to do violence to an accepted and wholly different practice.

We are aware that many young couples live together without the solemnization of marriage, in order to make sure that they can successfully later undertake marriage. This trial period, preliminary to marriage, serves as some assurance that the marriage will not subsequently end in dissolution to the harm of both parties. We are aware, as we have stated, of the pervasiveness of nonmarital relationships in other situations.

The mores of the society have indeed changed so radically in regard to cohabitation that we cannot impose a standard based on alleged moral considerations that have apparently been so widely abandoned by so many. Lest we be misunderstood, however, we take this occasion to point out that the structure of society itself largely depends upon the institution of marriage, and nothing we have said in this opinion should be taken to derogate from that institution. The joining of the man and woman in marriage is at once the most socially productive and individually fulfilling relationship that one can enjoy in the course of a lifetime.

· · ·

We conclude that the judicial barriers that may stand in the way of a policy based upon the fulfillment of the reasonable expectations of the parties to a nonmarital relationship should be removed. As we have explained, the courts now hold that express agreements will be enforced unless they rest on an unlawful meretricious consideration. We add that in the absence of an express agreement, the courts may look to a variety of other remedies in order to protect the parties' lawful expectations.

The courts may inquire into the conduct of the parties to determine whether that conduct demonstrates an implied contract or implied agreement of partnership or joint venture (see *Estate of Thornton* (1972) 81 Wash.2d 72, 499 P.2d 864), or some other tacit understanding between the parties. The courts may, when appropriate, employ principles of constructive trust (see *Omer v. Omer* (1974) 11 Wash. App. 386, 523 P.2d 957) or resulting trust (see *Hyman v. Hyman* (Tex. Civ. App. 1954) 275 S.W.2d 149). Finally, a nonmarital partner may recover in quantum meruit for the reasonable value of household services rendered less the reasonable value of support received if he can show that he rendered services with the expectation of monetary reward. (See *Hill v. Estate of Westbrook, supra,* 39 Cal.2d 458, 462, 247 P.2d 19.)

Since we have determined that plaintiff's complaint states a cause of action for breach of an express contract, and, as we have explained, can be amended to state a cause of action independent of allegations of express contract, we must conclude that the trial court erred in granting defendant a judgment on the pleadings.

The judgment is reversed and the cause remanded for further proceedings consistent with the views expressed herein.

WRIGHT, C. J., and McCOMB, MOSK, SULLIVAN and RICHARDSON, JJ., concur.

In the Matter of Baby M

109 N.J. 396, 537 A.2d 1227 (1988)

The opinion of the Court was delivered by
WILENTZ, C. J.

In this matter the Court is asked to determine the validity of a contract that purports to provide a new way of bringing children into a family. For a fee of $10,000, a woman agrees to be artificially inseminated with the semen of another woman's husband; she is to conceive a child, carry it to term, and after its birth surrender it to the natural father and his wife. The intent of the contract is that the child's natural mother will thereafter be forever separated from her child. The wife is to adopt the child, and she and the natural father are to be regarded as its parents for all purposes. The contract providing for this is called a "surrogacy contract," the natural mother inappropriately called the "surrogate mother."

We invalidate the surrogacy contract because it conflicts with the law and public policy of this State. While we recognize the depth of the yearning of infertile couples to have their own children, we find the payment of money to a "surrogate" mother illegal, perhaps criminal, and potentially degrading to women. Although in this case we grant custody to the natural father, the evidence having clearly proved such custody to be in the best interests of the infant, we void both the termination of the surrogate mother's parental rights and the adoption of the child by the wife / stepparent. We thus restore the "surrogate" as the mother of the child. We remand the issue of the natural mother's visitation rights to the trial court, since that issue was not reached below and the record before us is not sufficient to permit us to decide it *de novo.* . . .

I
FACTS

In February 1985, William Stern and Mary Beth Whitehead entered into a surrogacy contract. It recited that Stern's wife, Elizabeth, was infertile, that they wanted a child, and that Mrs. Whitehead was willing to provide that child as the mother with Mr. Stern as the father.

The contract provided that through artificial insemination using Mr. Stern's sperm, Mrs. Whitehead would become pregnant, carry the child to term, bear it, deliver it to the Sterns, and thereafter do whatever was necessary to terminate her maternal rights so that Mrs. Stern could thereafter adopt the child. Mrs. Whitehead's husband, Richard, was also a party to the contract; Mrs. Stern was not. Mr. Whitehead promised to do all acts necessary to rebut the presumption of paternity under the Parentage Act. *N.J.S.A.* 9:17-43a(1), -44a. Although Mrs. Stern was not a party to the surrogacy agreement, the contract gave her sole custody of the child in the event of Mr. Stern's death. Mrs. Stern's status as a nonparty to the surrogate parenting agreement presumably was to avoid the application of the baby-selling statute to this arrangement. *N.J.S.A.* 9:3-54.

Mr. Stern, on his part, agreed to attempt the artificial insemination and to pay Mrs. Whitehead $10,000 after the child's birth, on its delivery to him. In a separate contract, Mr. Stern agreed to pay $7,500 to the Infertility Center of New York ("ICNY"). The Center's advertising campaigns solicit surrogate mothers and encourage infertile couples to consider surrogacy. ICNY arranged for the surrogacy contract by bringing the parties together, explaining the process to them, furnishing the contractual form, and providing legal counsel.

The history of the parties' involvement in this arrangement suggests their good faith. William and Elizabeth Stern were married in July 1974, having met at the University of Michigan, where both were Ph.D. candidates. Due to financial considerations and Mrs. Stern's pursuit of a medical degree and residency, they decided to defer starting a family until 1981. Before then, however, Mrs. Stern learned that she might have multiple sclerosis and that the disease in some cases renders pregnancy a serious health risk. Her anxiety appears to have exceeded the actual risk, which current medical authorities assess as minimal. Nonetheless that anxiety was evidently quite real, Mrs. Stern fearing that pregnancy might precipitate blindness, paraplegia, or other forms of debilitation. Based on the perceived risk, the Sterns decided to forego having their own children. The decision had special significance for Mr. Stern. Most of his family had been destroyed in the Holocaust. As the family's only survivor, he very much wanted to continue his bloodline.

Initially the Sterns considered adoption, but were discouraged by the substantial delay apparently involved and by the potential problem they saw arising from their age and their differing religious backgrounds. They were most eager for some other means to start a family.

The paths of Mrs. Whitehead and the Sterns to surrogacy were similar. Both responded to advertising by ICNY. The Sterns' response, following their inquiries into adoption, was the result of their longstanding decision to have a child. Mrs. Whitehead's response apparently resulted from her sympathy with family members and others who could have no children (she stated that she wanted to give another couple the "gift of life"); she also wanted the $10,000 to help her family.

. . . On February 6, 1985, Mr. Stern and Mr. and Mrs. Whitehead executed the surrogate parenting agreement. After several artificial inseminations over a period of months, Mrs. Whitehead became pregnant. The pregnancy was uneventful and on March 27, 1986, Baby M was born.

Not wishing anyone at the hospital to be aware of the surrogacy arrangement, Mr. and Mrs.

Whitehead appeared to all as the proud parents of a healthy female child. Her birth certificate indicated her name to be Sara Elizabeth Whitehead and her father to be Richard Whitehead. In accordance with Mrs. Whitehead's request, the Sterns visited the hospital unobtrusively to see the newborn child.

Mrs. Whitehead realized, almost from the moment of birth, that she could not part with this child. She had felt a bond with it even during pregnancy. Some indication of the attachment was conveyed to the Sterns at the hospital when they told Mrs. Whitehead what they were going to name the baby. She apparently broke into tears and indicated that she did not know if she could give up the child. She talked about how the baby looked like her other daughter, and made it clear that she was experiencing great difficulty with the decision.

Nonetheless, Mrs. Whitehead was, for the moment, true to her word. Despite powerful inclinations to the contrary, she turned her child over to the Sterns on March 30 at the Whiteheads' home. . . .

Later in the evening of March 30, Mrs. Whitehead became deeply disturbed, disconsolate, stricken with unbearable sadness. She had to have her child. She could not eat, sleep, or concentrate on anything other than her need for her baby. The next day she went to the Sterns' home and told them how much she was suffering.

The depth of Mrs. Whitehead's despair surprised and frightened the Sterns. She told them that she could not live without her baby, that she must have her, even if only for one week, that thereafter she would surrender her child. The Sterns, concerned that Mrs. Whitehead might indeed commit suicide, not wanting under any circumstances to risk that, and in any event believing that Mrs. Whitehead would keep her word, turned the child over to her.

The struggle over Baby M began when it became apparent that Mrs. Whitehead could not return the child to Mr. Stern. Due to Mrs. Whitehead's refusal to relinquish the baby, Mr. Stern filed a complaint seeking enforcement of the surrogacy contract. . . .

The Whiteheads immediately fled to Florida with Baby M. They stayed initially with Mrs. Whitehead's parents, where one of Mrs. Whitehead's children had been living. For the next three months, the Whiteheads and Melissa lived at roughly twenty different hotels, motels, and homes in order to avoid apprehension. . . .

Eventually the Sterns discovered where the Whiteheads were staying, commenced supplementary proceedings in Florida, and obtained an order requiring the Whiteheads to turn over the child. Police in Florida enforced the order, forcibly removing the child from her grandparents' home. She was soon thereafter brought to New Jersey and turned over to the Sterns. The prior order of the court, issued *ex parte,* awarding custody of the child to the Sterns *pendente lite,* was reaffirmed by the trial court after consideration of the certified representations of the parties (both represented by counsel) concerning the unusual sequence of events that had unfolded. Pending final judgment, Mrs. Whitehead was awarded limited visitation with Baby M.

The Sterns' complaint, in addition to seeking possession and ultimately custody of the child, sought enforcement of the surrogacy contract. Pursuant to the contract, it asked that the child be permanently placed in their custody, that Mrs. Whitehead's parental rights be terminated, and that Mrs. Stern be allowed to adopt the child, *i.e.,* that, for all purposes, Melissa become the Sterns' child. . . .

[The trial court] held that the surrogacy contract was valid; ordered that Mrs. Whitehead's parental rights be terminated and that sole custody of the child be granted to Mr. Stern; and, after hearing brief testimony from Mrs. Stern, immediately entered an order allowing the adoption of Melissa by Mrs. Stern, all in accordance with the surrogacy contract. Pending the outcome of the appeal, we granted a continuation of visitation to Mrs. Whitehead, although slightly more limited than the visitation allowed during the trial. . . .

Mrs. Whitehead appealed. . . .

II
INVALIDITY AND UNENFORCEABILITY OF SURROGACY CONTRACT

We have concluded that this surrogacy contract is invalid. Our conclusion has two bases: direct conflict with existing statutes and conflict with the public policies of this State, as expressed in its statutory and decisional law. . . .

A. Conflict with Statutory Provisions

The surrogacy contract conflicts with: (1) laws prohibiting the use of money in connection with adoptions; (2) laws requiring proof of parental unfitness or abandonment before termination of parental rights is ordered or an adoption is granted; and (3) laws that make surrender of custody and consent to adoption revocable in private placement adoptions. . . .

(2) The termination of Mrs. Whitehead's parental rights, called for by the surrogacy contract and actually ordered by the court, 217 *N.J. Super.* at 399–400, 525 *A.*2d 1128, fails to comply with the stringent requirements of New Jersey law. Our law, recognizing the finality of any termination of parental rights, provides for such termination only where there has been a voluntary surrender of a child to an approved agency or to the Division of Youth and Family Services ("DYFS"), accompanied by a formal document acknowledging termination of parental rights, *N.J.S.A.* 9:2-16, –17; *N.J.S.A.* 9:3-41; *N.J.S.A.* 30:4C–23, or where there has been a showing of parental abandonment or unfitness. . . .

B. Public Policy Considerations

The surrogacy contract's invalidity, resulting from its direct conflict with the above statutory provisions, is further underlined when its goals and means are measured against New Jersey's public policy. The contract's basic premise, that the natural parents can decide in advance of birth which one is to have custody of the child, bears no relationship to the settled law that the child's best interests shall determine custody. . . .

The fact that the trial court remedied that aspect of the contract through the "best interests" phase does not make the contractual provision any less offensive to the public policy of this State.

The surrogacy contract guarantees permanent separation of the child from one of its natural parents. Our policy, however, has long been that to the extent possible, children should remain with and be brought up by both of their natural parents. That was the first stated purpose of the previous adoption act, *L.*1953, *c.* 264, § 1, codified at *N.J.S.A.* 9:3-17 (repealed): "it is necessary and desirable (a) to protect the child from unnecessary separation from his natural parents. . . ." While not so stated in the present adoption law, this purpose remains part of the public policy of this State. . . . This is not simply some theoretical ideal that in practice has no meaning. The impact of failure to follow that policy is nowhere better shown than in the results of this surrogacy contract. A child, instead of starting off its life with as much peace and security as possible, finds itself immediately in a tug-of-war between contending mother and father.

The surrogacy contract violates the policy of this State that the rights of natural parents are equal concerning their child, the father's right no greater than the mother's. . . .

The policies expressed in our comprehensive laws governing consent to the surrender of a child . . . stand in stark contrast to the surrogacy contract and what it implies. Here there is no counseling, independent or otherwise, of the natural mother, no evaluation, no warning. . . .

Under the contract, the natural mother is irrevocably committed before she knows the strength of her bond with her child. She never makes a totally voluntary, informed decision, for quite clearly any decision prior to the baby's birth is, in the most important sense, uninformed, and any decision after that, compelled by a pre-existing contractual commitment, the threat of a lawsuit, and the inducement of a $10,000 payment, is less than totally voluntary. Her interests are of little concern to those who controlled this transaction.

Although the interest of the natural father and adoptive mother is certainly the predominant interest, realistically the *only* interest served, even they are left with less than what public policy requires. They know little about the natural mother, her genetic makeup, and her psychological and medical history. Moreover, not even a superficial attempt is made to determine their awareness of their responsibilities as parents.

Worst of all, however, is the contract's total disregard of the best interests of the child. There is not the slightest suggestion that any inquiry will be made at any time to determine the fitness of the Sterns as custodial parents, of Mrs. Stern as an adoptive parent, their superiority to Mrs. Whitehead, or the effect on the child of not living with her natural mother.

This is the sale of a child, or, at the very least, the sale of a mother's right to her child, the only mitigating factor being that one of the purchasers is the father. Almost every evil that prompted the prohibition on the payment of money in connection with adoptions exists here. . . .

First, and perhaps most important, all parties concede that it is unlikely that surrogacy will survive without money. Despite the alleged selfless motivation of surrogate mothers, if there is no payment, there will be no surrogates, or very few. That conclusion contrasts with adoption; for obvious reasons, there remains a steady supply, albeit insufficient, despite the prohibitions against payment. The adoption itself, relieving the natural mother of the financial burden of supporting an infant, is in some sense the equivalent of payment.

Second, the use of money in adoptions does not *produce* the problem—conception occurs, and usually the birth itself, before illicit funds are offered. With surrogacy, the "problem," if one views it as such, consisting of the purchase of a woman's procreative capacity, at the risk of her life, is caused by and originates with the offer of money.

Third, with the law prohibiting the use of money in connection with adoptions, the built-in financial pressure of the unwanted pregnancy and the consequent support obligation do not lead the mother to the highest paying, ill-suited, adoptive parents. She is just as well-off surrendering the child to an approved agency. In surrogacy, the highest bidders will presumably become the adoptive parents regardless of suitability, so long as payment of money is permitted.

Fourth, the mother's consent to surrender her child in adoptions is revocable, even after surrender of the child, unless it be to an approved agency, where by regulation there are protections against an ill-advised surrender. In surrogacy, consent occurs so early that no amount of advice would satisfy the potential mother's need, yet the consent is irrevocable.

The main difference, that the unwanted pregnancy is unintended while the situation of the surrogate mother is voluntary and intended, is really not significant. Initially, it produces stronger reactions of sympathy for the mother whose pregnancy was unwanted than for the surrogate mother, who "went into this with her eyes wide open." On reflection, however, it appears that the essential evil is the same, taking advantage of a woman's circumstances (the unwanted pregnancy or the need for money) in order to take away her child, the difference being one of degree. . . .

The surrogacy contract is based on, principles that are directly contrary to the objectives of our laws. It guarantees the separation of a child from its mother; it looks to adoption regardless of suitability; it totally ignores the child; it takes the child from the mother regardless of her wishes and her maternal fitness; and it does all of this, it accomplishes all of its goals, through the use of money.

Beyond that is the potential degradation of some women that may result from this arrangement. In many cases, of course, surrogacy may bring satisfaction, not only to the infertile couple, but to the surrogate mother herself. The fact, however, that many women may not perceive surrogacy negatively but rather see it as an opportunity does not diminish its potential for devastation to other women.

In sum, the harmful consequences of this surrogacy arrangement appear to us all too palpable. In New Jersey the surrogate mother's agreement to sell her child is void. Its irrevocability infects the entire contract, as does the money that purports to buy it. . . .

Nothing in this record justifies a finding that would allow a court to terminate Mary Beth Whitehead's parental rights under the statutory standard. It is not simply that obviously there was no "intentional abandonment or very substantial neglect of parental duties without a reasonable expectation of reversal of that conduct in the future," *N.J.S.A.* 9:3-48c(1), quite the contrary, but furthermore that the trial court never found Mrs. Whitehead an unfit mother and indeed affirmatively stated that Mary Beth Whitehead had been a good mother to her other children. 217 *N.J.Super.* at 397, 525 A.2d 1128. . . .

. . . We now must decide the custody question without regard to the provisions of the surrogacy contract that would give Mr. Stern sole and permanent custody. (That does not mean that the existence of the contract and the circumstances under which it was entered may not be considered to the extent deemed relevant to the child's best interests.) With the surrogacy contract disposed of, the legal framework becomes a dispute between two couples over the custody of a child produced by the artificial insemination of one couple's wife by the other's husband.

We note again that the trial court's reasons for determining what were the child's best interests were somewhat different from ours. It concluded that the surrogacy contract was valid, but that it could not grant specific performance unless to do so was in the child's best interests. The approach was that of a Chancery judge, unwilling to give extraordinary remedies unless they well served the most important interests, in this case, the interests of the child. While substantively indistinguishable from our approach to the question of best interests, the purpose of the inquiry was not the usual purpose of determining custody, but of determining a contractual remedy.

We are not concerned at this point with the question of termination of parental rights, either those of Mrs. Whitehead or of Mr. Stern. As noted in various places in this opinion, such termination, in the absence of abandonment or a valid surrender, generally depends on a showing that the particular parent is unfit. The question of custody in this case, as in practically all cases, assumes the fitness of both parents, and no serious contention is made in this case that either is unfit. The issue here is which life would be better *for Baby M, one with primary custody in the Whiteheads or one with primary custody in the Sterns.*

Our custody conclusion is based on strongly persuasive testimony contrasting both the family life of the Whiteheads and the Sterns and the personalities and characters of the individuals. The stability of the Whitehead family life was doubtful at the time of trial. Their finances were in serious trouble (foreclosure by Mrs. Whitehead's sister on a second mortgage was in process). Mr. Whitehead's employment, though relatively steady, was always at risk because of his alcoholism, a condition that he seems not to have been able to confront effectively. Mrs. Whitehead had not worked for quite some time, her last two employments having been part-time. One of the Whiteheads' positive attributes was their ability to bring up two children, and apparently well, even in so vulnerable a household. Yet substantial question was raised even about that aspect of their home life. . . .

The Sterns have no other children, but all indications are that their household and their personalities promise a much more likely foundation for Melissa to grow and thrive. There *is* a track record of sorts—during the one-and-a-half years of custody Baby M has done very well, and the relationship between both Mr. and Mrs. Stern and the baby has become very strong. The household is stable, and likely to remain so. Their finances are more than adequate, their circle of friends supportive, and their marriage happy. Most important, they are loving, giving, nurturing, and open-minded people. They have demonstrated the wish and ability to nurture and protect Melissa, yet at the same time to encourage her independence. Their lack of experience is more than made up for by a willingness to learn and to listen, a willingness that is enhanced by their professional training, especially Mrs. Stern's experience as a pediatrician. They are honest; they can recognize error, deal with it, and learn from it. They will try to determine rationally the best way to cope with problems in their relationship with Melissa. When the time comes to tell her about her origins, they will probably have found a means of doing so that accords with the best interests of Baby M. All in all, Melissa's future appears solid, happy, and promising with them.

Based on all of this we have concluded, independent of the trial court's identical conclusion, that Melissa's best interests call for custody in the Sterns.

VI

VISITATION

The trial court's decision to terminate Mrs. Whitehead's parental rights precluded it from making any determination on visitation. 217 *N.J.Super.* at 399, 408, 525 A.2d 1128. Our reversal of the trial court's order, however, requires delineation of Mrs. Whitehead's rights to visitation. It is apparent to us that this factually sensitive issue, which was never addressed below, should not be determined *de novo* by this Court. We therefore remand the visitation issue to the trial court for an abbreviated hearing and determination as set forth below. . . .

The judgment is affirmed in part, reversed in part, and remanded for further proceedings consistent with this opinion.

Note: The visitation issue was tossed in the lap of the Chancery Division, Family Part, of the Superior Court of New Jersey, Bergen County.

On April 6, 1988, that court rendered its decision, reported as In the Matter of Baby M, 225 N.J. Super 267, 542 A.2d 52 (1988). The court described the Sterns as "extraordinarily good parents," and called Melissa a "resilient child," capable of adjusting to complex family relationships, like the "thousands of children of broken marriages."

The specific decisions with regard to visitation were as follows:

Weekly Visitation. Mary Beth Whitehead Gould shall have unsupervised visitation one day each week between the hours of 10:30 a.m. and 4:30 p.m. commencing immediately. In order to provide a transition from supervised to unsupervised visitation, William Stern shall take Melissa to the Edna Conklin Youth Center on the initial three visits and give her directly to her mother. Her mother can then take her home and return her to the Sterns' residence. Thereafter, Melissa's father shall take Melissa to her mother's residence and the mother shall return Melissa to her father's residence. Commencing in September 1988, the weekly visitation shall be increased by one additional day every other week.

Overnight Visitation. Commencing April 1989, the additional biweekly visitation days shall be expanded to two days and Melissa shall remain overnight with her mother.

Holiday Visitation. The court recognizes that the parties have two distinct family units and finds that it is in Melissa's best interest that she spend Christmas Day, Mother's Day, and Father's Day with the Sterns. Because children normally have birthday parties with their friends, Melissa shall also spend her birthdays with the Sterns. Melissa shall spend one day during the Christmas holidays and the following alternate holidays with her mother: Easter Day, Memorial Day, Fourth of July, Labor Day, and Thanksgiving Day. Melissa shall spend Jewish holidays of her father's choice with him. When a conflict occurs between a regular visitation day and a holiday Melissa will spend with her father, a mutually-convenient day for visiting with her mother shall be substituted.

Vacation Visitation. Commencing with the summer of 1989, Melissa shall spend one two-week vacation period with her mother which shall be selected no later than March 1 each year.

Notes

PREFACE

[1] John G. Wells, *Every Man His Own Lawyer and Business Form Book* (1867), pp. 3–5.

1 WHAT IS A LEGAL SYSTEM?

[1] Donald Black, *The Behavior of Law* (1976), p. 2.
[2] H. L. A. Hart, *The Concept of Law* (1961), pp. 89–96.
[3] See *Los Angeles Times*, July 6, 1996, Part A, p. 1, "When the Rules of the Road Are a Big Blur."
[4] 408 U.S. 238 (1972). Legal citations, like this one, usually begin with a volume number (here 408). They then give the name of the collection of volumes of which the volume is a part. United States Supreme Court cases are collected in a series which is abbreviated "U.S." Lower federal cases are in series abbreviated "Fed." or "F.Supp." The second number in the citation is the page number in the given volume (here 238). Last comes the date.
[5] Richard L. Abel, "A Comparative Theory of Dispute Institutions in Society," *Law & Society Review* 8:217, 227 (1973).
[6] *New York Times*, April 10, 1996, Section A, p. 20. Rostenkowski admitted guilt to two charges of mail fraud. In one case, he sent official payroll checks from his office in Washington, D.C., to Chicago, to pay employees who did personal service for him but no official work.
[7] *Blanks v. Richardson*, 439 Fed.2d 1158 (5th Cir., 1971).
[8] *McIlvaine v. Pennsylvania State Police*, 454 Pa. 129, 309 Atl.2d 801 (1973). Note the abbreviation for the state ("Pa."), which identifies the series of volumes that sets out the decisions of the highest court of Pennsylvania. "Atl." stands for "Atlantic"; the reference is to a series of volumes which groups case reports by region of the country. (Pennsylvania, Delaware, and New Jersey are among the states in the Atlantic region). If there are many volumes in a series, the numbering sometimes starts over, with a second ("2d") or even third or fourth series. There are many other tricks and conventions of citation, but those listed in these notes are perhaps the most basic.

[9] 415 U.S. 968 (1976).

[10] John H. Merryman, *The Civil Law Tradition,* 2nd ed. (1985), p. 10.

[11] See Inga Markovits, *Imperfect Justice* (1995), for an account of the demise of East German law.

[12] For a perhaps too glowing account of Cuban socialist law, see Marjorie S. Zatz, *Producing Legality: Law and Socialism in Cuba* (1994).

2 LAW: FORMAL AND INFORMAL

[1] Lon L. Fuller, *The Morality of Law* (1964), p. 106.

[2] Quoted in Stewart Macaulay, "Private Government," in Leon Lipson and Stanton Wheeler, eds., *Law and the Social Sciences* (1986), pp. 445, 450.

[3] *U.S. News & World Report,* July 2, 1984, p. 45.

[4] "Thugs in Uniform," *Time,* March 9, 1992, p. 44.

[5] Frank Morn, *The Eye That Never Sleeps: A History of the Pinkerton National Detective Agency* (1982).

[6] *Goss v. Lopez,* 419 U.S. 565 (1975).

[7] *New York Times,* May 5, 1996, p. 1; May 6, 1996, p. 1.

[8] Leigh-Wai Doo, "Dispute Settlement in Chinese-American Communities," *American Journal of Comparative Law* 21:627, 647–48 (1973).

[9] These figures are from Anne S. Kim, "Rent-A-Judges and the Cost of Selling Judges," *Duke Law Journal* 44:166 (1994).

[10] The term is from Robert Mnookin and Lewis Kornhauser, "Bargaining in the Shadow of the Law: The Case of Divorce," *Yale Law Journal* 88:950 (1979).

[11] Austin Sarat and William L. F. Felstiner, *Divorce Lawyers and Their Clients: Power and Meaning in the Legal Process* (1995), especially p. 146.

[12] Vice Commission of Chicago, *The Social Evil in Chicago* (1911), p. 329.

[13] Richard Maxwell Brown, *Strain of Violence: Historical Studies of American Violence and Vigilantism* (1974), chap. 4; on the vigilantes, see also Lawrence M. Friedman, *Crime and Punishment in American History* (1993), chap. 8.

[14] Odie B. Faulk, *Dodge City: The Most Western Town of All* (1977), p. 152.

[15] Brown, *Strain of Violence,* p. 129.

[16] *New York Times,* May 23, 1988, Section B, p. 1.

[17] Ibid., May 3, 1992, Section 1, p. 1.

[18] Brown, *Strain of Violence,* pp. 150–51; Friedman, *Crime and Punishment in American History,* pp. 186–187.

[19] John C. Schneider, *Detroit and the Problem of Order, 1830–1880* (1980), pp. 26–27.

[20] See George P. Fletcher, *A Crime of Self-Defense: Bernhard Goetz and the Law on Trial* (1988).

[21] *New York Times,* April 24, 1996, p. A1.

[22] See Pauline Maier, "Popular Uprisings and Civil Authority in Eighteenth-Century America," *William and Mary Quarterly,* 3rd ser., 27:3–35 (1970).

[23] See Allen G. Bogue, "The Iowa Claim Clubs: Symbol and Substance," *Mississippi Valley Historical Review* 45:231 (1958).

[24] Peter A. Munch, "Sociology of Tristan da Cunha," in *Results of the Norwegian Scientific Expedition to Tristan da Cunha, 1937–1938,* Erling Christopher, ed., vol. 1 (Oslo, 1946), p. 305.

[25] Quoted in Lawrence M. Friedman, *Crime and Punishment in American History* (1993), p. 37.

[26] On this theme in general, see Lawrence M. Friedman, *The Republic of Choice: Law, Authority, and Culture* (1990).

[27] *Breen v. Kahl,* 419 Fed.2d 1034 (1969).

3 THE BACKGROUND OF AMERICAN LAW

[1] On the history of American law, see, in general, Lawrence M. Friedman, *A History of American Law*, 2d ed. (1985); Kermit Hall, *The Magic Mirror: Law in American History* (1989).

[2] On the legal history of slavery, see the comprehensive study by Thomas D. Morris, *Southern Slavery and the Law, 1619–1860* (1996).

[3] Douglas Greenberg, *Crime and Law Enforcement in the Colony of New York, 1691–1776* (1976), p. 43.

[4] See Friedman, *History of American Law*, pp. 82–85; on the system in general, see Richard B. Morris, *Government and Labor in Early America* (1946); on the fate of the indentured servitude system, see Robert J. Steinfeld, *The Invention of Free Labor* (1991).

[5] Julius Goebel, Jr., "King's Law and Local Custom in Seventeenth-Century New England," *Columbia Law Review* 31:416 (1931); see David Grayson Allen, *In English Ways* (1981), pp. 208–210.

[6] Richard B. Morris, *Studies in the History of American Law*, 2nd ed. (1959), pp. 75–81.

[7] See Herbert A. Johnson, *Imported Eighteenth-Century Law Treatises in American Libraries, 1700–1799* (1978).

[8] See Benjamin H. Hibbard, *A History of the Public Land Policies* (1924; reprint 1965), pp. 1–14.

[9] George Dargo, *Jefferson's Louisiana: Politics and the Clash of Legal Traditions* (1975), pp. 156ff.

[10] Leon Litwack, *North of Slavery: The Negro in the Free States, 1790–1860* (1961), p. 3.

[11] See Thomas Morris, *Southern Slavery and the Law*; on the criminal law of slavery, see Philip J. Schwarz, *Twice Condemned: Slaves and the Criminal Laws of Virginia, 1705–1865* (1988).

[12] On auction sales: Thomas D. Russell, *Sale Day in Antebellum South Carolina: Slavery, Law, Economy, and Court-Supervised Sales* (Ph.D. dissertation, Stanford University, Department of History, 1988).

[13] *Latimer v. Alexander,* 14 Ga. 259 (1853).

[14] See Jerome H. Skolnick, *House of Cards: The Legalization and Control of Casino Gambling* (1978).

[15] On this point see Lawrence M. Friedman, "Is There a Modern Legal Culture?" *Ratio Juris* 7:117 (1994).

[16] See Norma Basch, *In the Eyes of the Law: Women, Marriage and Property in Nineteenth-Century New York* (1982).

[17] See Pete Daniel, *The Shadow of Slavery: Peonage in the South, 1901–1969* (1972).

[18] Hibbard, *Public Land Policies,* pp. 102–3.

[19] Ibid., p. 118.

[20] On the rise of divorce in the nineteenth century, and other aspects of family law, see Michael Grossberg, *Governing the Hearth: Law and the Family in Nineteenth Century America* (1985); Richard G. Chused, *Private Acts in Public Places: A Social History of Divorce in the Formative Era of American Family Law* (1994).

[21] J. Willard Hurst, *Law and Social Process in United States Social History* (1960), p. 69.

[22] *Proprietors of the Charles River Bridge v. Proprietors of the Warren Bridge,* 11 Pet. 420 (1837).

[23] The case is discussed in Stanley I. Kutler, *Privilege and Creative Destruction: The Charles River Bridge Case* (1971).

[24] Oscar and Mary Handlin, *Commonwealth: A Study of the Role of Government in the American Economy: Massachusetts, 1774–1861* (1969), p. 62. An important recent

study of regulation and government activity in the nineteenth century is William J. Novak, *The People's Welfare: Law and Regulation in Nineteenth-Century America* (1996).

[25] Stuart Bruchey, *The Roots of American Economic Growth, 1607–1861* (1968), p. 132.

[26] See, for example, William Forbath, *Law and the Shaping of the American Labor Movement* (1991).

[27] ICC Termination Act of 1995, Public Law 104–88, December 29, 1995. Some of the functions of the ICC were transferred to a Surface Transportation Board, within the Department of Transportation.

[28] See, in general, Edwin B. Firmage and Richard C. Mangrum, *Zion in the Courts: A Legal History of the Church of Jesus Christ of Latter-Day Saints* (1988).

4 THE STRUCTURE OF AMERICAN LAW: THE COURTS

[1] Maureen Mileski, "Courtroom Encounters: An Observation Study of a Lower Criminal Court," *Law & Society Review* 5:473 (1971).

[2] Beatrice Moulton, "The Persecution and Intimidation of the Low-Income Litigant as Performed by the Small-Claims Court in California," *Stanford Law Review* 21:1657, 1662 (1969).

[3] See Roselle L. Wissler, "Mediation and Adjudication in Small Claims Court: The Effects of Process and Case Characteristics," *Law & Society Review* 29:323 (1995).

[4] John A. Goerdt, "The People's Court: A Summary of Findings and Policy Implications from a Study in 12 Urban Small Claims Courts," *State Court Journal* 17 (3):38 (Summer/Fall 1993); see also "The Iowa Small Claims Court: An Empirical Analysis," *Iowa Law Review* 75:433 (1990).

[5] Judicial Council of California, *1993 Report,* p. 41.

[6] Cal. Const., Art. 6, Sec. 11.

[7] See John A. Stookey, "Creating an Intermediate Court of Appeals: Workload and Policymaking Consequences," in Philip L. Dubos, ed., *The Analysis of Judicial Reform* (1982), p. 153.

[8] Administrative Office of the Illinois Courts, *1978 Annual Report,* pp. 104, 106.

[9] *State Court Caseload Statistics,* 1994, p. 128.

[10] There are also "senior judges," who have retired and taken "senior status" but may continue to be more or less on active duty, taking cases if they wish to do so.

[11] Gerhard Casper and Richard A. Posner, *The Workload of the Supreme Court* (1976), pp. 3, 59.

[12] These statistics are from "The Supreme Court, 1994 Term, Leading Cases," *Harvard Law Review* 109:111, 344 (1995).

[13] U.S. Const., Art. III, Sec. 2 (2).

[14] *Arizona v. California,* 373 U.S. 546 (1963).

[15] Neb. Rev. Stats., Sec. 24–204.

[16] On state court organization, see Bureau of Justice Statistics, *State Court Organization 1993,* which is the source of much of the material in the text.

[17] John H. Merryman, *The Civil Law Tradition,* 2nd ed. (1985), p. 109.

[18] Sheldon Goldman, "Judicial Appointments to the United States Courts of Appeals," *Wisconsin Law Review* 1967:186.

[19] U.S. Const., Art. III, Sec. 2 (2).

[20] Cynthia O. Philip, Paul Nejelski, and Aric Press, *Where Do Judges Come From?* (Institute of Judicial Administration, 1976), introduction, pp. i, ii.

[21] Lawrence Baum, *American Courts,* 3rd ed. (1994), p. 126.

[22] Harry Kalven, Jr., and Hans Zeisel, *The American Jury* (1966).

[23] Jeffrey Abramson, *We, the Jury* (1994), p. 254.

[24] See Theodore F. T. Plucknett, *A Concise History of the Common Law*, 5th ed. (1956), pp. 673–707.

[25] Herbert Jacob, *Justice in America: Courts, Lawyers, and the Judicial Process*, 3rd ed. (1978), p. 200.

[26] *Annual Report of the Maryland Judiciary 1992–1993*, p. 66.

[27] Richard E. Miller and Austin Sarat, "Grievances, Claims, and Disputes: Assessing the Adversary Culture," *Law & Society Review* 15:525, 544 (1981).

[28] See H. Laurence Ross, *Settled Out of Court*, 2nd ed. (1980), for a general description of the process in automobile-accident cases.

[29] Robert H. Mnookin and Lewis Kornhauser, "Bargaining in the Shadow of the Law: The Case of Divorce," *Yale Law Journal* 88:950 (1979).

[30] Judicial Council of California, *1995 Annual Report*, pp. 91, 93.

[31] State of New York, *Sixteenth Annual Report of the Chief Administrator of the Courts* (1994), pp. 26, 27.

[32] Michigan State Courts, *Annual Report 1992*, p. 16.

[33] Brian J. Ostrom and Neal B. Kauder, *Examining the Work of State Courts, 1994: A National Perspective from the Court Statistics Project* (National Center for State Courts, 1996), pp. 12–13.

[34] Wayne McIntosh, *The Appeal of Civil Law: A Political-Economic Analysis of Litigation* (1990), p. 124.

[35] Ostrom and Kauder, *Examining the Work of State Courts, 1994*, p. 28.

[36] Packing Company Cases, 105 U.S. 566 (1881).

[37] Robert A. Kagan et al., "The Business of State Supreme Courts, 1870–1970," *Stanford Law Review* 30:121 (1977).

[38] See Lawrence M. Friedman, *Total Justice* (1985).

[39] On jury research, see Rita J. Simon, *The Jury: Its Role in American Society* (1980); Valerie P. Hans and Neil Vidmar, *Judging the Jury* (1986); Jeffrey Abramson, *We, the Jury* (1994).

[40] Kalven and Zeisel, *American Jury*, pp. 286–97.

[41] Abramson, *We, the Jury*, pp. 58–59.

[42] Edward C. Voss, "Dissent: Sign of a Healthy Court," *Arizona State Law Journal* 24:643, 679–80 (1992).

[43] Lawrence M. Friedman et al., "State Supreme Courts: A Century of Style and Citation," *Stanford Law Review* 33:773, 785–92 (1981).

[44] Elliot E. Slotnick, "Media Coverage of Supreme Court Decision-Making: Problems and Prospects," *Judicature* 75:128 (1991).

[45] S. Sidney Ulmer, "The Political Party Variable in the Michigan Supreme Court," *Journal of Public Law* 11:352 (1962).

[46] See Elaine Martin, "Men and Women on the Bench: Vive la Différence?" *Judicature* 73:204 (1990); Donald R. Songer, Sue Davis, and Susan Haire, "A Reappraisal of Diversification in the Federal Courts: Gender Effects in the Courts of Appeals, *Journal of Politics* 56:425 (1994).

[47] See, generally, Joel B. Grossman, "Social Backgrounds and Judicial Decision-Making," *Harvard Law Review* 79:1551 (1966).

[48] James L. Gibson, "From Simplicity to Complexity: The Development of Theory in the Study of Judicial Behavior," *Political Behavior* 5:7 (1983).

[49] John Hagan, "Extra-Legal Attributes and Criminal Sentencing: An Assessment of a Sociological Viewpoint," *Law & Society Review* 8:357 (1974).

[50] On the research in general, see Michael Tonry, *Malign Neglect: Race, Crime and Punishment in America* (1995), pp. 68–70.

[51] Ilene H. Nagel, "The Legal/Extra-Legal Controversy: Judicial Decisions in Pretrial Release," *Law & Society Review* 17:481 (1983).

[52] See Walter F. Murphy, *Elements of Judicial Strategy* (1964).

[53] Henry R. Glick, *State Courts in State Politics: An Investigation of the Judicial Role*

(1971); see also James L. Gibson, "The Role Concept in Judicial Research," *Law & Policy Quarterly* 3:291 (1981).

[54] Louis J. Sirico, Jr., and Beth A. Drew, "The Citing of Law Reviews by the United States Courts of Appeals: An Empirical Analysis," *University of Miami Law Review* 45:1051 (1991).

[55] On citation trends, see Lawrence M. Friedman et al., "State Supreme Courts: A Century of Style and Citation," *Stanford Law Review* 33:773 (1981); John H. Merryman, "Toward a Theory of Citations: An Empirical Study of the Citation Practice of the California Supreme Court in 1950, 1960, and 1970," *Southern California Law Review* 50:381 (1977).

5 THE STRUCTURE OF AMERICAN LAW: STATUTES AND STATUTE MAKERS

[1] Christie Glenny, ed., *California Public Sector* (1995).

[2] 369 U.S. 186 (1962).

[3] James Bryce, *The American Commonwealth*, 2nd ed. (1891), vol. 1, p. 190.

[4] Glenny, *California Public Sector.*

[5] On this development, see Lawrence M. Friedman and Jack Ladinsky, "Social Change and the Law of Industrial Accidents," *Columbia Law Review* 67:50 (1967).

[6] Quoted in Charles M. Cook, *The American Codification Movement: A Study of Antebellum Legal Reform* (1981), p. 75.

[7] Private Law 103-6 (October 22, 1994); Private Law 102-8, 106 Stat. 5151 (September 30, 1992).

[8] Ala. Laws, 1849–50, Act No. 335.

[9] Ala. Laws, 1849–50, Act No. 392.

[10] Ill. Const. 1870, Art. IV, Sec. 22.

[11] 26 U.S.C.A., Sec. 170 (d) (2) (A).

[12] See, for example, on the allocation of radio channels, 47 U.S.C.A., Sec 303.

[13] For the background of the Sherman Act, see William Letwin, *Law and Economic Policy in America: The Evolution of the Sherman Antitrust Act* (1965).

[14] Ohio Code, Sec. 3715.59.

[15] 443 U.S. 193 (1979).

[16] *Adarand v. Constructors, Inc.*, 115 S. Ct. 2097, 2110 (1995).

[17] *McBoyle v. United States*, 283 U.S. 25 (1931).

[18] 59 Stats. 536, act of September 24, 1945.

[19] Ohio Code, Sec. 3763.01(A). "Betted" as the past tense of "bet" sounds strange to my ears, but apparently not to the people who drafted this statute.

[20] Karl Llewellyn, "Remarks on the Theory of Appellate Decision and the Rules or Canons About How Statutes Are to Be Construed," *Vanderbilt Law Review* 3:395 (1950).

[21] T. St. J. N. Bates, "The Contemporary Use of Legislative History in the United Kingdom," *Cambridge Law Journal* 54:127, 139 (1995).

[22] Quoted in Harry W. Jones, John M. Kernochan, and Arthur W. Murphy, *Legal Method: Cases and Text Materials* (1980), p. 432.

[23] Scalia, J., in *Conroy v. Aniskoff*, 113 S. Ct. 1562, 1567 (1993).

[24] Robert A. Dahl, *Pluralist Democracy in the United States: Conflict and Consent* (1967), p. 24.

[25] The lobbying and disclosure provisions are found in 2 U.S.C.A., Secs. 1603ff.

[26] John A. Ferejohn, *Pork Barrel Politics: Rivers and Harbors Legislation, 1947–1968* (1974), p. 2.

[27] See, in general, James Buchanan and Gordon Tullock, *The Calculus of Consent* (1962). This is largely a theoretical, model-building account; for empirical confirmation see Thomas Stratmann, "The Effects of Logrolling on Congressional Voting," *American Economic Review* 82:1162 (1992).

6 THE STRUCTURE OF AMERICAN LAW: EXECUTING POLICY

[1] Herbert Jacob, *Law and Politics in the United States,* 2nd ed. (1995), p. 259.

[2] Tenn. Code, Sec. 63-18-202 (3).

[3] 60 Fed. Reg. 54,190 (October 20, 1995).

[4] 60 Fed. Reg. 56,270 (November 8, 1995).

[5] J. Willard Hurst, *Law and Markets in United States History* (1982), p. 107.

[6] Leonard D. White, *The Federalists: A Study in Administrative History* (1948), p. 177.

[7] Quoted in Leonard D. White, *The Jacksonians: A Study in Administrative History, 1829–1861* (1956), p. 550.

[8] Laws Conn. 1822, ch. 2, pp. 3ff.

[9] Conn. Stats. 1854, p. 240.

[10] Spencer L. Kimball, *Insurance and Public Policy* (1960).

[11] Conn. Stats. 1866, p. 182.

[12] Ill. Laws, 1871–72, pp. 618, 635, 769.

[13] 94 U.S. 113 (1876).

[14] 24 Stats. 379, act of February 4, 1887.

[15] N.J. Laws, 1851, p. 37.

[16] N.H. Laws, 1858, Chap. 1777.

[17] Gabriel Kolko, *Railroads and Regulation, 1877–1916* (1965).

[18] Stephen Skowronek, *Building a New American State: The Expansion of National Administrative Capacities, 1877–1920* (1982), chap. 5.

[19] See, in general, Morton Keller, *Regulating a New Economy: Public Policy and Economic Change in America, 1900–1933* (1990).

[20] 78 Stats. 241, Tit. VII, 253, 258, act of July 2, 1964.

[21] Eugene Bardach and Robert A. Kagan, *Going by the Book: The Problem of Regulatory Unreasonableness* (1982), pp. 11–12.

[22] Texas Nat. Resources Code, Sec. 85.046(10).

[23] 49 U.S.C., Sec. 106(e).

[24] Cal. Bus. and Prof. Code, Secs. 3010, 3011. Members of the faculty of a school of optometry are also eligible, but no more than two of these can be on the board at the same time.

[25] Marver Bernstein, *Regulating Business by Independent Commission* (1955).

[26] David Serber, "Resolution or Rhetoric: Managing Complaints in the California Department of Insurance," in Laura Nader, ed., *No Access to Law: Alternatives to the American Judicial System* (1980), pp. 317, 339.

[27] See Eugene Bardach and Robert A. Kagan, *Going by the Book: The Problem of Regulatory Unreasonableness* (1982).

[28] 15 U.S.C.A., Sec. 45.

[29] *New York Times,* October 31, 1981, p. 10.

[30] 5 U.S.C. App.3, Sec. 1ff; originally 92 Stats. 1101 (act of October 12, 1978).

[31] Jeffrey S. Lubbers, "APA-Adjudication: Is the Quest for Uniformity Faltering?" *Administrative Law Journal of American University* 10:65 (1996).

[32] 38 U.S.C.A., Sec. 211a.

[33] On the development of rules of standing, see Richard B. Stewart, "The Reformation of American Administrative Law," *Harvard Law Review* 88:1669, 1723–1747 (1978).

[34] Posner, J., in *North Shore Gas Co. v. EPA,* 930 F.2d 1239, 1242–3 (C.A. 7th, 1991).

[35] 295 U.S. 495 (1935).

[36] William H. Allen, quoted in Walter Gellhorn, Clark Byse, and Peter L. Strauss, *Administrative Law: Cases and Comments,* 7th ed. (1979), p. 343.

[37] 467 U.S. 837 (1984).

[38] Peter H. Schuck and E. Donald Elliott, "To the *Chevron* Station: An Empirical Study of Federal Administrative Law," 1990 *Duke Law Journal* 984.

[39] See Ian Ayres and John Braithwaite, *Responsive Regulation: Transcending the Deregulation Debate* (1992).

7 FEDERALISM AND AMERICAN LEGAL CULTURE

[1] Leonard D. White, *The Federalists: A Study in Administrative History* (1948), p. 123.

[2] James S. Young, *The Washington Community, 1800–1828* (1966), pp. 28, 31.

[3] Mary K. Bonsteel Tachau, *Federal Courts in the Early Republic: Kentucky, 1789–1816* (1978).

[4] Thomas W. Church, Jr., et al., *Justice Delayed: The Pace of Litigation in Urban Trial Courts* (National Center for State Courts, 1978).

[5] Ibid., p. 83.

[6] See Jack W. Peltason, *Fifty-eight Lonely Men: Southern Federal Judges and School Desegregation* (1961); see also Michal R. Belknap, *Federal Law and Southern Order: Racial Violence and Constitutional Conflict in the Post-*Brown *South* (1987).

[7] *Edwards v. California,* 314 U.S. 160 (1941).

[8] U.S. Const., Art. IV, Sec. 2.

[9] Ibid.

[10] See Paul Finkelman, *An Imperfect Union: Slavery, Federalism, and Comity* (1981).

[11] "Defense of Marriage Act," 110 Stats. 2419 (act of Sept. 21, 1996).

[12] *Paul v. Virginia,* 75 U.S. 168 (1868).

[13] See, in general, Gilman M. Ostrander, *Nevada: The Great Rotten Borough* (1966).

[14] Lawrence M. Friedman, *A History of America Law,* 2nd ed. (1985), pp. 502–3; Glenda Riley, *Divorce: An American Tradition* (1991), pp. 62–67.

[15] See Jerome H. Skolnick, *House of Cards: The Legalization and Control of Casino Gambling* (1978).

[16] 247 U.S. 251 (1918).

[17] 156 U.S. 1 (1895).

[18] Civil Rights Cases, 109 U.S. 3 (1883).

[19] 379 U.S. 294 (1964).

[20] The case was *United States v. Lopez,* 115 S. Ct. 1624 (1995).

[21] *Bibb v. Navajo Freight Lines, Inc.,* 359 U.S. 520 (1959); *Southern Pacific Co. v. Arizona,* 325 U.S. 761 (1945).

[22] *Dean Milk Co. v. Madison,* 340 U.S. 349 (1951).

[23] *Wyoming v. Oklahoma,* 502 U.S. 437 (1992).

[24] *Philadelphia v. New Jersey,* 437 U.S. 617 (1978).

[25] *Maine v. Taylor,* 477 U.S. 131 (1986).

[26] *Baldwin v. Montana Fish & Game Commission,* 436 U.S. 371, 390 (1978).

[27] 64 Stat. 1100, act of September 30, 1950.

[28] 79 Stat. 27, act of April 11, 1965.

[29] On the development of the federal role in crime control, see Lawrence M. Friedman, *Crime and Punishment in American History* (1993), chap. 12.

[30] 82 Stat. 197, act of June 19, 1968.

8 INSIDE THE BLACK BOX: THE SUBSTANCE OF LAW

[1] See *Craft v. Elder & Johnston Co.,* 34 Ohio Abs. 603, 38 N.E. 2d 416 (1941).

[2] Stewart Macaulay, "Non-Contractual Relations in Business: A Preliminary Study," *American Sociological Review* 28:55 (1963). See "Symposium—Law, Private Governance and Continuing Relationships," *Wisconsin Law Review* 1985:461, assessing the Macaulay thesis some twenty or so years later.

[3] *Farwell v. Boston & Worcester Rr. Corp.,* 45 Mass. 49 (1842).

[4] See Lawrence M. Friedman and Jack Ladinsky, "Social Change and the Law of Industrial Accidents," *Columbia Law Review* 64:50 (1964).

[5] For a study of personal-injury law in the courts, see Randolph E. Bergstrom, *Courting Danger: Injury and Law in New York City, 1870–1910* (1992).

[6] Mark A. Peterson and George L. Priest, *The Civil Jury: Trends in Trials and Verdicts, Cook County, Illinois, 1960–1979* (1982), p. 13.

[7] Neil Vidmar, *Medical Malpractice and the American Jury* (1995), p. 25.

[8] Under Article VII of this constitution, men could vote for representatives if they possessed a freehold of the value of £20.

[9] Marvin B. Sussman, Judith N. Cates, and David T. Smith, *The Family and Inheritance* (1970), p. 63.

[10] Carole Shammas, Marylynn Salmon, and Michel Dahlin, *Inheritance in America: From Colonial Times to the Present* (1987), p. 17.

[11] See Richard H. Chused, *Private Acts in Public Places: A Social History of Divorce in the Formative Era of American Family Law* (1994).

[12] On the history of divorce, see, generally, Glenda Riley, *Divorce: An American Tradition* (1991).

9 Crimes and Punishments

[1] Ga. Code, Sec. 16-11-61.

[2] Ibid., Sec. 16-6-7.

[3] Cal. Penal Code, Sec. 17.

[4] E. Adamson Hoebel, *The Law of Primitive Man: A Study in Comparative Legal Dynamics* (1954), p. 28.

[5] Eric H. Monkkonen, "A Disorderly People? Urban Order in the Nineteenth and Twentieth Centuries," *Journal of American History* 68:539 (1981).

[6] Rhode Isl. Stats., Sec. 20-7-10.

[7] Fla. Stats. Ann., Sec. 370.12. This statute also protects porpoises and makes it unlawful for anyone to "destroy a manta ray."

[8] *Statistical Abstract of the United States, 1995,* Table No. 324, p. 207.

[9] Bureau of Justice Statistics, *Sourcebook of Criminal Justice Statistics, 1994,* Table 3.32, p. 245.

[10] San Francisco Police Department, *Annual Report, 1989–1990,* p. 26.

[11] See, in general, Lawrence M. Friedman, *Crime and Punishment in American History* (1993).

[12] Essex Institute, *Records and Files of the Quarterly Court of Essex County, Massachusetts,* vol. 1, *1636–56* (1911), p. 380.

[13] Mark T. Connelly, *The Response to Prostitution in the Progressive Era* (1980), p. 3.

[14] Ark. Laws, 1907, no. 380.

[15] 36 Stats. 825, act of June 25, 1910. A fine study of the origins of the Mann Act and its subsequent history is David J. Langum, *Crossing over the Line: Legislating Morality and the Mann Act* (1994).

[16] 38 Stats. 785, act of December 17, 1914.

[17] On the upsurge of interest in victimless crime, see Lawrence M. Friedman, *Crime and Punishment in American History* (1993), chaps. 6, 15.

[18] See John Kaplan and Jerome H. Skolnick, *Criminal Justice: Introductory Cases and Materials,* 5th ed. (1991), p. 111.

[19] Vera Institute of Justice, *Felony Arrests,* rev. ed. (1981), p. 3.

[20] Bureau of Justice Statistics, *Sourcebook of Criminal Justice Statistics—1994,* Tables 4.23, 4.24, pp. 406, 408.

[21] Tex. Code Crim. Proc., Art. 19.06.

[22] Cal. Const., Art. I. Sec. 28 (d).

[23] Cited in Lawrence Baum, *American Courts*, 3rd ed. (1994), p. 181.

[24] Bureau of Justice Statistics, *State Court Organization 1993* (1995), Table 37, p. 274.

[25] Minn. Rules Crim. Proc., Rule 26.02(6).

[26] See *Georgia v. McCollum*, 112 S. Ct. 2348 (1992); *Batson v. Kentucky*, 476 U.S. 79 (1986). The Minnesota criminal-procedure rules just quoted also provide that "[n]o party may engage in purposeful discrimination on the basis of race in the exercise of peremptory challenges"; Rule 26.02 (6a) (1).

[27] See Laurence J. Severance and Elizabeth F. Loftus, "Improving the Ability of Jurors to Comprehend and Apply Criminal Jury Instructions," *Law & Society Review* 17:153 (1982).

[28] Bureau of Justice Statistics, *State Court Organization 1993*, Table 37, pp. 276–77.

[29] Harry Kalven, Jr., and Hans Zeisel, *The American Jury* (1966), p. 56.

[30] Jeffrey Abramson, *We the Jury: The Jury System and the Ideal of Democracy* (1994), pp. 253–54.

[31] Rita J. Simon, *The Jury: Its Role in American Society* (1980), p. 70; Abramson, *We the Jury*, pp. 202–5.

[32] Bureau of Justice Statistics, *Sourcebook of Criminal Justice Statistics 1994*, Table 5.49, p. 486.

[33] Michael O. Finkelstein, "A Statistical Study of Guilty Plea Practices in the Federal Courts," *Harvard Law Review* 89:293 (1975).

[34] Herbert Jacob, *Urban Justice: Law and Order in American Cities* (1973), p. 103.

[35] See Anne M. Heinz and Wayne A. Kerstetter, "Pretrial Settlement Conference: Evaluation of a Reform in Plea Bargaining," *Law & Society Review* 13:349 (1979).

[36] Cal. Penal Code, Sec. 1170.12 (e). Sec. 1192.7 (a) of the code prohibits plea bargaining in any "serious felony," or one in which the defendant used a gun, or in drug or drunk-driving cases, unless "there is insufficient evidence to prove the people's case, or testimony of a material witness cannot be obtained, or a reduction or dismissal would not result in a substantial change in sentence."

[37] Milton Heumann and Colin Loftin, "Mandatory Sentencing and the Abolition of Plea Bargaining: The Michigan Felony Firearm Statute," *Law & Society Review* 13:392, 424–26 (1979).

[38] Teresa W. Carns and John A. Kruse, "Alaska's Ban on Plea Bargaining Reevaluated," *Judicature* 75:310 (1992).

[39] John H. Langbein, "The Criminal Trial Before the Lawyers," *University of Chicago Law Review* 45:263 (1978): Lawrence M. Friedman and Robert V. Percival, *The Roots of Justice: Crime and Punishment in Alameda County, California, 1870–1910* (1981), p. 194.

[40] Friedman and Percival, *Roots of Justice*, pp. 176–78.

[41] Raymond Moley, *Politics and Criminal Prosecution* (1930), pp. 159–64.

[42] Wilbur R. Miller, *Cops and Bobbies: Police Authority in New York and London, 1830–1870* (1977), p. 16.

[43] See Robert M. Fogelson, *Big City Police* (1977).

[44] Baum, *American Courts*, p. 208.

[45] See David J. Rothman, *The Discovery of the Asylum: Social Order and Disorder in the New Republic* (1971); Adam J. Hirsch, *The Rise of the Penitentiary: Prisons and Punishment in Early America* (1992).

[46] Quoted in Lawrence M. Friedman, "History, Social Policy, and Criminal Justice," in David J. Rothman and Stanton Wheeler, eds., *Social History and Social Policy* (1981), pp. 203, 209.

[47] Ibid., p. 207.

[48] Friedman, *Crime and Punishment in American History*, p. 412.

[49] Alfred Blumstein et al., *Research on Sentencing: The Search for Reform*, vol. 1 (1983), pp. 88ff.

[50] David A. Sklansky, "Cocaine, Race, and Equal Protection," *Stanford Law Review* 47:1283, 1288 (1995); see also Michael Tonry, *Malign Neglect: Race, Crime and Punishment in America* (1995), chap. 3.

[51] *Atlanta Journal,* December 31, 1995, p. 8e.

[52] See Austin Turk, *Criminality and Legal Order* (1969), p. 165.

[53] Bureau of Justice Statistics, *Sourcebook of Criminal Justice Statistics 1994,* Table 6.19, p. 540.

[54] Friedman, *Crime and Punishment in American History,* pp. 429–34.

[55] *Los Angeles Times,* April 30, 1992, p. A1; May 1, 1992, p. A1.

[56] See, in general, Jerome H. Skolnick and James J. Fyfe, *Above the Law: Police and the Excessive Use of Force* (1993).

[57] 384 U.S. 436 (1966).

[58] See David Simon, *Homicide: A Year on the Killing Streets* (1991), pp. 193–207.

[59] 372 U.S. 335 (1963).

[60] Kaplan and Skolnick, *Criminal Justice,* pp. 351–58.

[61] See John S. Goldkamp, "Danger and Detention: A Second Generation of Bail Reform," *Journal of Criminal Law and Criminology* 76:1 (1985).

[62] See Ronald Berkman, *Opening the Gates: The Rise of the Prisoners' Movement* (1979); Friedman, *Crime and Punishment in American History,* pp. 310–14.

[63] Malcolm Feeley, *Court Reform on Trial: Why Simple Solutions Fail* (Twentieth Century Fund, 1983), p. 208.

[64] Ibid., p. 128.

[65] See H. Laurence Ross, *Deterring the Drinking Driver: Legal Policy and Social Control,* 3rd ed. (1984), for American and foreign examples; H. Laurence Ross, "The Philadelphia Story: The Effects of Severe Punishment for Drunk Driving," *Law & Policy* 12:51 (1990).

[66] See *New York Times,* September 10, 1996, pp. A1, A15.

[67] Friedman and Percival, *Roots of Justice,* p. 325.

10 Constitutional Law and Civil Liberties

[1] 249 U.S. 45 (1919).

[2] 1 Cranch 137 (1803).

[3] 118 U.S. 356 (1886).

[4] 372 U.S. 335 (1963).

[5] 337 U.S. 1 (1949).

[6] Laurence H. Tribe, *American Constitutional Law,* 2nd ed. (1988), pp. 14–15.

[7] *Korematsu v. United States,* 323 U.S. 214 (1944).

[8] Fletcher M. Green, *Constitutional Development in the South Atlantic States, 1776–1860* (1966), pp. 285–86.

[9] See, for example, Indiana Const. 1851, Art. IV, Sec. 21.

[10] Lawrence M. Friedman, *A History of American Law,* 2nd ed. (1985), pp. 356–57.

[11] Cal. Const., Art. 2, Sec. 8.

[12] Ibid., Art. 13A, approved by the voters June 6, 1978.

[13] 1 Cranch 137 (1803).

[14] 60 U.S. 383 (1857).

[15] A masterful and exhaustive treatment of the case is Don E. Fehrenbacher, *The Dred Scott Case: Its Significance in American Law and Politics* (1978).

[16] 6 Cranch 87 (1810).

[17] 4 Wheat. 518 (1819).

[18] Charles Fairman, *Mr. Justice Miller and the Supreme Court, 1862–1890* (1939), p. 62.

[19] 198 U.S. 45 (1905).

[20] Howard Gillman, *The Constitution Besieged: The Rise and Demise of Lochner Era Police Powers Jurisprudence* (1993), p. 4.

[21] William Swindler, *Court and Constitution in the 20th Century: The Old Legality* (1969), pp. 344–45.

[22] 295 U.S. 495 (1935).

[23] See William E. Leuchtenburg, *The Supreme Court Reborn: The Constitutional Revolution in the Age of Roosevelt* (1995).

[24] 348 U.S. 483 (1955).

[25] *Griswold v. Connecticut,* 381 U.S. 479 (1965); *Roe v. Wade,* 410 U.S. 113 (1973).

[26] 408 U.S. 238 (1972).

[27] *New York Times,* October 30, 1981, p. 10.

[28] 290 U.S. 398 (1934).

[29] 1 Stat. 596, act of July 14, 1798.

[30] Va. Code, 1849, Tit. 54, Chap. 198, Sec. 22; Russel B. Nye, *Fettered Freedom* (1963) p. 156.

[31] Civil Rights Cases, 109 U.S. 3 (1883).

[32] 98 U.S. 145 (1878).

[33] See Stanley I. Kutler, *The American Inquisition: Justice and Injustice in the Cold War* (1982).

[34] See Peter Irons, *Justice at War: The Story of the Japanese-American Internment Cases* (1983).

[35] 7 Pet. 243 (1833).

[36] 302 U.S. 319 (1937).

[37] 110 U.S. 516 (1884).

[38] See Gerald N. Rosenberg, *The Hollow Hope: Can Courts Bring About Social Change?* (1991).

[39] Okla. Stats., Title 21, Sec. 1040.13.

[40] 354 U.S. 476 (1957).

[41] Paul S. Boyer, *Purity in Print: Book Censorship in America* (1968), p. 136.

[42] See, for example, *A Book Named "John Cleland's Memoirs of a Woman of Pleasure" v. Attorney General of Massachusetts,* 383 U.S. 413 (1966).

[43] *Jenkins v. Georgia,* 418 U.S. 153 (1974).

[44] 422 U.S. 205 (1975).

[45] *Miller v. California,* 413 U.S. 15 (1973).

[46] *Pope v. Illinois,* 481 U.S. 497 (1987).

[47] 219 U.S. 219 (1911).

[48] William Cohen, "Negro Involuntary Servitude in the South, 1865–1940: A Preliminary Analysis," *Journal of Southern History* 42:31 (1976).

[49] 347 U.S. 483 (1954).

[50] See Rosenberg, *The Hollow Hope.*

[51] *Adarand Constructors, Inc. v. Pena,* 115 S. Ct. 2097 (1995); see David A. Strauss, "Affirmative Action and the Public Interest," in 1995 *Supreme Court Review,* p. 1.

[52] See *Hopwood v. Texas,* 78 F.3d 932 (5th Circuit, 1996).

[53] David S. Clark, "Judicial Protection of the Constitution in Latin America," *Hastings Constitutional Law Quarterly* 2:405 (1975).

[54] See Allan Brewer-Carias, *Judicial Review in Comparative Law* (1989), chaps. 13, 22.

[55] An English translation of this decision can be found in *John Marshall Journal of Practice and Procedure* 9:605 (1976).

[56] *New York Times,* September 8, 1995, p. A10.

[57] See Lawrence W. Beer, "Japan's Constitutional System and its Judicial Interpretation," in John O. Haley, ed., *Law and Society in Contemporary Japan* (1988), pp. 14–17.

11 ON LEGAL BEHAVIOR

[1] On the effectiveness of Prohibition, contrast Andrew Sinclair's *Prohibition: The Era of Excess* (1962) with J. C. Burnham, "New Perspectives on the Prohibition 'Experiment' of the 1920s," *Journal of Social History* 2:51 (1968).

[2] John Kaplan, *Marijuana: The New Prohibition* (1970), p. 25.

[3] Bureau of Justice Statistics, *Sourcebook of Criminal Justice Statistics, 1994,* Table 3.70, p. 289.

[4] Marvin B. Sussman, Judith N. Cates, and David T. Smith, *The Family and Inheritance* (1970), p. 64.

[5] *Sunday Advocate,* (Baton Rouge), December 11, 1994 p.1H; *Greensboro News & Record,* July 18, 1994, p. 4.

[6] Uniform Commercial Code, Sec. 2-302.

[7] "Legal Knowledge of Michigan Citizens," *Michigan Law Review* 71:1463 (1973).

[8] Martha Williams and Jay Hall, "Knowledge of the Law in Texas: Socioeconomic and Ethnic Differences," *Law & Society Review* 7:99 (1972).

[9] June Tapp and Lawrence Kohlberg, "Developing Senses of Law and Legal Justice," *Journal of Social Issues* 27:65 (1971).

[10] *Tarasoff v. Regents of the University of California,* 17 Cal. 3rd 425, 551 P. 2d 334 (1976).

[11] See Daniel J. Givelber, William J. Bowers, and Carolyn L. Blitch, "Tarasoff, Myth and Reality: An Empirical Study of Private Law in Action," *Wisconsin Law Review* 1984:443.

[12] See Lauren B. Edelman, Steven E. Abraham, and Howard S. Erlanger, "Professional Construction of Law: The Inflated Threat of Wrongful Discharge," *Law and Society Review* 26:47 (1992).

[13] See Robert M. Hayden, "The Cultural Logic of a Political Crisis: Hegemony and the Great American Liability Insurance Famine of 1986," in *Studies in Law, Politics, and Society* 11 (1991), p. 95.

[14] 408 U.S. 238 (1972).

[15] See Gordon Tullock, "Does Punishment Deter Crime?" *Public Interest* 36:103 (Summer 1974).

[16] Herbert L. Packer, *The Limits of the Criminal Sanction* (1968), p. 39.

[17] See, for example, George Antunes and A. Lee Hunt, "The Impact of Certainty and Severity of Punishment on Levels of Crime in American States: An Extended Analysis," *Journal of Criminal Law & Criminology* 64:487 (1973).

[18] J. Chaiken, M. Lawless, and K. Stevenson, *The Impact of Police Activities on Crime: Robberies on the New York City Subway System* (1974), p. 23.

[19] See H. Laurence Ross, *Deterring the Drinking Driver: Legal Policy and Social Control,* 3rd ed. (1984).

[20] Malcolm Feeley, *The Process Is the Punishment* (1979), p. 199.

[21] Ted R. Gurr, *Rogues, Rebels, and Reformers: A Political History of Urban Crime and Conflict* (1976).

[22] H. Laurence Ross, "The Neutralization of Severe Penalties: Some Traffic Law Studies," *Law & Society Review* 10:403–4 (1976).

[23] See Franklin Zimring and Gordon Hawkins, *Incapacitation: Penal Confinement and the Restraint of Crime* (1995).

[24] In *Coker v. Georgia,* 433 U.S. 584 (1977), the Supreme Court held that the death penalty could not be imposed on a man whose crime was rape of an adult woman.

[25] Roger Lane, *Violent Death in the City: Suicide, Accident, and Murder in Nineteenth-Century Philadelphia* (1979), p. 79; *Statistical Abstract of the United States* (1996), pp. 202–3.

[26] *Statistical Abstract of the United States* (1981), p. 177; (1996), p. 201.

[27] Jack K. Williams, *Vogues in Villainy: Crime and Retribution in Ante-Bellum South Carolina* (1959), p. 100.

[28] Philip J. Schwarz, *Twice Condemned: Slaves and the Criminal Laws of Virginia, 1705–1865* (1988), p. 15.

[29] Michael S. Hindus, *Prison and Plantation: Crime, Justice, and Authority in Massachusetts and South Carolina, 1767–1878* (1980), pp. 156–58.

[30] 408 U.S. 238 (1972).

[31] 428 U.S. 153 (1976).

[32] Title VI ("Federal Death Penalty Act of 1994") of the "Violent Crime Control and Law Enforcement Act of 1994," 108 Stat. 1796, 1959, act of September 13, 1994.

[33] Friedman, *Crime and Punishment in American History,* p. 321.

12 LEGAL CULTURE: LEGITIMACY AND MORALITY

[1] Jay MacLeod, *Ain't No Makin' It: Aspirations and Attainment in a Low-Income Neighborhood* (1995), p. 28.

[2] Victor Eisner, *The Delinquency Label: The Epidemiology of Delinquency* (1969), p. 105.

[3] Johannes Feest, "Compliance with Legal Regulations: Observation of Stop Sign Behavior," *Law & Society Review* 2:447 (1968).

[4] Lionel I. Dannick, "Influence of an Anonymous Stranger on a Routine Decision to Act or Not to Act: An Experiment in Conformity," *Sociological Quarterly* 14:127 (1973).

[5] See C. W. Kohfeld and T. W. Likens, "Mass Compliance and Social Interaction: A Dynamic Formulation," *Law and Policy Quarterly* 4:353 (1982).

[6] See Lauren Edelman, "Legal Ambiguity and Symbolic Structures: Organizational Mediation of Civil Rights Law," *American Journal of Sociology* 97:1531 (1992).

[7] Alan Hyde, "The Concept of Legitimation in the Sociology of Law," *Wisconsin Law Review* 1983:300.

[8] Arthur H. Miller, "Political Issues and Trust in Government: 1964–1970," *American Political Science Review* 68:951 (1974).

[9] James D. Hunter and Carl Bowman, *The State of Disunion: 1996 Survey of American Political Culture* (Vol. 1, Summary Report, 1996), p. 18.

[10] See Austin Sarat, "Support for the Legal System: An Analysis of Knowledge, Attitudes, and Behavior," *American Politics Quarterly* 3:3 (1975).

[11] Harry V. Ball, "Social Structure and Rent-Control Violations," *American Journal of Sociology* 65:598 (1960).

[12] Tom Tyler, *Why People Obey the Law* (1990).

[13] Charles R. Tittle and Alan R. Rowe, "Moral Appeal, Sanction Threat, and Deviance: An Experimental Test," *Social Problems* 20:488 (1973).

[14] Harold G. Grasmick and Robert J. Bursik, Jr., "Conscience, Significant Others and Rational Choice: Extending the Deterrence Model," *Law & Society Review* 24:837 (1990).

[15] See, for example, H. L. A. Hart, "Positivism and the Separation of Law and Morals," *Harvard Law Review* 71:593 (1958).

[16] 410 U.S. 113 (1973).

[17] 36 Stats. 825, act of June 25, 1910.

[18] David J. Langum, *Crossing Over the Line: Legislating Morality and the Mann Act* (1994), ch. 11; on Johnson and Berry, see pp. 179–188.

13 THE AMERICAN LEGAL PROFESSION

[1] Barbara A. Curran and Clara N. Carson, *The Lawyer Statistical Report: The U.S. Legal Profession in the 1990s* (1994), p. 1.

[2] Anton-Hermann Chroust, *The Rise of the Legal Profession in America*, vol. 1 (1965), p. 72.

[3] Gerard W. Gawalt, *The Promise of Power: The Emergence of the Legal Profession in Massachusetts, 1760–1840* (1979), p. 14.

[4] B. Peter Pashigian, "The Number and Earnings of Lawyers: Some Recent Findings," *American Bar Foundation Research Journal* 1978:51.

[5] Curran and Carson, *Lawyer Statistical Report*, p. 1.

[6] *New York Times*, April 2, 1982, p. 31, col. 3.

[7] Curran and Carson, *Lawyer Statistical Report*, p. 7.

[8] Lawrence M. Friedman, *A History of American Law*, 2nd ed. (1985), pp. 309–10.

[9] Claude M. Fuess, *Daniel Webster* (1930), vol. 1, p. 232.

[10] Merle Curti, *The Making of an American Community* (1959), p. 23.

[11] On the practice relating to marine insurance, see Julius Goebel, Jr., ed., *The Law Practice of Alexander Hamilton: Documents and Commentary*, vol. 2 (1969), pp. 391ff.

[12] Quintin Johnstone and Dan Hopson, Jr., *Lawyers and Their Work: An Analysis of the Legal Profession in the United States and England* (1967), p. 35.

[13] James B. Stewart, Jr., "Inside the World's Largest Law Firm," *American Lawyer*, January 1980, p. 21.

[14] *National Law Journal*, October 9, 1995, p. C6.

[15] Ibid., October 9, 1995, p. C7.

[16] There is a classic study by Erwin O. Smnigel, *The Wall Street Lawyer: Professional Organization Man?* (1964); more recently, see Robert L. Nelson, *Partners with Power: Social Transformation of the Large Law Firm* (1988); Marc Galanter and Thomas Palay, *Tournament of Lawyers: The Transformation of the Big Law Firm* (1991).

[17] Marc Galanter, "Mega-law and Mega-lawyering in the Contemporary United States," in R. Dingwall and P. Lewis, *The Sociology of the Professions: Lawyers, Doctors and Others* (1983), p. 152.

[18] John P. Heinz and Edward O. Laumann, *Chicago Lawyers: The Social Structure of the Bar*, rev. ed. (1994), p. 26.

[19] *Bradwell v. State*, 83 U.S. 130 (1873).

[20] Maxwell Bloomfield, *American Lawyers in a Changing Society* (1976), pp. 302–39.

[21] Allan P. Sindler, *Bakke, DeFunis, and Minority Admissions: The Quest for Equal Opportunity* (1978), p. 141.

[22] *Hopwood v. Texas*, 78 F. 3d 932 (5th Circuit, 1996).

[23] Heinz and Laumann, *Chicago Lawyers*, pp. 186, 190.

[24] On apprenticeship, see Lawrence M. Friedman, *A History of American Law*, 2nd ed. (1985), p. 318.

[25] J. W. Shuckers, *The Life and Public Service of Salmon Portland Chase* (1874), pp. 30–31.

[26] Edward S. Martin, *The Life of Joseph Hodges Choate*, vol. 1 (1920), p. 81. See, in general, Robert Stevens, *Law School: Legal Education in America from the 1850s to the 1980s* (1983).

[27] Arthur E. Sutherland, *The Law at Harvard: A History of Ideas and Men, 1817–1967* (1967), pp. 149–50.

[28] Frances K. Zemans and Victor G. Rosenblum, *The Making of a Public Profession* (1981), p. 101.

[29] Jerold S. Auerbach, *Unequal Justice: Lawyers and Social Change in Modern America* (1976), pp. 65–66, 239.

[30] Ibid., p. 287.

[31] *Goldfarb v. Virginia State Bar*, 421 U.S. 579 (1976).

[32] 433 U.S. 350 (1977).

[33] See, for example, Michael J. Powell, *From Patrician to Professional Elite: The Transformation of the New York City Bar Association* (1988).

[34] Johnstone and Hopson, *Lawyers and Their Work*, p. 72.

[35] Deborah L. Rhode, "Why the ABA Bothers: A Functional Perspective on Professional Codes," *Texas Law Review* 59:689, 718 (1981).

[36] Richard L. Abel, *American Lawyers* (1989), p. 147.

[37] Attorney Registration and Disciplinary Commission of the Supreme Court of Illinois, *Annual Report* (1995), pp. 6, 11.

[38] Douglas Rosenthal, *Lawyers and Clients: Who's in Charge?* (1974), p. 100.

[39] See Brian W. Smith and M. Lindsay Childress, "Avoiding Lawyer Liability in the Wake of Kaye, Scholer," *St. John's Journal of Legal Commentary* 8:385 (1993).

[40] Chroust, *Rise of the Legal Profession,* vol. 2, p. 127.

[41] Stewart Macaulay, Lawrence M. Friedman, and John Stookey, *Law and Society: Readings on the Social Study of Law* (1995), p. 816.

[42] Andrew Blum, "Losing Its Allure: Lawyer/Legislators Are a Dying Breed," *National Law Journal,* September 7, 1992, p. 1.

[43] Stephen Barlas, "Where Have All the Lawyers Gone?" *National Law Journal,* January 19, 1981, p. 13.

[44] Macaulay, Friedman, and Stookey, *Law and Society,* p. 814.

[45] See Marc Galanter, "The Assault on Civil Justice: The Anti-Lawyer Dimension," in Lawrence M. Friedman and Harry N. Scheiber, eds., *Legal Culture and the Legal Profession* (1996), p. 79.

[46] Ibid., pp. 79, 92–93.

[47] Heinz Eulau and John D. Sprague, *Lawyers in Politics: A Study in Professional Convergence* (1964); J. Green, J. Schmidhauser, L. Berg, and D. Brady, "Lawyers in Congress: A New Look at Some Old Assumptions," *Western Political Quarterly* 26:440 (1973).

[48] One such study was P. O'Connor, R. Engstrom, J. Green, and C. Kim, "The Political Behavior of Lawyers in the Louisiana House of Representatives," *Louisiana Law Review* 39:43 (1978).

[49] See Charles R. Epp, "Do Lawyers Impair Economic Growth?" *Law and Social Inquiry* 17:585 (1992).

[50] Richard W. Rabinowitz, "Law and the Social Process in Japan," *Transactions of the Asiatic Society of Japan,* 3rd ser., vol. 10 (1968), pp. 5, 49–50.

[51] John O. Haley, *Authority Without Power: Law and the Japanese Paradox* (1991), p. 103.

[52] Ibid., p. 107.

[53] Kevin Tierney, *Darrow: A Biography* (1979).

[54] 372 U.S. 335 (1963).

[55] See, for example, Lisa J. McIntyre, *The Public Defender: The Practice of Law in the Shadows of Repute* (1987).

[56] John M. Maguire, *The Lance of Justice* (1928), p. 70.

[57] Joel F. Handler, Ellen J. Hollingsworth, and Howard S. Erlanger, *Lawyers and the Pursuit of Legal Rights* (1978), p. 70.

[58] *New York Times,* July 20, 1982, p. 30, col. 1.

[59] Roger K. Newman, "Public-Interest Firms Crop Up on the Right," *National Law Journal,* August 26, 1996, pp. A1, A22.

14 LAW AND SOCIAL CHANGE

[1] J. Willard Hurst, *Law and Economic Growth: The Legal History of the Lumber Industry in Wisconsin, 1836–1915* (1964).

[2] Ibid., p. 190.

[3] Ibid., p. 607.

[4] On the legal history of slavery, see Thomas D. Morris, *Southern Slavery and the Law, 1619–1860* (1996). There was, of course, slavery in the northern colonies too up to the time of the Revolution; see Lawrence M. Friedman, *A History of American Law,* 2nd ed. (1985), pp. 85–89.

[5] Morris, *Southern Slavery*, chap. 2.

[6] Herbert S. Klein, *Slavery in the Americas: A Comparative Study of Virginia and Cuba* (1967), p. 43.

[7] Va. Laws, 1662, Act XII.

[8] Va. Laws, 1667, Act III.

[9] Ira Berlin, *Slaves Without Masters: The Free Negro in the Antebellum South* (1975), pp. 372–74.

[10] See Pete Daniel, *The Shadow of Slavery: Peonage in the South, 1901–1969* (1972); Daniel Novak, *The Wheel of Servitude: Black Forced Labor After Slavery* (1978).

[11] 109 U.S. 3 (1883).

[12] See, in general, C. Vann Woodward, *The Strange Career of Jim Crow*, 2nd ed. (1966).

[13] 163 U.S. 537 (1896). On the background of this famous case, see Charles A. Lofgren, *The Plessy Case: A Legal-Historical Interpretation* (1987).

[14] Ark. Stats. 1903, Sec. 5901.

[15] 238 U.S. 347 (1915).

[16] *Voting: 1961 Commission on Civil Rights Report*, p. 143.

[17] 347 U.S. 483 (1954). On the background of the case, see Richard Kluger, *Simple Justice* (1976).

[18] J. Harvie Wilkinson III, *From Brown to Bakke: The Supreme Court and School Integration, 1954–1978* (1979), p. 65.

[19] *Swann v. Charlotte-Mecklenburg Board of Education*, 402 U.S. 1 (1971).

[20] *Heart of Atlanta Motel, Inc. v. U.S.*, 379 U.S. 241 (1964); *Katzenbach v. McClung*, 379 U.S. 294 (1964).

[21] *Regents of the University of California v. Bakke*, 438 U.S. 1 (1978).

[22] *Adarand Constructors, Inc. v. Pena*, 115 S. Ct. 2097 (1995).

[23] *Miller v. Johnson*, 115 S. Ct. 2475 (1995).

[24] The case is *Hopwood v. Texas*, 78 F. 3rd 932 (CA. 5, 1996).

[25] See, for example, Gerald N. Rosenberg, *The Hollow Hope: Can Courts Bring About Social Change?* (1991).

[26] Wis. Const., Art. 1, Sec. 18.

[27] Quoted in Leonard J. Arrington and Davis Bitton, *The Mormon Experience* (1979), chap. 9; see also Edwin Brown Firmage and Richard C. Mangrum, *Zion in the Courts* (1988).

[28] 12 Stats. 501, act of July 1, 1862.

[29] 98 U.S. 145 (1878).

[30] 406 U.S. 205 (1975).

[31] *Katz v. Superior Court of San Francisco*, 73 Cal. App. 3d 952, 141 Cal. R. 234 (1977); see Joseph E. Broadus, "Use of the 'Choice of Evils' Defense in Religious Deprogramming Cases Offends Free Exercise While Ignoring the Right to be Free from Compelled Treatment," *George Mason University Civil Rights Journal* 1:171 (1990).

[32] Joseph Gusfield, *Symbolic Crusade: Status Politics and the American Temperance Movement* (1963).

[33] See Cal. Penal Code, Sec. 387 (1881).

[34] David F. Musto, *The American Disease: Origins of Narcotic Control* (1973), pp. 219–20.

[35] Michael Tonry, *Malign Neglect: Race, Crime and Punishment in America* (1994), pp. 108–9.

[36] See the discussion in John Kaplan, *The Hardest Drug: Heroin and Public Policy* (1983).

[37] *Bowers v. Hardwick*, 478 U.S. 186 (1986).

[38] 18 Cal. 3d 660, 557 P. 2d 106, 134 Cal. R. 815 (1976).

[39] Bureau of the Census, *Marital Status and Living Arrangements: March 1978*, Current Population Reports, Series P-20, no. 338, May 1979, p. 3, Table D.

[40] *National Law Journal,* April 16, 1979, p. 14.

[41] Minn. Stats. Ann., Secs. 513.075, 513.076.

[42] Mike McCurley, "Same-Sex Cohabitation Agreements," in Edward L. Winer and Lewis Becker, eds., *Premarital and Marital Contracts: A Lawyer's Guide to Drafting and Negotiating Enforceable Marital and Cohabitation Agreements* (1993), p. 195.

[43] In the matter of Baby M, 537 A. 2d 1227 (N.J. 1988).

[44] See Lori B. Andrews, "Beyond Doctrinal Boundaries: A Legal Framework for Surrogate Motherhood," *Virginia Law Review* 81:2343 (1995).

15 EPILOGUE: THE FUTURE OF LAW IN THE UNITED STATES

[1] *U.S. News & World Report,* December 20, 1982, p. 58.

[2] Quoted in Marc Galanter, "The Assault on Civil Justice: The Anti-Lawyer Dimension," in Lawrence M. Fredman and Harry N. Scheiber, *Legal Culture and the Legal Profession* (1996), p. 87.

[3] Bayless Manning, "Hyperlexis: Our National Disease," *Northwestern University Law Review* 71:767 (1977).

[4] *U.S. News & World Report,* December 20, 1982, p. 58.

[5] David S. Clark, "Adjudication to Administration: A Statistical Analysis of Federal District Courts in the Twentieth Century," *Southern California Law Review* 55:65, 86–88 (1981).

[6] Administrative Office of the United States, *Federal Judicial Workload Statistics,* March 31, 1993.

[7] Wayne V. McIntosh, *The Appeal of Civil Law: A Political-Economic Analysis of Litigation* (1990), p. 165.

[8] Lawrence M. Friedman and Robert V. Percival, "A Tale of Two Courts: Litigation in Alameda and San Benito Counties," *Law & Society Review* 10:267 (1976).

[9] 22 Stats. 209, act of July 2, 1890.

[10] See Lawrence M. Friedman, "The Six Million Dollar Man: Litigation and Rights Consciousness in Modern America," *Maryland Law Review* 39:661–72 (1980); Administrative Office of the U.S. Courts, *1995 Federal Court Management Statistics* (1996), p. 167.

[11] Peter H. Schuck, *Agent Orange on Trial: Mass Toxic Disasters in the Courts* (1986), pp. 4–5.

[12] Robert Kagan, "The Routinization of Debt Collection: An Essay on Social Change and Conflict in Courts," *Law & Society Review* 18:323 (1984).

[13] Laura Nader, ed., *No Access to Law: Alternatives to the American Judicial System* (1980), p. 5.

[14] See Janice A. Roehl and Royer F. Cook, "The Neighborhood Justice Centers Field Test," in Roman Tomasic and Malcolm M. Feeley, eds. *Neighborhood Justice: Assessment of an Emerging Idea* (1982), p. 91.

[15] American Bar Association, *Dispute Resolution Program Directory* (1993).

[16] *Washington Post,* August 18, 1981, p. 1, col. 2; *New York Times,* June 16, 1980, p. 16, col. 2; November 3, 1979, p. 44, col. 4.

[17] *U.S. News & World Report,* December 20, 1982, p. 58.

[18] Friedman, "Six Million Dollar Man," p. 667.

[19] *New York Times,* September 26, 1992, p. 1, col. 2. The trial court granted his request; *New York Times,* September 26, 1992, p. 1, col. 2. An appeal court decided that Gregory had no right, as a minor, to sue on his own, but did find a way to affirm the decision terminating his parents' rights. *Kingsley v. Kingsley,* 623 So. 2d 780 (Fla., 1993).

[20] Nader, *No Access to Law,* p. 5.

Index